Female Characters in Fragmentary Greek Tragedy

How were women represented in Greek tragedy? This question lies at the heart of much modern scholarship on ancient drama, yet it has typically been approached using evidence drawn only from the thirty-two tragedies that survive complete – neglecting tragic fragments, especially those recently discovered and often very substantial fragmentary papyri from plays that had been thought lost. Drawing on the latest research on both gender in tragedy and on tragic fragments, the essays in this volume examine this question from a fresh perspective, shedding light on important mythological characters such as Pasiphae, Hypsipyle and Europa, on themes such as violence, sisterhood, vengeance and sex, and on the methodology of a discipline which needs to take fragmentary evidence to heart in order to gain a fuller understanding of ancient tragedy. All Greek is translated to ensure wide accessibility.

P. J. FINGLASS is Henry Overton Wills Professor of Greek and Head of the Department of Classics and Ancient History at the University of Bristol. He has published *Sophocles* (2019) in the series Greece and Rome New Surveys in the Classics, as well as editions of Sophocles' *Oedipus the King* (2018), *Ajax* (2011) and *Electra* (2007), of Stesichorus (2014), and of Pindar's *Pythian Eleven* (2007) in the series Cambridge Classical Texts and Commentaries; has (with Adrian Kelly) coedited *The Cambridge Companion to Sappho* (2021) and *Stesichorus in Context* (2015), and edits the journal *Classical Quarterly*, all with Cambridge University Press.

LYNDSAY COO is Lecturer in Ancient Greek Language and Literature at the University of Bristol. Her research focuses on lost and fragmentary ancient Greek tragedy and satyr play. She is writing a commentary on Sophocles' fragmentary Trojan plays, and is coeditor (with Anna Uhlig) of *Aeschylus at Play: Studies in Aeschylean Satyr Drama* (2019).

Female Characters in Fragmentary Greek Tragedy

Edited by

P. J. FINGLASS
University of Bristol

LYNDSAY COO
University of Bristol

CAMBRIDGE
UNIVERSITY PRESS

University Printing House, Cambridge CB2 8BS, United Kingdom

One Liberty Plaza, 20th Floor, New York, NY 10006, USA

477 Williamstown Road, Port Melbourne, VIC 3207, Australia

314–321, 3rd Floor, Plot 3, Splendor Forum, Jasola District Centre, New Delhi – 110025, India

79 Anson Road, #06–04/06, Singapore 079906

Cambridge University Press is part of the University of Cambridge.

It furthers the University's mission by disseminating knowledge in the pursuit of education, learning, and research at the highest international levels of excellence.

www.cambridge.org
Information on this title: www.cambridge.org/9781108495141
DOI: 10.1017/9781108861199

First published 2020

A catalogue record for this publication is available from the British Library.

Library of Congress Cataloging-in-Publication Data
Names: Finglass, Patrick, 1979– editor. | Coo, Lyndsay, editor.
Title: Female Characters in Fragmentary Greek Tragedy / edited by P. J. Finglass, Lyndsay Coo.
Description: New York : Cambridge University Press, 2020. | Includes bibliographical references and index.
Identifiers: LCCN 2019039791 (print) | LCCN 2019039792 (ebook) | ISBN 9781108495141 (hardback) |
    ISBN 9781108817059 (paperback) | ISBN 9781108861199 (epub)
Subjects: LCSH: Women in literature. | Greek drama (Tragedy)–History and criticism.
Classification: LCC PA3015.W65 F46 2020 (print) | LCC PA3015.W65 (ebook) | DDC 882/.0099287–dc23
LC record available at https://lccn.loc.gov/2019039791
LC ebook record available at https://lccn.loc.gov/2019039792

ISBN 978-1-108-49514-1 Hardback

Contents

Notes on Contributors

LUIGI BATTEZZATO is Professor of Greek Literature at the Università del Piemonte Orientale, Vercelli. He is the author of an edition of Euripides' *Hecuba* (Cambridge University Press, 2018), two monographs on tragedy (*Linguistica e retorica della tragedia greca*, 2008, and *Il monologo nel teatro di Euripide*, 1995), and *Leggere la mente degli eroi. Ettore, Achille e Zeus nell'Iliade* (2019). He has taught as a visiting professor at the Scuola Normale Superiore, Pisa, at the Istituto Universitario di Studi Superiori, Pavia, and at the École Normale Supérieure, Lyon.

JAMES H. KIM ON CHONG-GOSSARD is Senior Lecturer in Classics at the University of Melbourne. He is the author of *Gender and Communication in Euripides' Plays: Between Song and Silence* (2008) and of articles on various topics, including consolation in Greek tragedy, the reception of Euripides, sex scandals in the Roman Empire, fifteenth-century commentaries on Terence's comedies and fourteenth-century commentaries on Seneca's tragedies.

LYNDSAY COO is Lecturer in Ancient Greek Language and Literature at the University of Bristol. Her research focuses on ancient Greek drama, in particular the lost and fragmentary works. She is writing a commentary on the fragmentary Trojan plays of Sophocles, has published on Greek tragedy and satyr play, and is coeditor (with Anna Uhlig) of *Aeschylus at Play: Studies in Aeschylean Satyr Drama*, a themed issue of the *Bulletin of the Institute of Classical Studies* (2019).

ROBERT COWAN is Senior Lecturer in Classics at the University of Sydney, having previously held posts in Exeter, Bristol and Oxford. His research interests range over much of Greek and Latin poetry, and he has published on Sophocles, Aristophanes, Plautus, Lucretius, Catullus, Cicero, Cinna, Ticida, Virgil, Horace, Ovid, Columella, Martial, Suetonius and Juvenal, as well as ancient graffiti and the operatic reception of Greek tragedy. His main specialisms are Imperial epic and Republican tragedy.

P. J. FINGLASS is Henry Overton Wills Professor of Greek and Head of the Department of Classics and Ancient History at the University of Bristol, and Director of the Arts and Humanities Research Council South, West and Wales Doctoral Training Partnership. He has published a monograph *Sophocles* (2019) in the series Greece and Rome New Surveys in the Classics; has edited Sophocles' *Oedipus the King* (2018), *Ajax* (2011) and *Electra* (2007), Stesichorus' *Poems* (2014), and Pindar's *Pythian Eleven* (2007) in the series Cambridge Classical Texts and Commentaries; has (with Adrian Kelly) coedited *The Cambridge Companion to Sappho* (2021) and *Stesichorus in Context* (2015); and edits the journal *Classical Quarterly*, all with Cambridge University Press.

HELENE P. FOLEY is Claire Tow Professor of Classics, Barnard College, Columbia University. She is the author of books and articles on Greek epic and drama, on women and gender in antiquity and on modern performance and adaptation of Greek drama. Author of *Ritual Irony: Poetry and Sacrifice in Euripides* (1985), *The Homeric Hymn to Demeter* (1994), *Female Acts in Greek Tragedy* (2001), *Reimagining Greek Tragedy on the American Stage* (2012) and *Euripides: Hecuba* (2015) and coauthor of *Women in the Classical World: Image and Text* (1994), she has edited *Reflections of Women in Antiquity* (1981) and coedited *Visualizing the Tragic: Drama, Myth, and Ritual in Greek Art and Literature* (2007) and *Antigone on the Contemporary World Stage* (2011).

FIONA MCHARDY is Professor of Classics at the University of Roehampton. Her research focuses on aspects of gendered violence in ancient Greek literature, in particular revenge ethics in Homeric epic, Greek tragedy and Attic oratory. She is author of *Revenge in Athenian Culture* (2008) and has coedited four volumes: *Revenge and Gender in Classical, Medieval and Renaissance Literature* (2018), *From Abortion to Pederasty: Addressing Difficult Topics in the Classics Classroom* (2014), *Lost Dramas of Classical Athens* (2005) and *Women's Influence on Classical Civilization* (2004). She is currently writing a book on gender violence in ancient Greece.

CALEB SIMONE is Teaching Fellow and Doctoral Candidate in the Department of Classics at Columbia University. He has published on sound in Pindar and is currently writing a dissertation on the cultural discourse that emerges around *aulos* performance in ancient Greek literature and art.

NIALL W. SLATER is Samuel Candler Dobbs Professor of Latin and Greek at Emory University. His research focuses on the ancient theatre and its production conditions, prose fiction and popular reception of classical literature. His books include *Spectator Politics: Metatheatre and*

Performance in Aristophanes (2002), *Reading Petronius* (1990) and *Plautus in Performance: The Theatre of the Mind* (1985, 2000²), as well as the Bloomsbury Companion to Euripides' *Alcestis* (2013). His translations of various Middle and New Comedy poets are included in *The Birth of Comedy: Texts, Documents, and Art from Athenian Comic Competitions, 486–280*, edited by Jeffrey Rusten (2011). With C. W. Marshall he coedits the series Bloomsbury Ancient Comedy Companions. He is currently working on fragments of Roman Republican drama for the new Loeb *Fragmentary Republican Latin*.

ALAN H. SOMMERSTEIN is Emeritus Professor of Greek at the University of Nottingham. He has published extensively on Greek drama, literature, language and society; has produced editions of the plays and fragments of Aeschylus (2008), including commentaries on *Eumenides* and *Suppliants* (Cambridge University Press, 1989, 2019), of selected fragmentary plays of Sophocles (with Thomas Talboy and David Fitzpatrick, 2006–2012), of the eleven comedies of Aristophanes (1980–2001) and of Menander's *Samia* (Cambridge University Press, 2014); and is editor of *The Encyclopedia of Greek Comedy* (2019).

ANNA UHLIG is Associate Professor of Classics at the University of California, Davis. Her research focuses on the performance culture of Greek lyric and dramatic poetry in the archaic and classical periods. She is coeditor (with Richard Hunter) of *Imagining Reperformance in Ancient Culture: Studies in the Traditions of Drama and Lyric* (Cambridge University Press, 2017), and (with Lyndsay Coo) of *Aeschylus at Play: Studies in Aeschylean Satyr Drama*, a themed issue of the *Bulletin of the Institute of Classical Studies* (2019), and author of *Theatrical Reenactment in Pindar and Aeschylus* (Cambridge University Press, 2019).

MATTHEW WRIGHT is Professor of Greek at the University of Exeter. He has published widely on fragmentary Greek drama, and his books include *The Lost Plays of Greek Tragedy* (two volumes, 2016–2019) and *The Comedian as Critic: Greek Old Comedy and Poetics* (2012).

Preface

This book has its origin in the conference 'Fragmented Women: The Female Characters of Fragmentary Greek Tragedy' co-organised by the editors at the University of Nottingham in July 2016; the papers presented there have been revised for this volume (with the exception of papers by Lucia Athanassaki, Marco Catrambone and Erika Weiberg, which are to appear in other venues), and augmented by two further chapters, by K. O. Chong-Gossard and Caleb Simone. We are most grateful to Cambridge University Press for publishing the volume, to the two anonymous referees and to Michael Sharp for his advice throughout the publication process.

The conference was funded by the Leverhulme Trust through the award to Patrick Finglass of a Philip Leverhulme Prize; the Trust's generous support allowed us to offer many bursaries to postgraduate students and early career researchers, especially from overseas. Lyndsay Coo's participation in the conference, as well as that of two Bristol PhD students, was funded by the Institute of Greece, Rome, and the Classical Tradition at the University of Bristol. We thank administrative staff at the University of Nottingham, both at the School of Humanities and at Nottingham Conferences, for their support of the event.

Tragic fragments are cited using the numeration of *Tragicorum Graecorum Fragmenta*, although individual contributors take responsibility for the actual text that they print and are not bound by any editor's decisions. A dot under a letter indicates that it is not certain; a dot under empty space indicates that the letter in question cannot be identified. Gaps on a papyrus (or inscription) are represented by square brackets, [ ]; scholars' attempts to fill these gaps are found within the brackets. Angular brackets, < >, signify letters not found on the papyrus; curly brackets, { }, signify letters erroneously included on the papyrus. When a gap on a papyrus coincides with a quotation found in an ancient author, the text thus added to the papyrus text is placed within half square brackets, ⌊ ⌋. Ancient dates are BC unless otherwise indicated. Cross-references are given by citing the author's name in small capitals, with a page reference if needed.

PJFF
LMLC
Bristol, June 2019

LEVERHULME
TRUST _____

Patrick Finglass's work on this book was supported by the award of a Philip Leverhulme Prize by the Leverhulme Trust.

Abbreviations

Adler	A. Adler (ed.), *Suidae Lexicon*, 5 vols. Lexicographi Graeci 1. Leipzig, 1928–38
BAPD	*Beazley Archive Pottery Database* (www.beazley.ox.ac.uk/pottery/)
BNJ	I. Worthington (ed.), Brill's New Jacoby (https://referenceworks.brillonline.com/browse/brill-s-new-jacoby).
Breithaupt	M. Breithaupt (ed.), *De Parmenisco grammatico*. Στοιχεῖα 4. Leipzig and Berlin, 1915
Carey	C. Carey (ed.), *Lysiae orationes cum fragmentis*. Oxford, 2007
CEG	P. A. Hansen (ed.), *Carmina Epigraphica Graeca*, 2 vols. Texte und Kommentare 12, 15. Berlin and New York, 1983–9
CGFPR	C. Austin (ed.), *Comicorum graecorum fragmenta in papyris reperta*. Berlin and New York, 1973
Chantry	M. Chantry (ed.), *Scholia in Aristophanem. Pars III: Scholia in Thesmophoriazusas, Ranas, Ecclesiazusas et Plutum. Fasc. Ia, continens Scholia vetustiora in Aristophanis Ranas*. Groningen, 1999
D–K	H. Diels (ed.), *Die Fragmente der Vorsokratiker*[6], 3 vols., rev. W. Kranz. Berlin, 1951–2
Drachmann	A. B. Drachmann (ed.), *Scholia vetera in Pindari carmina*, 3 vols. Leipzig, 1903–27
EGM	R. L. Fowler (ed.), *Early Greek Mythography*, 2 vols. Oxford, 2000–13
F.	P. J. Finglass, 'Text and critical apparatus', in Davies and Finglass, 2014: 93–205
FGE	D. L. Page (ed.), *Further Greek Epigrams. Epigrams before A.D. 50 from the Greek Anthology and other Sources, not included in* Hellenistic Epigrams *or* The Garland of Philip, revised and prepared for publication by R. D. Dawe and J. Diggle. Cambridge, 1981

GEF	M. L. West (ed.), *Greek Epic Fragments from the Seventh to the Fifth Centuries BC.* Loeb Classical Library 497. Cambridge, MA and London, 2003
Harder	A. Harder (ed.), *Callimachus.* Aetia, 2 vols. Oxford, 2012
Holwerda	D. Holwerda (ed.), *Scholia in Aristophanem, Pars I. Prolegomena de comoedia, Scholia in Acharnenses, Equites, Nubes; Fasc. III 1, continens Scholia vetera in Nubes.* Groningen, 1977
Hordern	J. H. Hordern (ed.), *The Fragments of Timotheus of Miletus.* Oxford, 2002
IG II–III²	J. Kirchner (ed.), *Inscriptiones Atticae Euclidis anno posteriores*, 4 vols. Berlin, 1913–40
Jocelyn	H. D. Jocelyn (ed.), *The Tragedies of Ennius.* Cambridge Classical Texts and Commentaries 10. Cambridge, 1967
K–G	R. Kühner, *Ausführliche Grammatik der griechischen Sprache. Zweiter Teil: Satzlehre²*, 2 vols., rev. B. Gerth. Hannover and Leipzig, 1898–1904
Leone	P. A. M. Leone (ed.), *Scholia vetera et paraphrases in Lycophronis Alexandram.* Lecce, 2002
LSJ⁹	H. G. Liddell and R. Scott, *A Greek–English Lexicon⁹*, rev. H. Stuart-Jones *et al.* Oxford, 1940
Martin	J. Martin (ed.), *Scholia in Aratum vetera.* Stuttgart, 1974
Most	G. W. Most (ed., transl.), *Hesiod.* Theogony. Works and Days. *Testimonia.* Loeb Classical Library 57. Cambridge, MA and London, 2006
M–W	R. Merkelbach and M. L. West (eds.), *Fragmenta Hesiodea.* Oxford, 1967, supplemented in *id.* (eds.), *Fragmenta selecta, ap.* F. Solmsen (ed.), *Hesiodi Theogonia Opera et Dies Scutum.³* Oxford, 1990
Nauck, *TrGF²*	A. Nauck (ed.), *Tragicorum Graecorum Fragmenta.²* Leipzig 1889, reprinted with a supplement by B. Snell, Hildesheim, 1964 [1st edn 1856]
P.Berol.	*Berliner Papyri*
PCG	R. Kassel and C. Austin (eds.), *Poetae Comici Graeci*, 8 vols. to date. Berlin and New York, 1983–
P.IFAO	*Papyrus grecs de l'Institut français d'archéologie orientale*
PMG	D. L. Page (ed.), *Poetae Melici Graeci.* Oxford, 1962, corrected reprint 1967

P.Oxy.	B. P. Grenfell, A. S. Hunt *et al.* (eds.), *The Oxyrhynchus Papyri*, 83 vols. to date. London, 1898–
Rotstein	A. Rotstein, *Literary History in the Parian Marble*. Hellenic Studies 68. Cambridge, MA and London, 2016
Schwartz	E. Schwartz (ed.), *Scholia in Euripidem*, 2 vols. Berlin, 1887–91
SEG	J. J. E. Hondius *et al.* (eds.), *Supplementum Epigraphicum Graecum*, 63 vols. to date. Leiden, Amsterdam, Boston, 1923–
S–M	B. Snell and H. Maehler (eds.), *Pindari Carmina cum Fragmentis*, 2 vols. Leipzig, 1987–9, and *Bacchylides.* Leipzig, 1970
Stählin	O. Stählin (ed.), *Clemens Alexandrinus*, 4 vols. Leipzig, 1905–34
Theodoridis	C. Theodoridis (ed.), *Photii Patriarchae Lexicon* [Α–Φ only], 3 vols. Berlin and New York, 1982–2013
Thilo and Hagen	G. Thilo and H. Hagen (eds.), *Servii grammatici qui feruntur in Vergilii carmina commentarii*, 3 vols. Leipzig, 1878–1902
TrGF	*Tragicorum Graecorum Fragmenta*. Vol. 1 *Didascaliae Tragicae, Catalogi Tragicorum et Tragoediarum, Testimonia et Fragmenta Tragicorum Minorum*, ed. B. Snell, 2nd ed. rev. R. Kannicht. Göttingen, 1971[1], 1986[2]. Vol. 2 *Fragmenta Adespota*, ed. R. Kannicht and B. Snell. 1981. Vol. 3 *Aeschylus*, ed. S. L. Radt. 1985. Vol. 4 *Sophocles*, ed. S. L. Radt. 1977[1], 1999[2]. Vol. 5 *Euripides*, 2 parts, ed. R. Kannicht. 2004
TrGFS	J. Diggle (ed.), *Tragicorum Graecorum Fragmenta Selecta*. Oxford, 1998
Van der Valk	M. van der Valk (ed.), *Eustathii Archiepiscopi Thessalonicensis commentarii ad Homeri Iliadem pertinentes*, 4 vols. Leiden, New York, Copenhagen, Cologne, 1971–87
Voigt	E.-M. Voigt (ed.), *Sappho et Alcaeus. Fragmenta.* Amsterdam, 1971
Warmington	E. H. Warmington (ed.), *Remains of Old Latin, Volume II: Livius Andronicus. Naevius. Pacuvius. Accius.* Loeb Classical Library 315. London and Cambridge, MA, 1936.
Wehrli	F. Wehrli (ed.), *Die Schule des Aristoteles: Texte und Kommentar. Heft II: Aristoxenos.*[2] Basel and Stuttgart, 1967 [1st edn 1945]

Wendel	C. T. E. Wendel (ed.), *Scholia in Apollonium Rhodium vetera*. Leipzig, 1935
Wessner	P. Wessner (ed.), *Scholia in Iuvenalem vetustiora*. Leipzig, 1931
W–H	C. Wachsmuth and O. Hense (eds.), *Ioannis Stobaei Anthologium*, 5 vols. Berlin, 1884–1912
Wilson	N. G. Wilson (ed.), *Scholia in Aristophanem. Pars 1: Prolegomena de comoedia, Scholia in Acharnenses, Equites, Nubes. Fasc. I B, continens Scholia in Aristophanis Acharnenses*. Groningen, 1975
Xenis	G. A. Xenis (ed.), *Scholia vetera in Sophoclis Electram*. Sammlung griechischer und lateinischer Grammatiker 12 Berlin and New York, 2010

1 | Introduction

LYNDSAY COO AND P. J. FINGLASS

The study of women in ancient Greek tragedy has become a scholarly mainstay. The subject has launched a thousand undergraduate dissertations and PhD theses, has attracted some of the most eloquent scholars of recent generations, and, particularly through its intersection with gender studies, structural anthropology and feminist criticism, has been instrumental in keeping tragedy firmly in the vanguard of new critical approaches to ancient literature. Yet unsurprisingly this attention has focussed on those plays that happen to have come down to us in full, with certain characters – such as Aeschylus' Clytemnestra, Sophocles' Antigone and Euripides' Medea – coming to dominate our understanding of the representation of women in tragedy. There have been few systematic attempts to approach the study of female characters from the perspective of fragmentary tragedy. That is what this book attempts to provide.

The prevalent focus on extant tragedy, though hardly difficult to understand or explain, is increasingly difficult to justify. There has never been a better time to be working on fragmentary tragedy, with the last few decades having seen enormous advances in this field.[1] The monumental series *Tragicorum Graecorum Fragmenta*, whose first volume appeared in 1971, was completed in 2004; its five volumes, expertly edited by three of the greatest philologists of the modern era (Richard Kannicht, Bruno Snell and Stefan Radt), collect together the fragments and testimonia of the 'big three' tragedians Aeschylus (1985), Sophocles (1977[1], 1999[2]) and Euripides (2004, in two parts), as well as those belonging to other tragic poets (1971[1], 1986[2], addenda 2004) and the anonymous fragments (1981, addenda 2004). The previous complete text, by August Nauck (1856[1], 1889[2]), was in only one volume; the massively increased bulk of the modern edition reflects the huge growth in material thanks to the publication of papyri from the late nineteenth century onwards. It has also never been easier to incorporate the fragmentary tragedies into university curricula: we now have Loebs of the fragments of the 'big three' (Lloyd-Jones

---

[1] For the history of the collection of dramatic fragments see Kassel 1991a = 1991b: 88–98, ≈ McHardy *et al.* 2005: 7–20.

2003, Collard and Cropp 2008, Sommerstein 2008), Budé editions of the fragments of Euripides (Jouan and Van Looy 1998, 2000), and commentaries in the Aris and Phillips series on selected fragmentary plays of Euripides (Collard, Cropp, and Lee 1995, Collard, Cropp, and Gibert 2004), Sophocles (Sommerstein, Fitzpatrick, and Talboy 2006, Sommerstein and Talboy 2012), and the 'minor' tragedians (Cropp 2019). Introductory chapters on fragments are included in companion volumes to the main tragedians (Hahnemann 2012, Collard 2017). As Pat Easterling has reiterated, 'there is even less reason now to stick to interpretations of tragedy based on the notion that the thirty-three plays that survive are all that are worth taking into account'.[2]

Yet despite the increased availability and accessibility of these texts, work on the tragic fragments has tended to remain somewhat isolated. Much excellent scholarship has been accomplished in terms of commentary on individual fragmentary plays, and occasional edited volumes have taken the fragments as their focus.[3] But in general, these texts are seldom fully integrated into more wide-ranging interpretative enquiries, and works that purport to examine a particular theme 'in Greek tragedy' regularly omit the fragments entirely or only include them as a kind of afterthought or extra.[4] The reasons for this are not hard to find. The fragments are, simply put, difficult to work with: they are often lacunose or textually obscure, necessitating philological elucidation; the plots of the plays from which they derive are less familiar to a general audience and require laborious exposition (sometimes involving a fair amount of hypothesis); more often than not, their context is unknown, and sometimes wholly unguessable. In some cases, we simply do not have the basic information – such as speaker, addressee and immediate or wider context – that is fundamental in using these texts in any manner beyond plot reconstruction. At a more practical level, fragmentary plays tend to appear in different series and volumes, sometimes located in different sections of libraries and by different editors and publishers, compared to dramas that have survived complete. For all the achievements of recent scholarship on tragic fragments, there remains a powerful sense that 'the plays of Sophocles' (for

[2] Easterling 2013: 185.
[3] Hofmann 1991, Sommerstein 2003, McHardy *et al.* 2005, Cousland and Hume 2009.
[4] Notable exceptions include Alan Sommerstein's *Aeschylean Tragedy* (2010a), which fully integrates the fragments into its discussion, partly as a result of using the trilogy as its structuring principle, and Jacques Jouanna's *Sophocle* (2007 ≈ 2018), which includes a detailed appendix with summaries of the fragmentary plays.

instance) comprise *Trachiniae, Ajax, Antigone, Oedipus the King, Electra, Philoctetes* and *Oedipus at Colonus* – and nothing else.

In the field of ancient Greek drama, patterns of transmission have made this problem particularly pressing in the case of tragedy. With Old Comedy, the survival of complete plays by only one writer, Aristophanes, means perforce that anyone wanting to advance a generalisation about the genre can hardly avoid taking fragmentary evidence into consideration. And in the case of satyr play only one example, Euripides' *Cyclops*, has survived in full, again meaning that any study of that dramatic form must adopt a perspective that includes the fragments; it helps that the largest fragment of satyr drama, the papyrus of Sophocles' *Ichneutae* (*Trackers*), is substantial, containing roughly half the play. Tragedy, on the other hand, offers us thirty dramas from the three most prominent authors in that field (plus two more whose attributions are unknown, *Prometheus Bound* and *Rhesus*), whose production dates stretch from 472 into the fourth century; these plays provide ample material for scholars to approach all kinds of issues across different axes without the need to take fragmentary evidence into account. But the failure to do this can lead to the impoverishment of those debates, based as they are on less than the totality of the material that has come down to us; it has resulted in the establishment of scholarly modes of enquiry that rarely depart from the grooves laid down by the fully extant plays alone.

It remains true that the analysis of fragmentary drama, as of fragmentary evidence of any kind, needs to proceed with caution. However, while the texts that we call tragic fragments do present particular problems to interpreters, we must remember that *all* of the evidence that we have for Greek tragedy is fragmentary to one degree or another, as can be seen in several ways. First, the thirty-two 'complete' plays that we have today are known to us not by autograph copies written by their authors, but from manuscripts written more than thirteen centuries after their original composition. During the long process of transmission many, perhaps all, of those dramas have lost lines; so the opening of Aeschylus' *Choephoroe* (*Libation Bearers*) is missing its opening lines (some of which can be restored from other sources which quoted them before the passage was lost), the endings of Euripides' *Bacchae, Children of Heracles* and probably Sophocles' *Oedipus the King* are mutilated, and occasional lines are missing from within dramas as well. The scripts that we possess are therefore themselves 'fragmentary' – admittedly, far larger fragments than we are used to dealing with, but nevertheless incomplete, and sometimes in ways significant for their overall interpretation. Many will also have been afflicted by textual additions made by actors and other sources during the period of their transmission that can be difficult to detect.[5] Second, most, probably all, of the 'complete' plays were intended to be performed as part of a larger unit, which in most cases was a *didascalia* made up of three tragedies followed by a satyr play. Whether or not a given sequence of plays had a connected storyline (as with Aeschylus' *Oresteia*), dealt with distinct episodes of a broader mythical history (as with Euripides' 'Trojan trilogy' of 415), or had no particular mythical coherence (as with Euripides' plays of 431, where *Medea* was performed with *Dictys* and *Philoctetes*, the name of the satyr play being unknown), each play was designed to be experienced in that context, a context which for most dramas has totally disappeared. A third way in which even our 'complete' plays show fragmentary characteristics arises from our ignorance of so many of the basic conditions of their performance. The actors' gestures and tones of voice, the dancing, the staging, the music, the weather conditions, the hubbub of the audience, the ceremonies before the performances, the sights, sounds and smells of the theatre – all this is lost to us.

The fully extant plays may, then, convey a comforting impression of completeness, but this too is illusory. There is therefore a certain contradiction if we confidently put forward interpretations of the extant plays while simultaneously professing our inability to include any analysis of the fragments on the grounds that so much is unknown. Indeed, even those wary of overly positivist approaches to the interpretation of extant tragedy are often reluctant to engage with fragments precisely on account of the constant need to acknowledge the precariousness of any conclusions reached and the slenderness of the evidence that one can accumulate. This is a wariness that must be overcome if we are to begin to use these texts in more sustained and meaningful ways in our readings of the genre. It may well be that we have to adjust our notion of the roles that 'certainty' and 'provisionality' should (or could) play in the formulation of a literary interpretation. For example, Matthew Wright, in a recent discussion of the methodology of working with tragic fragments, has highlighted the 'fragmentariness' of all our evidence more widely, and has outlined a mode of reading fragmentary texts that is not afraid to engage (albeit with due caution) with creativity, imagination and multiple, exploratory and simultaneously held interpretations – approaches that would usually be

[5] Finglass 2015a, 2015b, Lamari 2015, 2017.

considered undesirable when working with a 'complete' text.[6] Engaging with fragments is thus not only worth doing in its own right, but also has the potential to sharpen our methodologies for interpreting ancient literature more generally. As Douglas Olson has put it, with reference to the study of dramatic fragments, 'the recognition of what we do not know or cannot know about our texts, and an explicit acknowledgment of the degree to which our readings merely represent an agreement to work in a consensus environment forged by previous scholarship going back to the Hellenistic world, is a significant contribution this tiny subfield, with its difficult and puzzling material, can make to the modern discipline of classical studies'.[7]

We believe that the benefits of incorporating fragments into our regular discussions of tragedy in this way considerably outweigh any drawbacks. We look forward to a world where there are no 'fragments scholars' at all because everyone with an interest in this field, or any field for which the evidence is partially 'complete', partially fragmentary, discusses fragmentary evidence alongside less-fragmentary evidence as a matter of course.

***

In this volume, we bring some of the least-studied texts in the tragic genre into dialogue with one of its most-studied areas of modern scholarly enquiry: the representation of female characters. Our aim in doing so is twofold. From the perspective of the fragments themselves, we wish to re-examine them in the light of modern critical approaches, showing how they can open up insightful new ways of reading and interpreting these texts. And conversely, from the perspective of current trends in approaches to Greek tragedy, we ask how these neglected plays and characters might offer fresh perspectives on familiar questions, since turning to the fragments exposes the extent to which our ways of studying tragedy have been directed by a near-exclusive focus on the extant dramas. In other words, if tragedies such as *Agamemnon*, *Antigone*, *Hippolytus*, the *Electra* plays and *Medea* had not survived in full – but Aeschylus' *Nereids*, Sophocles' *Eurypylus* and *Tereus* and Euripides' *Antigone*, *Cretans*, *Hypsipyle*, *Ino* and *Protesilaus* had, what kind of traditions of thinking about tragedy would we have inherited, and what would it now mean to study 'women in tragedy'?

---

[6] Wright 2016: xi–xii, xxiii–xxvi. See also the dialogue of Baltussen and Olson 2017 for two contrasting approaches to the study of literary fragments, particularly in relation to the possibility and implications of the activity of recovering a lost 'whole'.
[7] Olson 2017: 138.

In both respects, we hope to show how the underused resources of the fragmentary tragedies have the potential to reshape the field, not only with regard to subjects that may appear more immediately connected to the theme of female characters (such as gender, sexuality, marriage and the family), but also by contributing to a better understanding of many issues central to the interpretation of ancient drama, including characterisation, ethical agency, politics, space and staging and *mousikê*.

In addressing the tragic representation of women, this volume intervenes in a field that has witnessed some of the most exciting and provocative scholarship of recent decades. The study of women and female experience in Greek tragedy was particularly reinvigorated from the 1970s onwards by the application of feminist interpretative frameworks to the texts; and the topic has been further enriched by readings and approaches that draw on, *inter alia*, psychoanalysis, structural anthropology and socio-linguistics.[8] Individual female characters from Greek tragedy have loomed large in debates in political and ethical philosophy: in particular, Sophocles' Antigone has been, and remains, a central figure in the discussion of kinship, ethics and, more recently, feminist politics.[9]

But in general, the engagement of this capacious and particularly fertile field of scholarship with the fragmentary plays has been restrained. This is partly down to the difficulties of dealing with fragments, as outlined above. But it is also due to the fact that the extant plays offer such a varied and complex range of characters that even restricting ourselves to these means that we already seemingly have 'enough' to be getting on with. One contribution in this area is illustrative: in his paper 'Sophocles and women', delivered in 1982 at the Fondation Hardt Entretiens on Sophocles, R. P. Winnington-Ingram begins his analysis of that tragedian's female roles with a fragment: *Tereus* fr. 583, Procne's lament on the miseries of marriage. After summarising its content in one sentence and hypothesising that the play might be dated to a relatively late period of Sophocles' career, his sole and concluding comment on the text itself reads: 'There is no lack of appropriateness to the dramatic situation, but we do not have the

---

[8] Zeitlin 1978 ≈ 1996: 87–119, 1985 ≈ 1996: 341–74 = Winkler and Zeitlin 1990: 63–96, Foley 1981b, 2001, Loraux 1985 ≈ 1987, des Bouvrie 1990, Rabinowitz 1993, Segal 1993, Seidensticker 1995, Wohl 1998, Ormand 1999, Mendelsohn 2002. For women's speech, song and communication in tragedy see McClure 1999, Griffith 2001, Mossman 2001, 2005, 2012, Dué 2006, Chong-Gossard 2008.

[9] Lacan 1986: 283–333 (lectures delivered 1960), translated in Lacan 1992, Irigaray 1974 ≈ 1985, J. Butler 2000, Honig 2013.

context and cannot say whether this speech bore on the total picture of the heroine. We had better turn to extant plays.'[10]

This reluctance to even attempt to engage with the fragments – to try to read them as literature, rather than a puzzle waiting to be reconstructed – is by no means untypical, even in a critic as insightful as Winnington-Ingram.[11] Strikingly, his structure and phrasing are echoed some thirty years later in Judith Mossman's chapter on women's voices in Sophocles for the Brill Companion: she also begins by looking at Procne's speech, but offers only a brief paragraph of discussion before concluding: 'Tantalizing though the fragments may be, it seems best to concentrate on the extant plays for the remainder of this chapter.'[12] In a pattern replicated in many other works, we find a tension here between the evident enticement and appeal of the fragment (which both scholars have, after all, elected to place first in their discussions) and its ready dismissal in favour of concentrating on the extant plays, where the chosen themes can be traced more fully, and with less need for uncertainty and speculation.

On the other end of the spectrum, the overconfident use of the fragments could be equally damaging to their acceptance into the scholarly mainstream. In his 1967 monograph on Euripides, T. B. L. Webster attempted to incorporate all the known plays, including the fragmentary ones, into his analysis, and his approach (typical of the period) relied on over-interpretation of the evidence in order to piece together detailed outlines and reconstructions of the lost works. In relation to the study of women in Euripides he at least attempted to draw together the totality of the evidence, but his main hypothesis to emerge from this endeavour – that in his early trilogies, Euripides followed the pattern of producing one play about a 'bad woman' (by which Webster generally means a woman who acts out of sexual desire), one play about an 'unhappy woman' and one play 'of a different kind' – has not aged well.[13]

There are other instances of the inclusion of fragmentary plays in discussions of gender and women in tragedy. For example, Froma Zeitlin's 'The politics of Eros in the Danaid trilogy of Aeschylus' takes the whole

---

[10] Winnington-Ingram 1983: 237.

[11] Similarly, Winnington-Ingram's great monograph on Sophocles (1980) is largely a fragment-free zone, with his reflections on humanity's relationship with the gods unaffected by the remarkable papyrus of Sophocles' *Niobe*, in which Apollo and Artemis slaughter the title character's terrified daughters, published only a few years before: Finglass 2019a: 29–34.

[12] Mossman 2012: 492.

[13] Webster 1967: 116. For the unfortunate afterlife of Webster's coinage of the phrase 'bad woman' in studies of tragedy see Mueller 2017: 502; for further criticism of his book see Burnett 1968.

trilogy into account, although given the exiguous remains of both *Egyptians* and *Danaids*, its focus is mainly on the single extant play, *Suppliants*.[14] The fact that the fragmentary tragedies preserve certain plot patterns that are not as well represented in the extant dramas has also led to their use in elucidation of those themes. In relation to the study of female characters, one notable example is the mythical pattern termed the 'girl's tragedy' by Burkert,[15] in which an unmarried girl is raped by a god and subsequently threatened or punished by her family when it is discovered that she is either pregnant or has given birth. Scholars have analysed this theme in fragmentary works such as Sophocles' *Tyro* and Euripides' *Antiope* and *Melanippe the Wise* alongside the extant *Ion*.[16] One fragmentary tragedy that has enjoyed more substantial critical attention is Euripides' *Erechtheus*, and the centrality of female characters to its plot – which includes a long and memorable speech by the Athenian queen Praxithea, in which she volunteers her daughter for sacrifice on behalf of the city – has helped the play find its way into scholarship on the representation of women's roles in Athenian civic and ritual identity.[17] But in the majority of those works that have been broadly influential in the study of gender and female characters in tragedy, it is fair to say that more often than not any mention of the fragmentary plays is brief, fleeting or simply absent.

***

In this volume, our contributors have approached the fragments under the directives outlined above: both to reveal new ways of reading and interpreting them, and to show how these plays might prompt a reevaluation of the kinds of questions and approaches that are current in tragic scholarship. We here offer a brief outline of the major findings of each chapter and their contribution to the broader landscape of the study of women in Greek tragedy.

One productive line of scholarly enquiry has been the attention given to the dynamics and symbolism of marriage. Viewed as a social transaction between men that transfers women from one household (the natal *oikos*) to another (the marital *oikos*), in tragedy the institution of marriage is particularly adept at exposing rifts and moments of tension in its surrounding

---

[14] Zeitlin 1992 = 1996: 123–71.

[15] Burkert 1979: 6–7.

[16] Scafuro 1990, Sommerstein 2006a.

[17] See Calame 2011 on the role of the male and female in the play's construction of Athenian autochthony, Goff 2004: 322–3 on ritual identity.

social structure, and at providing opportunities for female characters to voice their own subjective experiences and assert themselves as agents within their marital relationships.[18] In the extant plays, marriage rarely (if ever) manifests itself as a positive and straightforward transaction or state of affairs, and notably it is the women whose interventions generally help to bring things to a catastrophic end: so we find characters who cause death and destruction after their husbands introduce a mistress into the household (Clytemnestra, Deianira) or abandon them for another woman (Medea), wives who take or desire to take an adulterous lover (Clytemnestra, Phaedra) and women who commit suicide because of some aspect of their marriage (Deianira, Evadne, Jocasta, Phaedra). In addition, the overlapping imagery and symbolism of marriage and death means that we also find strong nuptial associations even in the cases of unmarried girls who die by suicide, sacrifice or murder (Antigone, Cassandra, Iphigenia, Polyxena, the daughter of Heracles).

The extant plays thus offer a rich variety of female roles in relation to their experience of marriage and sexual desire, but without taking the fragmentary plays into account, the picture is incomplete. Several contributions to this volume demonstrate how the fragments reveal variations and refinements of these well-known tragic models. In her chapter, Helene P. Foley ('Heterosexual Bonding in the Fragments of Euripides') provides a thorough survey of the theme of heterosexual love in the fragments of Euripides, demonstrating how many of these plays – particularly *Andromeda*, *Oedipus*, *Protesilaus* and *Antigone* – offer glimpses of a different permutation of tragic marriage. These plays dramatise marital or premarital relationships in which the female partner could play an active and sometimes assertive role, and which, even when placed within dramatic contexts that render the union itself problematic, may be termed reciprocal and even romantic. Foley's widening of the scope of enquiry demonstrates that the more positive portrayal of spousal bonds that we find in Euripides' *Helen* is not an anomaly within the genre: tragic marriage did not always have to be portrayed a site of friction and disaster, and in fact it was some of Euripides' most overtly erotic and romantic plays that left a distinctive mark on their original and later audiences.

Euripides did not, of course, restrict his portrayal of female sexual desire to that between husband and wife, or suitor and unmarried virgin; as is well known, he was lampooned in Aristophanes' comedies for creating

---

[18] For tragic marriage see Seaford 1987 = 2018: 257–99, Rehm 1994, Ormand 1999.

characters such as Phaedra and Stheneboea, married women driven by desire for a man who is not their husband. By contrast, the picture of Sophocles that we glean from the extant tragedies seems to characterise him as a playwright comparatively less interested in depicting female erotic expression and its consequences. Alan H. Sommerstein ('Women in Love in the Fragmentary Plays of Sophocles') shows that this picture is flawed: in at least three plays – *Phaedra*, *Oenomaus* and *Women of Colchis* – Sophocles did portray 'women in love' who experienced sexual desire for a male character and whose actions in pursuit of that desire resulted in the deaths of others. Sommerstein's chapter not only draws attention to this overlooked aspect of Sophoclean characterisation, but also deftly exposes the main differences between the typical Sophoclean and Euripidean models of such women: in Sophocles, none is deliberately betraying a husband, and this may be one reason as to why the playwright appears to have escaped the accusations of immorality and misogyny that comedy heaped upon Euripides.

As noted, in the extant plays we find examples of wives who react intensely and/or with violence to the introduction of a sexual rival into the *oikos* or to their abandonment by their partner for that rival. In her contribution, Fiona McHardy ('Female Violence towards Women and Girls in Greek Tragedy') fills in the gaps in our understanding of this pattern by taking into account the fragmentary plays in which women enact violence upon other women and girls. As she demonstrates, this most often occurs in the case of married women who perceive the introduction of a (younger) rival into their household as a threat to their own position and status, and it frequently takes the form of an attack upon this rival's physical beauty. McHardy shows that we should place less recognised figures such as Sidero, Dirce and the wife of Creon alongside the widely cited examples of Clytemnestra and Medea as tragic wives whose desire to maintain or restore their status leads them to violently target other women.

P. J. Finglass ('Suffering in Silence: Victims of Rape on the Tragic Stage') focuses on women who have themselves been the object of violence and who are linked by the theme of silence. The episode in *Trachiniae* in which Deianira is struck by the appearance of Iole has long been compared to the scene between Clytemnestra and Cassandra in Aeschylus' *Agamemnon*: in both cases, a silent woman, a target of male sexual lust, arrives at the home of her new master and is met by his wife. Finglass highlights the relevance of a third play for this pattern: Sophocles' *Tereus*, in which the mutilated Philomela, her tongue cut out, will have arrived at the palace of Tereus and his wife, her sister Procne. Finglass draws out the structural and thematic parallels between these three tragedies, showing how each offers a related but distinct configuration of the connection between female voice and voicelessness, suffering and power.

A further victim of rape – here, though, one who gives an account of her experience – is the subject of Niall W. Slater's chapter ('*Europa* Revisited: An Experiment in Characterisation'), which addresses the extensive fragment attributed to Aeschylus' *Carians/Europa*, in which the speaker Europa describes her rape by Zeus, the births of her three children and her fear for the safety of her son Sarpedon; this speech allows the audience 'to contemplate the sufferings of Europa over a woman's full lifecycle, culminating in her role as aged mother awaiting her only surviving son's return' (p. 137). Considering issues of lexicon and dramatic technique, Slater supports a date for the play in the 420s, noting with sympathy Martin West's argument this play's author was Aeschylus' son Euphorion.

The tragedians employed not only speech and silence in the creation of their female characters, but also song. Usually marking moments of elevated emotion, tragic song is used to powerful effect in the characterisation of both male and female (non-choral) characters, but is more strongly associated with the latter, in part owing to the associations of ritual lament as a women's genre.[19] In his chapter, Caleb Simone ('The Music One Desires: Hypsipyle and Aristophanes' "Muse of Euripides"') analyses a notable instance of female song in Euripides, the titular figure's monody in *Hypsipyle*. This character's song came to be viewed as so representative of the playwright's New Musical tendencies that she was parodied in Aristophanes' *Frogs* as 'the Muse of Euripides'. Simone's detailed reading of both the monody itself and Hypsipyle's Aristophanic reception blends the study of *mousikê*, aesthetics, synaesthesia and cult to show how Euripides' singing heroine absorbs the audience into her desire for a form of music that is marked as Asian, Orphic and citharodic, and which forges a continuous chain between the musical culture of Lemnos and Euripides' contemporary Athens. In this interpretation, Hypsipyle's song showcases not just the playwright's skill in the creation of a virtuosic female voice, but also his use of female song to create a link to the political realities of the world of the audience.

Greek tragedy often centres on families, and its female characters are viewed in their roles as mothers, wives, sisters and daughters. Given the particularly fraught and violent relationships that mark the families of

---

[19] Hall 1999 ≈ 2006: 288–320.

Greek myth, it is no surprise that these tragic women often face scenarios where the articulation and enactment of these different roles involve a conflict of loyalties, and that their ethical choices play out against a backdrop of social expectations determined by these familial roles and structures. In particular, the tension between their duty to their natal families and that owed to their (potential) marital families emerges as a key theme, and extant tragedy provides us with powerful paradigms of women who take decisive stances with regard to their own positioning within the family.

In the extant plays, both Antigone (in Sophocles' *Antigone*) and Electra (in Sophocles' *Electra* and Euripides' *Electra*) obsessively prioritise the memory of their dead or absent fathers and brothers over relationships with both their living female family members and their actual or potential marital partners; we see this solidarity of sister and brother also between Electra and Orestes in Euripides' *Iphigenia in Tauris* and *Orestes*. The prevalence in the extant plays of this particular model – the girl who is (excessively?) dutiful in her role as daughter to her father and sister to her brother – has left a strong stamp on our ways of thinking about tragedy, through both the legacy of Hegel's influential analysis of the family in *Antigone* and Freud's psychoanalytic theorising about the character of Electra. Lyndsay Coo ('Greek Tragedy and the Theatre of Sisterhood') instead draws attention to a familial relationship that has been treated as all but invisible: that between sisters. Although we find examples of this bond in our surviving tragedies (most notably in Aeschylus' *Suppliant Women* and Sophocles' *Antigone* and *Electra*), it has long been over-shadowed by a focus on male-female relations. Coo's discussion, prompted by the recent productive debate between the fields of classics and political theory over the sisterhood of *Antigone*, employs close readings of Sophocles' *Tereus* and Euripides' *Erechtheus* to bring out a feminist interpretation of these texts that places sisterhood front and centre. She shows not only that sisterhood was a more prevalent theme in Greek tragedy than is visible from the extant plays alone, but also that the fragments can be a rich source for scholars working in the area of feminist political theory.

A different focus on the family is found in Robert Cowan's chapter 'When Mothers Turn Bad: the Perversion of the Maternal Ideal in Sophocles' *Eurypylus*'. In this tragedy, known to us from extensive but lacunose papyrus fragments, the Mysian queen Astyoche receives news of the death at the hands of Neoptolemus of her son Eurypylus, whom she had sent to fight at Troy. Extant tragedy, of course, provides us with examples of 'bad' mothers, whose actions with regard to their children range from neglect

(Clytemnestra) to the extreme of murder (Medea). Cowan reads Astyoche through the intersection of maternal and patriotic values in what he terms the 'martial mother ideal', whereby women send the sons whom they have nurtured off to battle for the sake of the city. As he notes, in *Eurypylus* the mother's motivation is perverted – she sends her son not out of civic duty, but as the result of a bribe – and the outcome is inverted, as Eurypylus' resulting death does nothing to avert the fall of Troy. In drawing out the complex portrayal of Astyoche in relation to her role as mother, her manipulation of the categories of natal and marital family, and her violent self-condemnation, Cowan sheds new light on what must have been one of Sophocles' most compelling female characters.

The relationship between women and space in drama has also been a longstanding focus of critical attention. Michael Shaw's characterisation of any woman on the tragic stage (and hence in an outdoor space) as a 'female intruder' was challenged in the 1980s by Helene Foley, Froma Zeitlin and Pat Easterling, who argued for a more sophisticated conception than the binary that saw 'female' space as the hidden interior of the *oikos*, and 'male' space as the public, outdoor space of the *polis*.[20] The characterisation of theatrical space as gendered and the roles that female characters are able to play in creating, inhabiting, manipulating and traversing that space have continued to receive sophisticated analysis.[21] In her chapter ('Dancing on the Plain of the Sea: Gender and Theatrical Space in Aeschylus' *Achilleis* Trilogy') Anna Uhlig expands this discussion to encompass the relationship of non-human female characters to theatrical space, and considers how the matrix of gender and topography might have played out across the full span of a tragic production in the case of the conjectured Aeschylean trilogy of *Myrmidons*, *Nereids* and *Phrygians/The Ransoming of Hector*. Uhlig argues that the chorus of sea-goddess Nereids will have provided a contrasting female presence within the trilogy as a whole, usurping the roles of the male voices central to the plays' Iliadic source material, and her analysis demonstrates how their presence would have rendered the theatrical space unusually fluid, in both senses of the word. Her suggestion that other Aeschylean plays with female choruses may have been similarly imaginative in their manipulation of the representation of theatrical space, often involving configurations that move beyond the *oikos/polis*

---

[20] Shaw 1975; see Foley 1982, Zeitlin 1985 ≈ 1996: 341–74 = Winkler and Zeitlin 1990: 63–96, Easterling 1987.

[21] For women and space see Chong-Gossard 2008 (on gender, space and communication), Mastronarde 2010: 248–54 (on the indoors/outdoors binary).

opposition, posits an intriguing new connection between gender and the construction of space in tragedy.

Our volume also addresses the crucial nexus of female characterisation, ethics and agency. Since the 1980s, a particularly influential theory has argued that the women of tragedy are not meant to represent 'real' women, but rather an 'other' against whom the male characters (and audience) can construct their own ideas of selfhood and subjectivity. As Zeitlin has phrased it, in tragedy 'the self that is really at stake is to be identified with the male, while the woman is assigned the role of the radical other';[22] and along related lines, the seminal work of Helene Foley (2001) has argued that the tragedians' exploration of female characters permitted them to confront the implications of a subjective and gendered form of ethics.

Two of our contributors extend these explorations of female characterisation and agency to key figures in the fragmentary plays. In his contribution ('Fragmented Self and Fragmented Responsibility: Pasiphae in Euripides' *Cretans*'), Luigi Battezzato analyses the particularly complex representation of responsibility and selfhood present in the speech of Pasiphae in Euripides' *Cretans*, in which the queen defends her act of falling in love with the bull. Battezzato shows how Pasiphae is able to dissociate herself completely from her past actions by appealing to divine intervention, the role of her husband Minos and an understanding of human morality and motivation that is rooted in hedonistic principles. Pasiphae's defence thus relies on a concept of the fragmentation of the self that reveals her as one of Euripides' most philosophically sophisticated female speakers.

James H. Kim On Chong-Gossard's chapter 'Female Agency in Euripides' *Hypsipyle*' restores this play to a central place in discussions of female agency in tragedy by demonstrating how the intricacies of its plot result from a series of interconnected decisions made by women. At critical junctures both before and within the timeframe of the play itself, it is the female characters Hypsipyle, Eurydice and Eriphyle whose actions determine the course of the plot and have far-reaching implications for each other. Chong-Gossard's analysis shows how the play's happy ending – which sees Hypsipyle finally re-united with her twin sons – is made possible only because of a long series of choices enacted by these three women. In particular, Eurydice's decision to exercise forgiveness and spare Hypsipyle, whose neglect of her son Opheltes has led to his death,

---

[22] Zeitlin 1985: 66 ≈ 1996: 346 = Winkler and Zeitlin 1990: 68.

marks a powerful departure from the vengeful mothers that we find in other tragedies. Through these characters, Euripides articulates a view of women's experience and subjectivity that is no less rich and engaging than the male world of the unfolding expedition against Thebes, which forms this play's backdrop.

The influence of the extant plays has been so immense and far-reaching that it is easy to forget that other tragic versions of these characters existed. This is true above all in the case of Euripides' Medea, whose terrible, tortured act of infanticide is to many modern readers and audiences the single defining aspect of her tragic characterisation. In the final chapter ('Making Medea Medea'), Matthew Wright destabilises this preconception by drawing together evidence for the full range of tragic Medeas, including a play in which she is not guilty of the act that has come to define her, the killing of her own children. He recovers a more accurate picture of Medea on the tragic stage, and suggests that what 'made Medea Medea' for the ancient audiences was not her infanticide, but rather the sheer range and malleability of stories in which she featured. Wright's survey offers an important corrective to widespread conceptions of this iconic figure, and powerfully demonstrates how the legacy of a single surviving version has distorted our understanding of the kinds of female characters with which ancient tragic audiences would have been familiar.

***

We are aware of how much is left out. Important characters such as Ino, Melanippe and Niobe receive little or no attention here. And while Wright's contribution broadens the focus beyond the 'big three' tragedians (and Slater's raises the possibility that a major fragment attributed to Aeschylus could be by his son Euphorion), our volume does not do this systematically: female characters in plays by other classical tragedians, or in tragic fragments whose authorship is unclear, receive little coverage. In a discussion of fragmentariness which spans several disciplines, Glenn Most remarked of Rainer Maria Rilke's poem 'Archaic Torso of Apollo' (1918) that the object which it describes, 'precisely by being incomplete, ... stimulates our imagination to try to complete it, and we end up admiring the creativity that would otherwise have languished within us.'[23] So too we hope that the inevitable fragmentariness and incompleteness of our enterprise will stimulate the creativity of other scholars to fill the many

---

[23] Most 2009: 12.

gaps that we have left. Our hope is that this volume provides a starting point for further enquiry, and more important than any individual hypothesis advanced in its chapters is our overall conviction that the fragmentary plays need to be taken into account in any general theory of tragedy. Much of what we have outlined here could apply to the importance of fragmentary evidence for the discussion of any theme or idea in this extraordinarily rich genre. This is deliberate, as we are aiming to plot a course that others will follow in their interpretations. The regular, thorough and imaginative integration of the fragmentary plays can lead to nothing less than a realignment of how we do scholarship on Greek tragedy.

PART I

Themes

2 | Female Violence towards Women and Girls in Greek Tragedy

FIONA MCHARDY

While it has frequently been noted that violence did not usually take place on stage in Greek tragedy,[1] it is nevertheless a genre replete with examples of murderous acts and violent attacks of a physical nature, including torture, incarceration, blinding, beating and other forms of ill treatment, as well as psychological and emotional forms of abuse, such as intentional humiliation, neglect and infliction of distress.[2] Most of these instances involve harm inflicted upon members of the household, including kin-killing and intra-familial violence.[3] Examples of some of these acts of violence have been explored to discuss gendered power dynamics on the tragic stage and in other Greek literature. In his article on the imprisonment of women in Greek tragedy, Richard Seaford highlights how men sought to control their female kin who have become pregnant by a god.[4] David Schaps, in his article on wife-beating in the *Iliad*, also draws attention to men's desire to retain control over their wives as a reason for violence, noting that Zeus uses threats as a form of psychological abuse to control the behaviour of his wife.[5] In an article on instances of domestic violence during pregnancy, Susan Deacy and I argue that a sense of lack of control over women's sexuality might motivate men to act violently towards their intimate partners in an attempt to reassert their authority over the women's bodies.[6] Lloyd Llewellyn-Jones, too, focuses on the way in which men control their wives through violence in his exploration of the probable frequency of acts of domestic violence in ancient Greece.[7]

I would like to thank Lesel Dawson, Mike Edwards, Richard Seaford and the editors of this volume for their helpful comments on earlier versions of this chapter.

[1] E.g. Goldhill 1991: 15. Sommerstein 2004 = 2010b: 30–46 points out that both killing and hitting are absent from the stage (though present in descriptions by messengers and others), but other forms of violent behaviour such as dragging and manhandling do occur.

[2] Cf. Goldhill 1991: 19–20 on *hybris*.

[3] Belfiore 2000 argues that doing harm to friends is characteristic of tragic plotlines; cf. Arist. *Poet.* 1453b19–22.

[4] Seaford 1990; cf. McHardy 2008b.

[5] Schaps 2006; cf. Synodinou 1987.

[6] Deacy and McHardy 2013.

[7] Llewellyn-Jones 2011: 241–2.

In discussing Euripides' *Andromache*, he notes Hermione's fear of violence or death at the hands of her husband Neoptolemus (856–7) to suggest that there is an understanding in the text that husbands would be likely to act violently towards their errant wives to punish or discipline them.[8]

These discussions of family violence or domestic violence in ancient Greek texts focus on the behaviour of men, suggesting that they use physical and emotional violence in a controlling way to assert their authority over their female relatives. In this chapter, I explore gendered power dynamics on the Greek tragic stage from a new angle, examining the phenomenon of violence perpetrated by female characters against other female characters. An examination of instances from tragedy reveals that female violence against a woman or girl is typically generated following the introduction of a woman into the household either as a new wife or as a concubine, creating rivalry between the women involved. Underpinning a woman's acts of aggression is a feeling of anxiety about being replaced as a wife that can generate hostility and vengeful violence. The wife's actions are therefore primarily aimed at preserving her position in the household with the status and economic benefits that this position brings,[9] although she might also be concerned with preserving her relationship with her husband. Consequently, enacting aggression is frequently connected with perceptions of superior social status, and suffering violence with servitude. Some sources suggest that free mistresses were inclined to treat their female slaves with excessive violence to vent their own frustrations,[10] but in tragedy a gender dynamic where a woman demonstrates her power and status through violence is also at play, as Denise McCoskey has shown.[11] Enslaved women, upon whom violence is inflicted, are likened to animals, in particular to horses that must be tamed, if necessary through violence. Through this imagery, the power dynamics of the violent interchange are articulated.[12]

Attacks typically target the facial features and hair of a female rival, indicating the significance of sexual jealousy in the wives' aggression, but also demonstrating the power of feminine beauty in establishing social and economic standing within a household. Instances of violence between women are not typical in historical and legal texts of the period. Where

---

[8] Llewellyn-Jones 2011: 247.

[9] See Foxhall 1989 on the merits of establishing social and economic status through a good marriage for Athenian girls and women.

[10] P. Clark 1998: 122–6.

[11] McCoskey 1998.

[12] See Seaford 1987: 111 = 2018: 265–6 on the association of captured or tamed animals with brides.

such stories do occur, such as in the tale of Xerxes' wife described by Herodotus, the pattern of the violence is similar to that depicted in tragic texts, where a jealous wife brutally attacks the facial features of a perceived rival, mutilating and 'defacing' her out of anger at the way her own position has been challenged.[13] Several tragedies dwell on the emotions felt by a wife who is fearful about being replaced by another woman in her husband's affections.[14] Sexual jealousy is an especially potent force in generating violence influenced by the youth and beauty of the rival or the rival's daughter.[15] Examples across a range of ancient Greek texts indicate that sexual jealousy was perceived as the most compelling force driving men to commit violent and murderous revenge against a rival,[16] and the depiction of violence by a woman against a female rival in tragedy mirrors this common theme. Feelings of envy are also closely associated with female acts of violence, in particular regarding a rival's children or her fertility.[17] It is sometimes imagined that envy and sexual jealousy are combined with hatred and anger leading to the desire for revenge.[18] In some cases, anxiety is expressed that an envious wife or stepmother might act violently towards her husband's children as a way of retaliating against him or against her love rival. In other cases, the plays express anxiety about the vulnerability of women who have previously been attacked, either as war captives or as rape victims. Left without kin or protectors, these women who have been violently assaulted by men are subject to further, persistent abuse at the hands of the women of the house. The impact on these women, and the possibility that they too will turn to violence in revenge, is explored by the tragic dramatists.

Extant Plays

Female violence towards other women and girls is a plot element in a number of extant tragedies. Euripides' *Medea* features lethal violence

---

[13] Hdt. 9.108–13; see Sancisi-Weerdenburg 1983: 27–30 on the gendered power struggles in this text.

[14] See Sanders 2014: 130–56 on the emotions of Medea, Deianira and Hermione.

[15] In their study based on evolutionary psychology, Dijkstra and Buunk 1998 found a correlation between women's feelings of sexual jealousy and their perceptions of the attractiveness of their rival, concluding that jealousy is evoked in men by perceptions of dominance in a rival man, not by his attractiveness.

[16] McHardy 2008a.

[17] Research in social psychology indicates that feelings of jealousy about a female rival are heightened if that rival is of fertile age: Hurst *et al.* 2016.

[18] See McHardy 2008a: 61–4 on Medea's sexual proprietariness, anger and revenge.

against a female love rival together with an act of vengeful infanticide. At the start of the play, Medea is angry and hurt because her husband Jason has decided to make a new marriage with the daughter of Creon, king of Corinth (17–19, 489).[19] Jason acknowledges that it is only natural for a woman to become angry when her husband brings in a new wife (909–10), but Medea's feelings of anger and jealousy exceed his expectations, making her reaction unlike that of a typical Greek woman in his eyes (1336–43). During the course of the action, Medea determines to take revenge against her husband for his betrayal. At first she says that she will kill his new bride alongside her husband (374–5), but she later shifts her focus onto the bride and her own children, to ensure that Jason is deprived of future offspring (803–6). One of the emotions driving this decision is 'begrudging envy' as outlined by Sanders, who describes it as 'I am upset that you have something, and I want to deprive you of it'.[20] In this play, Medea's envy arises out of her anger and jealousy, and motivates her to take violent revenge by depriving her husband of his current children and the potential to have more in the future.[21] In this respect, Medea's attack on her female rival forms part of a larger plan to damage her husband by depriving him of his new wife.

At the same time, though, the mode by which Medea attacks the new bride, sending a gown and diadem covered in lethal poisons that cause the wearer to suffer extreme pain and physical mutilation, indicates the level of her hostility towards her rival.[22] The princess is a 'young girl' (νεάνιδος, 1150), has 'white cheeks' (λευκὴν ... παρηίδα, 1148), a mark of her beauty,[23] and a 'shapely face' (εὐφυὲς πρόσωπον, 1198). The destruction of the younger woman's physical beauty, through poisons that dissolve her skin, burn her hair and leave her face misshapen (1185–202), exposes the extent to which Medea wishes to destroy the features that she perceives

---

[19] See Sanders 2014: 138 for a list of twenty-one references to Medea's anger throughout the play; he also notes twelve references to hatred. For Euripides' handling of the story compared to other tragic treatments see WRIGHT.

[20] Sanders 2014: 16. Unlike other wives to be discussed in this chapter, Medea does not seek to consolidate her position of power in the household of Jason, but sets out to destroy him utterly after she has established that she can seek safety with Aegeus in Athens.

[21] Sanders 2014: 139.

[22] Seaford 1987: 110 = 2018: 263 notes that the gifts sent by Medea appear to be bridal attire but are transformed into funeral clothes.

[23] Hawley 1998: 44, Thomas 2002, Robson 2013: 45–6; also Soph. *Ant.* 781–4, which connects erotic love with an image of a maiden's soft cheeks. Dijkstra and Buunk 1998 note the link between attractiveness and fertility, potentially a point of relevance in Jason's choice to marry the princess (at *Med.* 562–7 he declares his intention to have children by her).

to be desired by Jason (556).[24] Her glee at the prospect that the princess and Creon suffered when they died (1134–5) reveals the depth of her hatred towards them.

Medea's power to do violence to her children and to her love rival, and thus to her husband, is made clear in the play even though she is 'isolated' and 'citiless' (ἔρημος ἄπολις, 255) and lacking in support from her father and brother (166–7, 252–8). She is also a foreigner exiled from her homeland, 'bereft of family/friends' (φίλων ἔρημος, 513; cf. 604), reducing her status even further.[25] While Creon and his daughter have the status and wealth that Jason desires, they are nevertheless unable to thwart the plots of Medea, who relies on her tried and tested murderous abilities, clever speech and deception to defeat her enemies from a position of apparent weakness.[26] At the same time, Medea makes use of the vulnerability of her own children to take revenge on her husband. As such, her violence can be seen as an expression of her desire to establish her superiority over her enemies through her ability to control them both physically and emotionally.

Elsewhere in tragedy, women are shown exploiting the social inferiority of their rivals or the vulnerability of their rival's children. A key example of this type of behaviour is shown in Euripides' *Andromache*, in which Neoptolemus' wife Hermione threatens his concubine Andromache and their son. Andromache is depicted as isolated, 'bereft of family/friends' (ἔρημος ... φίλων, 78; cf. 569–70), living far from her home in servile conditions. In the absence of Neoptolemus, this lack of support makes Andromache highly vulnerable to Hermione's violence (109–16). As an enslaved captive, she is also susceptible to violent treatment, as encapsulated in the imagery she uses to describe how she came to Greece as a slave 'dragged by the hair' (κόμης ἐπισπασθεῖσ', 402). A similar image, used by the chorus in Aeschylus' *Seven Against Thebes* to depict how women of all ages are taken captive in war, 'pulled by the hair like a horse' (ἱππηδὸν πλοκάμων, 328), illustrates how this treatment of enemy women by soldiers was meant to belittle and dehumanise them at the moment of their transition from freedom to slavery.[27]

Hermione is contrasted with Andromache in that she can call on her father Menelaus to support her; with his help she enacts her plan to get rid

---

[24] See Newton 1989 for how the princess's suffering is akin to experiencing *erôs*.

[25] See McHardy 2008a: 16 on the difficulties of exile, Ormand 2009 on gendered aspects of exile in Euripidean tragedy.

[26] See Gredley 1987 on the relative strength and weakness of Medea and Creon.

[27] For loose hair as uncharacteristic of a married woman see Cosgrove 2005: 682.

of Andromache and her child (675–7). Here, as in *Medea*, the combined force of the royal bride and her noble father threaten an isolated woman and her vulnerable offspring. Hermione first sets out her plans for how she wishes to treat Andromache, threatening to kill her (161–2), or at least to belittle her by treating her like the lowliest of slaves (164–8). When Andromache refuses to leave the sanctuary of the shrine in which she is hiding to avoid death, Hermione threatens to force her out by saying 'I will set fire to you' (πῦρ σοι προσοίσω, 257) and declaring that she will attack her physically, inflicting 'on your skin the pains of terrible wounds' (χρωτὶ δεινῶν τραυμάτων ἀλγηδόνας, 259) to make her leave her refuge. However, she does not enact this violence herself, but relies on her father to capture her rival, which he achieves by threatening to kill her son. Once Andromache has left the altar, Menelaus reveals that he will kill her, but that the fate of her son is in Hermione's hands (425–34). He later reveals that Hermione has decided to put the boy to death (517–19).

Hermione's motivation to treat her rival violently stems from her envy, which is driven by the gossip of other women (930–53), and because she believes that Andromache is intentionally making her infertile through use of potions (32–5, 155–60).[28] From her perspective, her treatment of Andromache functions as a counterattack to prevent the concubine from ousting the lawful wife from her husband's bed 'by force' (βίαι, 35) to become his only wife.[29] Through her aggression she seeks to reinforce her position as Neoptolemus' wife and hopes to strengthen her relationship with her husband by removing his concubine and son. So when her attempts to be rid of Andromache and her son are thwarted by Peleus, and her father has left, she is depicted inflicting violence on her own body by tearing her cheeks and hair (826–7), a physical demonstration of her grief. She is overcome by fear that she will be punished by her husband and either killed or made subservient to her own slave (854–60), a reversal of the situation at the start of the play when Hermione threatened Andromache with these two possibilities.[30] Through this depiction, Euripides shows that both Andromache and Hermione are tragic figures in their own way.[31] As such, Hermione's violent behaviour towards Andromache and her child is not straightforwardly evil, but generated out of her overwhelming

---

[28] McHardy 2018: 165.
[29] Sanders 2014: 151 argues that Hermione is right to fear Andromache as rival wife.
[30] Cf. Euripides' *Electra*, in which the victimised Electra participates in killing her mother.
[31] Pabst 2011.

emotions and her desperation about the fragility of her own position within her husband's household.

Evidence for the emotions and desperation experienced by a wife in this situation can be gleaned from a parallel story that appears in Andocides' oration *On the Mysteries* (400/399). He alleges that his rival Callias kept two women in his house at the same time, one his wife, a daughter of Ischomachus, the other her mother Chrysilla (1.124). In this instance, as in *Andromache*, the emotional state of the legitimate wife is tested by the relationship of her husband with an older woman who lives in the same household. We are told that the wife attempted suicide and eventually ran away (1.125), mirroring the behaviour of Hermione in Euripides' play; the older woman became pregnant, though the paternity of her child is questioned by the speaker (1.125–7). Andocides' tale primarily seeks to inform the jurors about Callias' shameless behaviour,[32] but in painting this picture of Callias, he makes clear the level of emotional abuse suffered by his wife. He also implies that the behaviour of her husband makes him a figure worthy of tragedy by likening him to 'Oedipus or Aegisthus' (Οἰδίπους, ἢ Αἴγισθος, 1.129).[33]

Both play and oration dwell on occasions when a mistress gives birth while a wife does not, a point of some significance in debates among Athenian men concerning civic identity, legitimacy and citizenship during the fifth century.[34] At the same time, Euripides highlights the emotions of a woman who is infertile, and suggests that 'fertility rivalry' of this type between women might lead to a threat to a man's offspring.[35] Since a woman's security and social status were dependent on her ability to produce children as heirs, particularly in elite households, she would have been expected to feel threatened by a more fertile rival. In tragedy, the emotions generated by these feelings lead to violent attempts to suppress any rivals or to attack their children.[36]

A murderous wife who threatens a captive concubine appears also in Aeschylus' *Agamemnon*. In this case though, the wife, Clytemnestra, achieves the murder of the concubine, Cassandra, without recourse to the aid of male relatives. Cassandra, like Andromache, is a war captive, reduced from an elite position in society to slavery. She is depicted as youthful and

---

[32] Cox 1996.

[33] See J. Roisman 1999 for the way that Andocides and other orators employ tragic motifs to influence the jurors.

[34] Vester 2009, Blok 2017.

[35] For 'fertility rivalry' and violence in tragedy see Suter 2004.

[36] See further n. 52 below on Euripides' *Ino*.

beautiful when Agamemnon refers to her as an 'exquisite bloom' (ἐξαίρετον | ἄνθος, 954–5) given to him by the army as a gift.[37] She is likened by the chorus to a 'newly captured animal' (θηρὸς ὡς νεαιρέτου, 1063) and Clytemnestra herself uses imagery associated with a captured horse to explain Cassandra's lack of ability to endure slavery, saying 'she does not know how to tolerate a bit' (χαλινὸν δ᾽ οὐκ ἐπίσταται φέρειν, 1066).[38]

In prophesying her own death, Cassandra sees Clytemnestra as a vengeful lioness who wishes to kill the new concubine whom her husband has brought into the household (1258–63).[39] Clytemnestra later refers to the sexual relationship between Agamemnon and Cassandra, offering it as part of the reason they had to die (1438–47). Certainly, this justification for killing Agamemnon seems rather thin given Clytemnestra's own extra-marital relationship with Aegisthus, as McCoskey has argued.[40] In this case, then, sexual jealousy does not seem the main motivator for Clytemnestra's violence, although it is a motivation she expresses. Rather, her desire to retain power after the return of her husband causes her to kill him. By framing her action as vengeful, emphasising Agamemnon's cruel slaughter of her offspring Iphigenia, she seeks justification in the eyes of onlookers.[41] Her choice to kill Cassandra is therefore apparently without a strong motivation. McCoskey explains this murder by suggesting that through violence towards Cassandra as a slave woman, Clytemnestra marks herself apart, as a free woman who deserves to retain power.[42] Here, as in Euripides' *Andromache*, violence is a signifier of power and being the victim of violence is emblematic of servile status.

The dynamics of status, gender and power are also at play in Euripides' *Alcestis*, which features a hypothetical situation in which a woman marrying into the household might be violent towards the children of her new husband. Alcestis sets out her fears about what a stepmother might do to her children in an impassioned speech to her husband Admetus shortly before she dies. She first explains her decision to die in his place, saying that she has no desire to marry again and live without Admetus, leaving her children orphaned (282–9). Her comments suggest that as well as acting as a devoted wife, Alcestis has considered the plight of her children carefully

---

[37] Cf. Hawley 1998: 42 on Deanira's sadness concerning the beauty of young war captives in Sophocles' *Trachiniae*. See also FINGLASS.

[38] See Seaford 1987: 128 = 2018: 294 on how this imagery also evokes marriage.

[39] Abbattista 2018: 208–11.

[40] McCoskey 1998: 45.

[41] McHardy 2008a: 106.

[42] McCoskey 1998: 39–40.

in making her decision to die in place of their father. As Dyson has noted, her first reported words in the play, addressed to the goddess Hestia, demonstrate her concern that the children should prosper even though she has died (163–9).[43] She then asks her husband not to marry again following her death (299–310). In explaining her request, she details the way in which she perceives a stepmother might threaten the couple's children.

Central to her thinking is the idea that a stepmother would be physically violent in her treatment of the children. Alcestis suggests that the woman would 'strike the children with her hand' (παισὶ χεῖρα προσβαλεῖ) 'out of envy' (φθόνωι) towards her and her superior position (306–7). In part, this feeling arises from the existence of the children as testament to the strength of the relationship between the previous wife and her husband, so the stepmother takes out the hostility she feels concerning her love rival on that rival's children. At the same time, a woman without children might feel hatred and bitterness towards her husband's children by another woman (cf. Eur. *Ion* 607–17). This, once again, is 'begrudging envy' which, alongside feelings of jealousy about her husband's relationship with another woman, generates the emotions that lead to violence.[44]

Perceived status also features as a significant part of the stepmother's motivation in Alcestis' speech. As Alcestis makes clear in her request to her husband, if he does not remarry, his children will maintain their position of lords in the house (304–5), but imposing a stepmother will threaten their status and position, making them vulnerable. After Alcestis has died, her son highlights the isolated position of the children left without a mother (406–7), offering a sense that without their mother the children are more susceptible to harm: a stepmother might be all too ready to take advantage of their vulnerability by advancing her own position through force. Hence the stepmother's violent treatment of the children can be seen as a demonstrable way in which she might go about diminishing them. Through corporal punishment, their bodies are treated like the bodies of slaves and she makes them servile to herself.[45]

Alcestis then stresses that she is particularly anxious about the fate her daughter might suffer at the hands of a stepmother (311–19).[46] Her fears

---

[43] Dyson 1988: 14.

[44] Sanders 2014: 127–9 describes how in Euripides' *Ion* Creusa's feelings of hatred and shame are combined with envy and jealousy leading to her violent impulses towards Ion.

[45] For the association of bodily punishment with treating a free person as a slave see Dem. 21.180, 22.55, 24.167; cf. Lys. fr. 279 Carey, V. Hunter 1994: 154–84.

[46] Dyson 1988: 16, Watson 1995: 54 n. 14.

centre on how a stepmother might seek to thwart a good marriage for her stepdaughter by spreading gossip about her.[47] Here again, as suggested above, the stepmother's motivation is part of her continued 'begrudging envy' towards her husband's former wife, but she might also be thought to act out of envy towards the girl herself, begrudging her a dowry for example.[48] Alcestis' speech suggests that there was a degree of social anxiety about whether girls who had lost a mother in childhood would be less likely to prosper in adulthood.[49] This concept of the danger of violence towards a young woman or girl who has lost her mother, who is beautiful, but powerless, yet is somehow conceived of as a threat to the wife and mistress of the household, appears to have been a prominent thread in the fragmentary tragedies to which I turn now.

Fragmentary Tragedies

My analysis of extant plays involving female violence against women and girls reveals that aggression between women in the household was frequently associated with feelings of envy and jealousy about the youth, beauty and fertility of one of the women. Violence is regularly associated with status and power dynamics, where a woman seeks to subdue or belittle her perceived rival by playing on her status as a slave or likening her to an animal through the use of psychological and emotional violence. A fragmentary play (*Alcmaeon at Corinth*) that appears to have referred to these elements is described by Apollodorus (*Bibl.* 3.7.7) in his account of what happened to the family of Alcmaeon after he had killed his mother and been driven mad by her Furies. According to Apollodorus, Euripides depicted Alcmaeon at the time of his madness giving his son Amphilochus and his daughter Tisiphone to Creon, king of Corinth, to raise them.[50] However, rather than achieving safety and protection as her father surely intended, Tisiphone was perceived to be a threat by Creon's wife who sold

---

[47] See McHardy 2018 on the power of women's gossip; Cohen 1991: 161–2 and V. Hunter 1994: 111–16 on gossip and conformity to social expectations.

[48] Cf. Watson 1995: 51–4 for the possible impact of inheritance issues on the relationship of stepdaughters and stepmothers at Athens; also Foxhall 1989 on dowry as women's 'inheritance'.

[49] McHardy forthcoming.

[50] Cf. Eur. fr. 73a.2 Ἀλκμέωνι δ' ἔτεκε δίδυμα τέκνα παρθένος, 'the maiden bore Alcmaeon twin children' (probably from the play's prologue).

her into slavery because she was afraid that her husband might wish to marry Tisiphone on account of her 'beauty' (εὐμορφία).[51] If accurate, this description suggests that Euripides' play featured a woman's fear that a beautiful maiden growing up with a foster-father might usurp her foster-mother's place in her husband's affections and simultaneously deprive her of her status and economic security within the household. As seen above in the discussion of the extant plays, fear of a beautiful, young rival, combined with a sense of anger at being replaced and feelings of envy or sexual jealousy, can lead to violence against the rival woman, the husband, his children or a combination of these characters.[52] In this case, instead, the response is to cause the rival woman to be enslaved, removing her as a threat within the household by selling her outside the home where she is unwittingly bought by her own father.

Selling an errant daughter overseas is a recurrent story pattern in plays featuring young women who have been impregnated by gods and whose fathers react angrily to their lack of chastity by attempting to drown them or give them to merchants to take overseas.[53] In one comparable tale, Herodotus says that Phronime's stepmother accused her of a lack of chastity and caused her father to sentence her to death by drowning, though she was spared and taken overseas by a merchant (4.154). In this story, as in the plotline associated with Tisiphone and the hypothetical behaviour of the stepmother in *Alcestis*, a woman who is supposed to care for and raise a girl instead treats her harshly and tries to get rid of her because she perceives her as a threat to her own position, or to the position of her own future offspring. Unlike the war concubines, the stepdaughter or foster-daughter does not come into the home as a slave, but like them she is treated as a rival, and because of this rivalry comes to be treated as if she were a slave, suffering harsh treatment through which the mistress of the house exerts her control over the situation and reinforces her own position of power in the household.

---

[51] Collard and Cropp 2008: I 87–8 suggest that these details would have been revealed in the prologue.

[52] The plot of Euripides' *Ino* (light on which has recently been shed by the publication of P.Oxy. 5131) appears to have explored the way two stepmothers each targeted the children of their rival, ultimately bringing about the destruction of the entire household (Hyg. *Fab.* 4); see McHardy 2005: 131–5, Collard and Cropp 2008: I 438–59, Finglass 2014, 2016a, 2017c, Kovacs 2016.

[53] McHardy 2008b, Finglass 2011 on Soph. *Aj.* 1295–7 (on Aerope, whose father Catreus, king of Crete, attempted to have her drowned after her seduction by a servant).

The ending of *Alcmaeon in Corinth* is uncertain, but a 'typical Euripidean recognition and reunion' seem likely.[54] It has been proposed that the queen revealed the identity of Tisiphone when she came with her father to the palace because she wished to ensure that her husband Creon did not take the girl back.[55] It appears from fr. 76 that Creon went into exile in a childless state, but the fate of the queen is not mentioned. Webster imagines she went with her husband, allowing the audience a sense of satisfaction that those who have done wrong are punished.[56]

Another fragmentary tragedy that might have ended with this same sense of satisfaction following the punishment of a violent woman is Sophocles' *Tyro*. The fairy-tale nature of the names of the violent woman and her victim are certainly suggestive, with Tyro the fair-complexioned 'Snow White' character,[57] persecuted by Sidero the 'iron' stepmother figure.[58] There is evidence that Sophocles wrote two tragedies entitled *Tyro*,[59] and that one ended happily with recognition and reunion,[60] but the scant fragments are insufficient to draw firm conclusions about the plot of either play. Carl Robert hypothesises that one play might have covered the early life of Tyro, her rape by Poseidon and the exposure of her twin boys, and the other could have featured Tyro's rescue by her adult sons.[61] Alternatively, Giuseppina Martino proposes that one of the plays might have covered the myth outlined in Hyginus, which features Tyro's murder of her children by her uncle Sisyphus, while the other play could have contained the version of Apollodorus, which includes the rape of Tyro by

---

[54] Collard and Cropp 2008: 1 87. Commentators have likened the play to New Comedy (cf. Van Looy *ap.* Jouan and Van Looy 1998: 98); Krappe 1924 compares this tale to the Apollonius Romance.

[55] Webster 1967: 268; cf. Van Looy *ap.* Jouan and Van Looy 1998: 98–9.

[56] Webster 1967: 268; cf. Arist. *Poet.* 1453a31–5. Gould 1991: 4 notes that acts of violence followed by revenge lead to a satisfying ending. Finglass 2016a: 306 comments that it is rare for the jealous woman to triumph in these tragedies; the exception is Medea.

[57] Cf. Diodorus Siculus (6.7.2) where Tyro ('cheese') receives her name because of her white skin and soft body (cf. Robert 1916: 302). Engelmann 1890 ≈ 1900: 40–51 assigned to *Tyro* a fragment that alludes to a fair-skinned girl (λευκὸν <γὰρ> αὐτὴν ὧδ' ἐπαίδευσεν γάλα, 'for white milk reared her like this', fr. 648).

[58] Watson 1995: 27 n. 28, A. Clark 2003: 84 n. 6.

[59] *TrGF* IV pp. 463–4.

[60] Σ Eur. *Or.* 1691 (1 241.8–14 Schwartz); cf. Martino 1996. Moodie 2003: 133–6 notes the similarity to Euripidean 'happy ending' plays and suggests that it is not impossible that Sophocles wrote his 'happy ending' *Tyro* earlier, casting doubt on the tendency to associate this plot style particularly with Euripides. For the 'ark' as means of recognition in *Tyro* see Ar. *Lys.* 137–9, Arist. *Poet.* 1454b25; also Men. *Epitr.* 325–33.

[61] Robert 1916: 300–2; cf. Sutton 1984: 153. Lloyd-Jones 2003: 313 suggests that both plays might have contained the same storyline, revised in the later play; *contra* Moodie 2003: 120–1.

Poseidon and her mistreatment by her stepmother.[62] If the play did follow the myth as outlined by Apollodorus, it could have featured Tyro being treated harshly by her stepmother Sidero before being rescued by her sons Neleus and Pelias. Apollodorus says that Pelias killed Sidero after the twins had chased her to the altar of Hera, 'because they discovered that their mother was being mistreated by her' (κακουμένην γὰρ γνόντες ὑπ' αὐτῆς τὴν μητέρα, *Bibl.* 1.9.8). Commentators have suggested that an ending of this nature would align the plot with Euripidean fragmentary plays such as *Melanippe Desmôtis*, *Hypsipyle* and *Antiope*, where a mother who has exposed her twin infants is rescued by them from a life of misery and servitude.[63]

Evidence from other ancient writers suggests that Sophocles staged the violent relationship between Tyro and Sidero in a striking and memorable way in at least one of the plays. In his catalogue of masks, Pollux places in a special section the distinctive mask worn by Sophocles' character that showed 'Tyro with bruised cheeks' (Τυρὼ πελιδνὴ τὰς παρειάς, 4.141).[64] He notes that her mask looked like this because of 'the blows she suffered at the hands of her stepmother Sidero' (ὑπὸ τῆς μητρυιᾶς Σιδηροῦς πληγαῖς πέπονθεν). Pollux's account indicates that Tyro would have articulated her suffering on stage in Sophocles' play, since it is improbable that the character would have worn such a mask without making reference to her wretched experiences. This brief mention of Tyro focuses on her physical appearance, as revealed by the mask, and hints at her marred beauty through reference to her cheeks, a body feature that is mentioned, alongside hair, in connection with the beauty of some of the women discussed above.[65] Her loss of status and identity is also implied within the imagery of the mask.[66] At the same time though, Pollux outlines the nature of the violence inflicted on Tyro by Sidero in a few short words, noting that she

---

[62] Hyg. *Fab.* 60, Apollod. *Bibl.* 1.9.8, Martino 1996: 202; cf. Engelmann 1890 ≈ 1900: 40–51.

[63] Wilamowitz-Moellendorff 1921: 76–7 = 1935–72: ɪ 455–6. Moodie 2003: 125–6 with n. 23 also compares Euripides' *Ion, Auge, Aegeus* and *Cresphontes* where the story features recognition of one offspring, and *IT* and *Helen*, which feature recognition between different relatives. For twins in Euripidean drama see Hourmouziades 1975 = 2003: 105–34.

[64] Calame 1986: 130. There is a striking resemblance here between the bruises suffered by Tyro and by her son Pelias, so-named, according to Apollodorus, because he was kicked by a mare as an infant and the hoof left a mark on his face.

[65] See n. 23 above. For marring of beauty through mourning see Soph. *Ant.* 526–30, where Ismene's beautiful cheek is reddened by her constant weeping. For self-injury through tearing of cheeks in mourning in tragedy cf. Aesch. *Cho.* 24–5, Eur. *Tro.* 280, *Hec.* 655 and above on Hermione's actions in *Andromache*. See Eur. *El.* 241 for Electra's shaven head as expression of her grief; also below on Soph. fr. 659.

[66] Hahnemann 2012: 179.

struck Tyro hard enough to cause visible bruising. The implication of the description is that Tyro suffered physical violence that hurt and disfigured her, but did not aim to kill her. In *Alcestis*, this scenario is mentioned as a hypothetical possibility when a girl is cared for by a stepmother. No further explanation is given for the rationale behind Sidero's vicious attack.[67]

Sidero's nature is further spelt out in one fragment where she is said to be ironlike as indicated by her name (fr. 658). Her iron name implies that she is strong, but insensitive and stubborn.[68] It also suggests that she was hardened, and perhaps somewhat manlike as implied by the use of μάχιμος, which associates her with 'warlike' physical aggression. This term is typically associated with fighting men, but Aristophanes' Lysistrata also uses this word of her fellow-women to suggest that they will fight physically against male attacks (452–4). This characterisation hints at how Sidero might have dominated Tyro through violence, and potentially aligns her with the 'manlike' Clytemnestra who inflicts violence on Cassandra in order to substantiate her position of power in the household.

Underlying the main surviving fragment spoken by Tyro are similar suggestions that violence and humiliation were used against her to subdue her and reduce her status.

> κόμης δὲ πένθος λαγχάνω πώλου δίκην,
> ἥτις συναρπασθεῖσα βουκόλων ὕπο
> μάνδραις ἐν ἱππείαισιν ἀγρία χερὶ
> θέρος θερισθῆι ξανθὸν αὐχένων ἄπο,
> 5   πλαθεῖσα δ' ἐν λειμῶνι ποταμίων ποτῶν
> ἴδηι σκιᾶς εἴδωλον αὐγασθεῖσά που
> κουραῖς ἀτίμως διατετιλμένης φόβην.
> φεῦ, κἂν ἀνοικτίρμων τις οἰκτίρειέ νιν
> πτήσσουσαν αἰσχύνηισιν οἷα μαίνεται
> 10   πενθοῦσα καὶ κλαίουσα τὴν πάρος χλιδήν.

And it is my lot to mourn my hair, like a foal, whom herdsmen have seized in the horses' stables with rough grip, and who has had the yellow mane reaped from her neck; and when she comes to the meadow to drink the water of the river, reflected in the water she sees her image, with her

---

[67] Watson 1995: 25 suggests that Sidero acted out of spite and hostility as a stereotypical stepmother. Diodorus Siculus (4.68.2) makes Sidero the second wife of Salmoneus and says that 'she treated Tyro harshly, because she was her stepmother' (αὕτη δὲ χαλεπῶς διετέθη πρὸς τὴν Τυρώ, ὡς ἂν μητρυιά). At 6.7.2–3, though, Salmoneus himself punishes his daughter harshly.

[68] Cf. Todd 2007: 686 on Lys. 10.20, who says that the term implies 'a combination of shamelessness [citing Ar. *Ach.* 492], insensitivity [citing Aeschin. 3.166] and also perhaps stubbornness [Hom. *Il.* 22.357]'.

hair shamefully hacked off. Ah, even a pitiless person might pity her, cowering beneath the outrage, as she madly laments and bewails the luxuriant hair she had before!

Soph. *Tyro* fr. 659 (transl. Lloyd-Jones)

The fragment appears to refer to Sidero's harsh treatment of Tyro.[69] Tyro compares herself to a young horse shorn of its mane (lines 1, 4) and speaks of the 'wild hand' of the men who shear the foal (lines 2–3), indicating their aggression in performing the act. In part, the shearing is an act of dominance that signifies control.[70] Unmarried women's hair is loose when young (*Hom. Hym.* 2.177–8) and tied back at marriage, but can be cut short for slaves.[71] The cropping of a free girl's hair likens her to a slave and humiliates her in public, as the fragment makes clear through mention of the dishonour and shame that comes of having hair shorn (lines 7, 9). Clark further suggests that the violence could be seen as a punishment for lack of chastity inflicted on Tyro by Sidero soon after she had given birth.[72]

Another possible interpretation is that Sophocles made Sidero the wife of Tyro's paternal uncle Cretheus, as suggested in Apollodorus, where Tyro was reared by her uncle Cretheus after the death of her parents.[73] If Sidero were in the role of uncle's wife, her violence towards Tyro could be explained by her fear of Tyro as a love rival, causing her to seek to destroy her rival's famous fair complexion and fair hair to make her less alluring to her husband.[74] In this play, as in those analysed above, a beautiful young woman is submitted to violent treatment that targets her beauty, hinting at envy and jealousy as possible motivating factors, as seen in *Medea*, where Medea targets the physical features of her rival. At the same time, by attacking Tyro physically, Sidero, like Hermione in *Andromache*, could be conceived of as treating Tyro like a slave to reinforce the status boundaries between herself as mistress of the house and Tyro as a perceived

---

[69] A. Clark 2003; cf. Moodie 2003: 133.

[70] A. Clark 2003: 94–5 compares Menander's *Perikeiromene* in which Glykera's hair is shorn, making her look like a slave, prostitute or flute girl. The cutting of Glykera's hair is an act of controlling domestic violence in an intimate partner relationship.

[71] Cosgrove 2005; cf. Griffith 2006b: 315–17. For the previously veiled hair of a married woman flowing loose when captured in war cf. Diod. Sic. 17.35.5–7; for slaves' short hair cf. Eur. *El.* 107–10.

[72] A. Clark 2003.

[73] Apollod. *Bibl.* 1.9.8. Cf. Hom. *Od.* 11.235–59, [Hes.] fr. 30.24–30 M–W, Diod. Sic. 4.68.3, where Tyro is said to be the wife of Cretheus.

[74] See Robert 1916: 280 for discussion of the ambiguity over Sidero's spouse in Apollodorus; cf. A. Clark 2003: 83–4.

threat to that status. Like the captive women discussed above, Tyro is associated with an animal that is subdued through humiliation.[75] By acting forcefully against her female rival, the mistress of the house hopes to dominate or to eliminate her. This reading would also align the play with *Alcmaeon at Corinth*, where the queen appears to have treated a perceived rival in the household as a slave to limit her ability to take her place.

Another play that apparently featured a violent wife maltreating and subduing her husband's niece is Euripides' *Antiope*.[76] Commentators have noted the common story pattern where twins, exposed at birth after their mother's rape by a god, return as adults to rescue her from an abusive situation and punish her abuser.[77] If we accept the plot for Euripides' *Antiope* as summarised by Hyginus,[78] Zeus is attracted to Antiope because of her beauty and makes her pregnant with the twins Amphion and Zethus. Her lack of chastity makes her father Nycteus furious and he threatens to harm his daughter, causing her to run away and get married to Epaphus. On his deathbed, Nycteus implores his brother Lycus to punish his errant daughter. According to Hyginus, Lycus is active in pursuing and capturing Antiope, but once again, as in *Tyro*, it is his wife Dirce who takes over as the main persecutor of the girl. Likewise, it is ultimately she who is punished by Antiope's adult sons, although they also threaten Lycus. While this summary explains the reason for Nycteus' anger and why his brother is motivated to act on his behalf, it does not provide any clear motivation for Dirce's actions. It is implied that Antiope was treated as a slave in her uncle's household and stated that Zethus mistook her for a runaway slave. Apollodorus' version (*Bibl.* 3.5.5) is similar, although he spells out more clearly that Lycus enslaves Antiope when he kills her husband and brings her as a 'war captive' (αἰχμάλωτος) to his house where she is mistreated by Dirce.[79] Underlying both these versions is the idea that an enslaved woman is passed over to the mistress of the house. As seen in other tragic texts, the mistress typically perceives the captive as a rival and a possible threat to her

---

[75] Xenophon (*Eq.* 5.8) suggests that cutting the mane of a mare diminishes her status and feelings of freedom, making her more servile and obedient; cf. Arist. *HA* 572a8–b29. Aelian (*NA* 2.10, 11.18), who preserves the fragment, makes similar points regarding status and cutting of hair; cf. Griffith 2006b: 315–17. Semonides' horse woman (fr. 7.57–70 *IEG*) dedicates herself to her looks, especially her hair, rather than working and being 'slavish' (cf. Gregory 2007: 205–6).

[76] Robert 1916: 280 compares the trio of Tyro, Cretheus and Sidero to Antiope, Lycus and Dirce.

[77] See above, n. 63, and cf. Paus. 9.25.3.

[78] *Fab.* 8, on which Luppe 1984; cf. Webster 1967: 205–11, Kambitsis 1972: xvii–xx, Van Looy *ap.* Jouan and Van Looy 1998: 213–39, Collard and Cropp 2008: i 171–5, Finglass 2014: 70–1. Cf. Σ Ap. Rh. 4.1090 (pp. 304.28–305.11 Wendel).

[79] Cf. Apollod. *Bibl.* 2.7.7 for Iole, 3.10.7 for Aethra taken as war captives.

own position, especially if she is younger and more beautiful. Through violence against Antiope, Dirce asserts her power and authority, as well as punishing Antiope for her lack of chastity.

In Propertius' version of the myth, it is said that Dirce attacked Antiope because of her sexual relationship with her husband Lycus.[80] He adds, 'Ah, how often the queen tore out her beautiful hair, and attacked her delicate face with savage hands' (*ah quotiens pulchros vulsit regina capillos,* | *molliaque immitis fixit in ora manus!*, 3.15.13–14), a mode of violence akin to Sidero's attacks on Tyro. The appearance of similar motivating forces in Hyginus' alternate story of Antiope (*Fab.* 7) perhaps suggests that Euripides did not make Dirce act out of sexual jealousy towards Antiope, but the presence of the etymology of the twins' names in *Fab.* 7, in similar fashion to fragments from Euripides' play (frr. 181–2), opens up the possibility that elements derived from Euripides' *Antiope* appear in both of Hyginus' summaries.

The fragments attributed to *Antiope* do not record how Dirce was violent towards Antiope, but three fragments referring to slaves' lack of status and weak position (frr. 216–18) may refer to Antiope and her suffering as a slave in the household of Lycus.[81] However, two fragments contain material referring to the punishment of Dirce, one of which appears to belong to a messenger's speech and the other to the final scene of the tragedy. Another fragment details how when Dirce was tied to the bull, 'if it happened to twist around anywhere <...> it dragged along with it woman, rock, oak tree, continually changing direction' (εἰ δέ που τύχοι | πέριξ ἑλίξας <...> εἶλχ' ὁμοῦ λαβὼν | γυναῖκα πέτραν δρῦν μεταλλάσσων ἀεί, fr. 221), giving a vivid picture of the horrifying way in which Dirce died. In the other fragment, Lycus is told that his wife has been killed by being dragged along by a bull (fr. 223.60–2).

It seems plausible that in Euripides' play the sons of Antiope rescued their mother as she was being dragged away by Dirce and then tied Dirce to the bull by her hair to kill her, as Hyginus describes.[82] The summary suggests that Euripides could have mirrored the image of a woman being dragged away by her hair as a slave with the image of her violent mistress

---

[80] López Cruces 2010, 2011: 468–9 suggests that Dirce makes use of the Dionysiac festival to disguise her genuine motive for trying to kill Antiope, namely sexual jealousy.

[81] Van Looy *ap.* Jouan and Van Looy 2000: 233, Collard 2004b: 324. Kambitsis 1972: 98 suggests that in fr. 216 Dirce could be addressing the herdsman. Cf. also Pacuvius fr. 13–14 Warmington.

[82] *Fab.* 8.5 *Dircen ad taurum crinibus religatam necant* ('they killed Dirce, tied to the bull by her hair').

dragged along by a bull by her hair. It is possible that a fragment of Pacuvius' *Antiopa*, which describes a woman being dragged away by the hair over the rocks, echoes a Euripidean scene involving Antiope being dragged away by Dirce (*agite ite evolvite rapite, coma | tractate per aspera saxa et humum, | scindite vestem ocius!*, fr. 18–20, 'Come you all! Move along! Seize her, roll her out! Haul her by the hair along the ground and over the rough rocks. Rend her garments, quickly!', transl. Warmington).[83] There has also been considerable debate over the attribution of P.Oxy. 3317, which refers to a woman wearing a fawnskin and roaming in the wild, to either Euripides' *Antiope* or his *Antigone*.[84] The fragment describes the threat to 'drag' a sheltering woman away 'by the hair' (ἕλκωσι ... [ἐ]θείρας, fr. 175.2–3), conjuring an image of a woman being dragged into slavery. The speech that follows has been reconstructed to suggest that the threatened woman states that she is free and should not be touched by a slave. Possibly this speech belongs to Dirce as she is to be dragged away by the sons of Antiope, since other sources say that Dirce came as a maenad to the place where Antiope had run. If Luppe's suggestion that this fragment correctly belongs to *Antiope* is accepted, it is possible to hypothesise that in typically Euripidean style the character who was inflicting the punishment becomes the punished.[85]

Even without attributing this fragment to *Antiope*, it is possible to hypothesise that Antiope called on her sons to mete out revenge by treating Dirce as she had treated their mother.[86] Potentially, as the scholiast on Euripides' *Phoenician Women* suggests, when Dirce 'handed over Antiope to them to be pulled apart by bulls, because they recognised their mother they saved her and caused Dirce to be pulled apart by bulls' (παρέδωκεν αὐτοῖς τὴν Ἀντιόπην ἐπὶ τῶι διὰ ταύρων διασπάσαι. οἱ δὲ γνόντες αὐτὴν μητέρα αὐτῶν αὐτῆς μὲν ἐφείσαντο, τὴν δὲ Δίρκην ὑπὸ τῶν ταύρων διέσπασαν).[87] Here again the mirroring of the crime and the punishment is striking. In many respects the punishment reflects the Dionysiac ritual in which Dirce is said to participate, since the bull is thought to run

---

[83] López Cruces 2011: 466.

[84] *Antiope*: Luppe 1981, 1989, Collard 2004b: 311–12, López Cruces 2011: 469–81. *Antigone*: Scodel 1982, Kannicht, *TrGF*. Possibly not Euripidean: Xanthakis-Karamanos 1986.

[85] See above on Hermione in *Andromache*; also e.g., Eurystheus in *Children of Heracles*, Polymestor in *Hecuba*, Pentheus in *Hippolytus*.

[86] Scodel 1982: 38 argues that this works better without the attribution of P.Oxy 3317 to *Antiope*, since the recognition should happen before the violent revenge.

[87] Σ Eur. *Phoen.* 102 (ɪ 262.22–4 Schwartz).

wildly through the country and to tear apart the body of the woman who is tied to it.[88] At the same time, the punishment that Dirce seems to have imagined for Antiope is excessively violent, designed to kill her in a painful way and to destroy her attractiveness completely.

López Cruces suggests that Pausanias refers to Euripides when he comments on the way Dionysus was angry with Antiope following the death of Dirce because 'excessive acts of revenge are always hateful to the gods'.[89] According to this interpretation, Euripides presented an angry and vengeful Antiope who acted brutally in retaliation towards Dirce by urging on her sons to inflict violence and humiliation similar to that which she had suffered and was about to suffer.[90] This image of an aggressive Antiope who instructs her sons to attack her erstwhile tormentor and gain revenge finds parallels in other Euripidean plays, such as *Children of Heracles* where Alcmene demands violent revenge against her captured enemy Eurystheus, shifting sympathy from the mother of Heracles to her tormentor towards the end of the play. The possible reversal from violent abuser to abused appears in *Andromache* where Hermione fears she will suffer what she previously inflicted. Similarly, in Euripides' *Medea* the apparently isolated and exiled Medea achieves violent revenge making use of her own sons. It is conceivable, then, that this play, like Euripides' *Electra*, contained not one violent woman, but two, and that rather than ending happily with reconciliation and reunion, the audience was left to reflect on the way in which hatred, anger, envy and jealousy generated by fear of a rival might twist the behaviour of women, causing them to treat their perceived rivals with brutal violence, and leading them in turn to incite or execute excessive acts of revenge.

This consideration of examples from fragmentary and extant tragedy reveals that while common themes and associations recur, the tragedians were creative in their use of these themes, and that there was potential to offer the audience a feeling of satisfaction from punishment done to an evil,

---

[88] For links to Dionysus see Scodel 1982: 39 n. 3, Seaford 1990: 84, Zeitlin 1993: 176–7, López Cruces 2011: 467.

[89] López Cruces 2011: 469–70; Paus. 9.17.6 ἐπίφθονοι δὲ ἀεί πως παρὰ θεῶν αἱ ὑπερβολαὶ τῶν τιμωριῶν εἰσι. Pausanias paraphrases Hdt. 4.205 ὡς ἄρα ἀνθρώποισι αἱ λίην ἰσχυραὶ τιμωρίαι πρὸς θεῶν ἐπίφθονοι γίνονται, a comment on how divine punishment follows excessive revenge by a woman, including violence against other women: Pheretima is said to cut off the breasts of her enemies' wives and hang them on the city walls alongside their impaled husbands. See McHardy 2008a: 38–9.

[90] López Cruces 2011: 470.

violent woman, or to leave them feeling unsettled by a reversal of fortunes in which victim becomes aggressor and takes violent revenge.

Conclusion

By drawing on fragmentary evidence, far from conclusive though it is, we can see how richly the picture of female violence against other women and girls was imagined on stage by Athenian dramatists. The most prominent examples in extant tragedy, Medea and Clytemnestra, are killers, one of whom slays her husband, the other her children, alongside their female rivals. The women of fragmentary tragedy employ more subtle techniques of oppression through violence that do not result in the death of their rivals. Yet through examining the plays together common imagery and associations are revealed.

The depiction of violence by women against other women and girls in Greek tragedy plays on interconnecting assumptions about what might cause a woman to act violently. These assumptions largely mirror ideas about intimate partner violence or family violence committed by men, which are typically generated out of a combination of powerful emotions and desire for control. There is a strong association between female aggression and feelings of anger, envy and hatred, and a suggestion that women might act violently in revenge when experiencing a combination of these emotions. In particular, fear of a beautiful rival frequently stimulates sexual jealousy, which causes female characters to act violently to attack their perceived rival. The modes of attack tend to be associated with women (such as poison, deception or asking a relative for aid), and the fact that some of the women specifically target the hair and cheeks of their victims indicates that the violence is underpinned by female concerns. At the same time, the depictions of female violence are regularly associated with imagery concerning the treatment of slaves and animals, indicating that the violence is generated from a desire to demonstrate dominance, power and status over a rival. Through the use of such oppressive violence against a female rival, a woman aims to maintain her position as a wife and, along with it, her standing in the household and in society.

In depicting stepmothers and foster-mothers in the role of mistresses, the plays reflect an anxiety associated with the plight of girls who have lost their mothers making them isolated and vulnerable. The prominence of female violence in plotlines where a woman has been raped by a god or by a victorious warrior indicates that susceptibility to violent treatment by a woman is associated with women who are already in a vulnerable position, having previously been sexually assaulted and treated violently by a man or god. With her loss of chastity or married status comes loss of protection, and sometimes outright hostility from her own kin. This loss of social status exposes her to the brutal treatment of a woman who considers herself socially superior and expresses her dominance through her violent actions.

Greek Tragedy and the Theatre of Sisterhood

LYNDSAY COO

'Unfortunately, little can be said about the relations of sisters.' Thus begins the section on sisters in a key study of the ancient family, which devotes over six pages to 'Brothers' and over thirteen to 'Brothers and Sisters', but just over one to 'Sisters', describing the sources available as 'slim pickings'.[1] However, while we have little evidence for the real-life relationship between sisters in classical Greece, we find an abundance of sisters in myth and literature.[2] Sisterhood – I use the term throughout this chapter to denote the relationship between sisters, as opposed to that between sister(s) and brother(s) – is a family relationship for which the majority of our ancient sources deal with the mythical and supernatural rather than the actual.

When we turn to Greek tragedy, another asymmetry emerges. Critical approaches to tragic sisters have tended to privilege the relationship between sister and brother, elevated to the ideal male-female bond by Hegel and other eighteenth- and nineteenth-century thinkers, while the relationship between sisters has been comparatively neglected. Furthermore, scholarship has concentrated on the sisters of tragedy rather than the *sisterhood* of tragedy, with analysis frequently centred on the characterisation of the Sophoclean pairs Antigone and Ismene in *Antigone* and Electra and Chrysothemis in *Electra*. Ismene and Chrysothemis are commonly viewed as 'foils': normative female figures whose main dramatic purpose is to highlight their sisters' transgressive behaviour.[3] This mode of enquiry, prevalent since antiquity,

---

[1] Golden 1990: 135. The revised second edition published twenty-five years later adds just one update (Coo 2013a) to this section (Golden 2015: 114–15 with 188 n. 84). See also the brief discussion of sororal relationships at Cox 1998: 113; she notes of the sources that 'although informative about relations between brothers and between brothers and sisters, they say very little about relations between sisters' (108).

[2] For the ubiquity of (often large) groups of sisters in myth see Lewis 2011: 452–3; for sisters in heroine cult see Larson 1995: 109–10.

[3] For a representative view, see Griffith 2001: 129 on Ismene: 'Her role has been to articulate "normal", conventional female attitudes and expectations, in order to throw into even sharper relief Antigone's extreme and unconventional behavior and views. And once Antigone's portrait is complete, and her fate sealed, Ismene has no further function to perform.' Recent discussions have shown more interest in Ismene, but still tend to view her primary dramatic purpose as being to enhance Antigone's characterisation: see e.g. H. Roisman 2018 on Antigone/Ismene and Electra/Chrysothemis.

has come at the expense of examination of sisterhood itself.[4] The tragedies that do not fit this pattern – such as Sophocles' *Oedipus at Colonus*, which presents a harmonious relationship between Oedipus' daughters, and Aeschylus' *Suppliant Women* with its chorus of united Danaids – are seldom analysed in terms of sisterhood.

However, in recent years the study of sisterhood in Sophocles' *Antigone* has burgeoned in the fields of political theory and philosophy. This has taken the form of a turn to Ismene, the sister frequently dismissed as weak, passive and apolitical, with scholars attempting to reclaim her as a positive model of ethical and political action.[5] This trend has intersected with classical studies through the productive dialogue of Simon Goldhill and Bonnie Honig, who have clashed over the meaning of Ismene's role for the politics of *Antigone*.[6] Whereas Goldhill highlights Antigone's dismissal of Ismene and notes how most feminist critics have repeated her move, Honig offers an interpretation of the play that sees both sisters as making co-ordinated ethical choices under extreme constraint. In Honig's provocative reading, Ismene is responsible for the first burial of Polynices, and the sisters conspire in front of Creon through coded language and gesture: when Antigone seems to reject Ismene, she is actually saving her life. Thus, in response to Phelan's statement that, 'cast firmly in an Oedipal tragedy, Antigone and Ismene nonetheless point to a different form of theatre sisters might one day invent',[7] Honig argues that attentiveness to their subtle conspiracy reveals that this new kind of sororal theatre, based on sisters' desire for one another, is already present in *Antigone*.[8] By re-interpreting both women as ethical agents, she brings sisterhood to the forefront of a tragedy that is usually interpreted in terms of the sister-brother relationship.

---

[4] See Σ Soph. *El.* 328 (pp. 162–3 Xenis): Sophocles pairs a stronger sister with a weaker one 'for the purpose of adding variety' (ἕνεκα τοῦ διαποικίλλειν). For the perceived similarity of Sophocles' Ismene and Chrysothemis already in the early fourth century see Coo 2013b.
[5] For example, Frank 2006: 339–40 identifies Ismene with 'the human practice of justice'. Kirkpatrick 2011 focuses on the political choices of the weak and disenfranchised, and, like Honig 2011, argues that Ismene carried out the first burial of Polynices. Rawlinson 2014, 2016: 83–105 emphasises the fact of Ismene's survival, seeing this sister, with her adherence to life and the living, as the one who should be praised as a feminist symbol instead of the death-obsessed Antigone. See also the analysis of Ismene's desire by Engelstein 2011, 2017.
[6] Goldhill 2012: 231–48, a revision of Goldhill 2006 that responds to Honig 2011; Honig 2013: 151–89, a revision of Honig 2011 that responds to Goldhill. See also Goldhill 2014.
[7] Phelan 1997: 15–16.
[8] Honig 2013: 184 ≈ 2011: 64.

Goldhill describes Honig's interpretation as 'an extraordinary act of wilful reading against the grain',[9] and it is certainly true that her theory of sororal conspiracy is implausible, in the sense that it is not likely to have been the implication of the play's first performance. But Honig's self-styled 'interruption' of traditional modes of reading *Antigone* is more concerned with unearthing new interpretative possibilities latent in the text (particularly those that reveal themselves in performance) and showing how these can speak directly to issues of current political thought, and it prompts the question of whether the sisterly theatre that she seeks may be found more readily elsewhere in tragedy. My discussion situates itself in part as a response to this recent congruence of classical literary criticism and feminist political theory, where both fields have found common but contested ground in reading *Antigone* as a text of sisterhood. By turning to the fragments and exploring the traces of sisterhood in tragedies that have not enjoyed the critical attention lavished on *Antigone*, I aim to both broaden and reposition this debate. Can we discern among the fragmentary plays any evidence of this new theatre of sisterhood – the depiction of sisters who act primarily because they *are* sisters, because *of* their sisters, and *for* their sisters?

My chapter first gives an overview of sisters in tragedy, including the lost and fragmentary plays in which sister pairs or groups are attested or plausible. It then offers new readings of Sophocles' *Tereus* and Euripides' *Erechtheus*, both of which, I argue, dramatise a theatre of sisterhood in their portrayal of women driven to subversive action by their duty to their sisters. As well as examples of sorority as a spur for radical female interventions, these plays may be read as exploring the link between sisterhood and the female experience (*Tereus*), or revealing how male-centred political systems attempt to neutralise sisters' subversive actions (*Erechtheus*).

Three concentric methodological frameworks inform this investigation. The first engages with a cross-disciplinary concern to interrogate sisterhood's applicability as a metaphor for feminist and female experience. Sisterhood is rarely a straightforward relationship of female solidarity, and as well as intimacy and loyalty it can encompass jealousy, rivalry, betrayal and the fractious negotiation of power.[10] In addition, the use of sisterhood as a feminist metaphor, with its implications of commonality

---

[9] Goldhill 2012: 247.
[10] For challenges to, and refinements of, the idea of 'sisterhood' from different disciplinary perspectives see Downing 1988, Michie 1992, Mauthner 2002, 2005.

and group identity, tends towards the problematic erasure of hierarchy and diversity, while also positioning women within further familial structures – for example, in relation to a father figure – that are themselves fraught with difficulty.[11] The second framework derives from the relentless search in political theory for paradigms of ethical and political action in the culturally privileged literature of classical Greece, and my study offers an intervention by pointing beyond the canon for these exemplars. Finally, the third framework addresses the need to develop a mode of reading tragic sisterhood that moves past issues of characterisation towards a more nuanced analysis of sisterhood itself, and that pays attention to how the choices made by sisters are situated within a complex of other familial and social bonds, such as that between parent and child, husband and wife or individual and *polis*.

Tragic Sisters

Pairs and groups of sisters featured in many tragedies by the three major dramatists, as seen in the overview at Table 1 (extant plays) and Table 2 (fragmentary plays). The list of extant plays includes only those sisters who fulfil one of the following criteria: 1) they appear on stage in either a speaking or non-speaking role; 2) they do not appear on stage, but are spoken about and thought of as being 'just off stage' (i.e., as a real, living character within the immediate world of the play); or 3) they are dead or otherwise absent, but their sister(s) appear on stage, and they are mentioned within the play. So, for example, the entry for Euripides' *Trojan Women* includes Cassandra's sister Polyxena, who has recently been killed off stage, but is spoken about on stage; but the list does not include Atossa's dream of the sisters Europe and Asia in *Persians*, who are not 'real' characters within the world of the drama.

With regard to the fragments, there are few examples of securely attested on-stage sisters, and so this list relies on conjectures based on examining the play's titles, the myths dramatised and the evidence of the fragments

---

[11] The emergence of sisterhood as the primary metaphor for (Western) feminism is widely attributed to the publication in 1970 of *Sisterhood is Powerful*, a compilation of radical feminist writings edited by Robin Morgan (followed in 1984 by *Sisterhood is Global*, and in 2003 by *Sisterhood is Forever*). Almost as soon as *Sisterhood is Powerful* appeared, however, the sisterhood metaphor was criticised for its propensity to flatten out and overlook issues of difference within women's experience.

Table 1 *Sisters in extant tragedy*

Ch.	= chorus
italics	= character who is mentioned but does not appear on stage (may be dead or far away)
[ ]	= spuriously attributed to author
AESCHYLUS	
Agamemnon	Clytemnestra, *Helen*
Eumenides	Erinyes (Ch.)
Supplices	Danaids (Ch.)
Septem	[Antigone], [Ismene]
[PV]	[Oceanids (Ch.)]
SOPHOCLES	
Antigone	Antigone, Ismene
Electra	Electra, Chrysothemis, *Iphianassa*, *Iphigenia*
OT	Antigone, Ismene
OC	Antigone, Ismene
EURIPIDES	
Bacchae	Agave, *Ino*, *Autonoe*
Electra	Electra, *Iphigenia*
Hecuba	Polyxena, *Cassandra*
Heraclidae	'Macaria', *Heraclids*
Hippolytus	Phaedra, *Ariadne*
IT	Iphigenia, *Electra*
Orestes	Electra, *Chrysothemis*; Helen, *Clytemnestra*
Troades	Cassandra, *Polyxena*

and testimonia.[12] The list includes only those plays where there is some positive reason to believe that sisters featured, and as a result it is dominated by the dramatists for whom we have the most evidence: Aeschylus, Sophocles and Euripides. In most cases, even when we are fairly certain that a tragedy must have featured sisters, we have insufficient evidence to say whether they appeared in speaking roles or were described as off-stage characters. However, even taking all this into account and allowing for a due degree of caution, we can still observe certain patterns, and these outline a fuller range of sisterhood models than can be gleaned from the extant plays alone.

First, we see that all three major dramatists wrote tragedies in which sisters played a role, but each tended towards a distinctive practice. With Aeschylus we find a predominance of groups, sometimes as the chorus, and many examples of supernatural sisters, such as nymphs or monsters. With

[12] The evidence (not including, however, the latest papyri) is summarised in Sommerstein 2008: III for Aeschylus, Lloyd-Jones 2003 for Sophocles, Collard and Cropp 2008 for Euripides.

Table 2 *Sisters in fragmentary/lost tragedy*

PHRYNICHUS	
Aegyptioi	Danaids[13]
Danaides	Danaids (Ch.?)
AESCHYLUS	
Aetnaeae	Thaleia, nymphs of Aetna (Ch.)?[14]
Aegyptioi	Danaids
Bassarides	Muses?[15]
Danaides	Danaids (Ch.); Hypermnestra
Heliades	Heliades (Ch.)
Nereides	Thetis, Nereids (Ch.)
Niobe	Niobids
Xantriae	Minyades?[16]
Hoplon Krisis	Thetis*, Nereids?[17]
Phorcides	Graeae, Gorgons[18]
Phineus	Harpies
SOPHOCLES	
Thamyras	Muses (Ch.?)[19]
Niobe	Niobids, (one role*)[20]
Polyxena	Polyxena, Cassandra?[21]
Rizotomoi	Peliades?[22]
Sundeipnoi	Thetis*, Nereids[23]
Tereus	Procne*, Philomela
Phineus 1 or 2	Harpies

[13] Fr. 1 indicates that this play was about the sons of Aegyptus and so the Danaids must have featured, whether or not any of them appeared as speaking characters.

[14] For the suggestion that the Aetnaeae of the title are both nymphs of Aetna and sisters of Thaleia see Sommerstein 2008: III 6.

[15] Eratosth. *Catast.* 24 seems to indicate that in this play the Muses gathered Orpheus' limbs and buried them.

[16] The play certainly featured Bacchants (fr. 169), but their identity is unclear. For the suggestion that they are the Minyades see Jouan 1992: 77, 83–4, Sommerstein 2008: III 171.

[17] The testimonium for fr. 174, an address to Thetis, says that the speaker was 'inviting the Nereids to come [out of the sea] and judge [the contest of the arms]', but there is reason to doubt the accuracy of this statement (Sommerstein 2008: III 177).

[18] This play appears to have featured both sets of Phorcys' daughters, probably as off-stage characters (fr. 262).

[19] The attested Sophoclean title *Muses* may be an alternative name for this play.

[20] At least one of Niobe's daughters had a speaking role (fr. 442.10–11). Fr. 444 may be addressed to one of the daughters, possibly the sole survivor, Chloris (Lloyd-Jones 2003: 229, 235).

[21] The role of Cassandra is a conjecture based on the evidently prophetic content of fr. 526 (Sommerstein 2006b: 56–7, Coo 2011a: 186–7).

[22] The subject of this play is unknown, but may have been about the killing of Pelias, in which case the Peliades would have featured.

[23] See fr. 562, where Thetis states that she has left the Nereids dancing in the sea.

Table 2 (cont.)

EURIPIDES	
Aeolus	Canace, Aeolids
Erechtheus	Erechtheids
Theseus	Ariadne, Phaedra[24]
Cressae	Aerope*, Clymene?[25]
Peliades	Alcestis?, Peliades (Ch.?)[26]
Phaethon	Heliades?[27]
APHAREUS	
Peliades	Peliades

This table does not attempt to distinguish between on-stage and
off-stage characters.
* = attested as an on-stage (non-Choral) character
? = role possible but not certain

Sophocles, we see pairs of sisters and examples of groups, but only one
uncertain instance of a chorus. By contrast, we have no completely unam-
biguous evidence that Euripides ever put two or more sisters on stage
together. The broad trends of extant tragedy thus hold true for the fragmentary plays too, namely that Aeschylus tends towards the sisterly collective (especially the divine group); the pairing of two sisters is a
distinctively Sophoclean practice; and Euripides shows comparatively less
interest in the on-stage interaction of sisters.

In some of these plays, sisters act as a female collective in their role as
mourners. The Heliades grieve for their half-brother Phaethon, Antigone
and Ismene for Polynices and Eteocles, and the Nereids accompany their
nephew Achilles in lamenting for Patroclus;[28] in Bassarids, the Muses
probably buried the dismembered limbs of Orpheus. Elsewhere we find
sisters acting together with violent results. This violence is always directed
towards men, often members of their own natal or marital families. The
Danaids (with the exception of Hypermnestra) murder their cousin-
bridegrooms; Agave dismembers her son with her sisters' aid; Medea tricks

---

[24] The hypothesis suggests that Ariadne was an on-stage character and that a deus ex machina
announced Theseus' future marriage to Phaedra (Collard and Cropp 2008: I 416).

[25] Aerope certainly appeared, and her sister may also have been mentioned (test. v; fr. 466 may
contain a reference to both women if Bekker's παῖδας οὐ is adopted for παῖδά σου).

[26] Collard and Cropp 2008: II 61–2, 69 consider that fr. 603 may be an address to one of the sisters,
Alcestis, and that, despite the play's title, it is unlikely that the Peliades formed the chorus.

[27] The Heliades did not appear on stage, but it seems likely that one of them is the bride that
Phaethon is about to marry, and their eventual metamorphosis may have been predicted at the
end of the play (Diggle 1970: 155–60, Collard and Cropp 2008: II 327–8).

[28] For the mourning of the Nereids in Aeschylus' Nereids see UHLIG, pp. 113–16.

the daughters of Pelias into killing their father. The plot of *Xantriae* ('Wool-Carders') is unclear, but one possibility is that it featured the daughters of Minyas tearing apart one of their sons. We also find sisterly aggression directed outside the family in the case of three divine groups: the Erinyes persecute Orestes, the Muses punish the hybristic musician Thamyras and the Harpies torment Phineus. Sisters may themselves be targets of violence. The Danaids are coerced into marriage; the daughters of Niobe are slaughtered because of their mother's boast; the Graeae have their one eye stolen by Perseus; the Harpies are killed. Alternatively, violence may be directed at one sister, as we see with Perseus' slaying of the Gorgon Medusa, and the sacrificed daughters of Agamemnon, Priam and Erechtheus; in *Cretan Women*, Aerope (and perhaps also her sister Clymene) seems to have been threatened with death.

In general, the extant plays do not offer many compelling examples of women who act out of sisterhood, or even who demonstrate any sustained affection for their sisters. There is a flash of sisterly solidarity in *Agamemnon* when Clytemnestra rebukes the chorus for their attack on Helen (*Ag.* 1464–7), prompting them to lament the disastrous similarity of these two adulterous sisters (1468–71). In *Orestes*, Helen expresses sadness at Clytemnestra's death and sends libations and offerings of hair to her tomb (*Or.* 77–125); however, her expressions of grief are hardly extravagant, and Electra notes that she has only cut the very ends of her hair, so as not to mar her appearance (128–9). In *Hippolytus*, Phaedra situates her own suffering within her family history by briefly bemoaning the fate of Ariadne (339), and in *Iphigenia in Tauris*, after Iphigenia and Orestes have celebrated their reunion, the first question Iphigenia asks is for news of Electra, saying that the subject is 'dear' (φίλα, 914) to her. Alongside these brief moments of sisterly concern, we also find unsuccessful appeals and disintegrating bonds of sisterhood: in *Antigone*, Ismene's care for her sister is not reciprocated by Antigone, and in Sophocles' *Electra*, Chrysothemis refuses to partake in Electra's plan to kill Aegisthus. Perhaps most strikingly, Electra earlier claims to speak on behalf of both her father and the dead Iphigenia, before launching into an explanation of why she believes her sister's killing to have been justified and necessary (554–5, 558–76).

In the extant plays, when sisters either act or consider taking action together, this is usually related to their roles as daughters to their fathers, or as sisters to their brothers. In Aeschylus' *Suppliant Women*, the Danaids are certainly a united group, but beyond their frequent invocation of their shared kinship with Io, they do not appeal to each other in terms of their own sisterhood. Their actions are driven not by horizontal sister-sister relations but by the vertical father-daughter one, as seen in their claim that they fled from Egypt under instruction from Danaus, their 'father and head counsellor and chief overseeing the pieces on the gameboard' (πατὴρ καὶ βούλαρχος | καὶ στασίαρχος τάδε πεσσονομῶν, *Suppl.* 11–12). Similarly, in the collaborative sisterhood of Antigone and Ismene in *Oedipus at Colonus*, their primary motivation is concern for their father rather than sisterly relations, and the appeals of Sophocles' Antigone to Ismene in *Antigone* and Electra to Chrysothemis in *Electra* are motivated by their sense of duty to their fathers and/or brothers, rather than to each other.

In order, then, to find sisters who act *because they are sisters*, it is necessary to look to fragmentary tragedy. I now turn in more detail to two case studies of women whose prioritising of the bond of sisterhood ahead of competing familial claims (such as parent-child and husband-wife) leads them to drastic and violent action.

'The Happiest Life of All Mortals': Sophocles' *Tereus*

Sophocles' *Tereus* insistently explores the bond of sisterhood and reveals its potential as an urgent and unsettling force. The myth of Procne and Philomela has frequently been used as stimulus for feminist thought, but seldom through direct engagement with Sophocles' text. For example, Patricia Klindienst Joplin's influential essay, 'The voice of the shuttle is ours',[29] uses the story of Philomela to articulate a feminist poetics: she sees her glossectomy as a metaphor for the patriarchal suppression of the female voice, her weaving as representative of art's power to constitute resistance, and the sisters' turn to violence as emblematic of how society blames women who challenge its structures. The essay takes its title from *Tereus* fr. 595 κερκίδος φωνή ('the voice of the shuttle'), but it does not discuss any fragment of Sophocles' play, engaging mainly with the Philomela story as found in Ovid. But if we turn our attention back to *Tereus*, it is possible to develop a reading in which this tragedy can become a foundational text for the idea of sisterhood as a metaphor for female experience.

The plot of *Tereus* is almost certainly represented by P.Oxy. 3013, a hypothesis to a Tereus drama; it is overwhelmingly likely that this refers to Sophocles' play, and not that of Philocles, the only other tragedy we know of on the theme.[30] The background and plot is briefly summarised as

---

[29] Klindienst Joplin 1984 = Higgins and Silver 1991: 35–64 = McClure 2002: 259–86.
[30] Parsons 1974, Coo 2013a: 352, Scattolin 2013, Meccariello 2014: 364–7, Finglass 2016b: 73–4.

follows. Procne, the daughter of Pandion, king of Athens, is married to the Thracian king Tereus. She misses her sister Philomela and asks Tereus to fetch her for a visit; but on his way back, Tereus rapes Philomela and cuts out her tongue. After an unspecified period of time, Philomela somehow reveals the truth to Procne though a piece of weaving. In revenge, Procne kills her son, Itys, cooks him and feeds him to his own father. Finally, the gods transform the three characters into birds: Procne becomes a nightingale, Philomela a swallow and Tereus a hoopoe.

Tereus is rarely brought into discussion of Sophoclean sisters, and when it is, it is usually assumed that Procne and Philomela must have been 'similar' to the paired sisters in *Antigone* and *Electra*.[31] In fact, this play presents a completely different model of sisterhood, one that is collective, collaborative and radical, and one where Procne destroys both her mother-child and wife-husband familial bonds in order to avenge her sister. But *Tereus* does more than offer an example of unusually violent sisters: it also presents a subtle exploration of a metaphorical connection between the idea of sisterhood and the shared experience of all women.[32]

In the following fragment, a speaker, who can only be Procne, laments the condition of women, who must leave the idyll of the natal home for the frightening and unfamiliar marital *oikos* (fr. 583+ P.Oxy. 5292):[33]

> νῦν δ' οὐδέν εἰμι χωρίς. ἀλλὰ πολλάκις
> ἔβλεψα ταύτηι τὴν γυναικείαν φύσιν,
> ὡς οὐδέν ἐσμεν. αἳ νέαι μὲν ἐν πατρὸς
> ἥδιστον, οἶμαι, ζῶμεν ἀνθρώπων βίον·
> τερπνῶς γὰρ ἀεὶ παῖδας ἄνοια τρέφει.   5
> ὅταν δ' ἐς ἥβην ἐξικώμεθ' ἔμφρονες,
> ὠθούμεθ' ἔξω καὶ διεμπολώμεθα
> θεῶν πατρώιων τῶν τε φυσάντων ἄπο,
> αἱ μὲν ξένους πρὸς ἄνδρας, αἱ δὲ βαρβάρους,
> αἱ δ' εἰς ἀγηθῆ δώμαθ', αἱ δ' ἐπίρροθα.   10
> καὶ ταῦτ', ἐπειδὰν εὐφρόνη ζεύξηι μία,
> χρεὼν ἐπαινεῖν καὶ δοκεῖν καλῶς ἔχειν.

---

[31] Post 1922: 51, Zacharia 2001: 110, March 2003: 154.

[32] This section develops a reading put forward in Coo 2013a.

[33] This fragment is made up of a citation recorded by Stobaeus (published in *TrGF* as fr. 583) and a papyrus (P.Oxy. 5292, for which see Slattery 2016, Finglass 2016b) that overlaps with that citation; for the full combined text, together with discussion, see FINGLASS, pp. 92–102. Here I follow Radt and others in printing ἀγηθῆ (a conjecture of Scaliger, modified by Van Herwerden) at line 10; for discussion of the papyrus reading, ἀήθη, see Finglass 2016b: 64–5.

νόμωι μὲν [

εἰ δ᾽ ἐκ τοιου[

15   ἴδοιμι και[

τὸ γὰρ ποθ. [

[Procne:]   But now, separated, I am nothing. Yet I have often regarded the female
sex in this way: that we are nothing. As young girls in a father's home, we
live, I think, the happiest life of all mortals; for ignorance always rears
children happily. But when we reach maturity and understanding, then
we are pushed out and sold, away from our family gods and our parents,
some of us to foreign husbands, some to barbarians, and some into
joyless homes, some to homes full of abuse. And this, once a single night
has yoked us, we have to approve of and seem to be doing well. By
custom ... but if from such ... I should see ... For ...

Procne moves from a focus on her own experience (οὐδέν εἰμι, 1) to the
experience of womankind in general (οὐδέν ἐσμεν, 3), and she uses first
person plurals (ἐσμεν, 3; ζῶμεν, 4; ἐξικώμεθ᾽, 6; ὠθούμεθ᾽ ... καὶ
διεμπολώμεθα, 7) to draw in the chorus – who must be female – as well
as addressing the entirety of the female race.[34] But what aspect of her
experience is she highlighting? Procne has evidently just been describing
some former and better aspect of her life: then she was happy, but now
(νῦν δ᾽, 1) she is nothing because she is χωρίς ('separated'). Given Procne's
limited range of past experiences, this can only refer to her separation from
her natal home and/or from Philomela.[35] But it is unlikely that the previous
lines contained a general description of the delight of the natal *oikos*, for that
is what we find in lines 3–5. Rather, Procne will have focussed on the specifics
of her own life – namely, her relationship with Philomela, the sister whom she
missed enough to ask her husband to fetch her all the way from from Athens.

As a result, Procne's following lines on the general condition of women
must be read as suggestive of her own childhood and that of Philomela.
The reference to happy and innocent girls in their father's home evokes the
life of the sisters in the house of Pandion before their forcible separation: even

---

[34] P.Oxy. 5292 confirms that Procne speaks these lines in the presence of the chorus, and so they
cannot have been male: Finglass 2016b: 66.

[35] It is unlikely that Procne describes herself in this way because she has just been told the false
news of Philomela's death (*pace* Curley 2003: 171, Fitzpatrick and Sommerstein 2006: 181),
since the shift from a lament for a recently deceased and beloved sister into this generalisation
on the lives of women would be too abrupt (thus Coo 2013a: 371, Finglass 2016b: 67–8). For
another possibility see Libatique 2018, who suggests a longer time frame, with Procne believing
that her sister has been dead for some time; he offers the plausible suggestion that the play is set
on an anniversary or some other commemoration of Philomela's 'death'.

in Procne's generalising statement, the language slips so that a plurality of young girls can be read as inhabiting just a single paternal household (αἳ νέαι μὲν ἐν πατρός, 3). Furthermore, Procne's complaint that some women are sold off to 'barbarians' is pointedly true in her case, since Tereus is barbarian not only in his Thracian nationality, but also, although she does not know this yet, in his horrific abuse of Philomela. Procne thus extrapolates from her own personal experience to generalise about the experience of all women.

Behind Procne's repeated use of 'we', therefore, we can catch an echo of the specific experiences of herself and Philomela, with the result that these sisters become a model for the sufferings of the entire 'race of women'. Sisters, who lead the 'happiest life of all mortals' (ἥδιστον ... ἀνθρώπων βίον, 4) together in the house of their father before being separated and married off, can thus be read a paradigm for the female experience, which is here defined by women's traumatic separation from each other and their 'selling' and subjugation by men. If women are 'nothing' (οὐδέν) when torn apart, it follows that they are 'something' when united. And indeed the play will show this to be devastatingly true, as the sisters reunite to take their awful revenge on Tereus. If we read the lines in this way, as both specific and generalising, this fragment models the idea of sisterhood as an under-current to the shared experience of all women. Sisterhood is here evoked as the ideal and idealised relationship, and placed in contrast to both the horror of the marital bond and the implicit condemnation of the father who 'pushes' out and 'sells' his daughters.[36]

The plotline of *Tereus* itself demonstrates the violence and power of a collective model of sisterhood, but this tragedy also explores the potency of the idea of sisterhood as a metaphor for female experience. Sisterhood here is certainly powerful: in the conspiracy between the speaking and the silenced sister, *Tereus* directly engages with the dynamic that Honig identifies as subtext in Sophocles' *Antigone*, namely a solidarity of purpose between women who have been suppressed and silenced, and who, despite their position of ostensible weakness, are able, through collaboration, to take action and bring about violent change.

'A Yoked Team of Three Virgins': Euripides' *Erechtheus*

Euripides' *Erechtheus* also centres on the Athenian royal family with its focus on Erechtheus, king of Athens, his wife Praxithea and their three

---

[36] For the lines' implied criticism of the father figure see Scattolin 2013: 125.

daughters (or possibly three out of a larger group of daughters).[37] We do not have any speech by these sisters, although a line in which children are exhorted to love their mother (fr. 358.1, below) suggests that at some point they appeared on stage. Nevertheless, the extensive fragments hint at how *Erechtheus* explored the power of sisterhood and its relationship to the *polis*. The Delphic oracle has told Erechtheus that the only way to save Athens from an invading Thracian force led by Poseidon's son Eumolpus is to sacrifice one of his daughters. One girl is duly sacrificed; her two sisters then join her by committing suicide, and in the ensuing battle, which repels the Thracians, Erechtheus is engulfed in a chasm made by Poseidon. Finally, Athena appears to a grieving Praxithea, founds the cults of Erechtheus and the Erechtheids, appoints Praxithea herself as priestess of Athena Polias and foretells the establishment of the Eumolpidae at Eleusis.

A central theme was evidently the family and the subversion of expectations with regard to its internal relationships, an issue particularly pertinent for the Athenian royal line, where the usual familial bonds have been destabilised by the element of autochthony.[38] One fragment emphasises the love of children for their mother as the greatest bond (fr. 358):[39]

> οὐκ ἔστι μητρὸς οὐδὲν ἥδιον τέκνοις·
> ἐρᾶτε μητρός, παῖδες, ὡς οὐκ ἔστ’ ἔρως
> τοιοῦτος ἄλλος ὅστις ἡδίων ἐρᾶν

> There is nothing more pleasing to children than their mother. Love your mother, children, since there is no other love that is more pleasing than this

This sentiment, with its focus on the love between mother and child, is drastically upended by the actions of Praxithea, who declares 'I love my children, but I love my homeland more' (φιλῶ τέκν’, ἀλλὰ πατρίδ’ ἐμὴν μᾶλλον φιλῶ, fr. 360a) and argues at length for the sacrifice of her own daughter, as discussed below. In another fragment, a character disparages the worth of adopted children (fr. 359):

---

[37] It is striking that in both of these tragic examples of women acting as sisters, the women are Athenian, and furthermore ancestors of two of the tribes of Athens, the Pandionids and the Erechtheids. According to the Parian Marble (A15 Rotstein), Erechtheus is a son of Pandion, and hence his daughters are nieces of Procne and Philomela; however, as Gantz 1993: 242 notes, it is 'not always a good idea' to join the dots like this, especially given the fluid and confused early genealogy of the Athenian royal family.

[38] For the implications of the autochthony of Erechthonius–Erechtheus see Calame 2011.

[39] Sonnino 2010: 293–4 suggests that this fragment comes from a scene in which Erechtheus tries to placate the two remaining daughters after he has agreed to their sister's sacrifice.

θετῶν δὲ παίδων ποῦ κράτος; τὰ φύντα γὰρ
κρείσσω νομίζειν τῶν δοκημάτων χρεών.

Where is the advantage in adopted children? It is necessary to consider those who are truly born better than mere make-believes.

This attitude is contrasted with Erechtheus' apparent adoption of a son, as shown by fr. 362 in which the king addresses a young man as τέκνον ('child') and refers to himself as πατήρ ('father').[40] How did sisterhood fit into this scrutiny of family relationships? I suggest that the play located the daughters of Erechtheus and Praxithea not only within the parent-child and individual-*polis* hierarchies, but also within a framework of sisterhood, and that this emerged as an unexpectedly subversive element in the play's wider exploration of familial and social relationships.

The major reversal of familial expectations is found with Praxithea, who persuades her reluctant husband to agree to their daughter's sacrifice. In the famous speech preserved by the fourth-century orator and statesman Lycurgus as an exemplar of patriotism, Praxithea proudly declares that she will give her daughter to save the city (fr. 360):

ΠΡ.	ἐγὼ δὲ δώσω παῖδα τὴν ἐμὴν κτανεῖν.	4
	(...)	
	ἔπειτα τέκνα τοῦδ' ἕκατι τίκτομεν,	
	ὡς θεῶν τε βωμοὺς πατρίδα τε ῥυώμεθα.	15
	πόλεως δ' ἁπάσης τοὔνομ' ἕν, πολλοὶ δέ νιν	
	ναίουσι· τούτους πῶς διαφθεῖραί με χρή,	
	ἐξὸν προπάντων μίαν ὕπερ δοῦναι θανεῖν;	
	εἴπερ γὰρ ἀριθμὸν οἶδα καὶ τοὐλάσσονος	
	τὸ μεῖζον, †ἑνὸς† οἶκος οὐ πλέον σθένει	20
	πταίσας ἁπάσης πόλεος οὐδ' ἴσον φέρει.	
	εἰ δ' ἦν ἐν οἴκοις ἀντὶ θηλειῶν στάχυς	
	ἄρσην, πόλιν δὲ πολεμία κατεῖχε φλόξ,	
	οὐκ ἄν νιν ἐξέπεμπον εἰς μάχην δορός,	
	θάνατον προταρβοῦσ'; ἀλλ' ἔμοιγ' εἴη τέκνα	25
	<ἃ> καὶ μάχοιτο καὶ μετ' ἀνδράσιν πρέποι,	
	μὴ σχήματ' ἄλλως ἐν πόλει πεφυκότα.	
	τὰ μητέρων δὲ δάκρυ' ὅταν πέμπηι τέκνα,	
	πολλοὺς ἐθήλυν' εἰς μάχην ὁρμωμένους.	
	μισῶ γυναῖκας αἵτινες πρὸ τοῦ καλοῦ	30

---

[40] This cannot be a biological son of Erechtheus and Praxithea, since the latter states that she has no sons (fr. 360.22–5). The identity of this adopted heir is unknown: for possibilities see Cropp 1995: 181, Sonnino 2010: 125–31.

†ζῆν παῖδας εἵλοντο καὶ παρήινεσαν κακά.
καὶ μὴν θανόντες γ᾿ ἐν μάχηι πολλῶν μέτα
τύμβον τε κοινὸν ἔλαχον εὐκλειάν τ᾿ ἴσην·
τῆμῆι δὲ παιδὶ στέφανος εἷς μιᾶι μόνηι
πόλεως θανούσηι τῆσδ᾿ ὕπερ δοθήσεται,
καὶ τὴν τεκοῦσαν καὶ σὲ δύο θ᾿ ὁμοσπόρω
σώσει· τί τούτων οὐχὶ δέξασθαι καλόν;
τὴν οὐκ ἐμὴν < > πλὴν φύσει δώσω κόρην
θῦσαι πρὸ γαίας.
(...)
χρῆσθ᾿, ὦ πολῖται, τοῖς ἐμοῖς λοχεύμασιν,
σώιζεσθε, νικᾶτ᾿· ἀντὶ γὰρ ψυχῆς μιᾶς
οὐκ ἔσθ᾿ ὅπως οὐ τήνδ᾿ ἐγὼ σώσω πόλιν.

35 / 50 lines marked.

Praxithea: I for my part will give my daughter to be killed. (...) Next, we give birth to our children for this reason: so that we might protect the gods' altars and our fatherland. There is one name for the whole city, but many live in it; how must I needs destroy them when I can give one to die for all? If I know my arithmetic and can tell greater from smaller, the fall of †one person's† household is not more powerful than that of an entire city, nor does it matter equally. If there was a male crop in our household instead of a female one, and the flame of war had gripped the city, surely I would not be refusing to send them out to battle, fearing death? No, may I have children who would fight and stand out amongst men, not mere pretences brought forth in the city in vain. Whenever mothers' tears send out their children, they feminise many as they set out into battle. I hate those women who choose life for their sons rather than what is noble, and encourage them to cowardice. And indeed, those who die in battle with many others obtain a communal tomb and an equal share of the glory. But my child, when she dies for this city, will be granted a single crown for herself alone, and she will save her mother, and you, and her two sisters; which of these is not a noble thing to receive? I will give this girl, who is not mine other than through her birth, to be sacrificed on behalf of our land. (...) Make use, citizens, of the child I gave birth to, be saved, win victory! In exchange for just one life, there is no way that I shall fail to save our city.

This speech echoes the fantasy of willing self-sacrifice that we find in Euripides' *Hecuba*, *Children of Heracles* and *Iphigenia at Aulis*, where a young girl, after some initial resistance, goes with dignity to a death that will benefit the (often predominantly or exclusively male) collective.[41]

[41] O'Connor-Visser 1987, Wilkins 1990, Rabinowitz 1993: 31–66.

But here the declaration of willingness is transferred to her mother, and whereas Hecuba and Clytemnestra try desperately to save their daughters, Praxithea enthusiastically offers up hers. She claims this as her prerogative because she views her offspring, the product of her womb and labour (14, 50), as a personal possession that she is entitled to donate to others (δώσω, 4, 38; δοῦναι, 18). The emphasis throughout is on the vertical parent-child relationship and ways in which a mother can contribute to the *polis* through her children: in the case of sons, by dispatching them to battle and exhorting them to act courageously, and in the case of her daughter, giving her up for the 'use' of the citizens. Since Praxithea sees this decision as hers alone, she even makes the extraordinary declaration that she, personally, will save Athens (52). While the daughter's death may thus be political, insofar as it saves the *polis*, the girl herself does not emerge from this speech as a political actor. Rather, it is Praxithea who makes an unconventional female foray into the public arena.[42]

However, it becomes clear that Praxithea, in her privileging of the vertical parent-child bond, the duty of family to *polis* and a pragmatic approach to sacrifice and glory (the death of 'one' will save 'many'; individual honour is better than shared), has badly misjudged her daughters, who instead promote the horizontal bond between sisters, the power of relationships *within* the nuclear family and a mode of action that stems from individual desire rather than communal and political expediency. Praxithea assumes that, in dying, her daughter will save the lives of her parents and sisters (36–7), and she fixates on the individual glory that this will bring, rather than viewing her daughters as a sisterly collective. The decision of the two remaining sisters to commit suicide will therefore have been, at least from her point of view, a shock.[43]

Cropp states that the sisters 'probably killed themselves in such as way as to assist the sacrifice and the salvation of Athens' and suggests that the deaths were 'quasi-sacrificial',[44] but it is not apparent that this was the case, nor is it clear how the sisters might have accomplished this. According to the oracle, only one daughter's death is required to save the city; the two suicides, therefore, are gratuitous. Whereas the sacrificial victim will have

---

[42] For the merging of autochthony, motherhood, and civic values in Praxithea's speech see Loraux 1998: 13–15, Calame 2011: 5–8, 15–16. For Praxithea's 'hyper-civic' form of motherhood see Cowan, pp. 142–4.

[43] J. Schmitt 1921: 68 suggests that the sisters killed themselves without warning their parents beforehand, comparing how Menoeceus keeps his intended suicide a secret from his father in Euripides' *Phoenician Women*.

[44] Cropp 1995: 151.

been killed with a knife, the two sisters may have jumped from a great height,[45] and when Athena orders their communal burial, she specifies the location of their tomb as the spot where the sacrificial victim died (fr. 370.67) – not, for example, where 'the three of them' died. It seems that the two sisters did not offer themselves up for sacrifice at the same time as their sister, nor is it evident that their self-driven suicide, presumably in a different location and by a different means, could have been seen as contributing towards either the sacrifice or the war effort. Both their mother and Athena distinguish between the sacrifice and the two suicides, and specify only the former as being for the sake of Athens. At fr. 370.36–42, Praxithea seems to first address the bodies of the two sisters, then Erechtheus, and finally the sacrificed girl as 'you, who for the city …' (σὲ τὰν πρὸ πόλεως, 40).[46] Similarly, Athena's speech refers to the daughter who was 'sacrificed for this land' (τῆσδε χώρας … προθύεται, fr. 370.66), but in relation to the two suicides she mentions only their oaths to their sister, not any patriotic motive. It appears that these women acted not for civic reasons, but out of loyalty to their sister.[47]

This sisterly solidarity, perhaps suggested by their description as 'a yoked team of three virgins' (ζεῦγος τριπάρθενον, fr. 357),[48] is made clear at the end of the play, when Athena addresses the mourning Praxithea (fr. 370):

ΑΘΗΝΑ
…

σὺ δ',] ὦ χθονὸς [σώτειρα Κηφισοῦ] κόρη,
ἄκου' Ἀθάνας τῆς ἀμήτορο[ς λό]γους·
65 καὶ πρῶτα μέν σοι σημανῶ παι[δὸς] πέρι,
ἣν τῆσδε χώρας σὸς προθύεται [πόσι]ς·

---

[45] This is based on two details in Praxithea's lament: she mentions falling (fr. 370.27), and may describe the daughters' limbs as 'tender' (i.e. bruised, bashed?) at fr. 370.38 τακερὰ μέλεα, following Austin's reading (though not certain: Carrara 1977: 81); cf. Hyg. *Fab.* 238.2 *reliquae ipsius sorores ipsae se praecipitauerunt* ('her remaining sisters threw themselves from a height'). See Cropp 1995: 151, Sonnino 2010: 357, 363–4.

[46] Collard and Cropp 2008: i 393.

[47] Cf. the accounts of the sisters' suicide at Apollod. *Bibl.* 3.15.4 ἐπεποίηντο γάρ, ὡς ἔφασάν τινες, συνωμοσίαν ἀλλήλαις συναπολέσθαι ('for, as some said, they had sworn an oath among themselves to die together') and Hyg. *Fab.* 46 *Erechtheus Pandionis filius habuit filias quattuor, quae inter se coniurarunt si una earum mortem obisset ceterae se interficerent* ('Erechtheus the son of Pandion had four daughters, who swore among themselves that if one them were to meet with death, the others would kill themselves').

[48] The exact resonances of this phrase in its original context are unknown. The yoke metaphor may indicate group harmony and solidarity, but it also suggests compulsion, as in the yoke of necessity or slavery; cf. the common idea of the married couple as yoked together (as in Soph. *Tereus* fr. 583.11).

θάψον νιν οὗπερ ἐξέπνευσ᾽ ο[ἰκτ]ρὸν βίον
καὶ τάσδ᾽ ἀδελφὰς ἐν τάφωι τ[αὐτ]ῶι χθονὸς
γενναιότητος οὕνεχ᾽, αἵτιν[ες φί]λης
ὅρκους ἀδελφῆς οὐκ ἐτόλμησα[ν λι]πεῖν.   70
ψυχαὶ μὲν οὖν τῶνδ᾽ οὐ βεβᾶσ᾽ ['Αιδ]ην πάρα,
εἰς δ᾽ αἰθέρ᾽ αὐτῶν πνεῦμ᾽ ἐγὼ [κ]ατώικισα·
ὄνομα δὲ κλεινὸν θήσομαι κα[θ᾽ Ἑλ]λάδα
Ὑακινθίδας βροτοῖσι κικλή[σκε]ιν θεάς
ἐπεὶ[   ]κᾳοιχετητ[   ]μένη   75
τοῦ συ[   ] ὑακίν[θου γ]άνος
καὶ γῆν ἔσωσε, τοῖς ἐμοῖς ἀστο[ῖς λέγ]ω
ἐνιαυσίαις σφας μὴ λελησμ[ένους] χρόνωι
θυσίαισι τιμᾶν καὶ σφαγαῖσι [βουκ]τόνοις
κοσμοῦ[ντας ἱ]εροῖς παρθένων [χορεύ]μασιν·   80

Athena: ... [And you,] daughter [of Cephisus, saviour] of this land, listen to the words of motherless Athena. First I will give you instructions concerning your child, whom your [husband] sacrificed on behalf of this land. Bury her on the spot where she breathed out her pitiable life, and these sisters also in the same tomb of earth, because of their nobility, those who could not bring themselves to abandon their oaths to their dear sister. And so their souls have not gone down to Hades but I have settled their spirits in the heaven; and I shall establish for them a famous name, 'Hyacinthid goddesses', which mortals shall call them throughout Greece. And since ... the gleam of the hyacinth and saved the land, I say to my citizens to honour them, never forgetting over time, with annual sacrifices and the slaughter of [oxen], and arranging the holy dances of virgin girls.

The reference to the pledges (φί]λης ὅρκους ἀδελφῆς, 69–70) shows that the women had joined in a suicide pact with their 'dear sister', and Athena praises all three, decreeing that they will be buried together as a mark of their 'nobility' (γενναιότητος, 69). The goddess thus highlights a further irony in Praxithea's earlier speech: the belief that her daughter will attain the honour of an individual tomb, outstripping the glory of communally buried male soldiers. Athena now reveals that she will gain a shared tomb after all, but that this will in fact be a marker of extraordinary achievement, since it is as a collective that the sisters gain even greater glory through their transformation into the Hyacinthids.[49] The girls will become a

---

[49] According to Σ Aratus *Phaen.* 172 (p. 166.1–3 Martin), Euripides said that the Erechtheids became the star-goddesses, the Hyades, and so it is sometimes assumed that Athena also

powerful apotropaic force for Athens, receiving libations whenever the city is about to be attacked, and enemies will be forbidden from entering their sanctuary to petition for victory. In their deification, the sisters are celebrated as a group with no distinction made between the sacrificial victim who saved the city and the two who acted out of sisterly loyalty. It appears that while the death of one may have defended the city from Eumolpus and the Thracians on this occasion, it is all three sisters that will protect it in perpetuity.

At the opening of her speech, the goddess instructs Praxithea to listen to the words 'of motherless Athena' (Ἀθάνας τῆς ἀμήτορο[ς, 64). Just as in *Eumenides*, where Athena's vote to acquit Orestes of the crime of matricide is based on the priorities derived from her own parthenogenetic birth, the adjective in *Erechtheus* may serve in part to explain her lack of engagement with Praxithea's maternal grief.[50] Instead of dwelling on the disintegration of the mother-daughter relationship, the motherless virgin Athena consecrates the power of the sisterly collective, and it is no coincidence that one of the ways in which the Hyacinthids will be commemorated is through virgin dances (παρθένων [χορεύ]μασιν, 80), i.e. groups of young girls acting in unison.

However, we can also read the deification of the sisters as a suppression, as much as an exaltation, of the precise nature of their action. In the extant plays of Euripides that feature female sacrificial victims, the girls go willingly to deaths that will benefit the community, thereby participating in a system that ultimately re-affirms patriarchal values through the glorification of female self-sacrifice.[51] The deaths in *Erechtheus*, however, do not fit this pattern: in the case of sacrificed girl, the important declaration of compliance comes not from the victim herself, but from her mother; in the case of her sisters, they themselves choose and control the manner of their death, which is an act driven by individual desire. The translation of these deaths into a benefit for the *polis* is thus especially uneasy, and although the sisters are praised for the nobility manifest in their actions, their individual underlying motivations are erased by the imposition of a single model of commemoration. Just like Tellus, the Athenian honoured for his prowess on the battlefield by a publicly funded burial on the exact spot

---

predicted the catasterism of the Erechtheids/Hyacinthids as the Hyades (see fr. 370.107–8); *contra* Sourvinou-Inwood 2011: 123–34.

[50] See also Leitao 2012: 170–1 on Athena's motherless birth as a 'counterpoint to the ideology of autochthony' in the play.

[51] Rabinowitz 1993: 31–66.

where he fell (Hdt. 1.30.5), the sacrificial victim will be buried at the place where she was killed (67–8); and her sisters, despite the very different nature of their deaths, will be made to share in the physical space, meaning and function of her tomb.[52] Moreover, the language that Athena uses to announce the sisters' deification (71–2) echoes an epitaph inscribed on the public monument for the men who fell at Potidaea in 432, αἰθὴρ μὲν ψυχὰς ὑπεδέξατο, σώ[ματα δὲ χθὼν] | τῶνδε ('The air received the souls and the earth the bodies of these men'); the Erechtheid sisters are thus presented as models for the heroisation of the Athenian war dead.[53] In their communal burial and shared deification and commemoration, all of which elide the difference in nature between their deaths and that of their sister, the two suicides are assimilated into the political and military implications of their sister's public-facing sacrifice. Their suicide is celebrated and yet simultaneously suppressed as an act of sisterhood.

The collective sisterhood of the Erechtheids/Hyacinthids thus finds an important place within this play's subversive exploration of family relationships. These sisters emerge as being more in tune with one another than their mother is with her own children, and the latter half of the tragedy shifts its focus from Praxithea's unconventional motherhood to the Erechtheids' shocking act of sisterhood. Even without any text in which sisters themselves speak, we see that in *Erechtheus* sisterhood asserts itself as a force to be reckoned with: these sisters act of their own accord, without directives from their parents or the city, and are both sacrificed and make the ultimate sacrifice. At the same time, the manner in which their model of sisterhood becomes consecrated within and valuable to Athens can be read as exposing some of the tensions inherent in trying to find a place for collective sisterhood within the *polis*. The potential of women to act together out of sisterhood – driven by concerns that exclude the interests of their male relatives – can lead to violent and unpredictable results, and the transformation of the Erechtheids' sisterly sacrifice into the military-focussed public good of the Hyacinthid cult lays bare some of the uneasy negotiation that must take place when confronting this relationship.

---

[52] Loraux 1985: 80–1 ≈ 1987: 46–7.

[53] *CEG* I 10(iii).5-6 (spelling 'modernised'); see Sourvinou-Inwood 2003: 28, 2005: 338–40, Sonnino 2010: 382. Cf. Calame 2011: 10: 'These young girls, the Hyacinthids, who convey the eroticism of flowers, are assimilated into the masculine sphere that is war.'

The Theatre of Sisterhood

I have argued that both *Tereus* and *Erechtheus* offer a glimpse of a 'theatre of sisterhood': a tragic female mode of action motivated by sisterhood, in which sisters, acting together and for each other, take drastic action with public repercussions. This openness to the possibilities offered by the fragments can also help to uncover nuances in the extant plays. In Sophocles' *Electra*, believing their brother Orestes to be dead, Electra attempts to recruit Chrysothemis for the assassination of Aegisthus by describing the glory they will gain for doing the deed (Soph. *El.* 977–85):

> "ἴδεσθε τώδε τὼ κασιγνήτω, φίλοι,
> ὣ τὸν πατρῶιον οἶκον ἐξεσωσάτην,
> ὣ τοῖσιν ἐχθροῖς εὖ βεβηκόσιν ποτὲ
> 980 ψυχῆς ἀφειδήσαντε προὐστήτην φόνου.
> τούτω φιλεῖν χρή, τώδε χρὴ πάντας σέβειν·
> τώδ' ἔν θ' ἑορταῖς ἔν τε πανδήμωι πόλει
> τιμᾶν ἅπαντας οὕνεκ' ἀνδρείας χρεών."
> τοιαῦτά τοι νὼ πᾶς τις ἐξερεῖ βροτῶν,
> 985 ζώσαιν θανούσαιν θ' ὥστε μὴ 'κλιπεῖν κλέος.

'Look at these two sisters, friends, who saved their paternal house, who, taking no thought for their own lives, stood forth against their securely-established enemies in order to avenge their father's murder. Everyone should love them, everyone should show them reverence, everyone should honour them at feasts and among the whole body of the city on account of their courage!' Such things will be said of us by all mortals, so that both while we are living and when we are dead, our fame will never die.

Electra appeals to her sister by imagining their public veneration for the murder in terms that evoke the image of the tyrannicides Harmodius and Aristogeiton being celebrated for the murder of Hipparchus.[54] Scholars have pointed out the incongruity of her scenario – as Goldhill puts it, two women cannot be equal to two men, and so 'Electra and Chrysothemis cannot make a duo for heroic action'[55] – and it is often assumed that Chrysothemis (whom, like Ismene, the scholarship dismisses as weak, passive and feminine) would never have taken up her sister's challenge. Electra's attempt to persuade her through this fantasy scene is seen as

---

[54] Juffras 1991.
[55] Goldhill 2006: 156 = 2012: 244; see further 2012: 242–4 (correcting the discussion of Goldhill 2006: 153–6, which stated that the tyrannicides were brothers rather than lovers).

deeply misguided; and indeed, her appeal fails.[56] But if we re-read this scene through the prism of the texts analysed in this chapter, we see that such moments are not just inert and hopeless appeals by sisters to their less-masculine 'foils', but rather points at which the real and potent force of sisterhood threatens to erupt onto the tragic stage, just as it did in those plays that are now lost to us.

By taking this broader view of tragedy we can restore some of the full range of literary models for this neglected relationship, and this should encourage us to revise the simplistic template of 'the sister and her foil' often imposed on *Antigone* and *Electra*. By taking its prompt from Honig and other feminist theorists who have looked to ancient theatre in order to interrogate the connections between sisterhood, female solidarity and political action, this chapter has proposed ways in which fragmentary tragedy can speak to this debate by providing fresh paradigms for thinking about the power of sisterhood. The sisterhood relationships analysed here must be seen as inextricably entwined in networks of other familial and social obligations: those of father-daughter, mother-child, husband-wife and individual-*polis*. Sisterhood is not a simple relationship, and in these plays it derives its force and complexity precisely when set against these competing claims of love and duty.

---

[56] See e.g. Finglass 2007: 404 on 973–85: 'It is difficult to imagine . . . a prospect less likely to appeal to Chrysothemis.'

4 | Women in Love in the Fragmentary Plays of Sophocles

ALAN H. SOMMERSTEIN

Aeschylus in Aristophanes' *Frogs* notoriously asserts that, in contrast with Euripides, he had never in all his plays portrayed 'a woman in love' (ἐρῶσαν ... γυναῖκα, 1044). The validity of that claim depends on what 'in love' means. Aeschylus certainly did portray, perhaps for the first time in a tragic drama, the second most notorious adulteress in all Greek myth, Clytemnestra, who after murdering her husband boasts openly of her relationship with Aegisthus (*Ag.* 1431–7), and who on being told of Aegisthus' death calls him φίλτατε, 'dearest' (*Cho.* 893); but neither she nor any other female Aeschylean character was to our knowledge seen in the throes of unsatisfied passion, or engaging in active courtship, as were the Euripidean characters to whom the Aristophanic Aeschylus refers, Phaedra and Stheneboea (*Frogs* 1043). And Clytemnestra, too, had been terribly wronged by her husband when he deceived her into sending Iphigenia to Aulis (*Ag.* 1521–9), supposedly to be married to Achilles, and made her a human sacrifice there instead: neither Phaedra nor Stheneboea had grievances of anything like that gravity. Phaedra does complain about Theseus' sexual infidelities, but a wife was expected to tolerate these so long as the husband did not bring a mistress into the marital home.[1]

The structure of Old Comedy demands a straight fight between two antagonists, and in *Frogs* Sophocles is left to one side, admired (he is second only to Aeschylus) but unanalysed.[2] Is *he* prepared to put an ἐρῶσαν γυναῖκα on stage, and if so, how? Euripides may have portrayed the adulterous passions of Phaedra and of Stheneboea, but he brought both of them to a bad end: Stheneboea, and Phaedra in *Hippolytos Kalyptomenos*, die by violence, Phaedra by her own hand,[3] and their wickedness is exposed. The case of the Phaedra of the surviving *Hippolytos Stephanêphoros*, who is determined to die rather than yield to her passion,

---

[1] Plut. *On How Young Men Should Listen to Poetry* 28a; see for example the revealing discussion of Lysias' behaviour in [Dem.] 59.21–3.

[2] *Frogs* 786–94, 1515–23. The references to Sophocles in *Frogs* may be last-minute additions to take account of his death: Dover 1993: 7–9, Sommerstein 1996: 20–1.

[3] For *Stheneboea* see Collard 1995b; for *Hippolytos Kalyptomenos*, Barrett 1964: 10–45, Halleran 1995: 25–37, Talboy and Sommerstein 2006: 255–72, Collard and Cropp 2008: I 466–89.

is rather different, but even she is exposed posthumously as the cause of Hippolytus' death, which was an indirect result of that passion.

Two characters who are, or could be, relevant appear in the seven extant plays of Sophocles – for it is now generally accepted that Antigone is not portrayed, even momentarily, as being in love with Haemon,[4] though Eros is certainly a strong determinant of *his* actions. In the case of Clytemnestra in *Electra*, Sophocles is clearly not interested in her emotions towards Aegisthus, whom she mentions only twice, both times as a protector rather than a lover – once to threaten Electra with dire punishment at his hands (626–7) and once in a despairing cry for help against her killers (1409). Deianira in *Trachiniae* is another matter. In her past history erotic passion – hers, at any rate – has played no part: she was a passive spectator of the contest for her hand between Achelous and Heracles (18–27, 497–530), and equally passive when Nessus attempted to rape her and Heracles killed him (555–77). But now, after many years of marriage, she says that Eros rules her (443–4): she is hopelessly in love – with her husband. She has never condemned him for his many infidelities (459–67) and is not going to start now, even though she has been told that Iole is to be Heracles' 'wife' (δάμαρτα, 427–9); but she eventually finds that she cannot bring herself to endure such a situation (536–51) and to remedy it she resorts to desperate measures that prove fatal both to Heracles and to herself.

In the fragmentary plays[5] there are three certain cases of women in love; another one can probably be added to these despite a lack of unequivocal evidence. Of the four women concerned, one is married (though she wrongly believes her husband to be dead) and the other three are unmarried. In the three certain cases, from what we can judge, the women's passions are portrayed as vividly as those of either of the Euripidean Phaedras. All three are led by their passion to commit murder, and in two cases the victim is a blood relation – and strikingly, both these kindred-killers get away with it.

---

[4] Because the verse that had sometimes been thought to betray such feelings, 572 ὦ φίλταθ' Αἷμον, ὥς σ' ἀτιμάζει πατήρ ('Dearest Haemon, how your father slights you!'), is to be assigned to Ismene: Davies 1986, Sommerstein 1990–3 = 2010b: 202–8, Griffith 1999: 217.
[5] Griffith 2006a: 64–7 revives a nineteenth-century suggestion that some of the Sophoclean plays to be discussed below (perhaps all of them except *Phaedra*) may have been satyr-dramas rather than tragedies, arguing that romantic love was a common feature of satyr-drama well before it provably appeared in tragedy, and that Soph. frr. 474 and 941 (see below) are closely paralleled by fr. 149 from the undoubtedly satyric *Lovers of Achilles*. Against this view it may be noted (i) that romantic love (between Achilles and Patroclus) was already central to the Iliadic trilogy of Aeschylus (frr. 135–9), and (ii) that *Women of Colchis* and *Nausicaa* at least must have had female choruses, which a satyr-play cannot have.

One of the three is none other than Phaedra, in the play that bore her name.[6] As in all other accounts, she has fallen in love with her illegitimate stepson Hippolytus. Her husband Theseus is believed to be dead (cf. fr. 686), so her passion is not adulterous, though it is still improper: if she is indeed a widow, her first duties are to her children, to whom Hippolytus is a potential rival. That she is aware of the impropriety, though she feels herself unable to resist her passion, is evident from some surviving words of hers to the chorus:

> αἴσχη μέν, ὦ γυναῖκες, οὐδ᾽ ἂν εἷς φύγοι
> βροτῶν ποθ᾽, ὧι καὶ Ζεὺς ἐφορμήσηι κακά·
> νόσους δ᾽ ἀνάγκη τὰς θεηλάτους φέρειν.

Women, there could never be a mortal who could avoid shame, if Zeus unleashes evil against him; it is necessary to endure god-sent afflictions.

> σύγγνωτε κἀνάσχεσθε σιγῶσαι· τὸ γὰρ
> γυναιξὶν αἰσχρὸν σὺν γυναῖκα χρὴ στέγειν.

Have sympathy and maintain silence! For a woman ought to join in concealing what is shameful for women.

Soph. Phaedra frr. 680, 679

Phaedra probably persuaded her Nurse, after some resistance, to approach Hippolytus on her behalf;[7] it is most likely the Nurse, speaking to Hippolytus, who describes the power of Eros very much as her Euripidean counterpart (speaking to Phaedra) does the power of Aphrodite (fr. 684):

> Ἔρως γὰρ ἄνδρας οὐ μόνους ἐπέρχεται
> οὐδ᾽ αὖ γυναῖκας, ἀλλὰ καὶ θεῶν ἄνω
> ψυχὰς ταράσσει κἀπὶ πόντον ἔρχεται·
> καὶ τόνδ᾽ ἀπείργειν οὐδ᾽ ὁ παγκρατὴς σθένει
> Ζεύς, ἀλλ᾽ ὑπείκει καὶ θέλων ἐγκλίνεται.

For Eros does not only attack men, or women for that matter; no, he even stirs up the souls of the gods in heaven, and moves over the sea; even all-powerful Zeus is not strong enough to repel him, but yields and gives way willingly.

Hippolytus, however, does not yield. He 'spits out' the Nurse's words (fr. 678) and in disgust goes off on his chariot. While he is away, to general amazement (fr. 686), Theseus returns; Phaedra, fearing Hippolytus will

---

[6] For Sophocles' *Phaedra* see Talboy and Sommerstein 2006, Casanova 2007, Bañuls and Crespo 2008.
[7] Talboy and Sommerstein 2006: 276–9.

come back and denounce her (and rejecting the alternative of suicide for the sake of her children: fr. 685), denounces *him* to Theseus for attempted rape (and perhaps also for an alleged plot to seize power for himself: cf. fr. 683); Theseus promptly curses Hippolytus, and presently the report arrives of his death, brought about by Poseidon's bull coming from the sea. Perhaps by then the falsity of Phaedra's accusation has already been revealed, or perhaps this happens afterwards; at any rate the revelation is inevitably followed by the suicide of Phaedra.

It has generally, and rightly, been thought that Sophocles' play was not the earliest of the three known tragedies about Phaedra and Hippolytus – in other words, that it followed at least *Hippolytos Kalyptomenos*.[8] If so, Sophocles reduced (but did not eliminate) Phaedra's guilt in the matter of the approach to Hippolytus, and may have had her repent of her actions in the end if the truth was revealed through her own confession.[9] But he still showed Phaedra pursuing with determination and persistence a course that she herself regarded as shameful.

Perhaps the most graphic surviving description of the power of love in Greek drama, outside *Hippolytos Stephanêphoros*, is the description by Hippodamia, in Sophocles' *Oenomaus*,[10] of the passion she feels for Pelops (fr. 474):

> τοίαν Πέλοψ ἴυγγα θηρατηρίαν
> ἔρωτος, ἀστραπήν τιν᾽ ὀμμάτων, ἔχει,
> ἧι θάλπεται μὲν αὐτός, ἐξοπτᾶι δ᾽ ἐμέ,
> ἴσον μετρῶν ὀφθαλμόν, ὥστε τέκτονος
> παρὰ στάθμην ἰόντος ὀρθοῦται κανών.

> Such a magic charm to hunt down love does Pelops have, a sort of lightning in the eyes, by which he himself is warmed and I am roasted alive; he matches his glance to mine, as straight as a carpenter's rule is when he goes along a line.

Pelops has come to the palace of Hippodamia's father, Oenomaus, at Pisa in Elis to compete for her hand on the terms which Oenomaus set down for every suitor: a chariot-race all the way to the Isthmus of Corinth, in which the suitor is given a start (in most accounts he takes Hippodamia with him in his chariot) and Oenomaus pursues him. If the suitor wins the race, he has won Hippodamia; if Oenomaus overtakes the suitor, he kills him.

---

[8] Talboy and Sommerstein 2006: 287–8.
[9] Talboy and Sommerstein 2006: 274, 283–4.
[10] Talboy and Sommerstein 2012.

Oenomaus' horses, by the way, are as swift as the wind, and the skulls of thirteen would-be sons-in-law (give or take a few)[11] are exhibited on the palace eaves to prove it. Evidently, for one reason or another, Oenomaus is determined that his daughter shall never marry. Sophocles seems to have used the version of the story in which Oenomaus' charioteer, Myrtilus, was bribed to sabotage his master's chariot, and it is likely that the bribe came not from Pelops but from Hippodamia, and was of a sexual nature, Hippodamia pretending that she had fallen in love with Myrtilus.[12] The race cannot have been shown on stage, of course, though its start may well have been;[13] but its outcome must have been reported, and probably Oenomaus' corpse brought back. The messenger may also have reported that Pelops' chariot (given to him by Poseidon) took to the air, with Myrtilus joining the happy couple on board. He probably did not know, but the audience did, that Pelops soon afterwards threw Myrtilus off into the sea when he tried to claim his reward. No source suggests that Hippodamia suffers for her parricide and treachery; some accounts end with her suicide or exile, but this is connected with a quite separate episode, the murder of Pelops' bastard son Chrysippus by a conspiracy involving Hippodamia and her sons.[14] The curse of Myrtilus, however, will have devastating effects on Hippodamia's descendants. Having said this, all these consequences are beyond the scope of the play, which will have ended with

[11] Thirteen in [Hes.] fr. 259(a) M–W, [Epimenides] D–K 3 B 17, Pind. O. 1.79–80 (with Σ 1.127b = I 45.11–46.6 Drachmann, which offers alternative lists of six or fifteen suitors), Pind. fr. 135 S–M, [Lucian] *Charidemus* 19, Philostr. *Imag.* 1.17.4; twelve in Σ Eur. *Or.* 990 (I 196.13 Schwartz), and cf. Apollod. *Ep.* 2.4); fifteen in Paus. 6.21.10–11 (who notes that some sources add a further two).

[12] Talboy and Sommerstein 2012: 80–2, 87–8, 103–5; frr. 475, 477, 472 may all come from this scene. Both the other sources that speak of Hippodamia falling in love with Pelops (Apollod. *Ep.* 2.4, Σ Ap. Rh. 1.752–8 = pp. 64.11–65.7 Wendel) say she acted to secure Pelops' victory in the chariot-race by bribing Myrtilus (some other sources refer to such a bribe without explaining its motivation). The nature of her bribe is usually left unmentioned, but the one author who specifies it (Servius on Virg. *Georg.* 3.7 = III/1 273.10–11 Thilo and Hagen, whence *Mythogr. Vat.* 1.21, 2.169) makes it a sexual one, and several other accounts suggest as much by stating that Myrtilus, when escaping with the couple after Oenomaus had been killed, made advances to Hippodamia (Pherecydes fr. 37b EGM, Apollod. *Ep.* 2.8, Σ Lyc. *Alex.* 165a = p. 36.13–15 Leone, identical to Σ Eur. *Or.* 990 = I 196.6–197.5 Schwartz). Fr. 475 may come from a scene in which Hippodamia declared her pretended passion to Myrtilus, and in fr. 472 she may be about to make him swear to carry out the sabotage of Oenomaus' chariot and/or to keep the plot secret.

[13] For the appearance on stage of chariots and other wheeled vehicles, and of horses, in fifth-century tragedy see respectively Taplin 1977: 75–9 and Sommerstein 2010a: 28. This particular race was abnormal in that the two competitors started it separately, perhaps at an interval of several minutes (see p. 65 above; contrast *El.* 709–13), so it would not be necessary to bring both chariots and teams on stage together.

[14] Gantz 1993: 544–5.

the death of Oenomaus and the escape of Pelops and Hippodamia. As usual,[15] it seems, a father who insists on keeping his daughter unmarried must pay for it.

The third woman is Medea in *Women of Colchis*. Nothing in the little that survives of this play proves that love was Medea's motive for helping Jason to secure the Golden Fleece, but no source ever suggests any other motive. One fragment (fr. 339) implies a private conversation between them (or perhaps a conversation in the presence only of a complicit chorus) in which Medea makes Jason swear to do her a favour in return for the favour she is doing him; it is not clear whether she allows him to know, before making the oath, what favour he is to do. We know (fr. 343) that in this play Medea's brother Apsyrtus was killed in their father's palace – in other words his murder was part of the play, which is likely to have ended with the escape of the Argonauts, taking with them Medea and the Fleece. But we do not know anything more about it for certain. A passage in Euripides' *Medea* (1334–5), which also places the killing in the palace, implies that Medea was solely responsible, but another early account spreads the guilt more widely:

Φερεκύδης … ἐν ζ΄ τὴν Μήδειάν φησιν ἆραι μικρὸν ὄντα Ἄψυρτον ἐκ τῆς κοίτης, Ἰάσονος εἰπόντος αὐτῆι ἐνεγκεῖν πρὸς τοὺς Ἀργοναύτας· ἐπεὶ δὲ ἐδιώχθησαν, σφάξαι καὶ μελίσαντας ἐκβαλεῖν εἰς τὸν ποταμόν.

Pherecydes in Book 7 says that Medea roused Apsyrtus (who was a small boy) from his bed after Jason had told her to bring him to the Argonauts; and when they were pursued, they killed him, dismembered him, and threw the body parts into the river.

Pherecydes fr. 32a *EGM*

Sophocles cannot have adopted Pherecydes' version wholesale, for Pherecydes was explicit that Apsyrtus was killed on board ship ('when they were pursued'). If the killing took place in the palace, the actual perpetrator can only have been Medea, but she might still have been acting on Jason's specific instructions; it would be just like the Euripidean Jason to ignore this, and she was certainly acting for the purpose of facilitating his escape.

And though no love-related material survives that is actually attributed to *Women of Colchis*, we may nevertheless possess a love-related fragment of this play. Sophocles fr. 941, a fragment unattributed by its source to any particular play, is an extended (seventeen-line) rhapsody addressed to a

---

[15] Compare the case of Acrisius, and also that of his ancestor Danaus (discussed in Sommerstein 2010a: 102–3, 106–7, 2019: 4–10, 13–20, 26–7).

chorus of maidens on the universal power of Aphrodite over all living things including the gods:[16]

> ὦ παῖδες, ἦ τοι Κύπρις οὐ Κύπρις μόνον,
> ἀλλ' ἐστὶ πολλῶν ὀνομάτων ἐπώνυμος.
> ἔστιν μὲν Ἅιδης, ἔστι δ' ἄφθιτος βίος,
> ἔστιν δὲ λύσσα μανιάς, ἔστι δ' ἵμερος
> 5   ἄκρατος, ἔστ' οἰμωγμός. ἐν κείνηι τὸ πᾶν
> σπουδαῖον, ἡσυχαῖον, ἐς βίαν ἄγον.
> ἐντήκεται γὰρ †πλευμόνων†[17] ὅσοις ἔνι
> ψυχή· τίς οὐχὶ τῆσδε τῆς θεοῦ πόρος;
> εἰσέρχεται μὲν ἰχθύων πλωτῶι γένει,
> 10   ἔνεστι δ' ἐν χέρσου τετρασκελεῖ γονῆι,
> νωμᾶι δ' ἐν οἰωνοῖσι †τοὐκείνης πτερόν.†[18]
>   <   >
> ἐν θηρσίν, ἐν βροτοῖσιν, ἐν θεοῖς ἄνω.
> τίν' οὐ παλαίουσ' ἐς τρὶς ἐκβάλλει θεῶν;
> εἴ μοι θέμις – θέμις δὲ τἀληθῆ λέγειν –
> 15   Διὸς τυραννεῖ πλευμόνων, ἄνευ δορός,
> ἄνευ σιδήρου· πάντα τοι συντέμνεται
> Κύπρις τὰ θνητῶν καὶ θεῶν βουλεύματα.

Maidens, the Cyprian is not the Cyprian alone, but is called by many names. She is death, she is immortal life, she is raving madness, she is unmixed desire, she is lamentation; in her is all activity, all tranquillity, all that leads to violence. For she sinks into the vitals of all that have life; where is there not a pathway for this goddess? She enters into the swimming race of fishes, she resides within the four-legged brood upon dry land, and her wing ranges among birds. [*Lacuna*] ... among beasts, among humans, among the gods above. Which of the gods does she not fight and vanquish?[19] If it is proper for me – and it is – to tell the truth, she rules over the heart of Zeus, without spear, without iron. All the plans of mortals and gods are cut short by the Cyprian.

The speaker is clearly a woman. It is unlikely to be Phaedra, since a speech saying much the same thing (about Eros) is already known from her play (fr. 684);[20] it might be Hippodamia, but in view of her age (she ought to

---

[16] See the admirable discussion by Coo 2011b. The translation is based on that of Lloyd-Jones 2003.
[17] Lloyd-Jones 2003: 404 places πλευμόνων within obeli.
[18] Diggle, *TrGFS* p. 77 places τοὐκείνης πτερόν within obeli.
[19] Literally 'wrestle and throw three times'.
[20] Wagner 1852: 445.

have been married long since) a chorus of her contemporaries and confidants would probably have consisted of young wives rather than maidens.[21] Ahrens may well, therefore, have been right to attribute the passage to Medea in *Women of Colchis*.[22] In that case, all these three plays will have included a substantial speech about the power of love in general (*Phaedra*, *Women of Colchis*), or about its effects on the individual (*Oenomaus*), or both.

Medea, so far as we can tell, like Hippodamia, goes unpunished for the murder she committed to assist her lover; it is conceivable that she was represented as having some valid grievance against her father and brother, but we never hear of any, and it is quite possible, indeed likely, that Apsyrtus was represented as a mere child, as in Pherecydes (fr. 32a *EGM*) and apparently in Sophocles' *Scythians* (fr. 546) where, although the text is partly corrupt, he is clearly younger than Medea (he was born ἄρτι 'lately', Medea πρίν ποτε 'at an earlier time'). However, Medea's virtual immunity from punishment for her many misdeeds is a striking feature of almost the whole of her mythical profile. She will in the end lose both Jason and her children by him, whom probably she did not herself intentionally kill in any version known before 431.[23] But once again, that is beyond the limits of the play – far beyond them, in this case.

There is no other direct evidence for Sophoclean portrayals of women in love, but there is at least one further highly probable case, namely Nausicaa – a role that, according to Athenaeus (*Deipn.* 1.20f = T 28 *TrGF*), Sophocles played himself, suggesting that this was an early play (as is in any case made likely by the fact that it is hard to see what individual characters there can have been other than Nausicaa, Odysseus and possibly Athena). In the *Odyssey* it is plain that Nausicaa is greatly struck by Odysseus, at least after Athena has beautified him (6.227–46), and the speech she then makes to him is a masterpiece of indirect courtship.[24] Sophocles' play was based on *Odyssey* 6, as is evident from its alternative title Πλύντριαι, *Washerwomen*, denoting the chorus of Nausicaa's servants who went with her to the seashore to wash clothes, and from Athenaeus' reference to Sophocles as Nausicaa showing skill in ball-play (cf. *Od.* 6.100, 115–17); and it is, to say the least, plausible that Nausicaa was made to

---

[21] Talboy and Sommerstein 2012: 89 n. 71.

[22] Ahrens 1846: 325, though he was probably going too far when he actually printed it as a fragment of that play.

[23] Mossman 2011: 5–9, 23–8, WRIGHT.

[24] Hom. *Od.* 6.255–315, especially 273–88; see Woodhouse 1930: 54–8, Garvie 1994: 29–30, 141–53.

express her feelings to the chorus, in Odysseus' absence, rather more freely than Homer allowed her to do. The play certainly made a significant and lasting impact: it was parodied in comedy by Philyllius towards the end of the fifth century,[25] and by Eubulus probably no earlier than 380.[26]

There are a few other possibilities, none very strong. Tyro, in the play dubbed *Tyro Keiromene* by A. Clark (2003), is described by someone (probably her stepmother Sidero) as a nymphomaniac (καπρομανής, literally 'boar-mad': fr. 652); but that very fact, and the punishment (cropping of hair) described in fr. 659, implies that she was already known to be pregnant or to have given birth, so that any reference to her passion for the river-god Enipeus (*Od.* 11.235–40) must have been retrospective.

In *Lemnian Women*, Hypsipyle was no doubt an important character, but we have no idea how her relationship with Jason was treated. A clue, however, may be provided by the comparison between this play and Aeschylus' *Hypsipyle* in the scholia to Apollonius.[27] In Aeschylus' play the Argo, though caught in a storm, had not been allowed to put in to Lemnos until its crew swore that they would have intercourse with the Lemnian women as soon as they disembarked, the women mustering in arms ready to drive them away if they refused. This sounds less like ἔρως than biological necessity: there were no men on the island, and the arrival of the ship was providential for the women. In Sophocles too the women mustered in arms; we are not told whether they made the same demand as in Aeschylus, but if they did it was apparently refused, since the scholiast speaks of a hard-fought battle between the women and the Argonauts. It is difficult to believe that the women defeated such a distinguished band of heroes, but if the Argonauts had won a clear victory they would hardly have stayed long with the women on the island; probably then the battle ended in a truce with the Argonauts agreeing to the women's terms. However one looks at it, individual love can have played little if any part in the establishment of relationships. It remains possible that Hypsipyle was shown as having developed a strong amorous attachment to Jason, as Deianira did to Heracles over a longer period; but that is only a possibility, and nothing in our fragments tells for or against it.

---

[25] See Orth 2015: 178–82, who with perhaps excessive caution says that a direct connection with Sophocles' play 'would be possible' ('möglich wäre', p. 179). Only one word of Philyllius' play survives.

[26] R. Hunter 1983: 7–10.

[27] Σ Ap. Rh. 1.769–73 (p. 68.8–12 Wendel).

A last possibility is presented by the family of Amyntor, the father of Phoenix. In the *Iliad* (9.447–57) Amyntor's wife, angry that her husband was neglecting her in favour of a concubine, tells Phoenix to sleep with the concubine, which he does; the concubine's own feelings do not come into the picture at all. In Euripides' *Phoenix*, on the other hand,[28] the concubine (there named Phthia) accused Phoenix falsely of rape, which in folktale and tragedy normally implies that *she* had propositioned him unsuccessfully, as is made explicit in an Attic story narrated by Hieronymus of Rhodes (*Phoenix* test. iv.a) and said to be parallel to that of Euripides' play. The second scenario gives scope for making the concubine into a Phaedra-like character, if the dramatist so desires; the first would probably not be relevant to our concerns. Sophocles wrote a *Phoenix*, but we know little about it; his *Dolopes* probably deals with a different episode, since Phoenix was made ruler of the Dolopians by Peleus *after* being driven from his homeland (*Il.* 9.480–4). The only clue we have to Sophocles' portrayal of the two women is fr. 720, where one of them, presumably the concubine, is called a prostitute (φορβὰς γυνή, literally 'a woman who feeds herself'). Our source, Eustathius, says that this is 'comic' language and implies indiscriminate promiscuity.[29] Since the outcome of the story must necessarily be the exile of Phoenix (leading to his becoming a dependent of Peleus), it is easiest to place this evidently somewhat vulgar expression in the mouth of an angry Amyntor, denouncing both his concubine and Phoenix in a form of the story similar to Homer's. It may have been that she was more guilty, and Phoenix less so, than in the *Iliad*, but that is pure speculation.

So in the end, though there may well have been other women in love portrayed in fragmentary Sophoclean plays, there are at most four about whom we can say anything definite: Phaedra, the wife who thinks she is a widow but knows that she is acting shamefully; Hippodamia, the maiden who has been iniquitously denied the right to marriage; Medea, the barbarian sorceress; and probably Nausicaa. In contrast with the Euripidean Phaedra or Stheneboea, none of them is knowingly violating a marital bond. All four plays, like *Trachiniae*, had female choruses[30] in whom the enamoured woman could conveniently confide. At least three of the four contained set speeches describing the power of love in general and/or in

---

[28] Collard and Cropp 2008: II 405–21; also Sommerstein 2014: 169–71.

[29] Eustathius, *Commentaries on Homer's* Iliad 539.13 (II 57.2–3 Van der Valk, on *Iliad* 5.203).

[30] There is no direct evidence for the gender of the chorus in *Oenomaus*, but Hippodamia could hardly have spoken openly of her erotic feelings (fr. 474) or pursued her corruption of Myrtilus (frr. 472, 475) in the presence of a chorus of men of Pisa; see Talboy and Sommerstein 2012: 89, 101–5.

their particular case. Hippodamia was probably given two such speeches –
one about her genuine passion for Pelops (addressed to the chorus) and
one about her pretended passion for Myrtilus (addressed to Myrtilus
himself). Hippodamia, fourteen times offered as a bride and thirteen times
robbed of her bridegroom, would probably win much sympathy for her
plight if not for her methods; Nausicaa presumably, as in Homer, acted
towards Odysseus with as much propriety as was possible in the circumstances (it was not her fault that she met Odysseus in the absence of her
parents and, if Sophocles followed Homer, initially in the absence of his
clothes); even Phaedra's guilt is to some extent palliated by her not
knowing that Theseus was alive and by the need she feels neither to bereave
nor to disgrace her children.[31] Three of the four women commit murder,
or what is tantamount to murder: Phaedra pays for it with her life, the
other two do not pay for it at all, or not till many years later, beyond the
bounds of the drama. I suspect that if Euripides had created a character like
the Medea or even the Hippodamia of Sophocles, it would have been
touted as another example of his slandering of women and his condonation
of rank immorality; but then Euripides had broken a constraint that
Sophocles seems to have carefully observed. The younger dramatist put
on stage two married women who knowingly, deliberately and wantonly
sought adulterous liaisons, and allowed them to defend their actions
(because in Euripides everyone, even a character as vicious as Polymestor
in *Hecuba*, is routinely given a chance to state his or her case with the best
arguments available). Sophocles, so far as we can tell, never did such a
thing; and so he could portray a woman killing for love and getting away
with it – and himself get away scot-free with doing so.

---

[31] On her fear of leaving the children motherless, see fr. 685; on her fear of disgrace (which would
affect them as well as herself), frr. 679, 680.

5 | Heterosexual Bonding in the Fragments of Euripides

HELENE P. FOLEY

In the *Odyssey* Penelope and Odysseus renew their marital bonds in their bedroom during an extra long night of love (23.241–343). Extant Greek tragedy certainly contains some frustrated hopes for close marital or emerging premarital bonds. In Sophocles, the devotion of Tecmessa and Deianira to their partners is not actively reciprocated, nor, assuming that we give *Antigone* 572, 'O dearest Haemon, how your father dishonours you', to Ismene rather than Antigone, does Haemon's passion receive a direct response from his fiancée.[1] In Euripides, Alcestis' sacrifice for Admetus is represented more as a practical and ethical than as a romantic gesture. *Erôs* plays a role in Medea's feelings for Jason and Theseus' for Phaedra, but those impulses are not reciprocated by a partner on stage. Andromache is the model of a devoted wife in both *Andromache* and *Trojan Women*, but her husband Hector is dead. Megara in *Heracles* has been loyal to her husband and welcomes his rescue briefly before he goes mad and kills both herself and their sons. Yet in no case but that of Helen and Menelaus in *Helen* are spousal bonds actively represented on stage in a central recognition scene; here both references to Penelope and Odysseus' reunion (such as a private set of tokens known only to the couple, at *Helen* 290–1, if genuine) and on-stage embraces are pointed. Perhaps most romantic of all, Evadne in *Suppliant Women* passionately chooses suttee for her husband Capaneus to the horror of her father (and the chorus at 1074–5). Yet once again, the object of her devotion is already dead and cannot respond.

Extant tragedy, unlike epic, tends to represent dysfunctional or failed marriages, and shows little interest in either youthful or mature romance. Euripides' fragmentary plays suggest a more complex picture. Aristophanes in *Thesmophoriazusae* apparently takes advantage of novelty in parodying both the pseudo-epic reunion of the spouses in *Helen* and the romance at first sight staged in the fragmentary *Andromeda*, although we should note that neither play was preserved as part of the canon. Moreover, the striking romantic effects of *Andromeda* apparently continued to foster

[1] SOMMERSTEIN, p. 63.

'Euripidomania' for many centuries. Lucian tells us of an epidemic produced by the play at Abdera (in Thrace, eastern Macedonia) under the reign of Alexander's former general Lysimachus around 300:

> They say, my dear Philo, that in the reign of King Lysimachus the people of Abdera were smitten by an epidemic. These were the symptoms: at first every one of them fell ill of a fever, violent and obstinate from the start; about the seventh day it was broken, in some cases by a copious flow of blood from the nostrils, in others by heavy sweating; but their minds were left in a ridiculous state; they all went mad with tragedy, shouting iambics and creating a din; they mostly sang solos from Euripides' *Andromeda* [or 'sang as a solo Andromeda's part in Euripides' play'], rendering Perseus' speech in song; the city was full of these seventh-day tragedians, all pale and thin, roaring, 'Love, you tyrant of gods and men' [fr. 136.1] and the rest in a loud voice, hour after hour, day after day, until winter and a severe cold spell stopped their noise. Archelaüs the actor seems to me to be to blame for such goings on. He was popular then, and in the middle of the summer in the blazing heat had played the *Andromeda* for them, so that most of them brought their fever away from the theatre with them, and later when they left their beds relapsed into tragedy; the *Andromeda* kept haunting their memory, and his Perseus and Medusa's head still flitted round everyone's brain.
>
> Lucian, *How to Write History* 1 (transl. Kilburn 1959: 3–5)

Given the response to this same play in early fourth-century vase paintings as well,[2] it seems plausible, as Gibert (1999–2000) and others have argued, that *Andromeda* represented a genuine tragic novelty. Yet other Euripidean plays apparently gave serious attention to the possibility of deeper heterosexual bonds in couples than in our extant plays. In this chapter, I look at these glimmerings of reciprocal spousal or premarital bonds central to the dramatic action in Euripides' fragmentary plays and consider their possible implications.

As the later extensive literary response to the myth suggests, Euripides' highly fragmentary *Protesilaus* is likely to have represented a genuine marital romance. Protesilaus, first off the boat at Troy, was in every version of his myth the war's first victim. The Iliadic catalogue of ships mentions his leap to death and notes that he left behind a lamenting wife and a house half-completed (2.698–702). Two similar scholia describing Euripides' play tell us that that *Protesilaus* is a drama written by Euripides:

[2] Trendall and Webster 1971: §III.3,10–13, Schauenburg 1981, Jones Roccos, 1994: 342–5, Gibert 2004: 133, Taplin 2007: 174–85, Collard and Cropp 2008: I 124, 128–9.

λέγει [λέγεται] δὲ ὅτι γαμήσας καὶ μίαν ἡμέραν μόνην συγγενόμενος τῆι γυναικὶ αὐτοῦ ἠναγκάσθη μετὰ τῶν Ἑλλήνων κατὰ τῆς Τροίας ἐλθεῖν, καὶ πρῶτος ἐπιβὰς τῆς Τροίας ἐτελεύτησεν. καί φησιν [φασιν] ὅτι τοὺς κάτω δαίμονας ἠιτήσατο καὶ ἀφείθη μίαν ἡμέραν, καὶ συνεγένετο τῆι γυναικὶ αὐτοῦ.

And he says [it is said] that after marrying and consorting with his wife for just one day he was compelled to go with the Greeks against Troy, and died after being the first of them to land at Troy. He also says [They also say] that he entreated the powers below and was released for one day, and consorted with his wife.

Σ Aelius Aristides 3.365 = Σ Lucian 26.1 (test. ii);
variants in the Lucianic scholia recorded in square brackets[3]

Due to inconsistencies in the two scholia, it is not entirely certain that Euripides' play is being described at every stage, but given that all later references to the story involve a return of Protesilaus to his wife from the world below,[4] the play must have dwelt on this brief return. In Euripides' version Protesilaus, rather than his wife Laodamia, as in some other versions, took the initiative in requesting the return from the world below. It also seems probable that Hermes escorted Protesilaus to or from the world above.[5] Scanty fragments suggest that he then encountered both his father-in-law Acastus and his wife Laodamia.

Reconstructing what may have happened during the play's one-day return must draw on later versions of the myth, which tend to focus on Laodamia more than Protesilaus; but it is safe to say that Euripides' play created a couple who were equally desirous of their brief reunion, and probably concluded with Laodamia committing suicide to join her husband in the underworld, whether on her own initiative or persuaded to do so by Protesilaus.[6] A line from *Protesilaus* attributed by its source to Laodamia, 'I shall not forsake a loved one, even though he is lifeless' (fr. 655), apparently confirms her active devotion. Given that Protesilaus initiated the plot, the speculation that Laodamia may have briefly thought that her husband had actually returned to life before discovering the truth as in Apollodorus' version (*Ep.* 3.30) seems likely. What role Laodamia's father Acastus played remains uncertain, but the fragments suggest a debate, perhaps between Acastus and Protesilaus, on the value of marriage, with

---

[3] Translations of Euripidean fragments and testimonia are cited from Collard and Cropp 2008 unless otherwise noted.
[4] Cat. 68.73–86, 105–18 focuses entirely on Laodamia's loss of her husband.
[5] This interpretation of fr. 646a is confirmed in Hyg. *Fab.* 103.2.
[6] Fr. 656, *TrGF* v/2 633–5.

Acastus denigrating the institution in a typically Euripidean fashion that threatens to undermine the romantic implications of the plot (fr. 653), and Protesilaus defending the possibility of a good wife (fr. 657): 'Anyone who puts all women together and blames them indiscriminately is foolish and not wise. There are many of them, and you will find one bad while another is of noble character, as this one is [*or* was].'[7] This last fragment might have come from someone commenting on Laodamia after her death, however.

Moreover, in most later versions of the story, Laodamia, actually carrying out a plan proposed by Admetus in *Alcestis* (348–56), had constructed an image (εἴδωλον) of her husband with which she consorted to some degree or other (προσωμίλει, Apollod. *Ep.* 3.30). Scholars have argued that Acastus may have insisted on destroying the image in an effort to persuade his daughter, in conformity with Attic views about widows of childbearing age, to remarry and give up her grief before Protesilaus' arrival on stage. In my view, contrary to other more adventurous reconstructions, the fragments only permit us to go as far as identifying possible elements in Euripides' play.[8] However, whether or not Euripides, as some think, surprised his audience by offering the first version of the story of Protestilaus' one-day return in the Greek poetic tradition, it is the lovers' spectacular devotion that left an enduring impression on later Greek and Latin literature. In Apollodorus (*Ep.* 3.30), the gods pitied Laodamia's desire (ἤρα) and brought Protesilaus back to her. In Hyginus' extravagant version (*Fab.* 103–4), the gods gave her three hours with Protesilaus; unable to restrain her grief after his return to Hades, she feigned religious devotion to a bronze image of her husband. A servant spied on her embracing and kissing the statue and informed her father that she had a lover. Her father burnt the image and Laodamia threw herself on the burning pyre. Virgil locates Laodamia with the other lovelorn in the Mourning Fields of the underworld, Catullus cannot plumb the depth of her love, Propertius measures his own love for Cynthia by Protesilaus' standard, and Ovid's Laodamia laments his departure, tends his image and promises to follow him wherever fate directs.[9]

Helen, Evadne and, it seems, Laodamia express direct passion to reunite with their husbands or partners, but other wives or consorts in the fragments express a devotion that suggests an intense memorable bond.

---

[7] Cf. Eur. *Captive Melanippe* fr. 494.22–9.

[8] Collard and Cropp 2008: ii 106–9 summarise previous views with further bibliography.

[9] Virg. *Aen.* 6.447 with Servius (ii 69.9–12 Thilo and Hagen), Cat. 68.73–86, 105–18, Prop. 1.19.7–12, Ov. *Her.* 13; also Canciani 1994.

Hypsipyle in *Hypsipyle*, as the chorus remarks, apparently spends her days of slavery commemorating in song the Argonauts' visit to the island of Lemnos and the pursuit of the Golden Fleece (fr. 752f). Presumably the most memorable if unstated part of this visit was her relation to Jason. She later evokes the memory of the Argo in desperation after she has allowed her nursling Opheltes to be killed by a snake, and finally, in the recognition scene with her sons, the report of Jason's death brings tears to her eyes.[10]

Far more spectacular, however, is the possible devotion of Jocasta to her son/husband in Euripides' *Oedipus*. Of course, Jocasta's incestuous relation to Oedipus (ironically) reflects mutual devotion in virtually every tragedy in which she appears. Sophocles' spouses have deep mutual respect, and Oedipus' blinding with Jocasta's brooches significantly occurs in the bedroom after he embraces his dead wife and exposes her body. Euripides' Jocasta in the extant *Phoenician Women* has survived and devotedly cares for her blind husband (1549–50), even after she has recognized his unwitting crimes. But Euripides' (metrically) late play *Oedipus*, which according to the sixth-century AD writer John Malalas (*Chronicles* 2.17 = test. ii) focussed on Oedipus, Jocasta and the Sphinx, may have had Jocasta outdo even Euripides' Andromaches (in *Andromache* and *Trojan Women*) as she outlines the degree of devotion expected of the ideal wife. In this brief discussion, I shall not engage with the controversial attempts to reconstruct the play as a whole, but simply examine the possibility that Jocasta did offer some version of the following speech to her husband.

The critical fr. 545a comes from Clement of Alexandria (*Miscellanies* 4.20.125.1–126.4, II 303.18–304.15 Stählin), who cites without naming a specific play lines 7–8, 9–10, 11–12, 1–3 and 4–6 separately and in this order. Clement attributes lines 7–12 to Euripides, lines 1–6 to 'tragedy'. If the speech is not by Jocasta, it may have been offered by another Euripidean tragic wife to her husband in a different play; Clement quotes six of the lines saying 'Euripides gives a dignified sketch of a wife who loves her husband'. I include it in this discussion because other fragments also attributed to the play (frr. 543, 544, 545, 548, mentioned below) seem to have focussed, however ambiguously, on the spousal relation in a fashion that could synchronise with this speech, and because of its possible relevance to the themes of this chapter concerning spousal bonding regardless of its attribution to Euripides' *Oedipus*.[11]

---

[10] Frr. 757.844–5, 759a.1617–18. For *Hypsipyle* see further Chong-Gossard, Simone.

[11] Liapis 2014 offers an extensive argument against attributing any of the fragments discussed here to *Oedipus*. Space does not permit addressing his argument, which has been thoroughly

οὐδεμίαν ὤνησε κάλλος εἰς πόσιν ξυνάορον,
ἀρετὴ δ' ὤνησε πολλάς· πᾶσα γὰρ κεδνὴ γυνή,
ἥτις ἀνδρὶ συντέτηκε, σωφρονεῖν ἐπίσταται.
πρῶτα μὲν γὰρ τοῦθ' ὑπάρχει κἂν ἄμορφος ᾖ πόσις,
5   χρὴ δοκεῖν εὔμορφον εἶναι τῆι γε νοῦν κεκτημένηι,
οὐ γὰρ ὀφθαλμὸς τὸ <ταῦτα> κρῖνόν ἐστιν, ἀλλὰ νοῦς.
εὖ λέγειν δ', ὅταν τι λέξηι, χρὴ δοκεῖν, κἂν μὴ λέγηι,
κἀκπονεῖν ἂν τῶι ξυνόντι πρὸς χάριν μέλληι πονεῖν.
ἡδὺ δ', ἢν κακὸν πάθηι τι, συσκυθρωπάζειν πόσει
10   ἄλοχον ἐν κοινῶι τε λύπης ἡδονῆς τ' ἔχειν μέρος.
σοὶ δ' ἔγωγε καὶ νοσοῦντι συννοσοῦσ' ἀνέξομαι
καὶ κακῶν τῶν σῶν ξυνοίσω, κοὐδὲν ἔσται μοι πικρόν.

Beauty benefits no wife with her husband, but virtue benefits many. Every good wife who has melted (συντέτηκε) in union with her husband knows how to be sensible (σωφρονεῖν). For this is the first fundamental: even if a husband is unhandsome, to a wife with sense at all he ought to seem handsome; for it is not the eye that judges (these things), but the mind. She must think, whenever he says anything, that he speaks well, even if he does not; and work to achieve whatever she means to work at to please her partner. It is pleasing too, if he experiences some trouble, for a wife to put on a gloomy face with her husband, and to join in sharing his pain and pleasure. (*To Oedipus*) You and I: I will endure sharing your guilt as my own, and bear your troubles; and nothing will be (too) harsh for me.[12]

Eur. *Oedipus* fr. 545a[13]

In another fragment also in trochaic tetrameter, Jocasta may have asserted that 'every sensible wife is her husband's slave; a wife without sense despises her partner out of folly'.[14] Fr. 548 may have had Jocasta add that 'it is the mind one must watch, the mind! What use is handsomeness, when a man does not have good sense?'. If she delivered this speech to Oedipus

challenged by Finglass 2017a. I would add that, given Jocasta's willingness to stand by her husband in *Phoenician Women*, I see no reason why (contrary to Liapis, p. 341) that she could not have done the same in this play, and the other relevant fragments mentioned below are specifically cited by Stobaeus as belonging to Euripides' *Oedipus*. Finglass 2017a: 19 would not attribute fragment 545a to Euripides' *Oedipus*, however.

[12] For similar sentiments about desired behaviour on the part of the ideal wife cf. Eur. *Andr.* 207–8, *El.* 1052–3, *Suppl.* 1028–30, *Phrixus* fr. 823.

[13] This ordering of the lines was first suggested by Musgrave; Kannicht in *TrGF* prints them in the order that they appear in Clement.

[14] Fr. 545. Finglass 2017a: 16–17 supports Cropp's suggested translation of the first phrase as 'the sensible wife is wholly her husband's slave'; he cites Euripidean parallels for viewing marriage as a form of slavery.

after he has been blinded,[15] the unusual emphasis on beauty in a husband would plausibly offer a response to Oedipus' disfigurement. Finally, in fr. 543 a character, possibly Oedipus, asserts that: 'Children and a wife are a great kingdom (τυραννίς) for a man. For it is an equal disaster for a man, I say, to lose children, fatherland, and money, as (to lose) a good wife, since his money alone <...> Truly it is better for a man, if he gets a virtuous (σώφρον') (wife)'.[16] If τυραννίς means despotic power, rather than kingdom, as translated here, the statement would reflect ambiguities also present in fr. 544, where a character argues that 'a woman/wife is the hardest of all things to fight'. Yet both fragments could also reflect Oedipus' gratitude for Jocasta's support.

The range of unmarried couples represented as at least to some degree in love in Euripides does not consistently suggest reciprocity in the feelings of the couple, but their relation is central and critical to the plot in each play discussed below. It seems likely that in Euripides' *Theseus*, Ariadne played an active role in pursuing and supporting the hero. The fragmentary hypothesis mentions the desire (ἐπιθυμίας) of Ariadne, who aided (συναγωνιώσης) Theseus in his struggle with the Minotaur.[17] She apparently – possibly on stage – persuaded her father, outraged over the death of the Minotaur, or Theseus himself, to consider a proposed plan that enabled Theseus to sail away with her on board. Fr. 388 recommends love that is moderate, just and temperate, perhaps in contrast to that of the typically Cretan Ariadne, vulnerable like her mother Pasiphae to inappropriate love. If so, Ariadne would then be more justifiably abandoned by Theseus on the return trip to Athens. At the same time, Theseus may have misled Ariadne or at least allowed her to take the risk of aiding him (συναγωνιώσης suggests shared action) and planning her departure. Even if this romance was relatively or entirely one-sided, it differs from those Euripidean plays where a married woman simply aims to seduce a younger man, like Stheneboea, especially given the extensive later literature that dwells on Ariadne's critical role in Theseus' Cretan adventure.

Equally tricky to interpret is the incestuous relation between Canace and Macareus, the children of Aeolus, that formed the basis of the plot in Euripides' *Aeolus* (dated before 423 since it was cited in *Clouds*). In a

---

[15] In this play Oedipus might have been blinded by the servants of Laius (fr. 541, Σ Eur. *Phoen.* 61 = I 258.14–16 Schwartz, although this fragment is not explicitly attributed to Euripides). See further Finglass 2017a: 9–13. In the view of some scholars (see Collard and Cropp 2008: I 2–7), he may also have been threatened with exile.

[16] Translation from Collard 2004a: 119; see further Finglass 2017a: 14–16.

[17] P.Oxy. 4640 col. i.1–17 (test. iii *TrGF*). For the play see Simon 1963: 14–16, Mills 1997: 252–5.

mythical prefiguring of a New Comic plot (the couple here involves two
mortals, not the typical divine male and mortal female, which again puts a
new emphasis on heterosexual bonding), Macareus, who according to the
hypothesis had fallen in love with (ἐρασθείς) and imposed himself on and
impregnated his sister Canace, apparently attempted to persuade his father
to allow the siblings to marry.[18] As Scafuro has pointed out, the verb
διαφθείρειν (destroy, ruin, undo) used to describe Macareus' act does not
necessarily make clear the degree of violence involved.[19] Given that the two
are siblings, and fr. 14 includes a reference to Tyro's falling in love with the
River Enipeus, perhaps we could infer less resistance on the part of
Canace.[20] The father-son debate (again prefiguring a topos in New
Comedy probably influenced by Euripides) seems to have weighed
the merits of wealth and nobility in making both marital and political
decisions. Macareus' speech to his father apparently included an ambiguous line in defence of incestuous marriage: 'What is shameful, if it does not
seem so to those practising it?' (fr. 19). In this case Aeolus seems to have
been dubious about marital partners of the same age, since women age
faster (fr. 24). The hypothesis to the play also tells us that Aeolus eventually
agreed to Macareus' plan, but a lottery gave Canace to the wrong son. The
hypothesis breaks off with a line suggesting that the couple then rushed to
meet each other in the same (agreed upon) place (?) and the nurse did
something (presumably with their newborn infant son?): συνδραμόντες
δ' εἰς τὸ αὐτ[ὸ] κουτ.[ ].ι τὸ μὲν γεννηθὲν ἡ τροφὸς [(33–4). Later sources
conclude that Aeolus discovered the child that Canace was trying to
conceal and probably sent her a sword. Macareus may have pleaded for
the couple, arrived too late to save Canace and committed suicide over
her body. (The child, contrary to the version found in Ovid, may have
survived.)[21] Whether or not Canace herself appeared on stage, her reported
rush to meet Macareus mentioned in the hypothesis suggests that the
couple shared the goal of consolidating their marriage and protecting the
child, despite the initial rape or even seduction, and that she was active in
trying to conceal the child with the help of her nurse. Ovid's *Heroides*
11 emphatically depicts the couple's passion as mutual (25–32) and gives

[18] P.Oxy. 2457.18–34 (test. ii *TrGF*).

[19] Scafuro 1990: 128, discussing the term in the context of the 'girl's tragedy' plot. Creusa in *Ion* is
raped by Apollo, as the use of the term βία by Hermes makes clear (10–11).

[20] Collard and Cropp 2008: I 14 go too far in linking Canace to bad married women who try to
seduce young men like Stheneboea.

[21] Webster 1967: 159, Gantz 1993: 169, Plut. *Greek and Roman Parallel Stories* 312c–d. Hom. *Od.*
10.1–12, by contrast, has Aeolus unite his incestuous children in happy marriage.

Canace a pre-suicidal monologue.[22] A Lucanian hydria dated to the 410s depicts a dying Canace on a couch with knife in hand; on the right Aeolus with staff points angrily at a bound Macareus on the left. A youth stands behind Macareus and an old woman (the nurse?) behind Aeolus.[23] However this relationship began or ended, it appears that the couple at least actively shared a final goal due to their offspring.

Euripides' *Meleager*, which again visits in detail the question of proper marriage partners, has Meleager (son of Althaea and Ares or Oeneus), who is in love with and hoping to marry Atalanta, present the hide of the Calydonian boar to her. This gesture led to the quarrel of Althaea's brothers over the hide and to their death, which was followed by Althaea's decision to kill her son by burning the fatal log coterminous with his life. For my purposes here, the play offers an interesting variation on courtship, in that Meleager defends to his mother his proposal to marry the unfeminine Atalanta while the virginal Atalanta insists that she has no interest in marriage. Meleager probably argues here for virtue (ἀρετή, fr. 526) and nobility (γενναιότης, fr. 527) as critical to marriage (fr. 520): 'So I reckoned, if one joined an inferior spouse with a man of worth, one would not get good children – but if both were good (ἐσθλοῖν δ' ἀπ' ἀμφοῖν), their offspring would be good'. Althaea in opposition favours wives who stay at home and avoid the outdoors (γυναῖκ' εἶναι χρεὼν | ἐσθλήν, fr. 521); women should stick to their proper ἐπιστήμη ('expertise'), the κερκίδων πόνος ('work of the shuttle') and not be overcome by the pleasures of fighting (fr. 522). Atalanta seems to have been present at the debate between mother and son because, despite her rejection of marriage, she asserts in her defence that those who toil at strenuous activities bear stronger children (fr. 525): 'And if I embarked on marriage – which I hope may never happen – I would bear stronger children than women who spend all their days at home. A father and mother who toil at strenuous activities will have children who are stronger.' Althaea may come back at Atalanta with (fr. 528): 'I detest every woman – and you above all of them – who has done wicked deeds and then speaks fine words.' While this striking three-way debate did not lead to the marriage for which Meleager hoped, most scholars think that Atalanta did accept the hide from the love-struck Meleager after the boar hunt that followed this scene (rather than before it, as Webster suggested),[24] and that Meleager's killing of his

---

[22] See also Ar. *Ran.* 1081, which links Canace with other 'bad' tragic women.

[23] Trendall and Webster 1971: §III.3,4, Giudice 1981: §1, Taplin 2007: 168–9.

[24] Webster 1967: 235–6 versus Gantz 1993: 328–39, Collard and Cropp 2008: I 615.

uncles may have been in defence of her retaining it. Perhaps only a virginal resister of love could be included in a debate during which Meleager indirectly woos Atalanta while fending off maternal objections.

Vase paintings possibly inspired by the play include images of Eros or Aphrodite. In particular, Eros hovers over a scene on an Apulian amphora of c. 330 attributed to the Painter of the Naples Europa Amphora in which Meleager gives the hide to Atalanta with an Eros hovering above and Aphrodite standing behind Atalanta; on the far left is a Fury with a torch and sword and an old messenger figure.[25] A related Apulian volute-krater attributed to the Suckling Group dated to the 340s shows Althaea rushing towards the dying Meleager supported by Tydeus and Deianira; Peleus, Theseus and Oineus lament below and Aphrodite and Phthonos appear at far right.[26] Moreover, if the possibly late alternative tradition that the Parthenopaeus who fought in the battle of the Seven Against Thebes was a son of Meleager and Atalanta, rather than of Talaus, Melanion or Hippomanes, the alternative of a consummated romance might lurk behind Atalanta's resistance in this play even if it is not fulfilled.[27]

Unfortunately one of the two most probably romantic young couples in Euripides is nearly inaccessible.[28] From Aristophanes of Byzantium's hypothesis for Sophocles' *Antigone*, we hear that the play's plot (μυθοποιία) is also found in Euripides' *Antigone*, except that there Antigone is detected (or 'stolen away', φωραθεῖσα) in company with Haemon, is joined with him in marriage and gives birth to a child Maeon. If μυθοποιία here really refers to a variation on the Sophoclean plot, Haemon, once again in love with Antigone (fr. 162), probably shared in the attempted burial of Polynices. (The hypothesis uses the same verb, ἐφωράθη, for Antigone detected in the burial of Polynices in Sophocles.) Two fragments suggest that Dionysus, indirectly answering the Sophoclean chorus's futile call for the god's help (*Ant.* 1115–54), could have made a final appearance on the machine to rescue the couple for marriage and predict the birth of a son (frr. 177–8; 178 could have been part of Dionysus' prophecy). Once again, there might have been a debate with Creon on what makes a suitable marriage, with Haemon taking the position that couples close in age are preferable (fr. 162a): 'For I shall have a marriage which it is right should do well,

---

[25] Trendall and Webster 1971: §III.3,39.

[26] For that tradition see Hyg. *Fab.* 70, 99, 270, Suet. *Tib.* 44.2, Trendall and Webster 1971: §III.3,40, Taplin 2007: 196–8.

[27] Gantz 1993: 337 suggests the name could have appeared with that of Tydeus in the *deus ex machina* speech that probably concluded the play (fr. 537).

[28] Webster 1967: 181–4, Gantz 1993: 520–1, Collard and Cropp 2008: I 156–9.

I tell you, with a wife with whom I shall grow old'. This quotation comes under a chapter labelled by Stobaeus 'The need to consider similar ages in those who marry.' The play could, however, have reflected some version of an otherwise unknown story in Hyginus (*Fab.* 72) where Antigone was handed over by Creon to Haemon for punishment; Haemon conceals and marries her, producing a son who grows up and is recognised by a birthmark during athletic games. Heracles failed to intercede for Haemon with Creon, and Haemon killed himself and Antigone. An Apulian amphora from Ruvo dated to the 350s shows Heracles at the centre of a shrine; to the left is Antigone with her hands bound and escorted by a guard, and behind them a veiled, dejected Haemon. On the right is Creon, a boy (possibly Maeon), an old woman (possibly a nurse), and above right Ismene with an open box. (The major characters are labelled.) Given the presence of Heracles, who does not appear in the Euripidean fragments, the vase could relate to a play that shared some features with Hyginus' version rather than Euripides' *Antigone*.[29] All we can conclude here is that any version of Euripides' play probably relied on a romance between Antigone and Haimon. *Antigone* fr. 161 could even be translated as 'they were in love [ἤρων; rather than 'I was in love']; and that showed that love is madness for mortals'.

   Andromeda (412) has been much and well discussed by others;[30] several features of the play are relevant to this discussion. First, Perseus, after a spectacular arrival on the machine, falls in love with Andromeda on stage and acts on his response to rescue her. His address to Eros mentioned earlier (fr. 136) sent the Abderites into their tragic fever. This dramatised love at first sight was probably novel and striking in itself.[31] Vase paintings that may have responded to Euripides can represent an exchange of gazes between the two. An Attic kalyx-krater from Capua of *c.* 390 shows Andromeda in suggestively tragic dress bound to a rock, with Perseus crowned by Aphrodite on the right gazing toward her while her father Cepheus and Hermes appear on the left.[32] Second, Perseus' decision to

---

[29] Taplin 2007: 185–6 considers a reference to Euripides possible. The *Antigone* of Astydamas the younger was performed in 341, too late to be referred to on this vase. See further Collard and Cropp 2008: i 158.

[30] Collard and Cropp 2008: i 124–9.

[31] Gibert 1999–2000 stresses the probable novelty of the theme. We do not know what happened in Sophocles' *Andromeda*; however, Sophocles' *Oenomaus* seems to have presented Hippodamia as falling in love with her suitor Pelops (fr. 474; see Talboy and Sommerstein 2012: 101–3 and SOMMERSTEIN, p. 65) and acting on her feelings. This story offered a far less innocent romance, however.

[32] Trendall and Webster 1971: §III.3,10, Schauenburg 1981: §8.

rescue Andromeda developed in a dialogic exchange. Fragments show that
Andromeda, after initial silence and maidenly reserve (fr. 126), addressed
her plight with Perseus and may have asked for pity and freedom from her
bonds (fr. 128). Yet while Perseus seems to be extracting from her a
promise of χάρις or gratitude if he saves her (fr. 129; the term χάρις could
have sexual implications), Andromeda, despite an apparently desperate
subservience, craftily hints at marriage from the start (fr. 129a): 'Take me
stranger, whether as a servant, wife, or slave'. This line suggests that she
may have committed herself to Perseus without parental support and
permission (though her father could have appeared at some point in this
scene). Later sources affirm that Andromeda stuck to her commitment to
Perseus regardless of probable opposition from father, mother, or a local
suitor, which is reflected in traces of arguments against the marriage
that raised questions about (Perseus'? or his prospective offspring's?)
bastardy and foreign status (fr. 141). Pseudo-Eratosthenes' *Catasterisms*
17 (test. iiia(a)) tells us that: 'by her own choice she left for Argos with
Perseus, a noble decision (εὐγενές τι φρονήσασα)'. Two unplaced fragments
also discuss the possibilities for those falling in love; love is pronounced a
source of pleasure when the objects of love are good/noble (ἐσθλῶν, fr. 138);
another fragment attests to love's unreliability (ἔρωτα δεινὸν ἔχομεν, fr. 138a).
The plural in both cases could suggest hints of mutual feeling in the couple,
but these references to *erôs* may only have been understood to apply to male
figures. At the very least, the play seems to have offered sympathy for
Andromeda's loyalty and found her decision to depart with him acceptable.

Given Euripides' practice elsewhere, each case of heterosexual bonding
discussed here is or was very likely embedded in dramatic contexts that
undercut or made it ambiguous. Male initiative and desire seem to have
predominated. Yet in varied ways female figures seemed to have offered
a sometimes fairly assertive response to courtship or expressed strong
emotional loyalty to bonds with partners. True, Hypsipyle remains devoted
to the memory of a consort who left her behind and took her twin sons;
Jocasta or another Euripidean wife perhaps defends her devotion to a
possibly disfigured and guilty Oedipus (or an ugly spouse); Canace very
possibly began as a rape victim rather than as a willing partner in incestuous love, but then seems to have joined forces with her lover; Atalanta
rejects Meleager's suit but perhaps takes later advantage of it; and Ariadne
may have justified her coming abandonment partly by her aggressive
pursuit of Theseus, who may nevertheless have accepted her involvement.
Yet it remains almost certain that the plays *Protesilaus*, *Andromeda* and
perhaps *Antigone* stressed a mutual response in couples that retained

positive dimensions even if Laodamia disobeyed her father and committed suicide, Andromeda's marriage provoked controversy for family and possible suitors, and Creon was likely to have been hostile to the couple's actions in *Antigone*. The ever-dangerous tragic *erôs* of other Euripidean dramas aside from *Helen* apparently functions in a more complex fashion in these works. In addition, in the fragmentary plays that focus on young couples, debates on what makes a suitable marriage seem to be pervasive. Whether this theme reflects evolving views in Attic society on this topic remains unprovable, but worth further consideration, especially as this theme re-emerges in New Comedy.

A second question is the legacy of these lost plays. Scenes possibly related to theatre performances of *Andromeda*, *Hypsipyle*, *Aeolus* and *Meleager*, and more controversially *Antigone* and *Oedipus*, left their mark on (largely) post-fifth-century vase paintings.[33] *Andromeda* won an immediate response for its titillating (erotic) novelty in Aristophanes' *Thesmophoriazusae* and *Frogs* (52–4); Aristophanes also alluded to *Aeolus* in *Clouds* and *Peace*, *Theseus* in *Wasps*, and *Hypsipyle* and *Meleager* in *Frogs* (1304–28, where Euripides' erotically scandalous music and choral lyrics are mocked). Among later Greek tragedians Lycophron (third century) wrote an *Aeolus*, *Aeolides* and *Andromeda*; Phyrnichus II also wrote an *Andromeda*. The early Roman tragedians Livius Andronicus, Ennius and Accius wrote plays called *Andromeda*; Pacuvius and Titius/Titinius each reportedly wrote a *Protesilaus* that was said to have influenced Ovid;[34] Accius wrote a *Meleager*.[35] Hypsipyle made important appearances in the *Argonautica* poems by Apollonius of Rhodes and Valerius Flaccus and in Statius' *Thebaid* books 4–6. References to Protesilaus' story, as mentioned above, appeared in Catullus, Virgil and Propertius as well as in Statius, *Silvae* 2.7.120–31; Ariadne plays a central role in Catullus 64.52–264. Roman poetry seems to have been especially receptive, if not necessarily directly, to Euripides' legacy; in particular, Ovid's *Heroides* includes letters from Hypsipyle (6), Ariadne (10), Canace (11) and Laodamia (13), while Andromeda appears in the *Metamorphoses* (4.668–5.249) and Ariadne reappears at *Ars Amatoria* 1.527–64. Ovid's poetic response alone cemented these figures' erotic and romantic legacy.

[33] See the relevant sections of Taplin 2007.
[34] Volscus 1481 (near beginning of commentary on Ovid, *Heroides* 13) makes this claim, though it has later been questioned.
[35] One cryptic fragment of Accius' *Antigone* (93–4) suggests a possible relation to Sophocles' version; hence Astydamas' *Antigone* (above, n. 29) may be the only known possible response to Euripides' version.

In the autumn of 2015, New York's Classic Stage Company's Greek Festival invited several playwrights to write new plays based on Greek tragic fragments. Ellen McLaughlin, who has written a number of adaptations and new versions of Greek tragedy,[36] chose to dramatise *Protesilaus*. In her version, Laodamia took the initiative and did choose to join her husband in the underworld at the end. But what happened during the brief reunion in the world above remains in the case of both Euripides and McLaughlin the most tantalising part of the story and, as far as can be conjectured, the most important example of active and shared heterosexual bonding in Euripides.[37]

[36] McLaughlin 2005.

[37] Romance could have occurred in earlier tragedies, however. For example, although the relevant play from Aeschylus' *Suppliant* trilogy is fragmentary, the Danaid Hypermestra's choice not to kill her husband Lynceus on their wedding night because she fell in love may have received some direct on-stage attention.

6 | Suffering in Silence

Victims of Rape on the Tragic Stage

P. J. FINGLASS

One of the most moving scenes in Sophocles takes place immediately after the first choral song of his *Trachiniae* (141–496). To the chorus, who have entered to console Deianira as she longs for the return of her husband Heracles, Deianira describes the sorrows of marriage; in her view, marriage brings pain to a woman because it constantly causes her anxiety for her husband or her children. A Messenger suddenly enters with good news: Heracles is alive, having recently triumphed in a battle, and is shortly to return. At Deianira's encouragement the chorus sing a lyric of joy; then another messenger, Lichas, enters, bringing with him a crowd of women, spoil from Eurytus' city Oechalia, which Heracles has recently sacked, holding Eurytus responsible for his year-long servitude to the Lydian queen Omphale. Despite her happiness, Deianira expresses her pity for these women, who have so recently made the awful transition from slave to free. One in particular catches her eye, a young woman of particularly striking appearance: she asks Lichas who she is and who her parents are, but he claims to know nothing.

After Lichas takes the women inside, the original Messenger intervenes, telling Deianira that the cause of Heracles' sack of Oechalia was not his time in Lydia, but his passion for Eurytus' daughter Iole, whom Eurytus refused to hand over to him as his concubine. When Lichas re-enters, keen to return to Heracles, the Messenger questions him closely about the young woman's identity; he continues to deny knowledge of her, though it becomes clear that he is lying. Deianira herself now intervenes, telling Lichas that he should speak the truth: she has coped with Heracles' infidelities in the past, and in any case feels compassion for the beautiful woman whose looks have destroyed her life. Lichas admits that he had been lying to protect her feelings; Deianira takes him inside to present him with gifts and a message to Heracles.

The heart of this complex and affecting scene, full of dramatic revelations and powerful displays of emotion, lies at the meeting of Deianira with the as yet nameless Iole. As Deianira says, addressing the chorus:

ἐμοὶ γὰρ οἶκτος δεινὸς εἰσέβη, φίλαι,
ταύτας ὁρώσηι δυσπότμους ἐπὶ ξένης
300   χώρας ἀοίκους ἀπάτοράς τ' ἀλωμένας,
αἳ πρὶν μὲν ἦσαν ἐξ ἐλευθέρων ἴσως
ἀνδρῶν, τανῦν δὲ δοῦλον ἴσχουσιν βίον.
ὦ Ζεῦ τροπαῖε, μή ποτ' εἰσίδοιμί σε
πρὸς τοὐμὸν οὕτω σπέρμα χωρήσαντά ποι,
305   μηδ', εἴ τι δράσεις, τῆσδέ γε ζώσης ἔτι.
οὕτως ἐγὼ δέδοικα τάσδ' ὁρωμένη.
ὦ δυστάλαινα, τίς ποτ' εἶ νεανίδων;
ἄνανδρος, ἢ τεκνοῦσσα; πρὸς μὲν γὰρ φύσιν
πάντων ἄπειρος τῶνδε, γενναία δέ τις.
310   Λίχα, τίνος ποτ' ἐστὶν ἡ ξένη βροτῶν;
τίς ἡ τεκοῦσα, τίς δ' ὁ φιτύσας πατήρ;
ἔξειπ'· ἐπεί νιν τῶνδε πλεῖστον ὤικτισα
βλέπουσ', ὅσωιπερ καὶ φρονεῖν οἶδεν μόνη.

A terrible sense of pity has come upon me, my friends, as I see these ill-
fated women wandering to a foreign land, deprived of their home and
deprived of their fathers – women who before, perhaps, were the offspring
of free men, but who now have the life of a slave. O Zeus who turns
battles, may I never see you approaching my seed in this way, or if you
will do so, do not while I am still alive! That is the fear that I have as
I behold them. O wretched woman, who among girls are you? Are you
unmarried, or a mother? As regards your appearance you are without
experience in all these matters, but you are some noble person. Lichas,
who among mortals does the foreign woman belong to? Who is her
mother, who the father who begot her? Speak out – since I pitied
her most of these when I saw her, in as much as she alone knows how
to behave.

Soph. *Tr.* 298–313

Deianira begins by surveying the women as a whole, before focussing on
the sorrow of one particular, distinctive girl. How exactly this was staged
we cannot say;[1] but somehow Iole must have been distinguished from the
mass of girls brought in by Lichas. The final line of Deianira's speech
suggests that either Iole's mask or her deportment set her apart – for
without some such physical indication, it is hard to see how Deianira could
have made this inference about her character.

A great part of the tension rests in Iole's silence. The audience would not
be expecting Iole to speak, at least in the present scene, since three speaking

[1] See Mastronarde 1979: 76–7, Easterling 1982 on 313 for suggestions.

actors were already on stage and a fourth was not normally permitted by the rules of the contest.[2] Yet for a non-speaking character, Iole becomes the focus of attention to an unusual degree, especially as she is (from one perspective) merely one of a group of women who have just entered the stage. The very refusal of the rules of the genre to allow her to speak is poignant, especially when the full story of her life becomes known: she is the wretched victim of Heracles' passion, the object of lust who, through no personal fault, has brought destruction on her father's city and on the women whom the audience can see processing across the stage. Like Deianira, Iole passively suffers the consequences of *erôs*; both are victims, in their own way, of the unbridled force of Heracles' lust.[3] Yet unlike Deianira, whose eloquence and individual speaking style contribute so much to the drama's overall impact, she is given no voice to express her sorrow. Because of Deianira's perseverance in her compassion for Iole even after it is discovered that she is her rival, Iole's pitiable state does not go undescribed, despite her silence; indeed, one scholar even comments that Iole's speaking 'would in fact be unnecessary, since Deianeira attributes her own feelings to her to such an extent that she effectively speaks for her.'[4] Deianira's capacity to speak for both women establishes her as a truly empathetic person, cognisant of the feelings even of a silent rival; by the end of the play, the contrast with the articulate but entirely self-centred Heracles, who lacks concern for the feelings even of his own son, will be clear. Yet Iole's very silence, too, has its own eloquence; in a scene where deceit is so prominent, her saying nothing provides an all too reliable testimony to her innocent victim-hood, to her inability to combat the mighty forces in which she has been caught up.

The meeting between Deianira and Iole has often been compared to the confrontation between Clytemnestra and Cassandra in Aeschylus'

---

[2] It was not completely unprecedented for such a non-speaking actor to speak – Pylades' dramatic intervention in Aeschylus' *Libation Bearers* (900–2), a play that otherwise has only two speaking characters on stage, is proof of that – but the solitary nature of that exception means that we can fairly talk about a rule.

[3] Cf. Wohl 1998: 17–18 'Iole is in the play's present what Deianira was in the past ... The sublimation of Deianira as Iole is facilitated by the many parallels between the two women', which she goes on to describe, and Foley 2001: 95 'Iole is a younger double of herself, as each incurred suffering due to their beauty (465, 523–28)'. See also Thumiger 2013: 34–5 on *erôs* and sexual jealousy in *Trachiniae*, and McHardy for this phenomenon in tragedy more generally.

[4] Mossman 2012: 496.

Agamemnon,[5] a play that *Trachiniae* presupposes in various ways and whose first performance, we can safely say, must have preceded it, though probably not by long.[6] Aeschylus' Cassandra is brought back from Troy by Agamemnon as the spoils of war, just as Iole is Heracles' prize from the sack of Oechalia; the advent of this concubine precedes (and to varying extents brings about) the destruction of her recently acquired master at the hands of his spouse.[7] There are differences between the two, naturally. So Iole is sent on ahead by Heracles, but Agamemnon arrives with Cassandra in his train; and Cassandra's concubinage is a by-product of the Trojan War, whereas Iole's was the whole purpose of Heracles' endeavour. One fundamental similarity, however, involves the silence of the two women when confronted by the rival that each could potentially displace. As we have seen, Iole makes no response to Deianira's inquiries, which have to be answered, falsely, by Lichas. So too, Cassandra ignores Clytemnestra, making no reply to her words and disobeying her demands to come into the house. The queen is confused, wondering whether Cassandra can speak Greek at all; in the end she herself returns inside, unsuccessful in her purpose for the first and only time.

The effect of this allusion has been much discussed. For one scholar, it 'serves to emphasize the difference between the two women already so clear by the contrast in their language: Clytaemestra the great manipulator of words, Deianeira the hesitant one, stumbling and sometimes rambling';[8] for another, whose more positive description of Deianira seems more persuasive, her 'understanding and gentleness are at the opposite extreme from Clytemnestra's smoldering hatred. In Deianeira Sophocles' audience could recognize the humane spirit of fifth-century civility at its best ... The woman whose situation she recalls, however, is a figure whose raw power, violent passion, immense hyperboles are in touch still with the rougher energies of a harsher, heroic age.'[9] From the point of view of this chapter,

---

[5] Aesch. *Ag.* 1035–68. See Kapsomenos 1963: 68–79, Mastronarde 1979: 76, Wohl 1998: 110–11, Montiglio 2000: 213, Easterling 2005: 31, Davidson 2005: 206–7 (putting the silence of Iole and Cassandra in the context of other effective silences), Mossman 2005: 354–5, 2012: 495–6, Rood 2010: 358, de Paco Serrano 2011: 137 (highlighting Cassandra's connexions with other tragic figures, including Iole), Coo 2013a: 358–9, Mattison 2015.

[6] Webster 1936a: 168, 177, Easterling 1982: 21–2. For the relatively early date of *Trachiniae* see Finglass 2011: 1–11; relative, that is, to the other surviving plays, since if the play does date to 457 or later Sophocles would already have had more than a decade's experience as a playwright.

[7] See Sanders 2013: 56 n. 68 and MCHARDY on the 'rival for legitimate wife' scenario in tragedy.

[8] Mossman 2012: 496.

[9] Segal 1995: 40. Cf. Webster 1936a: 168 'We are meant to compare the true nobility of Deianira with the superficial sympathy, the pride and brutality of Clytaemnestra', Easterling 2005: 31.

the silences in both scenes particularly repay comparison. In Aeschylus the young concubine is at first silent, baffling and defeating her conqueror's wife, and thus technically her rival; subsequently she sings and speaks, with a startling eloquence that her auditors, the chorus, nevertheless find impossible to understand.[10] Sophocles' twist on this scene in *Trachiniae* involves presenting the concubine as silent throughout. Iole's encounter with Deianira, which makes up the whole of her on-stage part, corresponds to Cassandra's with Clytemnestra (the latter's exchange with the chorus finds no place in Sophocles, except insofar as the chorus explicitly pity Cassandra at 1069, immediately after Clytemnestra departs, just as Deianira's reaction to Iole is one of compassion); but whereas Aeschylus' queen is manifestly defeated by the concubine, in Sophocles the point is rather the extraordinary understanding and sympathy that Deianira shows towards the woman who has shared her husband's bed, a sympathy all the more poignant because it arises purely out of Deianira's nature, not through any persuasive verbal power exerted by Iole.

The precise reasons for Iole's silence are not explored, but her failure to say anything hardly conveys defiance; if anything, it rather suggests a woman completely traumatised, a passive victim who has in no way recovered from her experience.[11] And although Sophocles' play shows a 'conversation' in which only one party speaks, it is hard to imagine an ordinary interlocutor taking as much account of a fellow participant in a conversation as Deianira does of Iole and her suffering; we are a world away from the sharp commands of Clytemnestra. Sophocles thus evokes the Aeschylean scene but directs the format towards his own poetic purpose.[12] The decision to move the subordinate character in the direction of permanent rather than temporary silence shows a (merited) confidence in his ability to create an emotional encounter between two characters only one of whom actually says anything.

---

[10] Aeschylus would become famous for characters who spoke only some time after their original entrance, especially at the start of the play (cf. Ar. *Ran.* 832–4, 911–30 with Dover 1993 on 911–12); for an intriguing instance from the *Iliad* see the discussion of that poem's Helen in H. Roisman 2006.

[11] Rood 2010: 361 takes a more optimistic view, arguing that while 'most readers pass over Iole's silence with the assumption that it approximates the impossibility of articulating the boundlessness of her despair and isolation ... her plot, like her silence, remains open-ended, with the promise of new life in a new generation'; but that takes too sanguine a position with regard to her forthcoming union with Hyllus (see p. 101 below).

[12] Cf. Mattison 2015: 13 'Sophocles re-focuses the scene where wife meets concubine so that it becomes entirely centred not on questions of power and control but on questions of marriage, family, and love.'

In 2016 a papyrus of Sophocles' *Tereus* was published that sheds new light on the scene from *Trachiniae* and its portrayal of a silently suffering woman. *Tereus* described how Tereus, king of Thrace and husband of the Athenian princess Procne, rapes Procne's sister Philomela while bringing her from Athens to Thrace in response to her sister's desire to see her; he additionally cuts out her tongue to prevent her from denouncing him. In time the sisters meet, and Philomela uses weaving to inform her sister what has happened to her; they conspire to kill Tereus' son by Procne, Itys, and serve him as a meal to his father. Once he discovers the truth, he pursues them, and all three are turned by the gods into birds: Tereus into a hoopoe, Procne and Philomela into a nightingale and a swallow respectively.

The papyrus overlaps with a twelve-line fragment quoted by the fifth-century paroemiographer Stobaeus; quotation and papyrus together yield the following text:

<Πρόκνη>   . . .

νῦν δ' οὐδέν εἰμι χωρίς. ἀλλὰ πολλάκις
ἔβλεψα ταύτηι τὴν γυναικείαν φύσιν,
ὡς οὐδέν ἐσμεν. αἳ νέαι μὲν ἐν πατρὸς
ἥδιστον, οἶμαι, ζῶμεν ἀνθρώπων βίον·
5   τερπνῶς γὰρ ἀεὶ παῖδας ἄνοια τρέφει.
ὅταν δ' ἐς ἥβην ἐξικώμεθ' ἔμφρονες,
ὠθούμεθ' ἔξω καὶ διεμπολώμεθα
θεῶν πατρώιων τῶν τε φυσάντων ἄπο,
αἱ μὲν ξένους πρὸς ἄνδρας, αἱ δὲ βαρβάρους,
10   αἱ δ' εἰς ἀήθη δώμαθ', αἱ δ' ἐπίρροθα.
καὶ ταῦτ', ἐπειδὰν εὐφρόνη ζεύξηι μία,
χρεὼν ἐπαινεῖν καὶ δοκεῖν καλῶς ἔχειν.
νόμωι μὲν [
εἰ δ' ἐκ τοιου[
15   ἴδοιμι καὶ[
τὸ γὰρ ποθ.[

Χο<ρός>   ἀλλ' εὖ τελ[
χρηστὴν φ[

Ποιμ<ήν>   δέσποινα[.].[
20   θέλων τι[

<Πρόκνη>   οὔκουν δ[
λόγων με[

<Ποιμήν>   ὅρκον γαρ[
φράσειν α[

25   <Πρόκνη>   λέξασα.[
κοινον.[

<Ποιμήν>   εἷρπον μ[

ἀλλ' ἐξ ἀγρα[ς
ὃς ἦμιν ερ[
στείχων δ[30
ἔνθεν χοαι[
ἔστην ὑπο[
τ̣ε̣ρ̣α̣μν' ὑπ̣[
]..π̣α̣ρ̣.[
    . . .

[Procne]   ... As it is, I am nothing on my own. But I have often
            regarded the nature of women in this way, seeing that we
            amount to nothing. In childhood in our father's house we live
            the happiest life, I think, of all mankind; for folly always rears
            children in happiness. But when we have understanding and
            have come to womanhood, we are pushed out and sold, away
            from our paternal gods and from our parents, some to foreign
            husbands, some to barbarians, some to unfamiliar homes, and
            some to homes that are opprobrious. And this, once a single
            night has yoked us, we must approve and consider to be a
            good thing ... custom. But if after such ... I should ... see ...
            too. For what ...

Chorus: Well, ... end ... good ...
Shepherd: Lady ... wishing ... something ...
[Procne:]   Then ... words ...
[Shepherd:] ... an oath ... shall speak ...
[Procne:]   By speaking ... For ... shared ...
[Shepherd:] I was making my way ... but from a hunt ... who ... to
            us ... things ... Travelling ... from where libations ...
            I stood ?under ... hut ...
                                            Soph. *Tereus* fr. 583+P.Oxy. 5292[13]

The twelve lines quoted by Stobaeus (lines 1–12 above) make up one of the
best-known fragments of Greek tragedy: a woman's lament, addressed to
other women, about the miseries of marriage as experienced by a woman.
The lines seem so sincere, and so affecting, that it is easy to forget that they
were written by a man, for delivery by a man, before audiences that
probably had a preponderance of males.[14] 'We do not know the context
of this speech', lamented Bernard Knox;[15] but the papyrus now gives us an

[13] Text from Finglass 2016b: 63, translation from ibid. 82 (where in addition some *exempli gratia*
supplements are also translated). For the *editio princeps* see Slattery 2016.
[14] For the gender composition of tragic audiences see Finglass 2017b: 314–17.
[15] Knox 1977: 221 = 1979: 312. Cf. Winnington-Ingram 1983: 237, cited in Coo and Finglass
above, pp. 6–7.

insight into precisely that. For while at first sight the extra text granted us by the sands of Egypt is less than impressive (not a single complete line, not a single piece of what we might think of as striking poetry), this precious find turns out to be most revealing as regards the construction of the drama.[16] It confirms that the speech is delivered by Procne, as had long been thought: no other female character in a *Tereus* play could be addressed 'mistress' (δέσποινα) by a shepherd. It reveals that her speech is delivered to the chorus, and no one else; for if another auditor were present, it would be astonishing for such a friend to utter no words of consolation in response to Procne's sentiments. It shows that Procne is unaware of any suffering undergone by her sister at this point: for if she possessed such knowledge, or even suspected anything of the sort, she would certainly have referred to this towards the end of her speech rather than conclude with general reflections on the state of married women; and yet the papyrus indicates that she delivers only four lines beyond the section preserved by Stobaeus, four lines which cannot be restored so as to mention any suffering by her sister. This additionally suggests that Procne's speech comes from early in the drama, because her discovery of her sister's experience led to the main action and so cannot have occurred late within it;[17] since the prologue is not a possibility (because the chorus are already on stage), the speech probably occurred in the first episode, immediately after the chorus's entrance song, which is where we find comparable speeches from Deianira in *Trachiniae* and Medea in Euripides' play.[18]

Moreover, the papyrus shows that after her speech, a new arrival, a Shepherd, enters to bring Procne news grave enough to prompt him to swear an oath as to its truth. While the nature of that news cannot be established for certain, a highly attractive possibility is that it involves the discovery of the mutilated Philomela. It is not clear what other serious news would suit this myth and the Shepherd's desire to confirm his message with an oath; moreover, the fragmentary word 'hut' in line 33, if correctly restored (and no alternative has so far been proposed) would fit

---

[16] The account that follows of what we can infer from the papyrus is an abbreviated version of the argument set out in Finglass 2016b: 66–75. For subsequent discussion see Libatique 2018.

[17] Sophocles' *Electra*, where the mutual recognition of Electra and Orestes takes place at a very late stage, is no counterexample; in that play Orestes' vengeance plot is underway at the opening of the drama, since Clytemnestra's offence is already well known, whereas in *Tereus* the conspiracy cannot begin until Procne learns of Philomela's suffering.

[18] Milo 2008: 38–9. For *Tereus* and *Medea* see Finglass 2016b: 77–9, 2019b: 17.

such a scenario perfectly, since that hut could be where Philomela had been confined after the rape. Such imprisonment is attested in other versions of the myth; the evidence of the papyrus suggests that it originated with Sophocles. And if that is correct, we may additionally infer that the Shepherd's speech to Procne announcing Philomela's discovery (whether or not the Shepherd correctly identified her) was followed not long afterwards by Philomela's arrival on stage, brought either by the Shepherd himself or by associates of his. The basic framework of the story, whereby the two sisters Procne and Philomela conspire to punish Tereus by killing Itys, his son by Procne, requires the sisters to meet; and if, as it seems, Philomela's discovery is only now being announced, that meeting has not yet taken place, and so must happen before long.

The upshot is that Procne is confronted first with a messenger, announcing important news, followed by the entrance of a woman who, through no fault of her own, has shared her husband's bed: exactly the same basic structure that we find in *Trachiniae*, and indeed in *Agamemnon*. That encounter between the two women will have been an extraordinary moment in *Tereus*, just as the comparable scene is in *Trachiniae*.[19] In both cases, the women's encounter leads to action by the first woman that wreaks a terrible punishment on her husband. And in both cases, only one of the women speaks. If *Tereus* had survived and *Trachiniae* were fragmentary, we would not have known this for sure; Iole's silence is the consequence of Sophocles' personal dramatic choice, not a mandatory part of the story. But because the cutting out of Philomela's tongue was an essential element of the myth, and indeed is all but confirmed for Sophocles' play by the fragment preserved by Aristotle that refers to 'the voice of the shuttle' (κερκίδος φωνή, fr. 595), we may infer that Philomela said nothing during the dramatic reunion with her sister.[20] Exactly how that encounter was staged cannot be determined; but given that Philomela was an active participant in the plot against Tereus (her metamorphosis would make no sense otherwise, and indeed fr. 589.1–2 refers to unspecified 'women' having acted even more mindlessly than Tereus himself), she must signalled her participation through assenting gestures. Her pitiful silence would have been accompanied by eloquent speeches on the part

---

[19] Finglass 2016b: 76–7.

[20] Hartman 1969: 240 = 1970: 337 asks of this fragment 'What gives these words power to speak to us even without the play?'; the papyrus may not restore the play, but it at least hints at the dramatic context in which the weaving featured.

of her sister, expressing both her distress and her plan for revenge; the chorus too must have voiced their opinion of the conspiracy.

The formal similarity between the scenes in *Tereus* and *Trachiniae* is so striking that it is fair to posit an allusion by the later play to the earlier. Which came first, however, we cannot say for sure. Perhaps *Trachiniae* is more likely, partly because it is probably relatively early in Sophocles' oeuvre,[21] partly because *Tereus* was satirised in Aristophanes' *Birds* of 414 and so (we might imagine) unlikely to predate *Birds* by forty years or more. Yet nothing prevents *Tereus* from coming from some time before 457 (the earliest possible year for *Trachiniae*); and Aristophanes satirises one play fully thirty-three years after its first performance,[22] so a gap of forty years or more cannot be ruled out, not least as Sophoclean plays, perhaps including *Tereus*, were already seeing reperformances in the fifth century.[23] *Trachiniae* indeed briefly references the Procne myth, when the chorus compare Deianira in her longing for Heracles to 'some wretched bird' (οἵα τιν' ἄθλιον ὄρνιν, 105), which can only be the nightingale,[24] though that does not tell us anything about chronology: the nightingale's lament was already an established part of the mythological tradition by this time,[25] and Sophocles could have used it in *Trachiniae* without previously having composed a *Tereus*. Accordingly, the discussion in this chapter takes no view either way on the issue of relative priority.

Whichever way round the plays were chronologically, in each case the differing treatments of female silence would have encouraged comparison of the two dramas by attentive spectators. In *Trachiniae*, at least, silence has a broader thematic significance. So the Deianira who encounters the silent Iole was herself once the passive prize of Heracles' might, sitting silently during the noisy contest between the hero and Achelous for her hand;[26] and later in the play Deianira's return to silence, remarked on by the

---

[21] See n. 6 above.

[22] Wright 2012: 147 refers (among others) to how Euripides' *Telephus* of 438 is satirised in *Frogs* of 405.

[23] Finglass 2015a, Lamari 2017: 35–8.

[24] Wohl 1998: 204 n. 66.

[25] Hes. *Op.* 568, Finglass 2007 on Soph. *El.* 107, Weiss 2017.

[26] Cf. Rood 2010, Kitzinger 2012: 123 'Iole's silence ... makes her an unknown whose point of view we are free to imagine ... there is in Iole's silence the same kind of fear that we witnessed in Deianeira'. There is no explicit reference to silence in the relevant passage (517/18–530), but it seems nevertheless to be implied by the juxtaposition of sonic terms describing the battle (πάταγος, στόνος; 'the duel itself was a confusion of violence and noise', as Easterling 1982 remarks on 517–30) with their complete absence in the depiction of Deianira. There may even be a shift in the sound of the Greek, with a profusion of hard consonants, particularly velars, in the battle description, which are toned down in the section that follows.

chorus (813–14), will mark the destruction of her hopes and imminent end of her life. In *Tereus*, the two women will themselves be reduced to silence at the play's end, or at least silence as far as human speech is concerned, through their metamorphosis into birds; but to what degree the play explicitly employed silence as a thematic feature, here or elsewhere, remains unknown.

Silence in each play causes problems of communication whose ultimate source lies in the male offender's actions. In *Trachiniae* Heracles does not instruct Lichas to lie to Deianira (479–83), but nevertheless acts in such a way that his herald, terrified by Deianira's likely response, feels that his only choice is to keep the truth from her. In *Tereus*, by contrast, the removal of Philomela's tongue, and her seclusion in a hut, are both intended to ensure, with the greatest possible security, that she never reveals what has happened to her. (Both plays involve different mixtures of force and deceit throughout. So while Iole and Philomela have both been taken from their fathers, the former is seized by force, resulting in the sacking of her city and enslavement of her people, whereas the latter is entrapped through guile; yet Lichas' lies ensure that truth and falsehood are prominent motifs in *Trachiniae* too, while Tereus does even more violence to Philomela's person than Heracles does to Iole.) The truth eventually comes out, in both cases at least partly by chance – thanks to the first Messenger in *Trachiniae*, who just happens to come to Deianira with the news of Heracles' return, and so was in a position to give her a true account after Lichas' deceit; and through the fortunate discovery by the Shepherd in *Tereus* of the abused woman in a hut in the countryside, which he seems to have stumbled across when wandering the fields on the way back from a hunting expedition. The problem of Iole's silence is then overcome when the Messenger speaks on her behalf; Philomela, by contrast, uses weaving to communicate the reason for her distress, taking advantage of the opportunity with which chance had provided her. Such weaving may have taken place off stage, presumably during a choral ode. (Alternatively, Philomela brought with her a piece of weaving, or had it brought on by the Shepherd or an associate before she came on stage, but it is hard to see what opportunity she would have had to fashion such an item; Tereus will hardly have equipped her hut with a loom.) As a result *Tereus*, like *Trachiniae*, involves a piece of cloth wielded by a woman with fatal consequences for a man – one cloth steeped in the blood of a centaur (himself an attempted rapist: *Tr.* 562–5), the other embroidered with the barbarous deeds of a monster.[27]

---

[27] Here too *Agamemnon* remains parallel to the Sophoclean dramas, Clytemnestra's slaying of Agamnemnon being assisted by the dreadful robe in which she enfolds him (Finglass 2017d).

The destructive plan that follows the encounter of each pair of women involves in one of the plays, but not in the other, the silent woman's participation. Just as Philomela actively reveals her suffering to her sister, so too she joins in the conspiracy against Tereus. Iole, on the other hand, remains passive: just as she took no steps to communicate her treatment at Heracles' hands, so too the reaction to this news (i.e., the sending of the robe) comes solely from Deianira, with no involvement from her. That suits a plan, of course, intended not to destroy Heracles or to punish him for his rape of Iole (or disrespect of Deianira), but to restore his love for Deianira, a love recently diverted in the direction of the younger woman. But each plan leads to destruction, even though that is intended in only one of the dramas. Assisted by Philomela, Procne makes a tragic choice in full knowledge to kill her child. Deianira, by contrast, is merely mistaken, and acts to restore good relations between herself and her husband rather than to rupture them for good. That does not mean, however, that audiences would have found only Deianira's plight sympathetic. Procne endures an appalling trauma in learning that her sister was raped and mutilated by her own husband; the audience indeed sees her discover this on stage, witnessing its emotional impact unmitigated by the passage of time. Her decision, grim though it is, becomes at least understandable; moreover, the involvement of her sister Philomela would have had the same effect, making the killing of Itys not just the murder of an innocent child (though it would be that), but also the sole means whereby a pair of abused women could achieve any kind of redress. Unable to speak, and sexually violated, Philomela was nevertheless capable of inflicting a merited punishment on her abuser: amid all the suffering, there is at least some satisfaction, however appalling, in that.[28]

The location of these women is also of crucial importance in the audience's reactions to them. Each play emphasises how the action is set far from the women's homeland. Early in *Trachiniae* Deianira remarks 'we live at a stranger's house here in Trachis, driven away' (ἡμεῖς μὲν ἐν Τραχῖνι τῆιδ' ἀνάστατοι | ξένωι παρ' ἀνδρὶ ναίομεν), where of ἀνάστατοι Jebb remarks 'the word would not suit a voluntary migration'.[29] As Segal says, 'The setting of the play in remote Trachis and the lack of indications of civic life add to this sense of the suspension or precariousness of normal civilized procedures. The Sophoclean Trachis appears as something of a frontier town, a place in which to envisage the breakdown of the most

---

[28] Finglass 2016b: 78–9.
[29] *Tr.* 39–40 with Jebb 1892 *ad loc.*

fundamental institution of society. Here both Deianeira and Heracles release their potential sexual violence, covertly and indirectly in the one case, shamelessly and with gross disregard for human lives in the other.'[30] The same word highlighted by Jebb is used later when Lichas tells Deianira how Heracles 'captured with his spear the land, so that it was sacked, of the women whom you see with your eyes' (ᾗρει τῶνδ' ἀνάστατον δορὶ | χώραν γυναικῶν ὧν ὁρᾷς ἐν ὄμμασιν, 240–1): 'Deianeira and Iole are both "uprooted" ... : the repetition draws attention to the thematically import-ant equivalence between the situations of the two women.'[31] Both women, thanks to Heracles, are away from their οἶκος, the usual locus of female activity, and both are diminished as a consequence; the male relatives on whom they could rely are distant or defeated.

The little that we have of *Tereus* indicates that location played an important part in that drama too. Procne's lament 'we are pushed out and sold, away from our paternal gods and from our parents, some to foreign husbands, some to barbarians, some to unfamiliar homes, and some to homes that are opprobrious' (7–10), although nominally a com-ment on the fate of all married women, has particular relevance to herself, a princess forced to leave Athens to live in the far-off and scarcely civilised land of Thrace; her dissatisfaction with day-to-day life there gives initial impetus to the plot, and is soon found to be all too justified when the very king of the country rapes her sister. That rape takes place on a journey that never reaches its intended conclusion, since Philomela is abandoned in the wild by Tereus rather than being taken to the palace to see her sister. Being outside the house gives Tereus, as it does Heracles, freedom both to indulge his depraved character and to keep his wife ignorant of his activities abroad; Procne and Philomela, on the other hand, like Deianira and Iole, are far from any of the usual sources of help to which they might turn, and find themselves virtually trapped in a land that is scarcely Greek, and whose civilisational deficiencies are personified in its ruler.

So Buxton's remark that 'developments in anthropology have alerted us to the uneasy tension between the barbarous and the civilized, the wild outside and the sheltered inside, which runs through *Trach<iniae>*, and growing scepticism about Sophoclean piety has enabled us to respond with more accuracy to the play's bleak dramatic landscape'[32] applies just as well to *Tereus*, we might think. In addition, though, the isolation of the two

[30] Segal 1995: 92.
[31] Buxton 1995: 9.
[32] Buxton 1995: 32.

women lends powerful justification to their course of action, alone as they are in the land of their enemy. Philomela's enforced silence and confinement are metaphorically emblematic of the sisters' situation: even after they meet, they remain confined in a far-off land, with no friends to respond to a cry for help.

The association of Iole with Aeschylus' Cassandra explored above prompts the question whether Philomela too can usefully be compared with the Trojan prophetess. The Tereus myth is invoked in Aeschylus' *Agamemnon*, when Cassandra is likened by Clytemnestra to the swallow, and by the chorus to the nightingale (1050–2, 1140–5); Cassandra rejects the latter comparison, noting that she, unlike Procne, will be executed, without the consolation of metamorphosis (1146–9). The comparison is significant: 'It is no surprise that Clytemnestra, mistress of deceiving words, should employ the conventional trope when she remarks that Cassandra speaks with a swallow's tongue. Like Philomela, Cassandra has had her ability to communicate wrested from her. Her voice and her visions of butchery prophesy the coming carnage: that which the audience both knows and awaits. But within the twisted world of the play the Chorus, echoing the Trojans before them, cannot understand her plainest statements.'[33] And as discussed in the case of *Trachiniae* above, *Tereus* does not need to predate *Agamemnon* for the reference to the myth to be understood, familiar as it was at the time; similarly, we can examine links between the three plays without taking a view on whether *Tereus* preceded one, both or neither. A couple of points can be highlighted, although the possibilities run much more widely.

First, all three dramas play with the idea of female powerlessness. The silent female initially seems in each play a mere victim, without even the resource of speech to defend herself, unable to do more than passively endure the violence of men. Yet in *Agamemnon*, Cassandra will turn out to be the only person who understands the true history of the house of Atreus and its significance, and correctly prophesies that her death at Clytemnestra's hands will be avenged (1279–81). In *Trachiniae* the voiceless Iole prompts in Deianira a profound worry that she is losing her husband's love, leading her to send the fatal robe that destroys the man who had seized Iole, destroying her people in order to do so; news of Heracles' agony prompts Deianira to kill herself, and as a result Hyllus regards Iole as solely responsible for his mother's death (μόνη | μεταίτιος,

---

[33] J. Williams 1997: 26.

1233–4), though that is an emotional response to the terrible situation, not a dispassionate judgment of Iole's culpability. In *Tereus* Philomela actively joins forces with her sister to punish her brother-in-law and rapist. The degree of agency demonstrated by each of the women differs across the three dramas, but each is involved, in one way or another, in the punishment of her tormentor; none of them is simply a victim.

Second, in all three plays, through a perversion of the usual process of wedding ritual, a woman receives into the house another woman intended by her errant husband to supplant her.[34] In Cassandra's case, Clytemnestra is genuinely the lady of the house: it is to her house that Agamemnon has brought the Trojan prisoner, and it is in her house where she will be struck down by a woman rather than marry a man. The Sophoclean plays use the same idea but with an additional twist: the 'receiving' woman is in front not of her own house, as we have seen, but of a dwelling in some foreign land to which she has been displaced. She welcomes – into a house that is not hers – the victim, not the bride, of the man who is not her son but her husband. The perversion of wedding ritual thus runs in triplicate, and continues to be explored in at least one of these plays, when at the end of *Trachiniae* Iole is assigned to a reluctant Hyllus not as his wife, but as his concubine: not as an act of kindness to her, but rather because Heracles regards her as his property to be disposed of according to his will; not by the father who would normally make such as assignation, but by the man who killed that father in order to seize his daughter.[35] But how *Tereus* explored the theme of marriage beyond what is noted above, if it did so at all, remains unknowable, at least for now.

Greek tragedy is full of lamentation, of both inarticulate cries and highly articulate expressions of distress, of loud and lengthy reactions to acts of appalling brutality. A whole book has been written with the title *The Captive Woman's Lament in Greek Tragedy*;[36] the title of a subsequent essay by its author, 'Lament as speech act in Sophocles', emphasises the link between lamentation and articulate speech.[37] Rape in particular was a crime that demanded a noisy response: the shouting of a woman at the time of her violation was regarded as important evidence that she was an unwilling participant in intercourse.[38] Yet in *Trachiniae* and *Tereus*,

---

[34] For the perversion (usually the welcoming was done by the groom's mother) see Seaford 1987: 128–9 = 2018: 294–6.

[35] MacKinnon 1971.

[36] Dué 2006.

[37] Dué 2012.

[38] Eur. *Tro.* 998–1001, Schulze 1918: 506–7 = 1966: 184–5; also Hom. *Il.* 2.355–6, 2.589–90 with H. Roisman 2006: 3, Soph. *Tr.* 565.

Sophocles presents us with two women who utter no sound at all, despite their recent traumatic experiences. That paradox is a central feature of *Trachiniae*, and seems to have been one in *Tereus* too, where, we may infer from the papyrus, the encounter between Procne and Philomela stood so close to – albeit with significant differences from – the Iole scene in the surviving play. Decades ago Webster claimed that '*Trachiniae* and *Tereus* must have been very much alike. Both had the diptych form; both dealt with the tragedy of a cultured woman married to a wild husband; in both the woman bewailed the lot of women. And there is close correspondence both of metre and thought between the choric fragments of the *Tereus* and the *parodos* of the *Trachiniae*';[39] his claim has aged well, and, as we have seen, *Agamemnon* too deserves to be considered alongside both of these dramas, not just with *Trachiniae*. Let us hope that one day a further *Tereus* discovery will provide new insights, both into the relationship between these plays, and into Sophocles' remarkable portrayal of female suffering.

---

[39] Webster 1936b: 4. Webster went on to date both plays to the period shortly before 431, but there is no need to infer that they must have been composed at the same time, and most scholars today would place *Trachiniae* rather earlier than that (see n. 6 above on the date).

PART II

Plays

7 | Dancing on the Plain of the Sea

Gender and Theatrical Space in Aeschylus' Achilleis *Trilogy*

ANNA UHLIG

The study of fragments, dramatic or otherwise, inevitably involves 'an element of creative fiction (which is not a dirty word)', as Matthew Wright has observed.[1] In this respect, at least, 'fragmentology' finds itself in methodological harmony with a rather different type of reconstructive project: the history and analysis of ancient dramatic performance. While much excellent work has been done in recent decades to expand our understanding of the conditions and structures which obtained in ancient theatrical productions,[2] scholarly discussions of ancient performance nevertheless still require a certain imaginative leap and the study of *opsis* retains something of its Aristotelian legacy as the least technical (*atechnotaton*) part of tragedy.[3] Like fragmentologists, those thinking about ancient performance must face the 'unavoidable hazard' of 'pil[ing] 'conjecture upon hypothesis', with results that are 'necessarily speculative at best'.[4] With regard to both of these speculative endeavours, I share Wright's view that the use of creativity and imagination in the face of irresolvable uncertainties does not, in and of itself, undermine the intellectual value of scholarship. Rather, as Wright urges, we can (and should) openly embrace the alternatives and multiplicities of creative speculation as a reminder that certain questions, and certain texts, demand that we pursue scholarship in the subjunctive mood.[5]

In what follows, I join the uncertainties of these two methods into a single, exuberantly speculative undertaking; piling the conjecture of fragmentology upon the hypotheticals of performance analysis to see how our

I owe a great debt of thanks to Marco Fantuzzi, Johanna Hanink, audiences at Nottingham and Santa Barbara, and to the editors and anonymous readers of this volume, all of whom have immeasurably improved my thinking about this chapter.

[1] Wright 2016: xxv.

[2] In addition to the seminal work of Taplin 1977, 1978, see also Hall 2006, Marshall 2006, 2014, Revermann 2006, Wiles 2007, Meineck 2011, Wyles 2011, Harrison and Liapis 2013b, Compton-Engle 2015, Mueller 2016.

[3] For the complexity of Aristotle's treatment of *opsis* see Sifakis 2013.

[4] Konstan 2013: 73; see also Harrison and Liapis 2013b: 11–13 on the use of iconographic fragments to illuminate tragedy.

[5] Wright 2016: xxv–xxvi, who observes (p. xxv): 'Even the most sober and restrained scholars are going to be using [fragments], essentially, to tell the stories that they want to tell, and so it is as well to clear the air by frankly admitting this.' See also COO AND FINGLASS, pp. 2–5.

understanding of tragic *opsis* might shift if we approach it from the vantage of fragmentary plays, rather than from the canonical works that have overwhelmingly shaped the inquiries of past decades. More specifically, I will ask how thinking about the performative dynamics and visual dimension of an exceedingly fragmentary play, Aeschylus' *Nereids*, might invite us to reconsider the relationship of space to gender in the Aeschylean corpus more broadly. In doing so, I invert the interpretive hierarchy that tends to treat *opsis* as a secondary characteristic; 'a handmaiden to the *muthos*' in the words of David Konstan.[6] At five fragments, totalling just over twenty words, and with little secure external evidence on which to reconstruct even the most basic details of the drama, Aeschylus' *Nereids* proves stubbornly resistant to interpretations based on questions of plot. But when viewed through the lens of *opsis*, these same fragments reveal themselves as a remarkably rich source for thinking about questions of performance and the complex ways that gender is encoded in tragic space.

My interpretive experiment with the fragmented *opsis* of *Nereids* is concerned with two simple questions. In the first section, I explore how the *dramatis personae* of a play – the bodies present in the theatre – call attention to powerful juxtapositions between what is seen and unseen, heard and unheard in the theatre. In the second, I examine how performing bodies transform the mimetic space of the theatre, producing an unexpected variety of imaginary landscapes. In both sections, my interpretations take shape through the lens of gender. I employ this fundamental (albeit complex and unstable) binary of the ancient theatre as a tool to shed light on other structuring elements in the drama.

Aristotelian Preamble

Despite my desire to read the fragments of *Nereids* without undue deference to *mythos*, some basic questions of plot must be broached. Although I have tried to treat them in as limited and open-ended a fashion as possible in the analysis that follows, I offer here a brief overview of the hypothetical scenarios that I adopt as a frame for interpretation.

Nereids is commonly thought to have been joined with two of Aeschylus' Trojan War themed plays, *Myrmidons* and *Phrygians*,[7] as part of a larger

---

[6] Konstan 2013: 73.

[7] Few convincing suggestions have been made regarding a satyr play to round out the tetralogy. Sommerstein 2010a: 34 suggests *Chamber-Makers*, a play about which virtually nothing is known. Simon 1982: 132–3 hazards *Propompoi* (*Escorts*), the title of an equally obscure drama.

Achilleis trilogy composed by the playwright at some indeterminate point in his career.[8] There are good reasons to be skeptical of modern critics' confidence regarding this trilogy grouping, but I will nevertheless work here on the assumption that *Nereids* formed part of a connected trilogy concerned with Achilles' actions before and after the death of Patroclus on the battlefield at Troy.[9]

The prevailing scholarly view situates *Nereids* as the second play in the *Achilleis* trilogy, centring on the immediate aftermath of Patroclus' death in which the hero is mourned (as in *Iliad* 18.35–69) by Thetis and her fellow Nereids.[10] It is generally assumed that the action would have extended as far as the presentation of Achilles' new armour and his (off-stage) slaughter of Hector.[11] This hypothesis places *Myrmidons*, in which Achilles' refusal to fight leads his lover, Patroclus, to take to the battlefield in his stead, as the first play of the trilogy, and *Phrygians*, which related the ransoming of Hector's body, as the final instalment of the series. The trilogy would thus map onto books 9–24 of the *Iliad*, concluding, as Homer's poem does, with lamentations for the slain Hector.[12]

The plots of *Myrmidons* and *Phrygians* undoubtedly correspond, albeit with significant deviations, to episodes narrated in the *Iliad*. The ample surviving fragments of *Myrmidons* give a relatively clear indication of its plot, and the alternate title of *Phrygians*, *The Ransoming of Hector* (Ἕκτορος λύτρα), leaves no doubt about its principal subject matter. *Nereids* presents a markedly less decisive picture. Indeed, the extant fragments of the play, together with its title, confirm only that the chorus was comprised of the eponymous Nereids and that Achilles, or at least his famous double-pointed spear (fr. 152), is mentioned at some point. The lack of clear evidence regarding the plot of *Nereids* led Martin West to argue that the play was actually the final instalment of the trilogy, and that its subject was not the aftermath of Patroclus' death, but rather the death of Achilles himself, mourned in grand style by his mother Thetis and her sisters as briefly recounted in the *Odyssey*.[13] The plots of the first two plays (*Myrmidons* and *Phrygians*) would remain the same, again corresponding

---

[8] The grouping was first proposed by Welcker 1824: 310, 415–30.
[9] Yoon 2016 makes a cogent case against our over-reliance on connected trilogies in the analysis of Aeschylus' fragmentary plays more generally.
[10] Thus originally Welcker; see Hadjicosti 2007: 97 n. 1 for bibliography.
[11] Sommerstein 2010a: 245–6.
[12] For the distinction between epic narration and the dramatic enactment of Aeschylus' trilogy see Moreau 1996: 5–7.
[13] Hom. *Od.* 24.47–9; West 2000: 341–3 = 2011–13: II 231–5.

to the second half of the *Iliad*, but rather than end where Homer does, Aeschylus would continue his tale as far as the death of the central hero, incorporating elements from the poems of the Epic Cycle. West's claim cannot be proven, but he offers no less plausible a reconstruction of *Nereids* than the traditional account that he seeks to challenge.[14] Thus, although scholars have been slow to embrace West's view, I will, nevertheless, entertain both possibilities without bias in what follows.

Bodies with Voices

Whether we consider *Nereids* as the second or third play in the progression, one feature distinguishes it from the other two plays assigned to the *Achilleis* trilogy, namely the gender of the chorus. As the titles of *Myrmidons* and *Phrygians* make clear, the choruses of the other two plays would have consisted of men: Greeks in the first instance, Trojans in the second. When we look to the *dramatis personae* of these plays, as far as they are known, the gender distinction becomes even starker, since in both *Myrmidons* and *Phrygians* the other dramatic roles seem also to have been filled exclusively by male characters.

Myrmidons

The extant fragments make clear that, in addition to Achilles and the chorus of his men, speaking parts in *Myrmidons* would have included Phoenix (as the army's ambassador to Achilles, fr. 132b) and later Antilochus (perhaps reporting the news of Patroclus' death, as in the *Iliad*, fr. 138). Our understanding of the plot all but guarantees that Patroclus was also given a speaking role, pleading unsuccessfully with Achilles to aid the Greeks, and then arming for battle himself. Amongst the many other figures that have been suggested,[15] only one is of concern here. Did Briseis, the female object at the heart of Achilles' Iliadic wrath, reprise her role – albeit in a significantly altered form – in Aeschylus' dramatic adaptation?

---

[14] The only substantive objection to West's position rests on the popularity of depictions of Nereids bearing armour to Achilles in fifth-century vase painting (so Sommerstein 2008: III 156–7). The complexity of adducing vase images as evidence for dramatic productions has long been recognised by scholars (e.g. Taplin 1997: 69–72), and the existence of these images cannot be claimed to confirm the plot of Aeschylus' play (see below, p. 116).

[15] Hadjicosti 2007: 113–14.

There is no indication in the surviving fragments of *Myrmidons* that Briseis, or any other woman, played a part in the drama. Some suggestion that Achilles' Iliadic spear-bride makes an appearance in *Myrmidons* (or somewhere in Aeschylus' *Achilleis*) arises from fragments of a kalyx-krater by Polygnotus dating between 450 and 440, thought to represent scenes from the trilogy.[16] On one fragment, an unnamed female figure at the side of Patroclus' bier has been tentatively identified as Briseis.[17] Since the vase fragment neither explicitly identifies Briseis nor demonstrates overt connections with Aeschylus' trilogy, there is ample ground for skepticism. Modern scholars' hesitation to include Briseis in *Myrmidons* tends to stem less from the unreliable nature of the evidence than from the difficultly of imagining how Briseis might be incorporated into the play.[18]

As Plato records in his *Symposium* (180a4–7), Aeschylus' *Myrmidons* cast the close bond between Achilles and Patroclus in explicitly erotic terms.[19] This feature is still evident in our extant fragments, where Achilles employs emphatically erotic language in describing his relationship with Patroclus.[20] Achilles' invocation of the kisses (fr. 135) and honour/congress of thighs (frr. 135 and 136 respectively) that bound him to Patroclus infuse the martial circumstances of the play with an overtly masculine sexuality (a pairing that, Plato suggests, resonated strongly with the drama's male spectators).[21] At the same time, if Achilles' erotically charged statements formed part of a much longer, formal lament,[22] Aeschylus may have used the scene to call (further) attention to the complex gender qualities of a figure whose heroism in the *Iliad* is, as scholars have observed, already characterised by an almost feminine embrace of lament.[23]

The focus on Achilles' love for his comrade may also have coloured the other male voices of *Myrmidons*. If, as Plato reports, Aeschylus cast Achilles as the older lover of a younger (and more beautiful) Patroclus,[24]

---

[16] Trendall and Webster 1971: §III.1,18–19.

[17] Trendall and Webster 1971: 54.

[18] So (tacitly) Taplin 2007: 277 n. 121 and (explicitly) Sommerstein 2010a: 243, Fantuzzi 2012: 125.

[19] Aeschylus' treatment of the romance between Achilles and Patroclus is studied in Michelakis 2002: 22–57, Fantuzzi 2012: 218–25.

[20] Hadjicosti 2007: 130–1.

[21] Moreau 1996: 18–19.

[22] West 2000: 340 = 2011–13: II 231.

[23] Monsacré 1984, Martin 1989: 86–7, Tsagalis 2004: 70, but see also the cautions of Van Wees 1998, Murnaghan 1999. For Aeschylus' Achilles and feminine lament see Michelakis 2002: 45, Hadjicosti 2007: 131–2.

[24] Moreau 1996: 19–20, Fantuzzi 2012: 226–31.

the past relationship between Achilles and the even older Phoenix (an important feature of their closeness in *Iliad* 9) may have been endowed with erotic elements in the dramatic retelling. Likewise, the presence of Antilochus, possibly reprising his Iliadic messenger role, may have included allusion (perhaps with erotic overtones) to the close bond that develops between him and Achilles in the wake of Patroclus' death in the epic tradition.[25] In a somewhat different vein, the voice of the Myrmidon chorus may also have been affected by the masculine focus of the play. As comrades of Achilles and Patroclus, the Myrmidons would have been participant in (as witnesses to and perhaps champions of) the erotic love of their leaders. And although our existing fragments furnish little evidence of the chorus' role in the play, it is plausible that their choral interventions would have reflected on, and served to enhance the power of, the passion between the best of the Myrmidons.[26]

Is there room for a female voice in such a play? A definitive answer eludes us, though the evidence in favour of a female role is slight. In the absence of female voices, *Myrmidons* would create a conspicuous frame for the male relationship at the heart of the play, calling even greater attention to the gender dynamics of the erotic pairing by situating it within an all-male drama. Athenian tragedy, as far as we can gauge, rarely excluded women outright. Even in overtly martial settings, female figures tend to find a way onto the stage, as in Sophocles' *Ajax*, where Tecmessa provides a critical female voice. Amongst our extant tragedies, only Sophocles' *Philoctetes* is entirely devoid of female voices, and the Lemnian setting of that play marks the absence of women as an unsettling aberration. We might venture, then, that the all-male bivouac of *Myrmidons*, if such it was, was a significant and unusual dramatic setting, and perceived as such by its audience.

But even the presence of Briseis in *Myrmidons* could not have entirely counteracted the play's radical restructuring of Homeric gender roles. In the *Iliad*, Achilles' attachment to his female captive Briseis motivates his anger and withdrawal from the battlefield. It is unclear how Aeschylus treated this element of the myth within the emphatically masculine erotics

---

[25] Sammons 2017: 115, who points out (n. 42) the highly speculative nature of neo-analytical treatments of this relationship.

[26] In frr. 131–2, generally thought to belong to the opening scene of the play, the chorus give voice to their frustration with Achilles (a frustration shared by Patroclus). Deschamps 2010: 191–9 and Fantuzzi 2012: 221–2 interpret these lines as reflecting Achilles' alienation from the collective, including his own men, but the tension between Achilles and the Myrmidons need not have persisted throughout the drama.

of *Myrmidons*. It seems unlikely, however, that Aeschylus' Achilles, guided as he is by his passion for Patroclus, would have reprised the sentiments of his Homeric forebear who lambasted the Atreidae for their hypocrisy:

ἦ μοῦνοι φιλέουσ᾽ ἀλόχους μερόπων ἀνθρώπων
Ἀτρεῖδαι; ἐπεὶ ὅς τις ἀνὴρ ἀγαθὸς καὶ ἐχέφρων
ἣν αὐτοῦ φιλέει καὶ κήδεται, ὡς καὶ ἐγὼ τήν
ἐκ θυμοῦ φίλεον, δουρικτήτην περ ἐοῦσαν.

> Do the sons of Atreus alone of men love their wives? Any man who is good and sensible loves and cares for his own woman, as indeed I loved this one from my heart, although she was spear-won.

Hom. *Il.* 9.340–3

Achilles' complaint in the *Iliad* is ultimately with Agamemnon, and the invocation of female companionship serves primarily as a means of asserting rank amongst men.[27] Nevertheless, the importance that Homer affords to Briseis serves to insert a female voice and perspective into the Greek camp that matches in quality, if not in quantity, the female voices that fill so much of the action inside the walls of Troy.[28] Aeschylus' dramatic treatment would seem to recalibrate the Homeric structure, setting a male romantic bond as the node around which the relationships of men take shape. The drama, as far as we understand it, seems to resist female influence or intervention. Yet the celebration of male erotic attachment in *Myrmidons* is defined as much by the absence of female voices and roles as it is by the male relationships that propel the dramatic action.[29]

Phrygians

Absent women are no less powerful a presence in *Phrygians*, though in a different fashion than in *Myrmidons*. The *dramatis personae*, insofar as we can identify them, suggest another all- or mostly male drama. The ancient *Life of Aeschylus* attests to an opening exchange between Achilles and Hermes, in which the god (unsuccessfully) instructs the hero to return Hector's corpse.[30] The main action of the drama likely centred on the dialogue between Achilles and Priam, accompanied by the eponymous chorus of Trojans. We cannot say if there were additional speaking parts

---

[27] Lyons 2012: 54–7.

[28] Easterling 1991.

[29] Deschamps 2010: 178 rightly observes that 'the audience's horizon of expectation' will have been formed in relation to Aeschylus' Iliadic model.

[30] Test. 1.6 *TrGF* (~ p. 365); the scene has been linked to fr. 266.

in the play. Those listed above are no fewer than are found in Aeschylus'
Seven Against Thebes (excluding the spurious ending), or, if one presumes a
messenger of some sort, in his *Persians* or *Suppliants*. Mention of a 'child of
Andraemon of Lyrnessus' in fr. 267 has led many to suggest a fourth,
female speaking part, generally identified as Andromache,[31] but the fragment itself proves neither the existence nor the gender of such a role.
Whether a female character was present in the drama is doubtful, but, as
with *Myrmidons*, the powerful reconfiguration of Iliadic gender roles in
Phrygians does not hinge on the total absence of female characters from the
play. Where *Myrmidons* exploited Achilles' erotic attachments to shift
focus to the relationships between male characters, it is the male chorus
who accompany Priam on his journey to Achilles' tent who contribute
most strongly to *Phrygians*' emphatically masculine disposition.

The presence of a chorus of Trojan men is logical enough given the
circumstances of *Phrygians*. The perilous journey into the enemy camp
could not reasonably have been undertaken by a group of women; nor
would the aged Priam have travelled without an attendant. In *Iliad* 24,
Homer's Priam is escorted by his servant Idaeus, whose function is loosely
replicated by the chorus of Aeschylus' play. There is, however, a subtle but
important alteration in the shift from Homer's single servant to Aeschylus'
chorus of Trojans (whether their status is that of servants, slaves or
otherwise is unclear).[32] Idaeus does relatively little to mitigate the isolation
of Homer's Priam, whose pathos is most powerfully felt through his one-
on-one confrontation with Achilles. Aeschylus' chorus of *Phrygians*, by
contrast, ensure that the Trojan king's entreaties are echoed by the collective voice of his companions, filling the Achaean camp with an abundance
of Trojan voices and perspectives, a particularly powerful effect if, as seems
credible, the chorus lamented the dead Hector once his body had been
ransomed.[33]

In *Iliad* 24 Priam returns to the Trojan citadel after ransoming his son's
body; there the epic draws to a close as the women of Troy sing Hector's
funerary lament. In transposing this scene to the Achaean camp, Aeschylus
upends not only the Iliadic geography but also the gender dynamics
surrounding this climactic scene. Where Homer (and possibly the cyclical
epics) foregrounded female voices – in particular those of Andromache,

---

[31] Garzya 1995: 46–7 with bibliography; Sommerstein 2010a: 248 favours Briseis, though as a mute
      character.
[32] Staltmayr 1991: 369–70.
[33] Staltmayr 1991: 372.

Hecuba and Helen – Aeschylus casts the lament in distinctly male tones. Female lament plays a crucial function in the *Iliad*, casting a stark light on the gendered binaries of the poem and the war at its centre and at the same time casting those same dichotomies into doubt.[34] While tragic lament is often, though by no means always, a female affair,[35] the gender dynamics of *Phrygians* take on particular significance against the unavoidable backdrop of Aeschylus' Homeric source material.[36] And, just as in *Myrmidons*, Aeschylus seems to have achieved this effect through the absence of female voices.

Nereids

The overwhelmingly, perhaps exclusively, male tenor of *Myrmidons* and *Phrygians*, both of which are further marked by their divergence from Iliadic paradigms, places unusual weight on the female characters who form the heart of the trilogy's remaining play. As noted above, we know little with certainty about this drama. But one can hardly doubt that the eponymous sea goddesses and their most famous sister, Thetis, played crucial roles. Although, as immortal goddesses, they are not precisely women, their presence unquestionably anchors *Nereids* in the female sphere. What might this emphatically female drama have entailed? How might the stark gender inversions developed in *Myrmidons* and *Phrygians* have been further explored through the female characters of this most obscure play of Aeschylus' otherwise conspicuously male trilogy?

If, as is generally accepted, *Nereids* comprised the second play of Aeschylus' *Achilleis*, the chorus of sea goddesses probably reprised, with some inevitable alterations, their role in *Iliad* 18, where they accompany Thetis to Achilles' camp in the wake of Patroclus' death. Despite the virtuosic catalogue with which they are introduced,[37] the Nereids' single appearance in the *Iliad* is treated rather succinctly: hearing of Thetis' grief,

---

[34] Murnaghan 1999, Ebbott 1999, Alexiou 2002, Tsagalis 2004, Perkell 2008.

[35] For the complex relationship between gender and lament in tragedy see Foley 1993 ≈ 2001: 19–55, Loraux 1998, Suter 2008a.

[36] The Trojan identity of the chorus in *Phrygians* should not be overlooked in this regard. Their markedly foreign character is attested by Ar. fr. 696 *PCG*, which recalls the strong impression made by their unusual dancing. The chorus's role as mourners would likely have emphasised the effeminate qualities that fifth-century Athenians often ascribed to eastern 'barbarians', as Hall 1993 has explored with regard to *Persians*. Nevertheless, the male chorus, however exotic their presentation, preempt the strong female voices that would have been a familiar component of this episode from its Homeric counterpart.

[37] Hom. *Il.* 18.39–49; Coray 2016: 33–7 ≈ 2018: 33–7, Rutherford 2019: 102.

they 'beat their breasts' (στήθεα πεπλήγοντο, 18.51) during their sister's lament before following her to Troy in tears (18.65–6). It is easy to imagine that this brief intervention in Homer's epic was greatly expanded in Aeschylus' tragic retelling, with the Nereids' virtuosic lamentation taking pride of place in the drama, perhaps through an elaborate choral duet with Thetis, or even a trio that included Achilles as well.[38]

If, as West conjectures, the Nereids' mourning in this play was for Achilles rather than Patroclus, the perceived quality of their threnody would be further enhanced by the fact, unmentioned by West, that the lament over Achilles' body is elsewhere almost invariably said to involve not only Thetis and her sisters but the very Muses themselves, as indeed is already the case in the *Odyssey*.[39] In the absence of the Muses, Aeschylus' Nereid chorus would be expected to present a spectacle of comparable excellence.[40]

Regardless of whose death they mourned, the Nereids situate the voice of lamentation in the female sphere, though importantly, not in the mouths of mortal women. Their virtuosic performance would counterbalance the all-male laments of *Phrygians* (and possibly also *Myrmidons*). If the Nereids' choral lamentation (for Patroclus) preceded that of *Phrygians*, then the mournful voices and bodies of mortal (and hyperbolically eastern) men adopting the roles played by women in the *Iliad* would be given shape by the same choreuts who had just filled the orchestra with a paradigmatic performance of female lament. Whether the mirroring would have further emphasised the aberrant quality of the chorus in *Phrygians*, or normalised their behaviour through assimilation to the idealised mourning of the Nereids, cannot now be determined. If, on the other hand, the chorus of *Phrygians* took up their threnody as a prelude to the Nereids' rendering of a similar scene of lament for Achilles, the resonances between the two performances may well have coloured the theatrical commemoration of the great hero. Perhaps Aeschylus deployed the assimilation as a further commentary on the gender attributes of the warrior, a quality that may have already been on display in *Myrmidons* in the wake of his lover's death.[41]

---

[38] The tripartite incantation of *Libation Bearers* and the (spurious) tripartite lament at the end of *Seven Against Thebes* suggest the power of such compositions.

[39] Hom. *Od.* 24.60–2; Burgess 2009: 40–1.

[40] Barringer 1995: 54–66 details the Nereids' various appearances as 'escorts of the dead' in literary and visual representations.

[41] Above, p. 109.

Whatever the ordering of the choral laments, or the dramatic effect of what are likely to have been two (or three) consciously articulated, extended mirror scenes,[42] the manipulation of gender roles throughout the *Achilleis* reflects a pointed engagement with the gendered voices of the *Iliad*. This concern will have been at work in the pairing of Nereid and Phrygian choruses; but it can also be discerned in the way that the famous silence(s) of Achilles himself (whether in *Myrmidons*, *Phrygians*, or both) place the power of silence at centre stage.[43] Alongside the conspicuously silent Achilles, who transformed the stage into a platform for wordless performance, Aeschylus' *Achilleis* trilogy is filled with other voices that remain unheard. And as with Achilles himself, lament is an essential vehicle for bringing these silences to light. *Phrygians* makes the substitution explicit, replacing the laments of Homer's Trojan women with those of an all-male chorus. A similar, albeit more subtle, effect arises around Briseis in *Nereids*.

Although Briseis' absence is most notable in the overtly erotic and emphatically male context of *Myrmidons*, the captive woman's critical role in the *Iliad*'s complex thematisation of lament makes her a potentially important absent figure in *Nereids* as well. Briseis' moving articulation of grief for Patroclus in *Iliad* 19 activates a broad network of associations, tying together the various strains of mourning within the poem through a pointed meditation on the nature of female vulnerability.[44] Aeschylus' continued silencing of Briseis in *Nereids* would thus be unavoidably implicated in the structuring of his own sequence of tragic lamentation,[45] all the more so if (as is generally assumed) *Nereids* depicted the mourning for Patroclus. The connection takes on added relevance in the light of the comparison drawn in the *Iliad* between Briseis' lament for Patroclus and that of goddesses (εἶπε δ' ἄρα κλαίουσα γυνὴ εἰκυῖα θεῇσιν, 'and, like goddesses, the woman spoke, lamenting', 19.286). Despite the formulaic language,[46] the line subtly suggests a comparison between Briseis' lament and that which was recently offered by the Nereids for the same fallen hero.

---

[42] For the critical role of mirror scenes in Attic tragedy see Taplin 1978: 122–39.

[43] For Achilles' noted silence see Taplin 1972: 58–76, Michelakis 2002: 30–9, Deschamps 2010: 179–90.

[44] Dué 2002: 5–20, Tsagalis 2004: 164.

[45] *Pace* Sommerstein 2008: III 262–3 who, as noted above, contends that Briseis may have had a speaking role in *Phrygians*, and Fantuzzi 2012: 125 who suggests, without evidence, though presumably on analogy with the *Iliad*, that she may have been heard from in *Nereids*.

[46] Edwards 1991: 268 notes that γυνὴ ἐικυῖα θεῇσι is formulaic, and a more generalised interpretation of the simile is supported by the comparison to Aphrodite at 19.282. Nevertheless, it is Briseis' lamentation (κλαίουσα) that unmistakably motivates the comparison

The two expressions of grief, one mortal and the other divine, are drawn into a shared realm. Homer's overt comparison of the mortal woman (γυνή) to the immortal goddesses (θεῆισι) becomes implicit in Aeschylus' dramatic retelling, as the absent Briseis is rendered as a shadow presence through her resemblance to the female surrogates who fill the orchestra, and as the divine voice of the Nereids gives shape to the mourning song that Briseis is not permitted to perform.

Those who place *Nereids* as the second play in the *Achilleis* trilogy assign a second role to the divine chorus of the play, as assistants to Thetis in delivering Achilles' new armour. The substantial number of vases depicting the Nereids furnishing Achilles' arms has generally been interpreted in support of this claim, though the evidence is far from conclusive.[47] In the *Iliad* the Nereids do not aid Thetis in the re-arming of Achilles; instead, the arms are revealed through an extended *ekphrasis* that details their creation, merging a vivid description of the weapons with the artistry of Hephaestus' labour in crafting them. Aeschylus' shift of focus from Hephaestus to the Nereids represents yet another inversion of Homeric gender roles. If male figures are brought to the fore through the erotic relationship of Achilles and Patroclus in *Myrmidons* and the lamentations of the male Trojan chorus in *Phrygians*, here we find a move from male to female. Control over the arms of Achilles is placed in the hands of a collective female chorus rather than the singular male divinity. It is almost as though Hephaestus' mute assistants, identified in the *Iliad* as female automata (presumably) of his own creation (18.417–20), are reimagined in the theatre as fully independent agents.

Taken collectively, the fragments of Aeschylus' *Achilleis* thus suggest an inversion of the Homeric model with respect to gender, with the chorus of *Nereids* likely standing alongside their sister, Thetis, as the sole female voices within the trilogy. Aeschylus uses the twinned motifs of silence and lament to draw attention to this concerted transposition, extending the power of theatrical non-speech to the women whose voices and presence seem to be excluded from his dramatic composition. If one adopts the traditional ordering of the trilogy, the chorus of *Nereids* do not simply reprise the gendered roles set out for them in the *Iliad*, but, like the male figures of the companion tragedies, appropriate important duties that Homer assigns to the opposite sex.

at 19.286, thus encouraging the recollection of the goddesses (the Nereids) who have most recently performed the same activity.

[47] Barringer 1995: 17–48; also the cautions of Taplin 2007: 84–5.

Bodies in Space

The sustained gender reversals of the *Achilleis* are not simply a question of *dramatis personae*, of assigning roles contrary to the gendered expectations set by Aeschylus' epic model. Rather, the novel perspective on familiar events promoted by the gender of the characters populating Aeschylus' trilogy is complemented by a correspondingly unsettled dramatic topography. In some cases, the landscape is marked as unconventional through implicit contrast with that of the *Iliad*. In others, it is the manipulation of the theatre space itself that destabilises the plays' spatial coordinates.

It is hard to reconstruct the spatial structure of ancient dramas even in those fortunate cases where plays have been preserved in their entirety. To attempt the task for a play like *Nereids*, where even basic features of plot are a matter of speculation, may seem foolhardy. Nevertheless, enough clues can be gleaned to justify a bit of creative reflection and the exercise itself is salutary insofar as it asks us to revisit many of the assumptions, explicit and otherwise, that guide our contemporary ideas about ancient drama.

As a starting point, I return to the possibility that the female chorus of *Nereids* were tasked with furnishing Achilles' new armour, transposing the Iliadic craftsmanship of Hephaestus into a new, distinctly choral form. An emphasis on choral performance is clearly reflected in the numerous fifth-century vases depicting Nereids mounted on dolphins and other marine creatures as they ferry new armour for their sister's son.[48] Such images participate in a broader iconographic tradition, elegantly explored by Eric Csapo, in which Nereids, dolphins and other sea creatures reflect the sinuous, circular movements of Dionysiac choruses.[49] As Csapo details, the strong associations between the Nereids, in their collective form, and choral performance regularly evince a distinctly marine flavour, as when Bacchylides vividly describes them as a chorus dancing 'upon wet feet' (ὑγροῖσι ποσσίν, 17.108), an elegant *adynaton* that assimilates the practical features of the terrestrial activity with the liquid qualities of its imagined underwater twin.[50] Whatever one imagines Aeschylus' Nereid chorus to have done in the orchestra, the fluid grace of the Dionysiac, choral sea is likely to have played an important part.

Hephaestus may be a great craftsman, but the lame god is no dancer. Homer's account of the construction of Achilles' arms emphasises the male

---

[48] Barringer 1995: 31–44.
[49] Csapo 2003.
[50] Fearn 2007: 250.

god's brute strength (18.372) and ungainly movements (18.411), attributes that contrast with the choral elegance of the Nereids. The substitution – graceful goddesses in place of lumbering god – can function as a comment on the choral nature of tragedy. By reimagining Homer's *ekphrasis* as a choral spectacle, Aeschylus adapts the epic *tour de force* to suit the strengths of his own art. The divergence is not, however, simply one of movement or gender, but also of environment, as the fiery enclosure of Hephaestus' house in the *Iliad* (built in bronze by the god himself, 18.369–71) is traded for the unstable expanses of the marine world of Aeschylus' Nereid chorus. The spatial contrast would be further heightened if, as we might conjecture, the Nereids' 'watery' dance with the arms was juxtaposed against a verbal description of the fiery furnace in which the objects were wrought, recalling the extended celebration of Hephaestus' command of fire and metal in the *Iliad* (18.468–77).

A glimmer of the way that Aeschylus may have used the spatial properties of his play to engage with his Homeric model is preserved in the intriguing anapaests of fr. 150, in which the Nereids (we presume, since anapaests are typically delivered by the chorus) speak of their marine journey to Troy:

> δελφινηρὸν πεδίον πόντου
> διαμειψάμεναι
>
> crossing the dolphin-filled plain of the sea

The metaphor πεδίον πόντου, which is the reason for the preservation of the fragment,[51] is hardly amongst Aeschylus' most challenging. The formulation is indebted to Homer's familiar εὐρέα νῶτα θαλάσσης ('broad back of the sea'), recalling the importance already assigned to the marine world in the *Iliad*. By shifting the metaphor from νῶτα (back) to πεδίον (plain), Aeschylus invokes a range of meaning distinct from that of his epic predecessor. Particularly striking, in the light of the shift in genre from monodic epic to choral lyric, is the obvious etymological link between πεδίον and πόδες (feet), the paradigmatic tools and symbol of choral performance.[52] Like the 'wet feet' of Bacchylides' Nereids, Aeschylus' 'plain of the sea' evokes the paradox of marine dancing – a quality that is further

---

[51] A scholium to Euripides' *Phoenician Women* (on 209 = I 279.4–8 Schwartz) compares the expression to that play's choral description of sailing 'the barren plains that flow around Sicily' (περιρρύτων | ὑπὲρ ἀκαρπίστων πεδίων | Σικελίας, 209–11). The scholiast also notes a similar usage by Ion (ὅταν δὲ πόντου πεδίον Αἰγαῖον δράμω, *TrGF* I 19 F 60).

[52] As Csapo 2003: 78–90 details, dolphins are often represented with human feet in vase images, and even in poetry, to indicate their status as choral dancers.

suggested in Aeschylus' usage by the adjective δελφινηρόν, with all of its Dionysiac connotations. Choral performance is an activity that, by rights, must take place on land, yet it is endowed with the fluid properties of the sea.

What might it mean for Aeschylus' Nereid chorus to inhabit this impossible space, on the 'plain of the sea?' Whether the dolphins invoked in fr. 150 are the literal mounts of the goddesses (as in the 'Nereid rider' pose common to their painted likenesses)[53] or, as seems more likely, a figurative representation of the chorus's own marine and Dionysiac character,[54] they endow the orchestra in which they perform with the properties of a marine space, transforming the ground under their feet into a location that cannot be entirely dry, that must, at least in part, belong to the sea.

The ambiguous, part-marine landscape of Aeschylus' orchestra space perhaps takes its inspiration from Homer, even as it reimagines the subterranean workshop of Hephaestus as the watery environment of the Nereids. In the *Iliad*, the Nereids perform their lamentations for Patroclus while still in the sea, before accompanying Thetis to the Trojan shore. Homer never says what the sea goddesses do once on land, but his description of their arrival may have influenced the marine character of Aeschylus' dramatic chorus.

> αἳ δὲ σὺν αὐτῆι
> δακρυόεσσαι ἴσαν, περὶ δέ σφισι κῦμα θαλάσσης
> ῥήγνυτο· ταὶ δ' ὅτε δὴ Τροίην ἐρίβωλον ἵκοντο,
> ἀκτὴν εἰσανέβαινον ἐπισχερώ, ἔνθα θαμειαί
> Μυρμιδόνων εἴρυντο νέες ταχὺν ἀμφ' Ἀχιλῆα.

> And they went with her in tears, and around them broke the wave of the sea. And when they arrived at the fertile land of Troy, they ascended the shore in a line (ἐπισχερώ), at the place where the ships of the Myrmidons were densely drawn up around swift Achilles.
>
> Hom. *Il.* 18.65–9

As Richard Janko has noted, the unusual adverb ἐπισχερώ was interpreted in antiquity along two distinct lines, 'one after another' and 'onto shore', both of which are fully applicable in the context.[55] Homer's polysemous term suggests a conflation between the ordered progression of the Nereids

---

[53] Barringer 1995: 31–44.
[54] Cf. Kowalzig 2013: 35.
[55] Janko 1979.

and their movement from sea to land. Whatever the original resonances of the epic usage, the description of Nereids progressing in a sequence 'one after another' is likely to have invoked choral formation to a fifth-century ear accustomed to the sea goddesses' status as a choral band *par excellence*. But the chorality envisioned in the Iliadic scene is, crucially, synonymous with the goddesses' position at the boundary between land and sea. It is, in other words, a concise but compelling template for a playwright seeking to incorporate the sea into the dancing floor of the theatre.

The transformation of the orchestra space of *Nereids* into a marine space has significant consequences for the way that we think about the *Achilleis* trilogy as a whole and, more broadly, the spatial dynamics of fifth-century tragedy. Within the context of the *Achilleis*, the unusual landscape of *Nereids* seems to fit into a larger program of spatial manipulation pursued throughout the trilogy. We might imagine, as has been claimed, that the action of all three plays of the trilogy takes place just outside the tent of Achilles at the centre of the *skênê*.[56] Around this single fixed point, the shifting identities of Aeschylus' choruses produce strikingly distinct perspectives, effectively restructuring the landscape of the theatre for each dramatic instalment. *Nereids*, as we have seen, draws the tent towards the sea, fixing the outer edges of the orchestra to the shoreline that is such an essential feature of the Homeric landscape. In *Phrygians*, by contrast, the Trojan chorus – their outsider status clearly signalled by their exotic dancing and, doubtless, costumes – draws the Myrmidon camp into spatial dialogue with the Trojan citadel, casting the orchestra space as an extension of the inland origin and disposition of the chorus. The binary between sea and land in *Nereids* becomes in *Phrygians* the invisible, but all-important border between improvised camp and fortified city, symbolised by the unseen, impregnable walls of Troy. *Myrmidons*, with its chorus of Achilles' own men, extends Achilles' tent out into the orchestra, suggesting a sympathetic unity to the space, if not outright harmony. The trilogy thus pivots at each turn. The close geographic connection in *Myrmidons* is replaced by the opposition between land and sea in *Nereids*, and again recalibrated as the conflict between Greeks and Trojans in *Phrygians* (or vice versa, depending on the order of the trilogy).

The marked shifts in the spatial coordinates of the *Achilleis* will have been all the more intensely felt if, as some have asserted, the action of *Myrmidons* or *Phrygians* or both was, in whole or in part, staged inside

[56] Sommerstein 2010a: 242.

Achilles' tent.[57] The landscape would thus not only veer from one orchestra perspective to another, but toggle between the intimate, interior environment of the hero's dwelling and the wild, even hostile, space beyond.

Such radical reconfigurations of theatrical geography have implications not only for the space in which the drama plays out, but also for the space in which the spectators witness it, as the audience's sense of their own spatial coordinates would be defined through their relationship to the imagined landscape before them. The spatial unity of *Myrmidons* would draw theatregoers into the heart of the Achaean camp, all the more so if the action took place within Achilles' tent, allowing the audience to inhabit – at least to some basic degree – the 'same' space as the drama played out before them. *Phrygians*, in turn, would draw the spectators 'inland', inviting them to view Achilles' tent through the lens of a now-Trojan orchestra space, drawing them into the ambit of the Trojan mourners, rather than their Greek foes. And the marine chorus of *Nereids*, positioned at the boundary of land and sea, would again recalibrate the audience's perception of the action playing out before them, allowing them to view the 'land' of Achilles' camp from beyond its shores. Through the mediating spatial perspective of the chorus, the spectators would find themselves 'at sea' within the mimetic world of the drama, viewing the performance from the same watery vantage as the Nereids.

Conclusion

It has now been over thirty years since Helene Foley argued against the simplistic model that held that dramatic women were in some fundamental way rejecting their normative gender roles simply by dint of their presence on the theatrical stage; that by abandoning the traditionally feminine sphere of the *oikos*, they had in some way 'intruded' into the male domin-ated space of the *polis*.[58] Echoing Foley, Pat Easterling called in 1987 for a recognition of the various ways in which 'tragedians, working on the basis of the traditional ideology in respect of women's roles, use the theatrical space in a flexible way to suit the particular themes and problems of each individual play'.[59] In the decades since these critical correctives were first

---

[57] Cf. Taplin 1972: 68–9, who places at least the opening scenes, and probably the whole performance, of *Myrmidons* in Achilles' tent.

[58] Foley 1982.

[59] Easterling 1987: 18.

issued, we have arrived at a far more nuanced understanding of the many spaces, real and imagined, that women were able to occupy in fifth-century Athens. But it may well be that we are still too restrained in our conception of the flexibility of theatrical space. Rather than serve as an end in itself, gender-based interpretations, like the one I have offered here, can serve as tools for coming to grips with those facets of our texts – like bodies and spaces – that currently occupy the margins of mainstream scholarship, as the study of gender once did.

Beyond furnishing a new lens through which to contemplate the fragmentary traces of Aeschylus' *Nereids*, a gender-based, *opsis*-lead interpretation of this play – provisional and hypothetical though it may be – may have broader implications for our understanding of Aeschylus' dramatic works. If we situate the spatial transformations of *Nereids* (the most unsettling and pervasive articulation of the geographic thematisation of the *Achilleis* trilogy as a whole, at least on the reading advanced here) within the more expansive frame of the Aeschylean corpus as it has been preserved for us, certain parallels, if not an outright pattern, begin to emerge. Within the playwright's more well-preserved dramas, similar inversions of the theatrical landscape suggest themselves in the unusual arrivals of two other choruses of female divinities. Most notable is the chorus of Erinyes, whose appearance in the opening scene of *Eumenides* has the effect, as Rush Rehm has argued, of flipping the orchestra so that theatregoers are transported to the inner sanctum of Apollo's temple at Delphi.[60] The arrival of the divine chorus reveals the hitherto concealed interior spaces of the *Oresteia*, transforming the theatre space in which the unseen is suddenly made visible. In a somewhat different vein, the Oceanid chorus of *Prometheus Bound* engineer a comprehensive restructuring of the theatre space into which they arrive, moving from their winged mounts into an orchestra simultaneously rendered liquid and uncertain by their presence.[61]

Turning to mortal women, the Danaid chorus of *Suppliants* participate in an analogous, if less comprehensive and unsettling, restructuring of the theatre space when a hitherto unnoticed harbour takes on sudden dramatic importance. As the chorus' Egyptian pursuers make their way to the Argive shore, Danaus narrates the arrival of their ship to his terrified daughters. Danaus draws attention to the fact that his is an eyewitness report (713–14, 719–20), but his perspective is not shared by the chorus. He can see the

---

[60] Rehm 1988: 294–6.
[61] Taplin 1977: 259–60, Griffith 1983: 109–10.

harbour, but the Danaids, gathered in the orchestra, cannot. As in *Nereids*, the spatial dynamics of the play extend to the audience as well, since the visual asymmetry of the mimetic world is not limited to the performers. The spectators share the Danaid chorus' inability to see the harbour. They too must rely on Danaus' eyewitness account, thus implicating themselves in the complex spatial structures of the drama.[62]

The picture of spatial flexibility within a single drama or connected trilogy that begins to take shape through the dynamic perspectives of these female choruses finds further encouragement in the ancient testimonium that records a staggering five scene changes in Aeschylus' *Women of Aetna*.[63] The internal recalibrations of theatrical space claimed for that play are paralleled in kind, if not in number, by the marked change of scene that takes place in *Eumenides* when the (already spatially unsettling) opening episode at Delphi gives way to the Athenian setting in which the remainder of the drama takes place. Scholars have posited similar shifts of location in both *Libation Bearers* (from tomb to palace) and in *Persians* (from palace to tomb), though the textual evidence for these shifts is less conclusive than for *Eumenides*.[64]

The majority of the dramas mentioned above are not structured around the *oikos*/*polis* binary typically associated with the Greek tragic theatre by modern scholars. In some cases a built structure seems to anchor the *skênê* (the impermanent tent of the *Achilleis* plays, the temple of the Delphi scene of *Eumenides*), but in almost all of these plays the *polis* is either entirely absent (*Myrmidons*, *Nereids*, *Prometheus Bound*, the Delphi scene of *Eumenides* – which then shifts to a *polis* without *oikos* in Athens) or far removed (*Phrygians*, *Suppliants*, portions of *Women of Aetna*(?)). Although these plays do not seem to reflect a landscape defined by gendered binaries (any more than the traditional *oikos*/*polis* model does), the choruses who find themselves positioned outside of the *oikos*/*polis* frame and/or who destabilise the mimetic geography of the theatre are disproportionately female. This fact may warrant some speculation when it comes to the many female choruses in Aeschylus' other fragmentary tragedies. Despite the partial and inevitably limited nature of the evidence, there are a number of plays featuring collectives of female divinities that seem to be located away from the traditional frame of either *oikos* or

---

[62] One might compare the asymmetrical vision of Neoptolemus and Odysseus at the beginning of Sophocles' *Philoctetes*, another play structured by an unseen coastline.

[63] P.Oxy. 2257 fr. 1.5–14, at *TrGF* III 126–7; Poli-Palladini 2001.

[64] Taplin 1977: 338–40, 105–7, with general remarks at 103–5.

polis: *The Judgement of Arms* (with Nereid chorus), *Phorcides*, *The Weighing of Souls* and possibly *Toxotides*.[65] Many plays with choruses of mortal women also strongly suggest unusual and/or non-urban settings, even if conclusive evidence is almost always lacking. A provisional list would include: *Bassarides*, *Daughters of the Sun*, *Thracian Women*, *Priestesses*, *Cretan Women*, *Lemnian Women*, *Wool Carders* and *Women of Salamis*. There is, of course, no way to confirm or refute the claim of an extra-urban setting for most of these plays, and despite the wild identities of many, the action in which they take part may nonetheless have been located inside a city (as is the case, for example, with Euripides' *Bacchae*). Nevertheless, these groupings would seem to encourage a maximally expansive view of the collocation of gender and theatrical space in *Aeschylean Tragedy*.

The diverse spatial dispositions and perspectives suggested by *Nereids*, and by many other plays in the Aeschylean corpus, hint at the broad spectrum of landscapes, and of the gendered structures of landscape, that took shape within the fifth-century theatre of Dionysus. The array of mimetic spaces created in these plays likely reflects only a small fraction of what theatregoers would have experienced during the heady, experimental first century of Attic tragedy. By imagining dramatic space through the fragmented lens of Aeschylus' *Nereids*, we can perhaps better appreciate the incomplete and fragmented vision of tragic performance that we have constructed around the handful of plays that have been preserved for us in their entirety.

---

[65] Both *The Judgement of Arms* and *The Weighing of Souls* are set, like *Nereids*, in the Greek camp at Troy. Aristotle seems to refer to the exotic setting of *Phorcides* when he classes it alongside plays 'set in Hades', though corruption of the passage renders interpretation difficult (*Poet.* 1456a2–3). It is unclear if the chorus of *Toxotides* are divine or mortal, but either way the setting of the play is likely the wilderness in which they hunt.

8 | *Europa* Revisited

An Experiment in Characterisation

NIALL W. SLATER

If it is a trial to be an icon, it must be even more of a burden to be an aetiological myth. We all know Europa – and that is the challenge when we turn to her depiction in the remains of Greek tragedy. Those remains are a single papyrus fragment, known for nearly a century and a half, but little re-evaluated in performative terms. Before listening to that fragmented voice, it will be useful to explore Europa in the visual and literary imaginary that preceded fifth-century tragedy as parameters for how an audience watching her on stage in Athens might have reacted to her, as well as the frames into which the earliest scholars studying the fragment sought to fit a new piece of text.

The ancient visual record directs us, as it must have Greek audiences, to one point in her life's narrative above all: the story of Europa's abduction by the bull. Numerous vases, though all from the red-figure period, portray this moment.[1] The sculptural record, though much more limited, is similarly focussed, with famous archaic metopes at Selinus perhaps from Temple Y as well as those at the temple of Athena at Assos and the Sicyonian treasury at Delphi.[2] Roman wall painting offers the opportunity to portray more bystanders,[3] but of representations of any other moment in Europa's story there are essentially none – apart from one or two vases subsequently associated with the fragment that is the focus of this paper.

---

[1] Boardman 1975: 224 ('particularly popular in the first quarter of the fifth century'). His fig. 147 illustrates the Berlin Painter's version (Oxford, Ashmolean Museum 1927.4502, *BAPD* §201990).

[2] Ridgway 1977: 242–51. She suggests that there might be 'some kind of saddle under Europa' on the Selinus metope; 'if so, the impromptu element of the story disappears, and the myth takes on the appearance of a fated event, which explains the fearless attitude of the heroine' (244). For the Selinus metope SM2 see Marconi 2007: 90–6 (with fig. 37), 120 (dating the small metopes *c.* 550), with a nice representation of the Sicyonian treasury metope as fig. 38 (dating it *c.* 560). For Assos and the Europe metope M5 there see Wescoat 2012: 176–9 and pl. 106; the temple date is highly controversial, but Wescoat ultimately opts for *c.* 540, though it could be a generation later (239). For Europa's iconography see Robertson 1988; for the literary tradition down to Stesichorus, Davies and Finglass 2014: 355–7.

[3] Perhaps the best example is from the House of Jason at Pompeii, well discussed in context and illustrated by Newby 2016: 177–84 with fig. 4.12 (Naples, Museo Archeologico Nazionale inv. 111475). The Portico of Pompey displayed a painting of Europa by Antiphilus (Plin. *NH* 35.114) and perhaps a statue of Europa on the bull by Pythagoras (an inference from Tatian, *Oration to the Greeks* 33.3–4). The Tomb of the Nasonii, late second or early third century AD, had another example in its complex of decoration: Newby 2016: 262–70.

Such differential survival seems unlikely to be accidental and suggests that for the ancient audiences as well, any other part of Europa's life must at a minimum have been less familiar.

The publication in 1879 of a papyrus fragment of the second century containing twenty-three lines of tragic verse spoken by a much older Europa, worrying about her absent son Sarpedon, suddenly pointed in a very different direction.[4] The text itself has many problems, virtually none of which can be our focus here, though it is worth keeping in mind Barrett's judgment on their source: 'the whole fragment, copied by a semi-literate schoolboy with his mind evidently on other things, is monstrously corrupt'.[5] The speaker was undoubtedly Europa, however, and the contents nonetheless immediately suggested that the source was a lost play recorded in the catalogue of Aeschylus' titles: *Carians* or *Europa*.

Yet that double title is itself in turn a source of speculation and frustration, carrying with it conflicting frames for the story of both Europa and the son she names in her speech, Sarpedon. Who are these Carians, and what is their function in the play? Many believe that where two titles are recorded for a play, one a plural group and the other a personal name, the former is more likely to be the original title naming the chorus and the latter an addition of the Hellenistic age.[6] Only two other fragments are attributed in antiquity to this play, both brief and neither illuminating for the identity of the chorus. The vexed question of the chorus merits a brief review of the possibilities. Given that all of our other sources associate Sarpedon with Lycia,[7] most would set the play there but then wonder why we have a chorus of Carians. Strabo supplies one possible simple answer: he claims that poets, especially tragedians, tended to mix up ethnic names, including for 'the Lycians, whom they also call Carians' (καὶ τοὺς Λυκίους Κᾶρας, 14.3.3). Strabo presumably had a specific example of this confusion in mind, and many are happy to think that this play supplied it: Carians are

---

[4] Louvre inv. 7172 recto coll. iv 10–v 9, published by Weil 1879: 18–22.

[5] Barrett 2007: 356, noting also (n. 19) 'We even know his name (Apollonios) and his age (not more than thirteen or fourteen)'. Lloyd-Jones 1957: II 599 suggests some errors resulted from Apollonios following dictation.

[6] Keen 2005: 67: 'It seems likely that *Cares was the original title* – it is generally presumed that titles denoting the chorus are earlier than the (presumably) Alexandrian versions that name the principal characters.' Sommerstein 2002a = 2010b: 11–29 argues that in general tragic titles were stable, though with important exceptions, and double titles perhaps a function of an incipient book trade (endorsing a suggestion of West), but in an addendum (2010b: 29) suggests that *Carians* or *Europa* is a problem case.

[7] Reviewed in Unwin 2017: 66–73, noting the intriguing suggestion of Durnford that 'Sarpedon' was derived from a Luwian name or title; cf. Bachvarova 2015: 171–2, 2016: 439 with n. 75.

thus Lycians by another name. Edith Hall, however, has remarked that Carian women were known as professional singers of laments (indeed Menander wrote a play called *Carinê* about such a mourner) and speculated that a chorus of Carian women assisted Europa in her eventual lamentations for the death of Sarpedon, who is certainly in this version of the myth her son.[8] These different possibilities highlight our ignorance of a key point: we have no idea whether the chorus was male or female, and to assume one or the other may strongly shape our interpretation. If the chorus was male, they are more likely to be Lycian elders,[9] perhaps quite similar to Aeschylus' *Persians*, with an eastern queen supported by elderly counselors in the absence of her son, the king.[10] If the chorus was female, they may have been either captives or mourners more emotionally connected to Europa. One of the two book fragments attributed to the play meditates on the destructiveness of war:

ἀλλ' Ἄρης φιλεῖ
ἀεὶ τὰ λῶιστα πάντ' ἀπανθίζειν στρατοῦ

But Ares is always in the habit of plucking off all that is best in an army.
Aesch. *Europa* fr. 100[11]

This might be Europa worrying over her son Sarpedon in another part of the speech to which we will soon turn, or perhaps in an exchange with the chorus. But it does not help identify the chorus, whose gender and status remain unknown – and we should beware of allowing presumptions about its nature to affect our interpretation of what survives.

The papyrus fragment introduces us to a Europa worrying about the fate of her only surviving son Sarpedon, off fighting at Troy – a relationship that must have surprised some in an Athenian audience, at least if they had been paying attention to details in the recitals of Homer at their festivals.

---

[8] Hall 1989: 131 'in choosing a Carian chorus to bewail Sarpedon's death in his *Cares*, therefore, Aeschylus may have been prompted rather by the fame of the Carian epicedian lament.'

[9] Though Gruber 2009: 533 somewhat curiously and very briefly suggests the male followers of Sarpedon as a chorus (and perhaps even a setting at Troy). While statistics are no guide to the gender of tragic choruses in general, men of military age are not common.

[10] Lyndsay Coo suggests a similarity to Astyoche and the chorus mourning for Eurypylus in Sophocles' eponymous play (also compared to *Persians*), though we cannot be sure of the gender of the chorus in that play. The messenger bringing the news of Eurypylus' death says the sorrow exceeds that for Memnon and Sarpedon (ὅσ' οὔτε Μέμγ[ω]ν οὔτε Σα[ρπηδὼν ποτε, fr. 210.80). Mette 1963: 108–12 compares Europa's mourning to Eos' for Memnon in Aeschylus' *Psychostasia*.

[11] τὰ λῶιστα is definitely an Aeschylean usage: *Suppl.* 962–3; *Ag.* 1053. It is also in the style of the *Prometheus Bound* poet (204). Translations of Aeschylus throughout are from Sommerstein 2008, unless otherwise noted.

In the Iliadic account, Sarpedon is the son of Zeus and Laodameia, and there is no connection to Europa. The version in which his mother is Europa, however, is attested in the competing Hesiodic tradition's *Catalogue of Women* – though not without its own internal problems:

ἔμ]ελλε τανισφύρωι Εὐρωπείηι,
] πατὴρ ἀνδρῶν τε θεῶν τε
10   νύ]μφης πάρα καλλικόμοιο.
ἢ δ' ἄρα παῖδ]ας [ἔτικτ]εν ὑπερμενέϊ Κρονίωνι
πο]λέων ἡγήτορας ἀνδρῶν,
Μίνω τε κρείοντα] δίκαιόν τε Ῥαδάμανθυν
καὶ Σαρπηδόνα δῖον] ἀμύμονά τε κρατερ[όν τε.
15   τοῖσιν ἑὰς τιμὰς δι]εδάσσατο μητίετα Ζ[εύς·
Λυκίης εὐρ]είης ἶφι ἄνασσε
πό]λεις εὖ ναιεταώσα[ς
πολ]λὴ δέ οἱ ἕσπετο τιμή
μεγαλή]τορι ποιμένι λαῶν.
20   τῶι δ' ἐπὶ τρεῖς γενεὰς ζώει]ν μερόπων ἀνθρώπων
δῶκεν ἐπεὶ   ἐφί]λατο μητίετα Ζεύς.
πολ]ὺν δ' ἐκρίνατο λαόν.
Τρ]ώεσσ' ἐπικούρους·
τοὺς ἄγε Σαρπηδὼν κρυεροῦ] πολέμοιο δαήμων.

] to long-ankled Europa he was going to [
] the father of men and of gods
10   ] from beside the beautiful-haired maiden.
She bore sons] to Cronus' very strong son
] commanders of many men,
sovereign Minos] and just Rhadamanthys
and godly Sarpedon,] excellent and strong.
15   To them their own honours] the counsellor Zeus shared out.
] mightily he ruled [broad Lycia
] well situated cities
] and much honour stays with him
] to the great-hearted shepherd of the people.
20   For to live for three generations] of speech-endowed human beings
he granted him, for   ] counsellor Zeus loved him
] and he chose a great host
] allies for the Trojans.
These Sarpedon led,] experienced in [chilling] war.
[Hes.] fr. 91.8–24 Most (with M.'s translation) ≈ 141 M–W

While supplying the missing names of both Minos and Sarpedon to the text here may be uncontroversial, rather trickier is the assumption in

Most's restoration that Sarpedon in this version already lived 'for three generations' of men. That bespeaks an attempt to solve a chronological problem: how could Sarpedon both be the founder of Lycia and yet remain ruler at the time of the Trojan War? Herodotus gives an account wherein strife between Minos and Sarpedon over the rule in Crete led the latter to found Miletus[12] and then Lycia (1.173.1–2):

οἱ δὲ Λύκιοι ἐκ Κρήτης τὠρχαῖον γεγόνασι (τὴν γὰρ Κρήτην εἶχον τὸ παλαιὸν πᾶσαν βάρβαροι). διενειχθέντων δὲ ἐν Κρήτηι περὶ τῆς βασιληίης τῶν Εὐρώπης παίδων Σαρπηδόνος τε καὶ Μίνω, ὡς ἐπεκράτησε τῆι στάσι Μίνως, ἐξήλασε αὐτόν τε Σαρπηδόνα καὶ τοὺς στασιώτας αὐτοῦ· οἱ δὲ ἀπωσθέντες ἀπίκοντο τῆς Ἀσίης ἐς γῆς τὴν Μιλυάδα· τὴν γὰρ νῦν Λύκιοι νέμονται, αὕτη τὸ παλαιὸν ἦν Μιλυάς, οἱ δὲ Μιλύαι τότε Σόλυμοι ἐκαλέοντο.

The Lycians came originally from Crete, which in ancient times was occupied entirely by barbarians. When the two sons of Europa, Sarpedon and Minos, quarrelled over the throne, Minos, who prevailed, expelled Sarpedon along with his partisans. The exiles reached the land of Milyas in Asia. For the land the Lycians now inhabit was known as Milyas at that time, and its inhabitants were called Solymi.[13]

Strabo offers more details, suggesting a two-stage process, from Crete to Miletus and thence to Lycia:

καὶ οἱ Κᾶρες δὲ νησιῶται πρότερον ὄντες καὶ Λέλεγες, ὥς φασιν, ἠπειρῶται γεγόνασι προσλαβόντων Κρητῶν, οἳ καὶ τὴν Μίλητον ἔκτισαν, ἐκ τῆς Κρητικῆς Μιλήτου Σαρπηδόνα λαβόντες κτίστην· καὶ τοὺς Τερμίλας κατώι-κισαν ἐν τῆι νῦν Λυκίαι· τούτους δ' ἀγαγεῖν ἐκ Κρήτης ἀποίκους Σαρπη-δόνα, Μίνω καὶ Ῥαδαμάνθυος ἀδελφὸν ὄντα, καὶ ὀνομάσαι Τερμίλας τοὺς πρότερον Μιλύας

Not only the Carians, who in earlier times were islanders, but also the Leleges, as they say, became mainlanders with the aid of the Cretans, who founded, among other places, Miletus, having taken Sarpedon from the Cretan Miletus as founder; and they settled the Termilae in the country which is now called Lycia; and they say that these settlers were brought from Crete by Sarpedon, a brother of Minos and Rhadamanthus, and that

---

[12] For Sarpedon's role in founding Miletus see also Strabo 14.1.6. Sarpedon is also mentioned briefly in a series of three variant accounts of the foundation of Miletus in a fragment of Herodorus of Heraclea (fr. 45 *EGM*; discussion in Fowler, *EGM* II 578–80, Mac Sweeney 2013: 70–2). Bachvarova 2015: 160–73 is a thorough analysis of all these accounts; note also her suggestion that 'we could interpret Herodotus' story as acknowledging that Lycian is a term applied by outsiders' (163).

[13] Translations of Herodotus from Romm 1998, here 66.

he gave the name Termilae to the people who were formerly called Milyae

Strabo 12.8.5 (transl. Jones 1969: 491)

None of this, however, will make chronological sense of a play in which Sarpedon is off fighting at Troy but his mother Europa is still alive at her new home in Lycia, and in truth we must leave the problem here.

Early scholarship on the fragment sought an action for the play that would accommodate Europa, her worries, and eventual news of Sarpedon. Herbert Weir Smyth, followed by many others, sought to make that action the sequel to the Homeric account of the death of Sarpedon, in which Zeus ordered Sleep and Death to carry his body back home to Lycia for burial, thus suturing together Homeric action and Hesiodic genealogy.[14] Like Europa, Sarpedon's story version is amply represented in the visual arts, and well before Aeschylus, most famously on the Euphronius krater.[15] Indeed, when the narrative moment can be determined, Greek art as on that krater most often depicts the removal of the body from the battlefield rather than its arrival in Lycia. In the early fourth century, however, an Apulian vase represents the arrival by air of Sleep and Death carrying a body and apparently delivering it to a seated female figure in Eastern dress.[16] Many have seen theatrical associations in this scene.[17] In the absence of labels for the figures it could be the delivery of Memnon's body to his mother, but opinion has favored Sarpedon and Europa. This vase may support the view that an early fourth-century reperformance of *Carians* or *Europa* ended with Sarpedon's body flown in by Sleep and Death on the *mêchanê* – though that is not probative for an original performance, and we shall return to that question as well.

While earlier scholarship was primarily grateful to have recovered one more bit of Aeschylus (and the *Europa* fragment was one of the first tragic fragments from Egypt to be published), both the mythic and visual novelty of staging a Europa from near the end of her life, fearing for and eventually mourning Sarpedon, cannot be denied. Let us consider an alternative frame for creating such a tragic heroine before turning at last to a linear consider-ation of her voice in the fragment. In recent years Martin West has made the challenging suggestion that this *Europa*, like *Prometheus Bound*, may

---

[14] Smyth 1922–6: II 415.

[15] Well illustrated in von Bothmer 1987: 34–7; Rome, Museo Nazionale Etrusco di Villa Giulia L.2006.10 (*BAPD* §187).

[16] Red-figure bell krater, from 400–380, attributed to the Sarpedon Painter; New York, Metropolitan Museum of Art 16.140.

[17] Taplin 2007: 72–4.

have been produced at Athens as a work of Aeschylus, but was in fact composed by the poet's son Euphorion.[18] We cannot re-examine all the issues of language and style in both plays that seem to West post-Aeschylean, but a few points about Euphorion are worth recalling before turning to details of the *Europa* fragment. Most of what we know about this son of Aeschylus comes from his entry in the *Suda* (ε 3800, *TrGF* I 12 T 1):

> Εὐφορίων, υἱὸς Αἰσχύλου τοῦ τραγικοῦ, Ἀθηναῖος, τραγικὸς καὶ αὐτός· ὃς καὶ τοῖς Αἰσχύλου τοῦ πατρός, οἷς μήπω ἦν ἐπιδειξάμενος, τετράκις ἐνίκησεν. ἔγραψε δὲ καὶ οἰκεῖα.

> Euphorion, son of Aeschylus the tragic poet; Athenian; a tragic poet himself. He was the man who won four victories with the plays of his father Aeschylus, which Aeschylus had not yet staged. He also wrote his own. (transl. Whitehead 2003, adapted)

The notion that Aeschylus left behind four unproduced tetralogies (at a minimum!) has bothered some.[19] Even more intriguing, however, is the fact that not a single fragmentary line or even word attributed to Euphorion himself survives, despite the fact that his tetralogy produced in his own name in 431 was victorious over both Sophocles and Euripides, whose entry included *Medea* (*TrGF* I 12 T 2, from the hypothesis). Aeschylus stood at the head of a multi-generational family of tragedians, including his nephew Philocles, great-nephew Morsimus, and two more descended from him, Astydamas the Elder and Astydamas the Younger.[20] These left at least some fragments that survive to us – but not Euphorion. The case for Euphorion's authorship of our *Europa* fragment can at best be a probability, to which the observations on the text below offer some support. If Euphorion wrote this *Europa*, however, whether intending to deceive the Athenian public about its authorship or not, this fragment would then give us not only a portrait of a familiar figure from myth at a most unfamiliar point in her life, but also show us how a fifth-century tragedian who was not one of the great three but was active in Athens in

---

[18] West 2000 = 2011–13: II 227–49. This follows up on his proposal (West 1990: 67–72) that Euphorion himself had composed most of a *Prometheus* trilogy produced in the 430s, including the surviving *Prometheus Bound*. Note also his intriguing suggestion that Euphorion could have used Aeschylus' *Prometheus Pyrkaeus*, from the tetralogy of 472 that included *Persians*, to conclude a *Prometheus* tetralogy produced in the 430s.

[19] E.g. *TrGF* I on 12 T 1 (p. 88): 'Aeschylum 4 tetralogias (i.e. 16 dramata) nondum actas reliquisse vix credibile (τετράκις = τετραλογίαι?)', but the suggestion that τετράκις in the *Suda* entry could mean 'with one tetralogy' seems scarcely possible Greek.

[20] Sutton 1987: 12–14.

the 440s and 430s (and thus competing with Sophocles and Euripides at the dramatic festivals) composed for a female voice.

Both the text and the translation (with likely supplementation) of the fragment used here come from Alan Sommerstein's superb Loeb edition (fr. 99):

ταύρωι τε λειμῶ ξένια πάμβοτον †παραντ†.
τοιόνδε μὲν Ζεὺς κλέμμα πρεσβύτου πατρός
αὐτοῦ μένων ἄμοχθος ἤνυσεν λαβεῖν.
τί οὖν; τὰ πολλὰ κεῖνα διὰ παύρων λέγω.
5   γυνὴ θεῶι μειχθεῖσα παρθένου σέβας
ἤμειψα, παίδων δ' ἐζύγην ξυνάονι.
καὶ †τριαγωνεις† τοὺς γυναικείους πόνους
ἐκαρτέρησ', ἄρουρα δ' οὐκ ἐμέμψατο
τοῦ μὴ 'ξενεγκεῖν σπέρμα γενναῖον πατρός.
10 ἐκ τῶν μεγίστων δ' ἠρξάμην φυτευμάτων
Μίνων τεκοῦσα <
                              >
Ῥαδάμανθυν, ὅσπερ ἄφθιτος παίδων ἐμῶν.
ἀλλ' οὐκ ἐν αὐγαῖς ταῖς ἐμαῖς ζόην ἔχει,
τὸ μὴ παρὸν δὲ τέρψιν οὐκ ἔχει φίλοις.
15 τρίτον δέ, τοῦ νῦν φροντίσιν χειμάζομαι,
Σαρπηδόν', αἰχμὴ μὴ 'ξ Ἄρεως καθίκετο.
κλέος γὰρ ἥκειν <
                              > Ἑλλάδος λωτίσματα
πάσης, ὑπερφέροντας ἀλκίμωι σθένει,
αὐχεῖν δὲ Τρώων ἄστυ πορθήσειν βία·
<
                              >
20 πρὸς οὓς δέδοικα μή τι μαργαίνων δορὶ
ἀνυπέρβατον δράσηι τε καὶ πάθηι κακόν.
λεπτὴ γὰρ ἐλπίς, ἥδ' ἐπὶ ξυροῦ μένει
μὴ πάντα παίσας' ἐκχέω πρὸς ἕρματι

[*My father unwittingly facilitated my abduction by welcoming Zeus's treacherous agent (?)] and <providing (?)>* for the bull a rich grazing meadow as a guest-gift. Such was the theft that Zeus succeeded in committing at the expense of my aged father, without moving from his place and without any toil. Well then, I shall tell the long tale of the past in a few words. I, a mortal woman, united with a god, gave up the honour of virginity, and was joined to a partner in parenthood; three times I endured a woman's pains in childbirth, and my fertile field did not complain nor refuse to bear to the end the noble seed of the Father. I began with the greatest of my offspring, giving birth to Minos ...

> [Secondly I bore] Rhadamanthys, who is the immortal one among my
> children; but the life he has is not seen by my eyes, and absence brings no
> joy to loved ones. The third child I bore was the one over whom I am now
> storm-tossed with anxiety, Sarpedon – anxiety lest an enemy spear-point
> may have pierced him. The story is that *<spear-wielding men (?),>* the
> best in all Greece, have come *<to fertile Asia (?)>*, men outstanding in
> martial strength, and boast that they will storm and sack the city of the
> Trojans.
>   *<My son has gone there at the head of his troops to keep the hostile army*
> *of the Argives out of Troy;>* I fear that against them he may go berserk
> with his spear and both do and suffer the greatest possible harm. My hope
> is slender, and it rests on the razor's edge whether I may strike a rock and
> lose everything

Our text therefore begins in the middle of a sentence as Europa is telling us
her story, in a manner much more like a Euripidean prologue than the style
of Aeschylus. There are at least three sections: the first few lines citing her
rape by Zeus, then the story of her marriage and three sons, and then with a
transition to the present her expression of anxieties over the fate of her sole
surviving son Sarpedon.

Versions of Europa's rape already current by the fifth century differed on
whether the bull that carried Europa off to Crete was Zeus himself transformed or simply an instrument sent by Zeus. It is not absolutely clear
here, but the adjective ἄμοχθος in the middle of line 3 strongly suggests the
latter version: Zeus remains both unmoved and untroubled (the standard
tragic meaning of the adjective[21]) while the bull does all the dirty work.[22]
The meadow was offered to the bull as ξένια, a guest gift, which Zeus Xenios
thus violated.[23] The rape itself is described as a κλέμμα, a theft, the first in
a series of verbal nouns in –μα scattered through this passage, and likely
one of the earliest attestations of this word. Queen Hecuba uses it with
typical Euripidean irony when she hopes to find some jewellery to adorn

---

[21] Cf. Soph. fr. 410 ἄμοχθος γὰρ οὐδείς ('no one is untroubled'), Eur. fr. 240.2 τίς δ᾽ ἄμοχθος εὐκλεής
   ('who gains glory without trouble?'), as well as Deianira's yearning for an 'untroubled life'
   (ἄμοχθον . . . βίον, Soph. *Tr.* 147). Translations of Sophocles are from the Loeb edition of Lloyd-
   Jones 1997, 1998, 2003, and the fragments of Euripides from the Loeb edition of Collard and
   Cropp 2008, unless otherwise noted.
[22] So Robertson 1957: 2 'the wording suggests that Aeschylus intended a deliberate tacit rejection,
   in the Pindaric manner, of the other version'.
[23] The first line of the fragment is particularly difficult. Sommerstein 2008: III 112 accepts West's
   readings λειμῶ and πάμβοτον.

Polyxena's body that another Trojan captive woman has stolen from her own home: εἴ τις τοὺς νεωστὶ δεσπότας | λαθοῦσ᾿ ἔχει τι κλέμμα τῶν αὑτῆς δόμων (*Hec.* 617–18: 'if by chance any has managed to steal from her own home, undetected by our new masters').[24] *Hecuba* likely dates to the later 420s,[25] close to Aristophanes' *Knights*, wherein the Sausage Seller employs a rather tragic-sounding jingle including two such verbal nouns in –μα to describe his theft of the Paphlagonian's oracles: τὸ μὲν νόημα τῆς θεοῦ, τὸ δὲ κλέμμ᾿ ἐμόν (*Knights* 1203: 'The Goddess thought it up, I pulled the job').[26] κλέμμα also means a stratagem or trick in war, as in Thucydides (e.g. 5.9.5). Both connotations may be present here as the now aged Europa describes the trauma not as an assault on herself but a crime against her father.

Cutting off any further memory of the rape, Europa promises to cover much of her history in few words (line 4). Decorous in language but vivid in structure, positioning μειχθεῖσα in the middle of line 5, she swiftly accounts for her three children by Zeus. No satisfactory account has been given for where the text preserves τριαγωνεῖς (7): is the poet inventing a new word here?[27] It does seem to mean something like 'triple suffering.' There follows the rather bizarrely structured claim that she, the embodied fertile field (ἄρουρα), did not reject or even blame the noble

---

[24] Translations of Euripides are from Kovacs 1994–2002, unless otherwise noted.

[25] With no firm external references, metrical criteria are the main hope for determining a date. Foley 2015: 14 and Battezzato 2018: 2–4 cite 424 as the most likely; Gregory 1999: xii–xv offers a range of possibilities clustering around the same time.

[26] Neil 1901: 159 *ad loc.* thinks it likely that this is tragic parody; Sommerstein 1981: *ad loc.* thinks it possible. Translations of Aristophanes are from Henderson 1998–2008 unless otherwise noted.

[27] This possible neologism might give some support to an intriguing suggestion by an anonymous referee who, noting that divine rapes are usually 'one-night stands', speculates that the three brothers Minos, Rhadamanthys and Sarpedon might be meant to be triplets. Europa's description of triple birth pangs could be consistent with three births in one labour. Survival of a triplet birth would increase Europa's heroic stature: Antipater of Thessalonica gives voice to a Polyxo who died giving birth to her triplets (*Anth. Pal.* 7. 168 = 647–52 *GP*). For multiple births in antiquity see Dasen 1997 (a reference that I owe to my colleague Sandra Blakely; also Dasen 2005 with Roman evidence), who notes over thirty instances of twins in mythology (51) but no triplets. No other figures who are certainly triplets are known to me from Greek mythology. Hesiod's *Theogony* lists more than one group of three sisters fathered by Zeus, including the Fates (904–5) and the Graces (907–11). Aglaea is later called the youngest of the Graces (ὁπλοτάτην Χαρίτων, 946; although Seneca, *Ben.* 1.3.6 calls her the oldest, *Aglaien maximam natu*), but this would not technically preclude them being triplets. The astrological work of Ptolemy says mothers conceive triplet girls under the influence of the Graces, though curiously he goes on to connect these with three heavenly bodies, one of whom requires a sex-change: τρεῖς δὲ θηλείας ὑπὸ τὴν τῶν Χαρίτων Ἀφροδίτη, σελήνη μεθ᾿ Ἑρμοῦ τεθηλυσμένου ('And three females under the [nativity] of the Graces, Venus and the moon [being arrayed] with Mercury made female', *Tetrabiblos* 3.8.3). On the other hand, Zeus certainly made separate visits to Leda to father Polydeuces, the divine one of the Dioscuri twins, and their sister Helen from the egg.

seed (σπέρμα γενναῖον) of Zeus. This is the traditional conception of the Greek wife and mother carried to an extreme. The extravagance of her expression may suggest some resonance with Medea's famous line rejecting such a role:

> ὡς τρὶς ἂν παρ' ἀσπίδα
> στῆναι θέλοιμ' ἂν μᾶλλον ἢ τεκεῖν ἅπαξ.

> I would rather stand three times with a shield in battle than give birth once.
> Eur. *Med.* 250–1

We may further note that she describes her offspring with another verbal noun in -μα, φύτευμα, infrequent but known from both Pindar and tragedy.[28]

Something has gone missing in this schoolboy's writing exercise between the mentions of Minos and Rhadamanthys, though we should perhaps pause to appreciate the point emphasized by Keen, that this was already a famous excerpt when young Apollonios was set the task of copying it: Europa's sense of duty may have been one of the things that made her suitable for edifying the boys. Minos must be dead, and Rhadamanthys is immortal (ἄφθιτος) but unseen (οὐκ ἐν αὐγαῖς ταῖς ἐμαῖς), therefore already in the Isles of the Blest; it is Sarpedon she is really worried about (12–16).

Europa now describes herself as storm-tossed by her thoughts and worries (φροντίσιν χειμάζομαι, 15). The passive verb in this metaphorical sense is well attested in both Sophocles and Euripides;[29] its only occurrence in the Aeschylean corpus, however, is *Prometheus Bound* (563). If this play is not (wholly?) by Aeschylus, the word and image would be at home with the Sophoclean and Euripidean usages as contempories.

In turning to her last remaining son, Europa must now rely on κλέος, on reports from elsewhere (17–23). The lacuna in line 17, accepted by Sommerstein, was first posited by W. S. Barrett.[30] Radically oversimplifed, the basis of Barrett's suggestion is that in the period when Aeschylus is composing, verbal forms in -μα, when describing people, are only used in conjunction with an expressed noun. The metaphorical λωτίσματα is such a form, and therefore, Barrett argues a concrete noun for the warriors must have been in a now missing section. The strength of such a case for the

---

[28] Pind. *O.* 3.18, Soph. *OC* 698.

[29] Soph. *Phil.* 1458–60, *Ichneutae* fr. 314.273, Eur. *Hipp.* 315, *Suppl.* 268–9, *Ion* 966. The use at Ar. *Frogs* 361 is probably paratragic; note also Cratinus' Χειμαζόμενοι.

[30] Barrett 2007: 355–6 (from a paper originally written in the early 1980s).

136   NIALL W. SLATER

lacuna would be undercut if the *Europa* fragment is post-Aeschylean, but Barrett calls our attention to such nouns, which seem unusually frequent in such a short passage. We have already met κλέμμα (with no Aeschylean precedent), the very common σπέρμα, the precedented but infrequent φύτευμα, and now the also unusual λώτισμα, the only other tragic example of which seems to be from Euripides' late play, *Helen* (1593).

Something else is certainly missing between lines 19 and 20 of our fragment, where we now find Europa stating her fears directly: that Sarpedon will lose himself in an uncontrolled heroic rage. Her verb, μαργαίνω, is distinctly Homeric and appears to be *hapax legomenon* in *Il.* 5.882 where Ares is complaining about Diomedes' uncontrolled *aristeia*, wherein he wounds Aphrodite and attacks Ares himself: μαργαίνειν ἀνέηκεν ἐπ' ἀθανάτοισι θεοῖσιν ('[she has incited Diomedes] to vent his rage on immortal gods'). The standard tragic verb is rather μαργάω, though found only in the participial form μαργῶν. Aeschylus certainly uses it thus in the *Seven against Thebes*: Τυδεὺς δὲ μαργῶν καὶ μάχης λελιμμένος ('Tydeus, lusting madly for battle', 380), with several similar examples in Euripides and one in Sophocles. Hence the poet's use of the Homeric *hapax* μαργαίνων here seems quite studied.

The last preserved couplet in the fragment is of particular interest for its depiction of hope.[31] λεπτὴ ἐλπίς (22), light or slender hope, is never well founded in tragedy and before too long becomes something of a cliché.[32] Light or floating hope is then rather queasily combined with an even more familiar metaphor for danger, the razor's edge (22),[33] only to crash on a rock in the very next line. That rock or reef, ἕρμα, is yet one more verbal noun in –μα, from εἴρω; it is, however, certainly good Aeschylean vocabulary (*Ag.* 1007), as is the verb in the clause of fearing, ἐκχέω (*Eum.* 653). The mind nonetheless struggles to reconcile the conflicting metaphors here, as floating hope balances on the razor's edge but then may run aground on the unseen reef or rock and spill forth all of its contents. The speech undoubtedly went on, but the fact that Apollonios' copying assignment ended here suggests that the schoolhouse reception saw this as the emotional climax at least of this phase of Europa's speech.

The aged Europa here is an appealing figure, dignified yet suffering. We cannot know whether the chorus had yet arrived to hear this speech, but

---

[31] See Slater 2018 on comic versus tragic hope in Greek performance.
[32] As it is at Ar. *Eq.* 1244, from a paratragic passage; cf. *Gerytades* fr. 156.11 *PCG*.
[33] Hom. *Il.* 10.172–4, [Simon.] *A.P.* 7.250 = 724–5 *FGE*, Hdt. 6.11.2, Soph. *Aj.* 786 with Finglass 2011 for further parallels.

she seems to speak as much directly to the spectators as to any on-stage audience. While her mention of the rape long ago may serve as much to identify her as anything else, she seems to have dealt with the trauma by framing it almost impersonally, as something that happened to her father the king rather than her – although when she characterises her father as then elderly (πρεσβύτου πατρός, 2), is she projecting something of her own sorrows in present old age[34] onto that past narrative? Everyone has left her: Zeus of course (her partner in parenthood, ξυνάονι, 6, here certainly ironic), Minos by death, Rhadamanthys to realms unseen, and now her only remaining son, whom she must have followed from Crete to Lycia. All she has left is κλέος (17), where the sense of hearsay must already be tinged with the irony of the κλέος that comes to Sarpedon through his death. Now she suffers storms of anxiety and fears insuperable evil (ἀνυπέρβατον ... κακόν, 21). In little more than twenty lines the poet of this play thus invites his audience to contemplate the sufferings of Europa over a woman's full lifecycle, culminating in her role as aged mother awaiting her only surviving son's return. Such a Europa might have spoken with striking effect in the war years of the 420s.

With full awareness of the dangers of circular reasoning, let us turn again briefly to the presumed ending of this play and its possible staging. The return home of Sarpedon's body from the field of battle (by the express command of Zeus as in the *Iliad*) seems the certain climax, and the most theatrically effective means would employ the *mêchanê*. The work of Mastronarde and others has built a strong case that this stage resource is first securely datable at the *Medea* performance of 431.[35] The next two decades see lively experimentation and development, including flying two actors at the same time in Euripides' *Heracles* and *Orestes*. Flying three figures, with two actors as Sleep and Death (though one almost certainly

---

[34] Lyndsay Coo raises the good (if ultimately unanswerable) question of whether Europa must necessarily have been considered 'old' in the play when other tragic women with grown sons and presumably past child-bearing are not so labelled. In one sense costume and mask might have answered that question in the original performance; in another it would be the actor's interpretation and emphasis in such passages as this that would portray her so. Of course, if the play made explicit reference to how Sarpedon could still be ruling, three generations after colonising Lycia, his mother can hardly have been other than elderly.

[35] Mastronarde 1990. Indeed the device that hoisted Medea, a chariot and (at least figures of) the bodies of the children into view (but with no necessary visible horizontal movement) may have been a different contraption from the later *mêchanê*. The assertion of Knox 1977: 206–7 n. 44 = 1979: 319 n. 44 of an 'exact correspondence of all the features of Medea's final appearance with the functions of the *deus* in the later plays' from which he seeks to show it is 'unlikely ... that this can have been the first use of this device' is not well founded.

mute) and a dummy corpse of Sarpedon, may well represent the techno-logical upper limit of what the *mêchanê* could support. All of this seems consistent with a production date for this play in the 420s.

Much in these lines does not seem Aeschylean in either language or dramaturgy, from the tricks of style that reach for tragic sonority but without overall archaic grandeur to the Euripidean directness of the appeal to the audience. Yet one can also believe that they would have been enough for an audience that, as West says, 'will have wanted to believe that they were getting more Aeschylus'.[36] This nobly suffering queen might well have appealed strongly to more traditional elements in the audience, for whom Euripides' women were too daring and perhaps even Sophocles' heroines too morally complex. If this fragment is indeed from an artist trying to compete with them, it does seem possible that, on any given festival day, he might have had his chance.

[36] West 1990: 69.

9 | When Mothers Turn Bad

The Perversion of the Maternal Ideal in Sophocles' Eurypylus

ROBERT COWAN

On Bad Mothers, Perversions and Inversions

'Bad mothers like Klytaimestra and Eriphyle are exceptions that prove the rule.'[1] Although Henderson cites in support of this sentiment an admirably broad range of mothers from fragmentary as well as extant tragedy, it is hard to agree with it, or with his reasons for excluding figures such as Medea, Procne, Ino and, most importantly for this chapter, Astyoche, from the category of bad mothers. Recent years have seen a growth in scholarship on the depiction of mothers in tragedy,[2] as part of the wider topic of the actual and idealised roles of mothers in Athenian society.[3] Some studies have concentrated on tragic women before and immediately following childbirth, but the focus of this chapter will be on mothers with grown-up children.[4] I explore how the fragmentary plays contribute to our understanding of the depiction of mothers and the maternal ideal in tragedy more broadly. The specific focus will be on what I shall term the martial mother ideal and its depiction, or rather perversion, in Sophocles' *Eurypylus*. First, however, it will be necessary to think a little about tragic bad mothers, about perversion and about the martial mother ideal itself.

The majority of bad mothers in Attic tragedy act in ways that are inversions rather than perversions of the maternal ideal. Although 'inverted' and 'perverted' are often used almost interchangeably in tragic scholarship, a distinction can, in many cases, usefully be drawn between instances where a character performs the precise opposite of normative behaviour, and those where that normative behaviour is enacted but in a distorted manner or to negative ends. Wright has written of 'tragedy's tendency to pervert positive experiences into negative ones' as part of his discussion of how the emotion of joy (χαρά and ἡδονή) in Sophocles' *Electra* is not inverted or replaced by grief or pain, but rather displayed

[1] Henderson 1987: 112.

[2] Foley 2001: 272–99, Bodiou *et al.* 2005, McHardy 2005, Sebillotte Cuchet 2006, Tzanetou 2012.

[3] Demand 1994, Loraux 1998, Damet 2011. Alaux 1995 focuses on sons, Leduc 2011 on the relationship between the two.

[4] Hall 2006: 60–98, especially 67–80, Zeitlin 2008.

in contexts, triggered by causes, and productive of effects far removed from the normative ideal.[5] Plot structures too can be perverted, as Dugdale writes of *Oedipus the King* that 'Oedipus' story is a perversion of the heroic journey'.[6] Again, we are not dealing with inversion, where the Sphinx kills Oedipus, or failure, where Oedipus does not return to Thebes, does not marry the royal bride, or is not recognised as the long-lost prince. Rather it is the successful fulfilment of all these plot-motifs, with awful results, which constitutes the perversion.

Probably the most common site of perversion in the plays themselves and in the scholarship on them is ritual. In particular, sacrifice is success-fully performed in tragedy, but its form (substituting human for animal, inside not outside) and results (division rather than solidarity) mark it as a perversion.[7] Perhaps most relevant to the current argument is the tragic perversion of marriage ritual. As Seaford in particular has shown, the tragic wedding does not arbitrarily substitute death as a grim perversion of the bridegroom, but rather permits the domination of the very anxiety about death whose suppression the wedding ritual dramatises.[8] The perversion, in a peculiarly tragic fashion, acknowledges the tensions and anxieties latent in a positive practice, experience or emotion, and enacts the worst-case scenario's surfacing and coming to fruition. It would be absurd to draw too sharp a distinction between inversion and perversion, and in many cases there is significant overlap or even blur-ring between the two. Yet for others, it is useful to note the difference between a norm that is replaced by its polar opposite and one that is fulfilled to negative ends. The maternal ideal – or at least one aspect of it – is one of these.

To return to bad mothers in tragedy, the majority of these, as noted earlier, are inversions of the maternal ideal. This inversion, primarily the tendency to harm or even kill offspring instead of nurturing or protecting them, is often explicit, combined with a denial that the mother deserves the name of mother. Both Aeschylus' and Sophocles' Electras describe

---

[5] Wright 2005: 178.

[6] Dugdale 2015: 432.

[7] For perverted sacrifice in tragedy see Zeitlin 1965, Burkert 1966 = 2001: 1–36 = 2001–11: VII 1–36, Vidal-Naquet 1972 ≈ 1988, Seaford 1989 = 2018: 3–14, 1994: 369–88, Henrichs 2000, Gibert 2003.

[8] 'The association with death, one of the negative tendencies which in a normal wedding would be overcome in the rituals of transition and incorporation, has in the tragedy emerged as a triumphant reality' (Seaford 1987: 110 = 2018: 264, on Creon's daughter in Euripides' *Medea*). For the tragic wedding see also Rehm 1994, Mitchell-Boyask 2006, Swift 2009.

Clytemnestra in these terms. The former calls her 'my mother, possessing an ungodly attitude to her children by no means suited to that name' (ἐμή γε μήτηρ, οὐδαμῶς ἐπώνυμον | φρόνημα παισὶ δύσθεον πεπαμένη, *Cho.* 190–1), while the latter declares that 'she is called "mother"; but she is in no way like a mother' (μήτηρ καλεῖται· μητρὶ δ' οὐδὲν ἐξισοῖ, *El.* 1194), summing her up with the famous oxymoron 'unmotherly mother' (μήτηρ ἀμήτωρ, 1154).[9] Only slightly less explicit is the exchange in Euripides' *Medea* between Medea and Jason following the infanticide:

> Ια. ὦ τέκνα φίλτατα. Μη. μητρί γε, σοὶ δ' οὔ.
> Ια. κἄπειτ' ἔκανες; Μη. σέ γε πημαίνουσ'.
>
> Jas.: O dearest children!   Med.: To their mother, but not to you.
> Jas.: And because of that you killed them?   Med.: Yes, to grieve *you*.
>
> Eur. Med. 1397–8

There is considerable complexity, if not contradiction, in Medea's position, as she denies Jason's relationship with their children while almost simultaneously declaring it her reason for killing them.[10] Yet, for the present issue, the key point is the way that Jason's κἄπειτα articulates the paradox, not just that someone would kill those dearest, most closely tied (φίλτατα) to them, but specifically that a mother (μητρί) should do so. It is virtually certain that several of the bad mothers of fragmentary tragedy were also inversions of the maternal ideal. Certainly Euripides' eponymous Ino and the Procne of Sophocles' *Tereus* kill rather than nurture their children, though whether the specifically inverted nature of their actions was explicitly articulated cannot be determined from the surviving fragments.[11]

---

[9] For Clytemnestra as mother in the *Oresteia* see Chesi 2014; in *Electra*, Strubbe 1993.

[10] Cf. Luschnig 2007: 116 on how 'the children go back and forth between their parents in this grotesque parody of care and nurture of children' as 'the two parents vie over love for the children and responsibility for their deaths'.

[11] *Tereus* fr. 589 shows someone, perhaps a *deus ex machina*, expressing moral disapproval of Procne and Philomela's actions. Yet the emphasis seems to be on the disproportionate retaliation against Tereus (ἄνους ἐκεῖνος· αἱ δ' ἀνουστέρ<ως> ἔτι, 'He was deranged but they [acted] still more derangedly', 1; μεῖζον ... τῆς νόσου τὸ φάρμακον, 'the remedy greater than the disease', 4) rather than the treatment of Itys, and in any case Procne's unmotherly behaviour is not explicitly mentioned in the surviving lines. If P.Oxy. 5131 is correctly attributed to Euripides' *Ino*, it offers a number of insights into the complex of infanticides already detailed in Hyg. *Fab.* 4 (on which see Finglass 2014, 2017c, and especially 2016a) but no clear indication of how the play depicted the eponymous character's actions, either in killing her son, Melicertes, or in engineering her rival Themisto's unwitting murder of *her* sons (Finglass 2016a: 309–11).

The Martial Mother and Her Inversions

This chapter will focus on perversion rather than inversion, and more specifically the perversion of one particular aspect of the maternal ideal, which for brevity and convenience I shall term the martial mother ideal. This aspect is clearly formulated by Mastronarde in his description of Theseus' mother, Aethra, in Euripides' *Suppliant Women*, as one who 'embodies the behavior expected of citizen women by the official discourse of the polis: to bear male citizens to fight for the city and to send them off willingly into danger'.[12] Other examples of the normative performance of this ideal are unfortunately lacking in extant tragedy and hard to reconstruct confidently from fragments, but it is clearly paralleled, and arguably even allegorised, by the more literal ritual sacrifice of offspring (male or, more often, female) to secure the divinely sanctioned salvation of the city.[13] The parallelism between the two is made explicit by Praxithea in Euripides' *Erechtheus*:

> εἰ δ' ἦν ἐν οἴκοις ἀντὶ θηλειῶν στάχυς
> ἄρσην, πόλιν δὲ πολεμία κατεῖχε φλόξ,
> οὐκ ἄν νιν ἐξέπεμπον εἰς μάχην δορός,
> θάνατον προταρβοῦσ'; ἀλλ' ἔμοιγ' εἴη τέκνα,
> <ἃ> καὶ μάχοιτο καὶ μετ' ἀνδράσιν πρέποι,
> μὴ σχήματ' ἄλλως ἐν πόλει πεφυκότα.
> τὰ μητέρων δὲ δάκρυ' ὅταν πέμπηι τέκνα,
> πολλοὺς ἐθήλυν' εἰς μάχην ὁρμωμένους.
> μισῶ γυναῖκας αἵτινες πρὸ τοῦ καλοῦ
> ζῆν παῖδας εἵλοντ' ἢ παρήινεσαν κακά.

> If there were in my household, instead of females, a male
> crop, and the fire of war had hold of the city,
> would I not send them out into spear-battle,
> fearing in advance their death? Rather let *me* have children
> who would both fight and be conspicuous among men,
> not merely images who have been born in the city.
> Whenever mothers' tears send forth children,
> they feminise many who are hastening to battle.
> I hate any women who, in preference to what is fine,
> choose that their children live or exhort them to wicked deeds.
> Eur. *Erechtheus* fr. 360.22–31

---

[12] Mastronarde 2010: 257, but note Foley 2001: 279 'In instilling military courage into her son, her actions are perhaps more typical in Greek tradition of the Spartan mother, who was famed for this role.'

[13] Foley 1985, O'Connor-Visser 1987, Kearns 1990, Wilkins 1990.

Praxithea justifies her willingness to sacrifice her daughters to save Athens from Thracian attack by asserting that, if she had borne sons, she would have similarly sent them to die in battle for the city.[14] The parallel with death in battle is also made by Menoeceus in *Phoenician Women*, who considers it shameful (αἰσχρόν) to run away when those unbound by oracles stand side-by-side behind their shields.[15] In assessing this maternal ideal, its inversions and perversions, it will be helpful to make use of example of literal sacrifice.

Examples of the inversion of the martial mother motif, where mothers (and sometimes fathers) refuse to sacrifice their offspring, literally or otherwise, to save the city, are reasonably common in extant and fragmentary tragedy. Creon in *Phoenician Women*, the eponymous hero in *Erechtheus*, and both Agamemnon and Clytemnestra in *Iphigenia at Aulis* are obvious examples of parental resistance to the literal sacrifice of, respectively, Menoeceus, the Erechtheidae and Iphigenia for the greater good.[16] A mother's refusal to send her son to war is exemplified in Euripides' *Scyrians*, whose hypothesis writes of the time 'when Thetis learned the fate of her son Achilles, wanting to keep him from the expedition against Ilion' (Θέτιδος τοῦ παιδὸς Ἀχιλλέω[ς τὴν εἱμαρ]μένην ἐπεγνωκυίας, τῆ[ς πρὸς ῎Ιλι]ον στρατείας αὐτον ἀ[πείργειν θέ]λουσα, test iia.12–15). Yet these inversions are clearly quite different from the total upending of the very idea of motherhood represented by the cruelty and neglect of a Clytemnestra or the infanticide of a Medea or Procne. Even proclamations of the ideal explicitly or implicitly acknowledge the conflicting maternal ideal, familial rather than political, natural rather than cultural, that a mother might wish to protect and save her offspring. Theseus in *Suppliant Women* bases his own resolve to fight at Thebes on the *a fortiori* argument that his enemies would criticise him if he should do otherwise when he is sent into battle *even by his mother*, i.e. one who might be expected to discourage him out of maternal feeling.[17] More stridently, Praxithea acknowledges the existence, even as she expresses her loathing, of

---

[14] For Praxithea see Harder 2006, Sebillotte Cuchet 2006, Calame 2011, Coo, pp. 51–9.

[15] Eur. *Phoen.* 999–1005. See also Wilkins 1990: 179–80, who further notes the connection between literal and non-literal self-sacrifice made at Plut. *Pelop.* 21–2.

[16] Creon: *Phoen.* 962–76; Agamemnon: *IA* 378–401; Clytemnestra: *IA* 1164–1208. Erechtheus' resistance can be deduced from Praxithea's refutation of objections in fr. 360, which is addressed to him (Kamerbeek 1991: 114).

[17] Eur. *Suppl.* 343–5 τί γάρ μ' ἐροῦσιν οἵ γε δυσμενεῖς βροτῶν, | ὅθ' ἡ τεκοῦσα χὐπερορρωδοῦσ' ἐμοῦ | πρώτη κελεύεις τόνδ' ὑποστῆναι πόνον; ('For what will those among men who are my enemies say of me, when you, who bore me and are afraid for me, are the first to command me to undertake this labour?').

mothers who choose that their children live. We are then dealing here with a civic maternal ideal which is itself an inversion of a personal – one might even dare to say natural – maternal ideal. Indeed, many critics have found Praxithea's willingness, or rather determination, to sacrifice her daughter deeply problematic.[18] The conflict between personal and civic maternal ideals in this area throws into question Tzanetou's otherwise attractive assertion that 'mothers who do not appear to act in concert with the aims of Athenian civic ideology are represented in negative terms, as vengeful, nonnurturing, and harmful toward their offspring'.[19] At one end of the spectrum we have the hyper-civic Praxithea, and at the other the hyper-personal Hecabe, who declares 'Polyxena is my *polis*'.[20] Each of these extremes, these mutual inversions of each other's ideal, enables audiences to interrogate the space in between, but another perspective is provided by perversions of the martial mother ideal.

Perverting the Martial Mother: Sophocles' *Eurypylus*

By the definition of perversion that we have already established, the external form of the ideal would be accomplished, but there would be something amiss about its motivation, enactment, result or all three. A perverted martial mother would be one who does send her son into battle but who does so either for reasons other than civic duty, by negative means or with an outcome that does not contribute to the salvation of the city. One potential candidate for such a role would be Eriphyle, who sent her husband Amphiaraus to war at Thebes as one of the Seven, and possibly also her son Alcmaeon as one of the Epigoni. Her motivation was not civic duty but bribery, first with the necklace of Harmonia by Polynices, and then by his son, Thersander, with the same queen's *peplos*.[21] Neither expedition was a glorious defence of the city, but rather fratricidal wars between claimants to the Theban throne. The outcome likewise was not

---

[18] E.g. Harder 2006: 157 '[Praxithea] denies herself her role as a mother, who is expected to protect and cherish her child'.

[19] Tzanetou 2012: 110.

[20] Eur. *Hec.* 280–1: 'an utterance that would be impossible and virtually forbidden to women in Athens outside of the theater – women, who do not have the title of "citizen" but must devote themselves to the city. Hecuba, it is true, is queen and barbarian . . .' (Loraux 1998: 40).

[21] The sources for the second bribery are late (Diod. Sic. 4.66.3, Apollod. *Bibl.* 3.7.2) and there are problems over the logic of the sequence of events (Gantz 1993: 524–5), but they are not insuperable; see further Sommerstein 2012: 26–34, Davies and Finglass 2014: 344–8.

salvation of the city but the failure and destruction of the Argive army in
the first war, and Alcmaeon's vengeful matricide of Eriphyle before or after
the second. Some aspect of the conflict between Eriphyle and her son was
almost certainly dramatised in Sophocles' and Euripides' *Epigoni* and the
former's *Eriphyle* (if indeed it was a different play from *Epigoni*), as well as
being an important part of the background to Alcmaeon's later career as
depicted in the latter's *Alcmaeon in Psophis* and *Alcmaeon in Corinth*.[22]
However, the surviving fragments of these plays offer little further indication of how these themes might have been developed and so we can only
speculate from the broad outline of the myth that Eriphyle's actions might
have been portrayed in this way.[23]

A more promising instance of the perverted martial mother is Astyoche
in Sophocles' *Eurypylus* and it is to a case study of this play that the
remainder of this chapter will be devoted. The story of the wife of Telephus
and sister of Priam, who was bribed by the latter to send her son Eurypylus
to fight at Troy, where he was killed by Neoptolemus, is already alluded to
in the *Odyssey* and the *Little Iliad*, passages to which we shall return.[24]
Unfortunately, there is minimal iconographic evidence to help flesh out the
picture.[25] However, a fragment of the mythographer Acusilaus, preserved
in a scholion on the *Odyssey* passage, provides a reasonably detailed and
early version of the story:

Εὐρύπυλος ὁ Ἀστυόχης καὶ Τηλέφου τοῦ Ἡρακλέους παῖς λαχὼν τὴν
πατρώιαν ἀρχὴν τῆς Μυσίας προΐσταται. πυθόμενος δὲ Πρίαμος περὶ τῆς
τούτου δυνάμεως ἔπεμψεν ὡς αὐτὸν ἵνα παραγένηται σύμμαχος. εἰπόντος
δὲ αὐτοῦ ὡς οὐκ ἐξὸν αὐτῶι διὰ τὴν μητέρα, ἔπεμψεν ὁ Πρίαμος τῆι μητρὶ
αὐτοῦ δῶρον {Ἀστυόχηι} χρυσῆν ἄμπελον. ἡ δὲ λαβοῦσα τὴν ἄμπελον τὸν
υἱὸν ἔπεμψεν ἐπὶ στρατείαν. Νεοπτόλεμος δὲ ὁ τοῦ Ἀχιλλέως αὐτὸν ἀναιρεῖ.

Eurypylus, the son of Astyoche and of Telephus the son of Heracles,
inheriting his father's dominion, ruled over Mysia. When Priam learnt

[22] For Sophocles' *Epigoni* see Kiso 1977, Mülke 2007 on P.Oxy. 4807, Sommerstein 2012.
[23] Soph. *Epigoni* fr. 189 does have someone, probably Alcmaeon, address a female character,
almost certainly Eriphyle, as 'O woman who has had the effrontery to do everything and more',
which Sommerstein 2012: 68 takes as a reference to the second bribe. However, in fr. 187.1
(ἀνδροκτόνου γυναικός, 'husband-slaying woman') Alcmaeon emphasises her crime towards
Amphiaraus rather than himself.
[24] I omit discussion of the substantial Eurypylus episode in Quint. Smyrn. *Posthom.* 6, which is so
late as to be of doubtful value for the interpretation of Sophocles, and in any case gives Astyoche
a very small role.
[25] Zagdoun and Gondicas 1988; but see Lloyd-Jones 1992 = 2005: 106–9 for a suggestion that two
late sixth-century hydrias by the Antimenes painter may depict Eurypylus as dying alongside
Helicaon, which would account for the reference to two corpses at fr. 210.47–53.

of his power, he sent to him to come to his side as an ally. When he said that he could not because of his mother, Priam sent to his mother a gift of a golden vine. She took the vine and sent her son to fight, and Neoptolemus the son of Achilles killed him.

Acusilaus fr. 40a EGM

Some elements of the story remain elusive, most tantalisingly the detail that Astyoche was initially a hindrance to Telephus' fighting at Troy (οὐκ ἐξὸν αὐτῶι διὰ τὴν μητέρα), which could suggest an internal conflict over her decision whether to accede to Priam's request. However, the outline is clear and corresponds closely to our definition of the perversion of the martial mother ideal, as a mother sends her son into battle for the wrong reasons with disastrous results. A *Eurypylus* by Sophocles is not attested in any testimonia, but the tragedy of that name listed by Aristotle among those deriving from the *Little Iliad* has been generally accepted as his.[26] The sole book fragment, from Plutarch (*On Controlling Anger* 458d), was massively added to by substantial fragments preserved on P.Oxy. 1175, published in 1912. The largest and most coherent parts of this contain a scene in which a messenger reports the aftermath of Eurypylus' death to Astyoche while she and the chorus react, and it is from this scene that most of the evidence for Sophocles' depiction of the perverted martial mother ideal comes. I shall discuss how the perversion is depicted through its result, its motivation and its means, before reflecting on the dramatic depiction of Astyoche's actions and drawing some provisional conclusions.

Perverted Result: Not Saving the City

To understand how Sophocles depicts the result of Astyoche's perversion of the martial mother ideal, we need to note *Eurypylus'* affinity with one more subgenre of tragedy. In addition to the sacrifice tragedies discussed earlier, the play also has much in common with what Christ has termed 'recruitment dramas', plays that depict the issues surrounding 'conscription and draft evasion', with obvious relevance to contemporary Athenian concerns.[27] While sacrifice dramas generally involve an immediate response to a war in which the prospective victim's *polis* is already engaged, the

---

[26] Arist. *Poet.* 1459b6. For the play see Goerschen 1975, Nicolosi 1976, Ozbek 2006, Iovine 2016, 2017, Finglass 2019a: 48–54.

[27] Christ 2004: 43–55, including discussion of both Sophocles' and Euripides' *Scyrians*, but not *Eurypylus*, perhaps because Eurypylus' recruitment probably preceded the action of the play.

background of *Eurypylus* deals with the eponymous hero's decision to travel from neutral Mysia to Troy and engage in a war to which he is not otherwise committed, a closer parallel to common scenarios in recruitment dramas. It is tempting to speculate that the play might have drawn parallels with the recruitment of his eventual killer, Neoptolemus, to fight against Troy.[28] Only tiny scraps of evidence for this survive, but the concentration within ten lines of the traces λυκο[('?Lycomedes', fr. 206.8), ἐλθόν[τ ('coming', 206.15) and Σκύρου.[('?from Scyros', 206.19) do indicate that Neoptolemus' journey to Troy from his grandfather's kingdom was at least mentioned. Any more elaborate description of Neoptolemus' recruitment involving the depiction of his mother Deidamia as a parallel or foil to Astyoche, perhaps alluding to Sophocles' own *Scyrians*, must remain speculative, though by no means improbable.[29] It also seems clear from a number of fragments that repeated references to Telephus and Achilles in the play set up the fatal duel between Eurypylus and Neoptolemus as a replay and perversion of the two confrontations, one violent, one healing, between their fathers. We shall return later to the wider significance of Telephus in the play, but this parallelism offers further support for the attractive possibility that the recruitments of the two young heroes were compared and contrasted.

Whether or not Neoptolemus' recruitment was emphasised in the play, it was surely Eurypylus' which was of central importance, and this brings us to one of the key criteria for the perversion of the martial mother motif: the failure of the intended outcome. Both plot patterns to which *Eurypylus* is closely related, the non-familial recruitment drama and the familial human-sacrifice drama, tend to be closely tied to the salvation of the city or other community.[30] In the only extant recruitment drama, Sophocles' own *Philoctetes*, Odysseus responds to Neoptolemus' question as to whether he does not think it disgraceful to lie by declaring 'Not if lying brings salvation' (οὔκ, εἰ τὸ σωθῆναί γε τὸ ψεῦδος φέρει, 109). While the ethics of Odysseus' tactics are, to say the least, problematised, we miss much of the moral complexity of the play if we lose sight of the fact that, however Machiavellian his means, his end is the admirable one of saving the Greeks at Troy from disaster, a fate to which the noble Philoctetes and Neoptolemus seem content to abandon them. The motif of saving the community, often with an explicit use of the verb σώιζω, recurs in all the

---

[28] For Neoptolemus' role in the play see Sommerstein 2010b: 265–6.
[29] Christ 2004: 52 cites evidence that, in *Scyrians*, 'Neoptolemus' grandfather, Lycomedes, and his mother, Deidameia, probably opposed his going'.
[30] For saving the city see Kearns 1990.

sacrifice dramas discussed above, as in Iphigenia's plea to Achilles, 'Let me save Greece, if I can.'[31]

Eurypylus' defeat and death at the hands of Neoptolemus is not in itself a mark of the plot pattern's perversion. Literal victims and 'sacrificial' warriors (though not necessarily other 'recruits') must by definition die as substitution sacrifices for the survival of the community. The problem with Eurypylus' death is that it does *not* save Troy. More than that, both imagery and explicit statement depict it as symbolising and even contributing to the city's destruction. Coo notes how Eurypylus fits into a pattern of parallelism in Sophocles' Trojan plays between the death of its champions and the fall of the city itself, so that his 'death is imbued with a strong sense of finality for Troy'.[32] An explicit articulation of this notion is made by Priam in the lament over his nephew's corpse, which a messenger reports to Astyoche and the chorus:

> "οἴμοι, τέκνον, πρ[ο]ύδωκά σ' ἐσχάτη[ν ἔ]χων
> Φρυξὶν μεγίστην <τ'> ἐλπίδων σωτη[ρία]ν."

'Alas, my child, I have betrayed you, having in you the last
and greatest salvation of the hopes for the Phrygians.'

Soph. *Eurypylus* fr. 210.76–7

Eurypylus' potential to act as a conventional city-saviour is asserted as he is called not even personal σωτήρ ('saviour') but abstract σωτηρία ('salvation'). However, Priam's betrayal leads to an inversion of the desired result, as salvation is not only not attained, but its very possibility – its last and greatest chance – thrown away. The inversion of the result does not mean that, within the terms set for this argument, this is the inversion rather than the perversion of the whole martial mother ideal. As with perverted sacrifice, the significant action is completed and the outcome, not the action itself, is inverted.[33] We might also compare Seaford's analysis of the tragic wedding, which dramatises the realisation of the underlying anxieties about death that normative wedding ritual acknowledges but overcomes.[34] In a similar fashion, the motif of the martial mother and her son the city-saviour acknowledges anxieties about the destruction of the city (conceptualised as men and not walls without

---

[31] Eur. *IA* 1420 ἔα δὲ σῶσαί μ' Ἑλλάδ', ἢν δυνώμεθα; cf. *Phoen.* 997, *Hcld.* 402, *Erechtheus* fr. 360.42.

[32] Coo 2011a: 11.

[33] Cf. Seaford 1994: 370 on Aeschylus' *Agamemnon*: 'In sacrificing Agamemnon Klytaimestra perverts the sacrifice, as an expression of household solidarity, into its opposite.'

[34] See n. 8 above.

men) through the fall of its young men in battle, but transmutes them into a form of substitution sacrifice whereby the death of the young leads to the salvation of the city as a whole. In *Eurypylus'* perversion of this motif, the anxiety is fulfilled as both youth and city fall.

Perverted Motive: Women's Gifts

Astyoche's failure to save the city by sending Eurypylus to war perverts the normative outcome of the martial mother motif, but its motivation is also perverted. Like Eriphyle, but unlike the normative martial mother, Astyoche does not send her son into battle from a sense of civic duty, but because she is bribed. This is the aspect of the story that is most prominent in other extant allusions, most notably in the early epic tradition, and although the surviving fragments of Sophocles' play preserve no explicit references to the golden vine, it is hard to imagine that it did not feature.[35] In the *nekyia*, when Odysseus is recounting Neoptolemus' achievements at Troy to the shade of his proud father, he gives special prominence to Eurypylus:

πάντας δ' οὐκ ἂν ἐγὼ μυθήσομαι οὐδ' ὀνομήνω,
ὅσσον λαὸν ἔπεφνεν ἀμύνων Ἀργείοισιν,
ἀλλ' οἷον τὸν Τηλεφίδην κατενήρατο χαλκῶι,
ἥρω' Εὐρύπυλον, πολλοὶ δ' ἀμφ' αὐτὸν ἑταῖροι
Κήτειοι κτείνοντο γυναίων εἵνεκα δώρων.
κεῖνον δὴ κάλλιστον ἴδον μετὰ Μέμνονα δῖον.

I could not recount nor name all those,
as great a mass as he slew defending the Argives,
and such a man as the son of Telephus he cut down with bronze,
the hero Eurypylus, and many comrades around him,
Keteians, were killed on account of women's gifts.
He was the most beautiful I saw after godlike Memnon.

Hom. *Od.* 11.517–22

The emphasis placed on Astyoche's role in the episode is surprising in the context of magnifying Neoptolemus' κλέος and underlines its motivic

---

[35] Lyndsay Coo and Guy Smoot have independently suggested to me the possible parallelism between the golden vine and the vine that Telephus tripped over before being wounded by Achilles (Apollod. *Ep.* 3.17). That our play might have mentioned the episode is perfectly possible but the only potential surviving trace is the word σφαλῇις ('you tripped'?) at fr. 219a.79.6.

significance, perhaps resonating with Agamemnon's sufferings at the hands of Clytemnestra and Odysseus' anxieties about Penelope. Certainly the phrase γυναίων εἴνεκα δώρων is not only allusive, but ambiguous. The adjective suggests not merely gifts given to a specific woman but the sort of gifts women in general would accept, an implication supported by the generalising plural and confirmed by the use of exactly the same formula at 15.247 to refer to Amphiaraus' death as a result of Eriphyle's bribery with Harmonia's necklace.[36] Odysseus genders bribes as feminine. Astyoche may be perverting one maternal ideal, but she does so by fulfilling another female stereotype.

Yet however much Odysseus may generalise about 'women's gifts', the specifics of Astyoche's bribe are immensely significant. Like the necklace of Harmonia, which was Eriphyle's bribe, the golden vine combines the intrinsic value of precious metal, the prestige of divine craftsmanship and the ornamental quality of a trinket that would stereotypically appeal to a woman. Also like Harmonia's necklace, the golden vine has a history, as a fragment from the *Little Iliad* relates:

> ἄμπελον, ἥν Κρονίδης ἔπορεν οὗ παιδὸς ἄποινα
> χρυσείην, φύλλοισιν ἀγαυοῖσιν κομόωσαν
> βότρυσί θ', οὓς Ἥφαιστος ἐπασκήσας Διὶ πατρί
> δῶχ', ὃ δὲ Λαομέδοντι πόρεν Γανυμήδεος ἀντί.

> The vine, which the son of Cronus gave as compensation for his son,
> a golden one, tressed with noble leaves
> and grape-clusters, which Hephaestus fashioned and gave
> to Father Zeus, and which he gave to Laomedon in compensation for
>   Ganymede.

> *Little Iliad* fr. 6 GEF

The notion of the vine as a commodity offered in exchange for Laomedon's son Ganymede is overdetermined in this short passage (παιδὸς ἄποινα, Γανυμήδεος ἀντί) and the parallelism with Astyoche's acceptance of it in exchange for her son, Eurypylus is obvious. As Lyons puts it, 'the golden vine is twice called upon to induce a parent to part with a son'.[37] As well as being a sacrifice and an act of recruitment, Astyoche's transaction is also an instance of the tragic motif of perverted exchange.[38] Most studies focus on

---

[36] For possible relationships between the stories in early epic see Brown 1997: 42–3, Tsagalis 2014.

[37] Lyons 2012: 70. Her assertion of a strong contrast between the judgment placed on Laomedon and on Astyoche is less persuasive.

[38] For tragic exchange see Rabinowitz 1993, Seaford 1994, Wohl 1998, Ormand 1999, 2015, Lyons 2003, 2012.

the exchange – and hence objectification and commodification – of women, but the traffic in sons is also a feature of tragedy. The striking image from the first stasimon of Aeschylus' *Agamemnon* casts Ares as a 'gold-changer of bodies' (χρυσαμοιβὸς ... σωμάτων, 437/8) who exchanges men for ashes and urns, as 'the violence of commodity fetishism ... recoils upon the male exchangers, and ... men are weighed out to make up the price of a bad deal'.[39] Yet in *Eurypylus*, the transaction is more literally body for gold, a life's value balanced against precious metal. We cannot know if Sophocles used the *Little Iliad*'s image of ἄποινα, but if so, Astyoche is perversely receiving compensation for Eurypylus' death before he dies, or rather as a bribe to cause his death. It is also tempting to see more direct perversion of the martial mother ideal. The literal sacrifice of an Erectheid and the metaphorical sacrifice of an Athenian hoplite were conceptualised as substitutions, reciprocal exchanges with the gods of one life for the community.[40] As a variation on this, Menoeceus speaks of himself as 'about to give the gift of his death – no mean one – to the city' (θανάτου δῶρον οὐκ αἰσχρὸν πόλει | δώσων, Eur. *Phoen.* 1013–14) and Iphigenia as 'giving [her] body to Greece' (δίδωμι σῶμα τοὐμὸν Ἑλλάδι, *IA* 1397). Astyoche's exchange of Eurypylus, not for the city, but for the golden vine, and her acceptance of a gift *for* her son rather allowing him to offer himself, pervert both these motifs.

Perverted Motive and Means: Privileging Natal Over Conjugal Kin

Astyoche's action in exchanging son for vine not only parallels Laomedon's; it also reverses it. Laomedon's acceptance of the vine from Zeus validates the transaction whereby the male offspring Ganymede is lost to the Trojan royal household. Astyoche accepts the vine from the current head of the Trojan royal household, Priam, and provides a substitute male offspring to replace Ganymede. Yet in doing so, she removes Eurypylus from the Mysian royal household and from the *oikos* of Telephus, the more emphatically so if the play included the detail, preserved in a scholion on Juvenal, that Eurypylus' fighting at Troy broke an oath by Telephus henceforth to stay out of the

---

[39] Wohl 1998: 97.

[40] Eur. *Erechtheus* fr. 360.18 προπάντων μίαν ὕπερ δοῦναι θανεῖν ('to give one girl to die on behalf of all'), 51–2 ἀντὶ γὰρ ψυχῆς μιᾶς | οὐκ ἔσθ' ὅπως οὐ τήνδ' ἐγὼ σώσω πόλιν ('at the cost of a single life it is not possible that I will not save this city').

war.[41] Astyoche herself was of course born into the Trojan royal household. She is Laomedon's daughter, Priam's (and Ganymede's) sister, as well as Telephus' wife. As such, her action fits into the common tragic pattern whereby a woman privileges her natal over her conjugal kin.[42] Here we have the third way in which Astyoche perverts the martial mother ideal, a combination of dubious motivation and negative means.

Both extant and fragmentary tragedy offer examples of women privileging their natal over their conjugal families.[43] Such privileging, like incest, which is an extreme form of it, can be aligned with a discourse that values endogamy and the preservation of the royal or aristocratic *oikos* over the democratic associations of exogamy and the establishment of ties of *philia* with the wider *polis*.[44] Astyoche's action in this respect thus carries a considerable political charge. Figures such as Sophocles' Antigone and Aeschylus' Danaids are of course relevant here.[45] However, the most illuminating parallels are the mothers who kill their children because they place greater value on their natal family. Medea, as always, is something of an exception, and the multiple, shifting relationships that she constructs and destroys with her children, her husband Jason and her natal kin, as represented by her father Aeetes and especially her grandfather Helios make her a slippery comparand.[46] More suggestive are the figures of Althaea, who featured in Phrynichus' *Pleuronian Women* and the *Meleager* plays of both Sophocles and Euripides, and Procne in Sophocles' *Tereus*. Althaea demonstrates her preference for her natal kin when she kills her son Meleager to avenge his killing of her brothers. Procne avenges her husband Tereus' rape and mutilation of her sister Philomela (and perhaps the honour of their father, Pandion) by killing and serving to him the flesh of their son Itys.[47]

---

[41] Σ Juv. 6.655 (p. 118.11–23 Wessner). Sommerstein 2010b: 265–6 suggests that this is the reason for Astyoche's assertion that she has committed a capital crime, but her claim is amply justified by other aspects of her behaviour.

[42] Only McHardy 2005: 149–50 notes this aspect of the story, though I would disagree with her suggestion that Astyoche, along with Pacuvius' Iliona, 'show a more *subconscious* preference for their natal families' (p. 149; my italics).

[43] Visser 1986, Seaford 1990, S. West 1999, Holland 2003: 270–2, McHardy 2005, Coo 2013a.

[44] I use endogamy and exogamy here to refer to marriage inside and outside the *kinship* group, but within the wider *polis*. The distinction between marriage inside and outside the *citizen* group was quite differently valorised in fifth-century Athens.

[45] See especially *Ant.* 904–15 with Maitland 1992: 33 on 'the ties that married women must have retained with their natal households, ties potentially dangerous in a dynastic context. Nothing could be further removed from the interests of the community'.

[46] For Medea and her kin see Visser 1986, Holland 2003: 270–2, McHardy 2005: 135–41.

[47] Coo 2013a asserts the importance of Philomela for Procne's motivation in response to emphasis elsewhere (Burnett 1998: 184, 187, Fitzpatrick and Sommerstein 2006: 153–5) on Pandion. See

The parallels with Astyoche – sibling more important than husband and son – are clear, but the differences are not limited to that between actual murder and mere putting in harm's way. In the process of dissociating themselves from their conjugal families and realigning with their natal ones, Procne emphatically and Althaea more subtly also dissociate their sons from themselves and align them exclusively with their husbands. We might compare the process, particularly prominent in the *Oresteia*, whereby the relationship of son to mother is denied as a means of justifying matricide and more broadly privileging patriarchal and masculine values over maternal and feminine.[48] Here it is the mother who severs the tie in order to justify filicide. Procne punishes Tereus by murdering *his* son and thus avenging *her* sister. Althaea's vengeance is directed at Meleager himself rather than at his father Oeneus, but still involves an implicit or explicit denial of her own maternal relationship. Unfortunately, the surviving fragments of these plays offer no explicit statement of this notion, but we can, with due caution, note two suggestive lines from the Procne and Althaea episodes of Ovid's *Metamorphoses*, which do not merely treat the same stories, but are self-consciously 'tragic'.[49] Ovid's Procne says to Itys before she kills him, *a! quam | es similis patri!* ('Ah! How like your father you are!', 6.621–2), while his Althaea is determined that Oeneus should not enjoy his son's victory while Thestius is childless, conceptualising Meleager as exclusively his father's son.[50]

Astyoche's act, in marked contrast, dissociates Eurypylus from the house of his father, Telephus, and, in accordance with the series of transactions involving the golden vine, aligns him exclusively with her natal *oikos*, that of Priam and Trojan royalty. Unlike the situation with Althaea and Procne, this idea is clearly articulated in the surviving fragments of *Eurypylus*. There are a remarkable number of references to Telephus in the surviving fragments, mostly brief and elusive.[51] These must have repeatedly

---

now the new fragment (P.Oxy. 5292), which seems to prepare the way for Philomela's arrival on stage, something that leads to Procne's dreadful conspiracy (Finglass 2016b: 68–73).

[48] Zeitlin 1978 ≈ 1996: 87–119, Chesi 2014.

[49] For Ovid and tragedy see Curley 2013 and (for light shone by new papyrus discoveries) Finglass 2014: 76 with n. 81, 2016b: 70–1.

[50] Ov. *Met.* 8.486–7 *an felix Oeneus nato uictore fruetur, | Thestius orbus erit? melius lugebitis ambo* ('Is fortunate Oeneus to enjoy his son's victory, and will Thestius be childless? Better that you will both mourn').

[51] Frr. 210.24–7 Ἀ]χιλλέως |]ουσδ᾿ ἰωμένη | Τ]ήλεφον λέγω· | ἰ]άσατ[ο]· ('of Achilles ... healing ... it is Telephus I speak of ... healed'), 210.74 (discussed below), 211.10–13 ἰὼ δόρυ Τηλ[εφ | παιδὶ συνκυ[| ὦ λόγχα σώτ[ειρα |]ομουσαμ[('Alas the spear meeting with the child of Telephus ... O spear saviour ... ?our house ...'), 212.6–8 κοινόθακα λάξοα | Τη]λέφου

reminded the audience that Eurypylus was Telephus' son, including in situations where that status was contested. Fortunately, one such site of contestation has survived, in the messenger's introduction to Priam's lament over Eurypylus' corpse, whose opening couplet was discussed earlier:

ὁ δ' ἀμφὶ πλευραῖς καὶ σφαγαῖσι [κ]είμενος,
πατ[ὴρ] μὲν οὔ, πατρῶια δ' ἐξαυδ[ῶ]ν ἔπη,
Πρία[μος] ἔκλαιε τὸν τέκνων ὁμ[αί]μονα,
τὸν [π]αῖδα καὶ γέροντα καὶ νεαγ[ί]αν,
τὸν οὔτε Μυσὸν οὔτε Τηλέφου [κα]λῶν,
ἀλλ' ὡς φυτεύσας αὐτὸς ἐκκαλούμ[εν]ος·
"οἴμοι, τέκνον . . .

And, lying over his wounded side,
not his father, but speaking a father's words,
Priam lamented the blood-kin of his children,
the child and old man and youth,
calling him neither Mysian nor Telephus',
but calling on him as if he himself had begotten him;
'Alas, my child . . .

Soph. *Eurypylus* fr. 210.70–6

Both the messenger and Priam himself articulate here precisely the tendentious shift in Eurypylus' identity that we have seen as the result of Astyoche's privileging of natal over conjugal kin. Priam is not Eurypylus' father (πατ[ὴρ] μὲν οὔ) but nevertheless speaks a father's words (πατρῶια . . . ἔπη), laying verbal claim to a kinship status to which he has no right. He explicitly severs Eurypylus from his existing civic (οὔτε Μυσόν) and familial (οὔτε Τηλέφου) ties, addressing him instead as if he himself did not merely stand in adoptive *loco parentis*, but actually begot him (ὡς φυτεύσας αὐτός).

The close relationship between a young man and his maternal uncle, the so-called 'avunculate', is a feature that anthropologists have noted in many societies, and one whose importance in archaic and classical Greece has been discussed by Bremmer.[52] Indeed, Bremmer mentions the relationship of Priam and Eurypylus, but only very briefly as an apparently

---

ξυνουσίαν | δ]εῖπνα πλησιαίτατος ('shared seats hewn from stone . . . Telephus' company . . . banquets . . . nearest . . .'), fr. 218a.40.3 Τη]λέφου ('of Telephus'). 'A notable feature of the papyrus fragments is the number of times Telephus is mentioned . . . For some reason Sophocles seems to have wished to stress Eurypylus' paternity' (Sutton 1984: 49).

[52] Bremmer 1976, 1983.

unproblematic item in a list of 'cases which are indicative of a good relationship between a MoBr [mother's brother] and his SiSo [sister's son]'.[53] The relationship between Priam and Eurypylus may have been 'good' in terms of their mutual regard, but its outcome was ruinous for all concerned and loudly lamented by those still alive to do so. This extreme, limiting case of the avunculate – arguably a perversion in itself – contributes to the wider perversion of the martial mother ideal. Astyoche and Priam, sister and brother, mother and would-be father, have between them conspired to transfer Eurypylus from the house of Telephus and the polity of Mysia to those of Priam and Troy, with results that are disastrous for both houses, both polities, both siblings and for Eurypylus himself. This almost incestuous privileging of natal over conjugal kin constitutes the third and final way in which Astyoche perverts the martial mother ideal.

Staging Perversion: The Dramatic and Ethical Dimension

The audience is guided in its emotional and ethical response to these perverted actions of Astyoche's by explicit moral judgments, the generation of pathos and the manipulation of theatrical effects. The best-preserved scene from the *Eurypylus* is remarkable and in some ways unique. In particular, the interruption of the messenger speech by the *kommos* between Astyoche and the chorus is unparalleled in tragedy.[54] This structural innovation produces striking theatrical effects. It greatly intensifies the emotional colouring of the messenger-speech, which is focalised through Astyoche's and the chorus's response. Even more strikingly, it produces a parallelism between Astyoche's on-stage lament and Priam's off-stage lament as reported by the messenger.[55] Bers's study of incorporated speech in extant tragedy cites only one example of quoted, incorporated lament, two very brief outbursts by Jocasta in the final messenger speech of *Phoenician Women*.[56] However, the recipient of that speech, Creon, is largely unmoved and certainly offers nothing like the parallelism produced between Astyoche and Priam. Indeed, it is hard to find any passage of extant tragedy where on- and off-stage action mirror each other

---

[53] Bremmer 1983: 179.

[54] 'Caso unico nelle tragedie conservatesi, questo lungo racconto è interrotto da un κομμός, del tutto indipendente dalla ῥῆσις, tra il corifeo e Astioche' (Ozbek 2006: 30).

[55] For male lament in tragedy see Suter 2008a.

[56] Eur. *Phoen.* 1432–3, 1436–7, Bers 1997: 89.

so closely. The parallelism further contributes to the quasi-incestuous bond between brother and sister, who act together to lament Eurypylus just as they acted together to destroy him. Furthermore, it not only tropes their collusion in bringing about Eurypylus' death, but produces a complex, dynamic commentary on that collusion. Several of the motifs that mark Astyoche's perversion of the martial mother ideal are alluded to in Priam's lament, and they are depicted in terms that are both emotive and morally self-condemnatory. Priam 'betrayed' (πρ[ο]ύδωκα, fr. 210.76) Eurypylus, and the latter's short sojourn in Troy 'will provide a memory of many ills' (π[ολ]λῶν κακῶν | μνήμην παρέξεις, 78–9). The audiences – internal and external – are given ample cues to join Priam in his act of self-condemnation, which is also a condemnation of Astyoche's role in her son's death.

However, the clearest cue for the audience comes from Astyoche's own self-condemnation and the chorus' harsh endorsement of it. Astyoche's ethical assessment of her own actions is clear:[57]

> Πρια]μίδας καὶ το[ν
> Ἰδαῖον βασιλ[ῆα
> Πρίαμον, ὅς μ[ε
> πᾶσα κατάρ[ατον
> ἔπεισεν ἄβου[λον τόδ'
> ἔ[ργο]ν ἔρξαι.

> Priam's] sons and
> Ida's king
> Priam, who me
> ?wholly accursed
> persuaded this senseless
> deed to do

Soph. Eurypylus fr. 211.1–6

This is as close as the surviving fragments come to a clear reference to the bribe of the golden vine. Astyoche emphasises the role of Priam in persuading her but nevertheless takes full responsibility for the folly of her own action. Indeed the light oxymoron of ἔπεισεν ἄβου[λον foregrounds the perversity of the situation where persuasion is set in opposition to (good) counsel.[58] Yet the clearest note of self-condemnation comes with κατάρ[ατον, which carries both its metaphorical force of generalised

---

[57] Wilamowitz's supplement Πρια]μίδας is virtually certain and Diehl's κατάρ[ατον very likely. I have printed Brizi's ἄβου[λον τόδ' in marginal preference to Hunt's ἀβου[λίαι, but the key connection with folly is secure. For the text see now Iovine 2017: 307–10.

[58] For persuasion in tragedy see Buxton 1982.

censure and a gesture towards its more literal sense of an actual curse, which we shall see reflected in Astyoche's reference elsewhere to a malign *daimon*. The full force of Astyoche's words can only be understood in the context of the preceding main clause of which Πρια]μίδας and Πρίαμον are the objects, a clause which is unfortunately lost. There are two likely possibilities, each of which has interesting implications. Astyoche may be expressing similar sentiments to her brother Priam at fr. 210.76–7 (quoted above), that Eurypylus' death has confirmed the doom of Priam and the sons of Priam ('Ruin now awaits the Priamids . . .'). This would constitute yet another instance of the siblings' disturbing ὁμοφροσύνη (like-mindedness), but it would also juxtapose the futility of Astyoche's action as a martial mother (failure to save the city) with its immorality (bribery, folly, cursedness), comprehensively underlining its perversity.

Conversely, Astyoche may be cursing or otherwise vilifying the Trojan royal household ('I curse the Priamids'), bitterly lashing out at those she identifies as the cause of her son's death and her own misery. This would certainly fit with the relative clause, specifying Priam as the one who persuaded her to do the deed of folly. Such an imprecation would once more dissociate Astyoche from her natal family, and indeed the following lines include fragmented references to Telephus and the spear of Achilles that wounded and healed him, perhaps reasserting the bond of φιλία with her dead husband:

> ἰὼ δόρυ Τηλ[εφ   10
> παιδὶ συνκυ[
> ὦ λόγχα σώτ[ειρα
>
> Alas the spear . . . Telephus
> to his child ?together ?coming
> O spear saviour

Soph. Eurypylus fr. 211.10–12

The evocation of Telephus, the spear and his healing encounter with it in the hands of Achilles contrasts poignantly with the deadly encounter of Eurypylus with the same spear lethally wielded by Neoptolemus, associating the conjugal family with health and salvation, the natal with death and disaster. Salvation, saving the city, springs from the spear that healed Telephus (ὦ λόγχα σώτ[ειρα), not from Priam's betrayal of his pseudo-son (πρ[ο]ύδωκα . . . σωτη[ρία]ν, fr. 210.76–7). The conceptual reintegration of Astyoche and Eurypylus into the conjugal family underlines the perversity of her and Priam's attempt to make Priamids of them and of her action as a martial mother in sending him to fight at Troy.

One further passage illustrates not only Astyoche's self-condemnation but the chorus's endorsement of that verdict:

30 <ΑΣΤΥΟΧΗ>   οἰοῖ οἰ[οῖ].

        διπλοῦς ἀνεστέναξ[α   ]φα[ ]

<ΧΟΡΟΣ>   πατρὸ[ς   ]

        ραν· ἐπ[   ]μος ἴδε τέκνων.

<ΑΣ.>   τρίτην δ' ἐπ' ἐμ[ὲ   ] <ΧΟ.> κ[α]ὶ γὰρ οὖν

35   προσάγ[α]γ' ὡδὶ[ ]. ιγ[ ]ν διαίνεις·

        ἐπεὶ κτησίων φρενῶν ἐξέδυς.

<ΑΣ.>   ὦ δαῖμον ὦ δύσδαιμον, ὦ κείρας [ἐ]μέ.

<ΧΟ.>   ἀγχοῦ προσεῖπας· οὐ γὰρ ἐκτὸς ἑστὼς

        σύρει δὴ φύρδαν.

40 <ΑΣ.>   ἐπισπάσει δίκα<ι> με.

<ΧΟ.>   δίκαι ναί.

<ΑΣ.>   ἀλλ' ὡς τάχιστ' ἄριστα.

<ΧΟ.>   ἐέ·

        τί φήσομεν, τί λέξομεν;

45 <ΑΣ.>   τίς οὐχὶ τοὐμὸν ἐν δίκηι βαλεῖ κάρα;

<ΧΟ.>   δαίμων ἔκειρεν ἐν δίκαι σε δαίμων.

<Astyoche>: Ah, ah
        I groan aloud for twofold . . .

<Chorus>   . . . of the father . . .
        . . . ?Priam? . . . saw . . . of children.

<As.>:   Against myself the third . . . <Ch.>: Yes indeed, for
        it brought (?deployed) ?labour-pangs? . . . you moisten;
        since you abandoned the sense belonging to the household.

<As.>:   O spirit, O evil spirit, O one who destroyed me.

<Ch.>:   You address one near; for not standing outside he drags you
        indeed to ruin.

<As.>:   He will drag me justly.

<Ch.>:   Justly indeed.

<As.>:   But as soon as possible would be best.

<Ch.>:   Ah, what shall we speak, what say?

<As.>:   Who will not in justice bombard my head?

<Ch.>:   A spirit destroyed you in justice, a spirit.

Soph. *Eurypylus* fr. 210.30–46

Both Astyoche and the chorus insistently emphasise the justice of the former's punishment, with no fewer than four references in half a dozen lines to its being exacted with δίκη. On each occasion, the chorus almost antiphonally endorses Astyoche's self-condemnation, transferring the sense that her perversion of the martial mother ideal was unjust from the level of guilt-ridden self-flagellation to that of communal judgement.

In addition, Astyoche's mention of the δαίμων that destroyed her constitutes a fascinating instance of tragedy's recurrent engagement with ideas of divine causation and human responsibility.[59] It is not clear from her vague apostrophe whether she conceives of it as an external force acting upon her, like Aeschylus' Xerxes (according to Darius), or even through her, like his Clytemnestra, or as an internal working of her psyche, like Euripides' Phaedra.[60] However, the chorus emphatically situates the δαίμων – and with it full responsibility – within Astyoche (ἀγχοῦ ... οὐ ... ἐκτός). Intriguing though this assessment of Astyoche's guilt is, for the purposes of the present argument the key point is that her persuasion of Eurypylus to fight at Troy and its disastrous consequences are depicted as the result of the action of a ruinous δαίμων (however conceptualised), and thus put on a par with the mental aberrations that lead to kin-killing (like Clytemnestra) and the destruction of communities (like Xerxes), terrible acts that Astyoche has, in a sense, committed. To depict the sending of one's son to war in such terms is perhaps the ultimate indication that the martial mother ideal has been totally perverted. The uncharacteristically unsympathetic comments from the chorus, who might be expected to console rather than condemn, provide a final cue to the audience.

Conclusion

What then might Sophocles' *Eurypylus* contribute to our understanding of the martial mother ideal and indeed to the treatment of Athenian ideology more broadly in tragedy? We should stop short of a reading that treats it as constituting a pacifist condemnation of the horrors of sending one's sons to war, though it is more tempting to see the perversion of the martial mother ideal as an exploration of its limits and the tensions within it. To compare Euripides' *Erechtheus* once more, many have seen there a critique of Praxithea's strident insistence on sacrificing her daughter for the city, and indeed she does seem to come close to Astyoche's self-condemnation. Following the death of her daughters and husband, and the Athenian defeat that seems imminent in spite of them, Praxithea

---

[59] For the δαίμων as a figure of causation in tragedy and elsewhere see Padel 1983, 1992, Holmes 2010.

[60] Xerxes: Aesch. *Pers.* 725 φεῦ, μέγας τις ἦλθε δαίμων, ὥστε μὴ φρονεῖν καλῶς ('Alas, some great *daimon* came so that he did not have good sense'). Clytemnestra: Aesch. *Ag.* 1475–80. Phaedra: Eur. *Hipp.* 241 ἐμάνην, ἔπεσον δαίμονος ἄτηι ('I was insane, I fell because of the delusion of a *daimon*'). Cf. Padel 1992: 152 'tragic acts (like the murder of one's own child) are so numbingly destructive that they must be impelled, even perhaps performed, not by a human but by animal or daemonic agents, or by human beings "driven" by animal and daemonic passion'.

despairingly laments her loss in frantic dochmiacs, but not simply in terms of its cost to her, which could be set against her virtuous service to the city. She seems to question the moral validity of the sacrifice, in one breath describing it as 'on behalf of the city' (πρὸ πόλεως, fr. 370.40) and 'an unholy, unholy, unhallowed, unhallowed' death (ἀνίερον ἀνίερον <ἀν>όσιον ἀνόσιον, 41), a startling reevaluation that Diggle's attractive alternative text, 'holy, unholy, hallowed, unhallowed' (ἱερὸν ἀνίερον ὅσιον ἀνόσιον, TrGFS p. 108), with its characteristically tragic oxymora, only partially softens. Yet the differences between Praxithea and Astyoche are as significant as the similarities. Sophocles' Troy is indeed doomed and Eurypylus' death in vain, but Euripides' Athena, *ex machina*, invites Praxithea and the audience to alter their evaluation of the martial mother ideal yet again. Praxithea is addressed, according to a very probable supplement, as 'saviour of the land' (χθονὸς [σώτειρα, fr. 370.63), a striking reprise of the 'saving the city' motif, and more securely as one who has 'set upright again foundations of this city' (πόλεως τῆσδ' ἐξανώρθωσας βάθρα, 95). Praxithea's pain remains, and one of the two exiguous traces of her reply to Athena is the word 'pitiable' (ο]ἰκτροί, 119), but her action as a martial mother is shown to have been efficacious as well as well-motivated.

The contrast with Astyoche's comprehensively perverted 'sacrifice' of Eurypylus is telling. We should not expect a homogenous depiction of any ideologically charged issue in different tragedies, let alone in those by different tragedians. The contrasting settings in Troy and Athens may also be significant, and Wilkins has proposed a distinction between the positive depiction of voluntary self-sacrifice in Euripidean plays set in Athens (*Children of Heracles* as well as *Erechtheus*) and the more problematic picture in those set elsewhere (*Phoenician Women* in Thebes, *Hecuba* in Thrace, *Iphigenia at Aulis*).[61] This emphasis on the alterity of the world on stage is also central to Kelly's assertion that the depiction of institutions such as the care of war-orphans in Sophocles' *Ajax* does not critique the fifth-century Athenian practice by analogy but rather validates it by contrast.[62] Astyoche's perversion of the martial mother ideal undeniably

---

[61] Wilkins 1990: 189.

[62] 'One can agree wholeheartedly with Goldhill and others that an Athenian audience would notice the contact between the two worlds here, but would they have felt that a negative comment on their own customs and practices was any part of the poet's purpose? Instead, by pointing out the differences and distances between the Greek camp in Troy and the Athenian present, Sophocles appears to be suggesting that the contemporary form of this shared theme is actually preferable to that envisaged in the heroic world' (Kelly 2015: 70–1, with reference to Goldhill 1987 ≈ Winkler and Zeitlin 1990: 97–129; cf. Allan and Kelly 2013).

addresses anxieties inherent in that ideal, in particular its conflict with the more 'natural' maternal ideal of wishing to protect and preserve one's children. As with the tragic wedding, this perversion allows those anxieties to dominate within the world of the play. However, the differences and distances between heroic Troy and fifth-century Athens, between the avaricious, quasi-incestuous, ineffective Astyoche and the citizen mother who saves the city by sending her son into battle, are sufficient for the former to stand as a foil, not a mirror, for the latter. In Athenian ideology, though not in tragedy, bad mothers were indeed the exception that proves the rule.

10 | The Music One Desires

Hypsipyle and Aristophanes' 'Muse of Euripides'

CALEB SIMONE

Best known from the myth of the Argonauts as Jason's lover, Hypsipyle was the daughter of Thoas, king of the Aegean island of Lemnos and son of Dionysus; this gave her a connection to Dionysian cult in Athens as the god's granddaughter.[1] Euneus, Hypsipyle's son by Jason, becomes the founder of the Euneidae family in Athens. Closely associated with *kitharôidia* (solo singing to the cithara), the Euneidae provided the priest for the cult of Dionysus Melpomenos ('The Singer'), who played a leading role in the rituals at the City Dionysia festival where tragedies were performed.[2] In the wake of the disastrous end to the Sicilian expedition during the Peloponnesian War in 413, Euripides brought *Hypsipyle* to the Athenian stage, renewing the Dionysian cultural heritage that Athens had long shared with its Lemnian allies in the eastern Aegean.[3] In a move especially characteristic of his later tragedies, Euripides gives Hypsipyle a musically innovative monody.[4] While developments in musical style had long been underway in the fifth century, the so-called 'New Music' became

---

[1] Thoas appears as the king of Lemnos in the *Iliad* (14.230); in Euripides' play, Thoas is named as Hypsipyle's father (fr. 759a.1626) and as Dionysus' son (fr. 752a.7).

[2] Photius' *Lexicon* glosses the Euneidae under two separate entries, as follows: 'A musical family at Athens. Descended from Euneus, son of Jason and Hypsipyle' and 'There is a family thus named among the Athenians. They were citharodes, providing the liturgy for the performance of holy rites' (ε 2258–9 = II 215 Theodoridis). For a genealogy with discussion see Toepffer 1889: 181–206 with Cropp 2003: 139–41. Note the inscription from one of the seats in the theatre of Dionysus (*IG* II–III² 5056): ἱερέως Μελπομενοῦ Διονύσου ἐξ Εὐνειδῶν, 'the priest of Dionysus Melpomenos from among the Euneidae'.

[3] A scholion (on Ar. *Ran.* 53a = Eur. *Antiope* T ii) groups *Hypsipyle*, *Phoenician Women* and *Antiope* as three 'fine' plays produced 'just before' *Frogs* (405) and after *Andromeda* (412); see further Cropp 2004: 181–2. Cropp 2003: 136–43 discusses Lemnian–Athenian relations as they relate to the play's mythmaking; see Gastaldi 2010 for a more recent analysis of the epigraphic sources. Smarczyk 1986 discusses Athenian relations with the north Aegean near the end of the Peloponnesian War, emphasising Athenian attempts to reinforce ties with allied states at a time of widespread disaffection; genealogical reconstructions in Athenian drama, especially Aristophanes' *Lysistrata* and Euripides' *Ion*, were one strategy in achieving this goal (ibid., 48–55, 1990: 612–18).

[4] Csapo 1999–2000 shows that from the mid-420s onwards, actors' song becomes more prominent, a trend often connected with professionalisation and innovation in tragic music especially seen in Euripides' later plays; on actor's song, see further below.

162

especially associated with Euripides, among others.[5] The New Music involved tonal, melodic, instrumental and formal innovations in the music of dithyrambs, nomes and drama.[6] Prioritising sound over language, it tended toward melodic and rhythmic innovation, astrophic structure and exaggerated imitation (mimesis). Hypsipyle's New Musical performance was apparently so distinctive that the comic poet Aristophanes parodied her as an embodiment of Euripidean musical style.[7] In the contest between Aeschylus and Euripides in *Frogs*, Aeschylus summons a caricature of 'Euripides' Muse' on stage: the woman who 'claps with the potsherds'.[8] The scholiast's comment that this woman refers to *Hypsipyle* was confirmed with the recovery of new fragments from the play near the beginning of the twentieth century.[9]

Even though substantial passages of this once-lost monody have been recovered, the significance of its female singer for the play's broader aims has remained obscure. The New Musical style of Hypsipyle's song has cast a long shadow on its reception. Until recently, commentators had long disdained the New Music, negatively influenced by its aristocratic critics.[10] This bias contributed to a view of the *Hypsipyle* as 'melodramatic'.[11] Due to

---

[5] Modern scholars use the term 'New Music' as a convention, but the ancients did not refer to these stylistic innovations as 'new' or 'revolutionary', but rather as 'theatre' music (σκηνική or θεατρική): LeVen 2014: 71–3. For the movement, its development, and its innovations, see Csapo 2004, D'Angour 2006, Csapo and Wilson 2009, Kowalzig and Wilson 2013.

[6] Cf. Arist. *Pol.* 1342a15–22, Aristox. fr. 70 Wehrli, [Plut.] *On Music* 1140de, 1142c (cited by LeVen 2014: 71 n. 1).

[7] Weiss 2018: 3 reads this passage, among others in *Frogs*, as evidence 'not simply for the prominence of *mousikē* within a tragedy but for its reception in fifth-century Athens'.

[8] Ar. *Ran.* 1305–7 ποῦ 'στιν ἡ τοῖς ὀστράκοις | αὕτη κροτοῦσα; δεῦρο, Μοῦσ' Εὐριπίδου, | πρὸς ἥνπερ ἐπιτήδεια ταῦτ' ἄιδειν μέλη, 'Where is that woman, the one who claps with the potsherds? Come here, Muse of Euripides, yours is the fitting accompaniment for these songs to be sung to.' I have consulted Dover 1993, Sommerstein 1996; all translations are my own.

[9] Σ Ar. *Ran.* 1305c (p. 147 Chantry). The extensive *Hypsipyle* papyrus, discovered in 1906, was published as P.Oxy. 852 by Grenfell and Hunt 1908, with contributions from Ulrich von Wilamowitz-Moellendorff, Gilbert Murray and John Bagnell Bury.

[10] Already in antiquity the 'demise of music' (διαφθορὰ μουσικῆς) was ascribed to innovations in the dithyramb that spread to theatre music more broadly (Σ Ar. *Nub.* 333d, p. 84.1–7 Holwerda); see Franklin 2013. LeVen 2014: 71–188 discusses the cultural history of the reception of the New Music, especially the biases against it. Csapo and Wilson 2009 catalogue the modern critical reception of Timotheus the citharode specifically and the New Music more generally: e.g. 'mere fashion-mongering without permanence' ('bloße Moderichtung ohne Ewigkeitswert': Schmid 1946: 516), 'taste formed by the mob' (Segal 1985: 244), 'cheap café music' (Borthwick 1994: 27 = 2015: 202, referring to *Hypsipyle* specifically).

[11] Thus Borthwick 1994: 27 = 2015: 201, employing a category already established in Euripidean studies; cf. Michelini 1987: 22–6, 321–3. For the label 'melodrama' and its difficulties and advantages see Mastronarde 1999–2000: 37–8; Wohl 2015: 3 notes that such labels simply categorise the peculiarity of such plays without explaining them.

the general neglect of the fragmentary plays and to the particular bias against this parodied drama, Hypsipyle is rarely taken seriously among the female characters of the tragic stage.[12]

In extant tragedy, female characters of royal blood like Hypsipyle in fact make up the largest group of actors who sing monodies.[13] Lyrics tend to be reserved for female or feminised characters *in extremis*, a coincidence that reflects the feminine associations with lament more generally.[14] Hypsipyle's fragmentary monody, however, stands out from actors' songs in the canonical tragedies both for its framing of the female poetic persona and the ritual function it serves within the drama as a whole. Reading this fragmentary monody alongside its parody in the *Frogs*, I show how Hypsipyle's unique poetic persona as a female singer relates to the play's wider cultic and political framework.[15] Emphasising the musicality of her performance with marked flourishes, the singing heroine inspires the audience to desire the music that she herself desires, namely, 'Asian', Orphic *kitharôidia*. Through an eastern Aegean musical form especially relevant to the Euneidae and the Athenian cult of Dionysus Melpomenos, Hypsipyle recrafts a cultic connection between Lemnos and Athens.

Attending to the 'aural form' of tragedy in its sociocultural context, this chapter shows how Hypsipyle's monody musically embodies the cultic connections that Euripides forges in the play.[16] In the first section, I offer

---

[12] The play has generally been discussed alongside similar plays, especially *Antiope* and *Phoenician Women*, with a focus on the larger themes or male characters. Zeitlin 1993: 171–82 argues that in these three plays, 'a positive Dionysiac pattern can be shown to operate in a significant relation to Thebes, but only in displacement from its actual territory and the temporal frame of its usual sequence of events' (181). Lamari 2012 reads these three plays in terms of father–son relations in the context of its political setting, though it is not necessary to accept that the three were performed as a trilogy. Karamanou 2012 discusses *Hypsipyle* among other Euripidean plays sharing the 'family reunion' motif against the turbulent socio-political milieu of Athens in the late fifth-century; she concludes that such tragedies mirror this social and political crisis and in turn promote unity in Athens.

[13] Thus Hall 1999 ≈ 2006: 288–320, who sees the other major group as non-citizen, foreign males, which is to treat Creon, Heracles, Oedipus, Orestes, Peleus and Philoctetes as foreigners.

[14] Foley 1993 ≈ 2001: 19–55.

[15] For a contextual approach to *mousikê* as music, song and dance, see Murray and Wilson 2004. Recent work on Euripides' later canonical plays has emphasised the coherence between musical form, generic structure and literary content. Weiss 2018 for example treats *mousikê* as a formal feature closely connected with plot; Catenaccio 2017 examines the expansive and versatile formal use of monody. For a more technical perspective of the relationship between music and text see Phillips and D'Angour 2018.

[16] My discussion addresses what Hall 1999: 120 = 2006: 318–19 terms 'the relationship of tragedy's aural *form* – its actors' musical and metrical performance codes – to the society which produced it'. See Wohl 2015 on the politics of form in Euripidean tragedy more generally. Especially useful for my discussion of sensation and perception is S. Butler and Purves 2013a, which moves

a fresh reading of the monody, showing how Hypsipyle sets up her performance as a multi-sensory experience that fosters an attachment to its style through the psychagogic powers of tragic poetry. Appropriating a Sapphic persona, Hypsipyle enacts a rejection of other poetic modes, bringing the audience at last to a vision of the kind of music that she 'desires to see': namely the citharodic music of Orpheus in a distinctly 'Asian' style, one indigenous to her eastern Aegean home and foundational for the cult of Dionysus Melpomenos in Athens. In the second section, I turn to *Frogs* to consider this reading through the lens of Aristophanes' parody, taking into consideration the comic poet's broader representation of Euripidean style. In contrast to previous readings that have interpreted the parody as distancing Hypsipyle from Lesbian *mousikê*, I follow a more recent reading to show how the 'Lesbianising' joke reflects a musical style that fuses Hypsipyle's New Musical monody with an ancient cultic tradition.

Before turning to the fragments of Hypsipyle's monody, I offer a brief synopsis of the play. When the Argonauts visited Lemnos, Hypsipyle fell in love with Jason and bore him twin sons, Euneus and Thoas.[17] Jason took the boys on his departure, and on his death left them in the care of Orpheus in Thrace. When the Lemnian women infamously plotted the murder of the men of the island (the so-called *Lêmnia kaka*, the 'Lemnian troubles'), Hypsipyle refused to kill her father Thoas, instead fleeing to escape the repercussions.[18] In Euripides' play, the displaced Lemnian princess has become a slave to Lycurgus, the priest of the local sanctuary of Zeus at Nemea. Hypsipyle serves Lycurgus and his wife Eurydice as a nurse to their infant son, Opheltes. On a quest to find their mother, Hypsipyle's now mature sons receive hospitality in Lycurgus' house. The plot unfolds from Hypsipyle's encounter with the seer Amphiaraus, whom she meets as the seven Argive leaders pass through the isthmus at Nemea on their way to attack Thebes.[19] When assisting Amphiaraus in drawing water from the nearby spring, Hypsipyle leaves Opheltes unattended on the ground, where

---

beyond the readerly, text-oriented paradigm of strict 'visuality' to appreciate the senses more fully.

[17] Thoas may be Euripides' addition; the *Iliad* mentions only Euneus (7.468–9, 21.41, 23.744–7).

[18] Masciadri 2004 provides a structural analysis of the myth of the 'Lemnian troubles' in relation to Hypsipyle in particular. Other major references to this event include Aesch. *Cho.* 631–8, Eur. *Hec.* 886–7, Hdt. 6.138.

[19] Although we have a few lines, quoted by various sources, from the play's opening monologue featuring Hypsipyle's reference to Dionysus (fr. 752), P.Oxy. 852 begins around 130 lines into the play (fr. 752b–e), when Hypsipyle's sons arrive at Lycurgus' house where their mother, whom they do not yet recognise, is a slave. Hypsipyle's monody and her exchange with the

a monstrous serpent kills him. The baby's mother Eurydice calls for Hypsipyle's death, but Amphiaraus comes to her defence. Renaming Opheltes 'Archemoros' ('first to die'), the seer interprets the infant's death to mean that the Argives will die at Thebes. To honour the child's memory, Amphiaraus calls for funeral games, thus establishing the Nemean festival. When Hypsipyle's sons Euneus and Thoas participate in these games, they are finally reunited with their mother. The play ends with an appearance of Dionysus on the *mêchanê*.

Looking at Sound with Hypsipyle

Hypsipyle's monody is marked by contrasts. A princess from a heroic quest narrative, she is here notoriously cast as a foreign slave woman. Her song continually holds these roles in tandem as she reflects on her former high status and her present role as a nurse. The monody initially functions as a work song for her servile tasks: through its metaphors, the displaced heroine draws an analogy between her song-making and the more elevated activity of weaving. While emphasising her low status, the chorus women also invite her to enter a more elevated epic register through song. In the end, Hypsipyle rejects both work songs and epic conventions in favour of a vision of Orpheus' performance aboard the Argo, highlighting the kind of music she desires.

Near the beginning of the play, once Hypsipyle has welcomed her travelling sons (without recognising them) into her masters' house, she returns to her work: comforting the infant Opheltes (fr. 752f.8–14, ~194–201).[20]

> ἰδοὺ κτύπος ὅδε κορτάλων.
>
> <   >
>
> οὐ τάδε πήνας, οὐ τάδε κερκίδος
> 10   ἱστοτόνου παραμύθια Λήμνι' ἃ
> Μοῦσα θέλει με κρέκειν, ὅ τι δ' εἰς ὕπνον
> ἢ χάριν ἢ θεραπεύματα πρόσφορα
> π]αιδὶ πρέπει νεαρῶι,
> τάδε μελωιδὸς αὐδῶ.

chorus appears in the first most substantial continuous passage from P.Oxy. 852 (fr. 752f-k). See Cropp 2004: 170–9 for a full reconstruction.

[20] I have accepted the proposal of Battezzato 2005: 187 to make the overall syntax more coherent by reading an elided relative (Λήμνι' ἃ) at line 10, where Kannicht has Λήμνια, and similarly a relative ὅ τι in line 11 where Kannicht has ὅτι. In citations the tilde (~) indicates approximate line numbers for the play as a whole, as found in the Loeb edition by Collard and Cropp (2008).

> Look: here's the clack of the clappers . . .
> This is not for the weft-thread; this is not for the
> loom-stretching shuttle, no Lemnian consolations which
> the Muse wants me to weave, but that which for sleep
> or charm or satisfactory comfort
> suits the young child:
> this I tunefully sing.

Within the dramatic context of comforting the infant, Hypsipyle speaks directly to Opheltes. At the same time, Hypsipyle draws attention to the musical performance she enacts on stage.[21] From the start, Hypsipyle emphasises the acoustic qualities of her song. Blending the senses of sight and sound, she bids Opheltes – and the audience by extension – 'Look: here is the sound' (ἰδοὺ κτύπος, 8) of the castanets she plays. Just as sight directs attention to the sound, so too does the language: the percussive sound expressed through the onomatopoeic *ktupos* alliterates with the name of its source through instantaneous, velar *kappas* (κτύπος . . . κορτάλων). This mimetic interplay of sound and sense continues in the lines that follow, as the repetition of the dactylic *ou tade* with its dental consonants re-echoes the repetitive clack of the castanets. But Euripides' musical innovation does much more than simply draw attention to its own peculiar form. Hypsipyle's words 'Look: here is the sound' invite the audience to think about its function and significance. The demonstratives *tade* . . . *tade* . . . in these lines and later repeated at her monody's conclusion do not refer straightforwardly to the 'Lemnian consolations' (10); they point more broadly to the atmosphere of the musical accompaniment already marked out in line 8 as the 'here and now' of Hypsipyle's performance.[22] Although unusual in syntax, this use of the demonstrative is not unparalleled; a distinctive feature of the New Music is to bend structure in the service of style.[23] The immediate effect is to synchronise the audience (so to speak) with Hypsipyle's felt experience of caring for Opheltes, as both sight and language work together to focus attention on the sound. It becomes clear, however, that this actor's monody is about much more than the work enacted on stage.

---

[21] Weiss 2018: 8 describes such moments as instances of 'metamusicality', meaning 'references to song and dance that engage with the live musical performance'.

[22] Battezzato 2005: 184–6 discusses the function of τάδε, which does not refer to a neuter plural παραμύθια, but more broadly to 'this setting', specifically the sound of the castanets Hypsipyle has drawn attention to in the preceding lines. Bond 1963: 65 takes τάδε simply as 'here'.

[23] Csapo 2004: 225–6.

In what follows (9–14), Hypsipyle introduces other types of song as foils for her present performance. Beginning with the work songs that Lemnian women would sing at the loom, she proceeds to reject martial poetry as well before arriving at the kind of music she desires. Casting her performance in terms of weaving, Hypsipyle contrasts her current, servile 'work song' for Opheltes with consolatory work songs from the past: *paramuthia Lêmnia*, sung by Lemnian women to ease their work at the loom. Even as Hypsipyle rejects the Lemnian weaver's songs, her performance with its metaphors casts her into precisely this role: a Lemnian woman singing as she works to 'weave' the song that the Muse wants her to sing (Μοῦσα θέλει με κρέκειν, 11).[24] This mention of the Muse invites the question, 'What does the Muse want Hypsipyle to sing?'

The language of Hypsipyle's weaving metaphor introduces marked musical resonances and aural effects. The rare compound adjective 'loom-stretching' (ἱστοτόνου, 10) blends *histos* (the 'loom' or 'web') with *tonos*, a word that refers to 'tension', which in music conveys the tautness of a string; hence the use of the term for 'pitch'.[25] This blending of the physical loom with a decidedly musical term materialises Hypsipyle's act of sound-weaving. With the term *krekein* especially, these weaving and musical valences are held in tandem: the semantics of *krekein* centre on the sound produced when plying a plectrum over musical strings or a shuttle (κερκίδος, 9) over the loom.[26] Finally, *krekein* is a carefully chosen term with a potentially Lesbian resonance: it is not the standard term for weaving (*huphainein, plekein*) except in Sappho, where it occurs with *histos*.[27]

After Hypsiyple casts her current lullaby as a form of weaving with the Muse, the chorus of local Nemean women arrive, interweaving their entrance song with Hypsipyle's monody (fr. 752f.15–28, ~202–15):

15   τί σὺ παρὰ προθύροις, φίλα;
         πότερα δώματος εἰσόδους
         σαίρει[ς], ἢ δρόσον ἐπὶ πέδωι
         βάλλεις οἶά τε δούλα;

---

[24] See Chong-Gossard 2009 on the dynamics of consolation at work in Hypsipyle's monody.

[25] LSJ⁹ s.v. τόνος ιι 2. For the history and semantics of the musical term *tonos* see Rocconi 2003: 21–6. This 'web-stretching' imagery features prominently in Aristophanes' parody of Euripidean choral lyric at *Ran.* 1313–16.

[26] Restani 1995: 99–100 discusses the analogy between weaving and *barbitos*-playing specifically, noting similarities in posturing and string sound production these activities share.

[27] Sappho fr. 102.1 Voigt. Euripides also uses the term for weaving at *El.* 542; Stieber 2011: 315–34 treats Euripides' use of craft language for weaving more generally.

ἢ τὰν Ἀργὼ τὰν διὰ σοῦ
στόματος ἀεὶ κληιζομέναν   20
πεντηκόντερον ἄ[ι]δεις
ἢ τὸ χρυσεόμαλλον
ἱερὸν δέρος ὃ περὶ δρυὸς
   ὄζοις ὄμμα δράκοντος
φρουρεῖ, μναμοσύνα δέ σοι   25
   τᾶς ἀγχιάλοιο Λήμνου,
τὰν Αἰγαῖος ἑλί[σ]σων
κυμο⟨κ⟩τύπος ἀχεῖ;

What are you doing next to the doors, dear friend?
Are you sweeping the entrance to the house,
or casting drops of water about the floor
as a slave-woman does?
Or are you singing of the Argo, which is
ever celebrated in song by your lips,
that famed penteconter?
Or of the sacred golden-fleeced
hide about the oak's branches
which the serpent's eye
guards? And is your memory
of sea-girt Lemnos,
encircling which
the wave-thrashing Aegean resounds?

At their entrance, the chorus women capture the extremes of Hypsipyle's role. Their initial assumption – that she is performing mundane chores – maintains the vivid proximity to Hypsipyle's servile status that we saw in her monody. At the same time, the women evoke her more elevated mythic characterisation, offering a list of themes for song: the voyage of the Argonauts, the quest for the Golden Fleece, the island of Lemnos (19–28). Assuming that Hypsipyle desires a heroic narrative, the Nemean women invite the singing princess to witness a martial spectacle first-hand (fr. 752f.29–38, ~216–25):

δεῦρο δ' ἂν λειμῶνα Νέμει[ον·
ἀσ[τ]ράπ[τ]ει χαλκέο[ι]σ⟨ιν⟩
   ὅπλο[ις   30
Ἀργεῖον π[ε]δίον πᾶ[ν·
ἐπὶ τὸ τᾶ[ς] κιθάρας ἔρυμ[α,
   τὰς Ἀμφιονίας ἔργον [
ὠ[κυ]πόδας Ἄ[δρ]ασ[το]ς [⏑ – ⏑⏑

35   ὁ [δ'] ἐκάλεσε μένο[ς
          ποικίλα σάματα [
          τόξα τε χρύσεα [
          κα̣[ὶ] μονοβάμονε[ς

          Come now to the Nemean meadow:
          it glimmers with bronze arms,
          the whole Argive plain;
          against the cithara's bulwark,
          Amphion's work . . .
          swift-footed Adrastus . . .
          he summoned the might
          ornate insignia . . .
          and golden bows . . .
          and single-treading horses . . .

Given Hypsipyle's mythic associations (of which she has apparently sung in the past), the Nemean women invite her to witness the Argive contingent marching across the plain to Thebes.[28] This specific mode of female spectatorship evokes epic conventions, in particular Helen on the walls of Troy in the *Iliad*'s *teichoskopia*. In that poem, when Iris summons Helen to view and comment upon the Achaean army on the Trojan plain, she finds her weaving at the loom, embroidering 'the toils of the horse-taming Trojans and the bronze-coated Achaeans'.[29] Much like Helen, Hypsipyle has just been 'weaving' her song when the chorus women find her. By urging her to survey the Argive soldiers from the plain, the women position Hypsipyle for a role much like Helen's as a poetic weaver and epic viewer. The details that the chorus draw out convey the visuality of the scene, suggesting the desirability of armed men, elaborate insignia and war horses. With this enticing projection of the army that they intend the Lemnian singer to gaze upon, the chorus women evoke a mode of female viewership familiar from the opening of Sappho's famous priamel: 'some say a contingent of horses, others one of infantry, still others that one of ships is the most beautiful thing on the dark earth'.[30] In this exchange, the chorus thus dramatically stage an epic poetic role for the singing heroine who 'weaves the song that the Muse wants her to sing'.

---

[28] Scodel 1997 discusses this scene in view of Sappho 16 alongside scenes in *Phoenician Women* and *Iphigenia at Aulis* where Euripides stages women viewing an army.

[29] Hom. *Il.* 3.125–7 ἣ δὲ μέγαν ἱστὸν ὕφαινεν, | δίπλακα πορφυρέην, πολέας δ' ἐνέπασσεν ἀέθλους | Τρώων θ' ἱπποδάμων καὶ Ἀχαιῶν χαλκοχιτώνων.

[30] Sappho fr. 16.1–3 Voigt ο]ἰ μὲν ἰππήων στρότον, οἰ δὲ πέσδων, | οἰ δὲ νάων φαῖσ' ἐπ[ὶ] γᾶν μέλαι[ν]αν | [ἔ]μμεναι κάλλιστον.

By rejecting the chorus's invitation, Hypsipyle positions herself much like the female spectator of Sappho fr. 16 Voigt, as she sings about the kind of music she desires (fr. 752g.6–17, ~255–66):[31]

> τὸν ἁ τοῦ ποταμοῦ παρ–
>   θένος Αἴγιν' ἐτέκνωσεν
> Πηλέα, μέσωι δὲ παρ' ἱστῶι
> Ἀσιάδ' ἔλεγον ἰήιον
> Θρῆισσ' ἐβόα κίθαρις {Ὀρφέως}   10
> μακροπόλων πιτύλων
> ἐρέταισι κελεύσματα μελπομένα,
> τότε μὲν ταχύπλουν,
> τότε δ' εἰλατίνας ἀνάπαυμα πλάτα[ς.
> τ[ά]δε μοι τάδε θυμὸς ἰδεῖν ἵεται,   15
> Δαναῶν δὲ πόνους
> ἕτερος ἀναβοάτω.

> he whom the river's daughter
> Aegina engendered, Peleus,
> and by the mast mid-ship,
> the Thracian cithara of Orpheus
> cried out a plaintive Asian song,
> for the rowers of the long strokes
> singing commands, at one moment to sail fast,
> then at another, a rest from the pine oars.
> This, this my spirit desires to see,
> but the toils of the Danaans,
> let another proclaim that.

Here at the close of her monody, Hypsipyle recalls its opening by repeating the mimetic demonstrative: τάδε, τάδε (15). At the start, she defined her song in terms of what it was not: οὐ τάδε . . . οὐ τάδε. Now these demonstratives mark off her concluding lines with their vision of Orpheus' music aboard the Argo as precisely 'what her spirit desires to behold' (ἰδεῖν, 15), thus marking the conclusion of her priamel.[32] The visuality of Hypsipyle's ultimate desire parallels Sappho's: '[Anaktoria's] lovely gait and flashing,

---

[31] The text is uncertain at line 9: where Kannicht retains Ἀσιάς modifying Θρῆισσ' . . . κίθαρις, I have followed Beazley's suggestion of Ἀσιάδ' taken with ἔλεγον.

[32] My text retains the papyrus reading ἰδεῖν, 'to see'. Wilamowitz, defended by Battezzato 2005: 190, suggested the sensible emendation ὑδεῖν, 'to call; to name' on the grounds that calling or naming is more logically suited to Hypsipyle's performance. My discussion defends precisely the synaesthetic conceit of seeing sound and as a key component of Hypsipyle's monody, as well as the female viewership of Sappho's poetic persona.

brilliant face I would rather see (*idên*) than the chariots of Lydia and the infantrymen in all their arms'.[33] Similarly, Hypsipyle expresses what it is that she wants 'to see', while jettisoning the epic theme of the Seven for 'another' to sing (ἕτερος, 17).[34] In visualising Orpheus playing, Hypsipyle wants to re-embody the scene of the mythic musician plucking his elegiac Asian song on the cithara, sounding out orders for the Argonauts as they row.

In remarkably specific language, Hypsipyle here 'weaves' a finely wrought scene full of intricate details. She presents a particular kind of *kitharôidia* (stringed instrumental music with sung accompaniment) that is decidedly New Musical, and thus inspired by the musicality and function of the double reed pipes known as the *aulos*.[35] By using the enchanting cithara of the mythic Orpheus to choreograph the rowing Argonauts, the scene co-opts a role usually performed by the *aulos*.[36] Distinctive attributes of the *aulos* – its volubility, its elegiac character, its choreographic capacity – are here projected onto the cithara of Orpheus, whose song is specifically characterised as 'Asian' (9–10; see n. 31 above). With this epithet, Euripides fuses 'Thracian' Orpheus with a Lesbian tradition of the cithara's eastern provenance.[37] As one of our sources for music history reports, the 'Asian' epithet is attributed to Lesbos, 'because Lesbian cithar-odes who lived opposite Asia made use of it'.[38] This descriptor underscores a kind of eastern otherness often associated with the New Music, a point to which I return. At the same time, the 'Asian' cithara may suggest the kind of *avant-garde* innovation inspired by the *aulos* in stringed music associated with Timotheus the citharode.[39]

---

[33] Sappho fr. 16.17–20 Voigt τὰ]ς <κ>ε βολλοίμαν ἐρατόν τε βᾶμα | κἀμάρυχμα λάμπρον ἴδην προσώπω | ἢ τὰ Λύδων ἄρματα κἀν ὅπλοισι [πεσδομ]άχεντας.

[34] Cf. Scodel 1997: 91–3 on Hypsipyle's 'priamel of the type that shades into recusatio' (p. 93).

[35] Orpheus is not explicitly represented as singing in Hypsipyle's song; his cithara itself takes over this role as it 'cries out' the instrumental accompaniment for the rowers, imitating the *aulos*. For the auletic musicality of the New Music see Csapo 2004: 216–21, Franklin 2013; Wilson 1999 and Martin 2003 discuss the complex cultural debates over the *aulos*.

[36] Hardie 2012: 174.

[37] Euripides' characterisation of Orpheus in terms of ancient Lesbian *kitharôidia* has a New Musical resonance: cf. Timotheus' 'history of the lyric tradition' (fr. 791.221–33 Hordern) with LeVen 2014: 97–101. See Burkert 1994 = 2001–11: III 112–19 on Euripides' introduction of Orpheus into the play, especially in relation to the cult of Dionysus Melpomenos.

[38] [Plut.] *On Music* 1133c.

[39] See Csapo and Wilson 2009 and Power 2010: 516–54 on Timotheus and the New Music, as well as his possible associations with Euripides.

With such specific details about the soundscape that she desires, Hypsipyle encourages a synesthetic experience of this Orphic music.[40] That is to say, her song invites the audience to conjure this soundscape along with her through an imagined spectacle – a spectacle itself crafted through song. This blending of visual and aural modes recalls Hypsipyle's initial imperative to 'look' at the sound she performs, an activity she casts as 'sound-weaving'. Moreover, the Orphic performance that she yearns to see and thus hear is specifically a work song (κελεύσματα, fr. 752g.12, ~260) whose choreographic rhythms are meant to be felt as much as heard, since rowers maintain their bodily coordination by keeping time with the music.[41] The Orphic music that she desires is similar to the varieties of song she rejected in her priamel: a work song 'woven' by a Lemnian princess featuring a heroic quest narrative. Traces of each dismissed genre thus fold into her ultimate vision of song.

Hypsipyle's virtuosic monody thus constructs a *mise-en-scène* that invites the audience to picture enchanted, Orphic music actively working on bodies. Such a synaesthetic experience exploits tragedy's psychagogic power over the audience to an extreme.[42] As Plato suggests in the *Republic*, the musicality in tragedy especially, like colour in a painting, affects the mind through the senses.[43] Heightened with the anticipation of the Sapphic priamel and the intense musical desire Hypsipyle models for the audience, this monody fosters an attachment to the Asian sound of Orpheus' *kitharôidia* – the musical style connected to the cult that the play aetiologises.

In a fragment from the end of the play, Euenus explains that after their father Jason died, Orpheus cared for him and his brother, training Euneus in the music of the 'Asian cithara' (μοῦσάν με κιθάρας Ἀσιάδος διδάσκεται, fr. 759a.101, ~1622) and Thoas in the arms of Ares. Hypsipyle's musical desire – Orpheus and his Asian *kitharôidia* – thus takes on new life

---

[40] 'Synaesthesia' refers clinically to the condition of experiencing one sense through another; in performance, it refers to 'sensory blending' through metaphor or other devices (S. Butler and Purves 2013a: 1; for a theoretical perspective on the visceral experience of synaesthetic performance see Machon 2009).

[41] As mentioned above, Orpheus' enchanting cithara here performs the usual role of the *aulos*, which was used aboard triremes for choreographing rowers. The *aulos*-choreographed vessel appears in a highly New Musical choral passage in Euripides' *Electra* (432–41).

[42] Of all poetic genres, tragedy is 'the most pleasant to the many and most capable of moving the soul' ([Pl.] *Minos* 321a4–5). For *psychagôgia* ('soul-leading') as the means by which tragedy mediates its aesthetic form see Wohl 2015: 6–7.

[43] Pl. *Resp.* 601a4–b8. Cf. Gorg. *Hel.* 9 on the enchanting power of poetry.

through her son who was trained in this citharodic art by Orpheus himself.[44] As a paradigmatic citharode, Orpheus is particularly relevant to the Lesbian heritage of 'Asian' music Hypsipyle desires. At the same time, Orpheus also has ties to Dionysian cult.[45] This combination of eastern musical tradition with the Dionysian connection makes Orpheus an ideal mythic figure for uniting Lemnos and Athens into a shared musical culture – to say nothing of his role in the heroic narrative of Jason and the Argonauts. By anchoring Hypsipyle's performance around such a mythically charged figure, Euripides projects a continuity reaching from the ancient cult figure to the contemporary Euneidae family of citharodes.[46]

Aristophanes' 'Lesbianising' Hypsipyle

Building upon this reading of how Hypsipyle's monody functions on the tragic stage, I turn now to the lens that Aristophanes provides in the *Frogs*. In this early strand of literary criticism, Aristophanes casts Euripidean style as soft, slender and feminising, incorporating sophistic chatter and bookish learning.[47] Aristophanes' character Euripides discusses his own style as an embodied form, explaining that he 'took the weight off' of tragedy, slimming her down 'with little works and strolls and white beets, administering a juice strained off from chatty books'; then he 'nurtured her with a mixture of Cephisophon's monodies' (941–4). On this account, actor's song – like Hypsipyle's monody – carries much of the 'substance' of Euripidean tragedy. When Aristophanes' Aeschylus later introduces the caricatured Hypsipyle as the 'Muse of Euripides', he has just accused Euripides of culling his music from low-register sexual or sympotic contexts, as well as foreign, specifically 'eastern' or 'Asian' sources (1298–1303). Especially in view of her own poetic self-fashioning on the tragic stage, the singing Hypsipyle makes the ideal target for this low-brow, orientalising, feminising embodiment of Euripidean style, a parody that turns on Hypsipyle's musical accompaniment

---

[44] Wilamowitz *ap*. Grenfell and Hunt 1908: 28 suggested that Dionysus at the play's end bids Euneus to go to Athens to establish the *genos Euneidae*.

[45] Ghidini 2013 distinguishes a Dionysian strand of Orphic music from a more Apollonian one. See also Power 2010: 355–67 on Orphic *kitharôidia*.

[46] Csapo 1999–2000, 2004, 2008 argues that the New Music marked a resurgence in traditional Dionysian cult, including appeals to the mystery cult figure Orpheus. Cf. LeVen 2014: 97–101, which discusses Timotheus on the citharodes Orpheus and Terpander.

[47] For Euripidean style in Aristophanes see O'Sullivan 1992, Worman 2015: 114–45; also Farmer 2017 on the 'culture of tragedy' as represented on the comic stage.

and style. Reading this comically embodied 'Muse' in the light of the fragments, this section focuses on the musical implications of one criticism especially: that 'Euripides' Muse' is 'Lesbianising'.[48]

When the potsherd-clacking caricature of Hypsipyle appears on stage at Aeschylus' invitation, Dionysus responds with wry sarcasm: αὕτη ποθ᾽ ἡ Μοῦσ᾽ οὐκ ἐλεσβίαζεν, οὔ; (1308).[49] His remark offers stylistic commentary: '*That* Muse never had any Lesbian charm at all, did she?' with the ribald twist, '*That* Muse never sucked it, did she?'[50] While critics have tended to take this comment to mean that Hypsipyle must have been stylistically distanced from Lesbian poetry and sexually unattractive, one argues precisely the opposite, offering a reading more in line with the broader critique of Euripidean style in the passage's context.[51] Dionysus' sarcasm suggests that Hypsipyle had a strong flair of Lesbian style, one that might be easily mocked and doubled with a sexual joke. This Lesbian style has been read in terms of the parody that follows, which has an Aeolic rhythm.[52] But Dionysus' one-liner can be interpreted in terms of Hypsipyle's monody, a connection that Aristophanes invites by specifying 'this Muse' (i.e. the castanet-playing caricature of Hypsipyle).

As noted above, Hypsipyle positions herself much like the female spectator of Sappho fr. 16, performing an extended priamel that culminates in the music she 'desires to see'. Sapphic imagery also appears in Hypsipyle's language for her poetic weaving (fr. 102 Voigt; p. 168 n. 27 above). Her castanets however, are especially singled out in the parody (Ar. *Ran.* 1305–7). While castanets do often appear in popular scenes – a fact that Aristophanes exploits – they also feature in a more elevated context in Lesbian poetry. In Sappho's scene of the wedding of Andromache and Hector, the *krotala* accompany the lyre, *aulos* and choral song in

---

[48] For female personifications in comedy see Hall 2006: 170–83, especially 173–4 on 'Euripides' Muse'. Note also the discussion in Gilhuly 2015 ≈ 2018: 92–116 of the Lesbian 'Muse' on the comic stage as a figure created through literary discourse who blends transgressive new musical styles with transgressive female behaviour.

[49] I take the line as a sarcastic question with an emphatic double negative, as the scholiasts were inclined (De Simone 2008).

[50] Dover 1993 *ad loc.* discusses the double entendre in *lesbiazein* as referring to oral sex as well as to behaving or performing (musically) in a 'Lesbian' style, as a verb ending in –ιάζειν; see further Gilhuly 2015 ≈ 2018: 92–116, Worman 2015: 133 with n. 96. See also Henderson 1991: 183–4 for a discussion of the sexual practice, with apposite parallels among sympotic flute-girls (*aulêtridai*).

[51] De Simone 2008.

[52] Henderson 1991: 183, De Simone 2008.

an atmospheric performance.[53] Another decidedly elevated register for
castanets is the eastern cult worship of Cybele and Dionysus.[54] In the
hands of Dionysus' granddaughter in tragic performance, this connection
could hardly fail to resonate. On the tragic stage then, Hypsipyle's New
Musical castanets could convey a Dionysian cultic association with an
eastern, possibly even Lesbian style. Aristophanes mocks Euripides' affinity
for the common by representing Hypsipyle's *krotala* as an impromptu
instrument of ostraca, which – the scholia comment – would be a particularly vulgar accompaniment for song.[55] On this point however, a Lesbian
tradition may be at play even in Euripides' characterisation of Hypsipyle as
a slave woman. According to this account, the Muses were seven Mysian
(i.e. 'eastern') servant girls (θεραπαινίδαι), who were brought to Lesbos and
taught to play the cithara.[56]

Several Lesbian features thus colour Hypsipyle's performance. While it is
difficult to determine precisely which aspect of 'Euripides' Muse' was felt to
be 'Lesbianising', the reference certainly invites consideration of what this
would mean from a musical perspective.[57] Neighbouring the island of
Lemnos in the Aegean, Lesbos played a key role in the reception of
citharodic performance from the Near East in the early archaic period.[58]
This style of *kitharôidia* was especially associated with Apollo, Orpheus
and the eastern-influenced tradition of the miraculous powers of the
cithara.[59] During the rise of the New Music in the fifth century, the
'Asian' cithara (as Orpheus plays in Hypsipyle's monody) has ties to

[53] Sappho fr. 44.25–6 Voigt καὶ ψ[ό]φο[ς κ]ροτάλ[ων … ἴκα]νε δ' ἐς αἴθ[ερα. See West 1992: 123 on
the history of the castanets, although I read the sonic atmosphere in Sappho as more of a
distinctive musical style than as a reflection of historical practice for 'popular, festive music-
making', as he does. The elevated ensemble of lyre, *aulos*, and choral song – without the
castanets – appear frequently in Pindar's victory songs (*O.* 3.8–9, 10.93–4, *N.* 9.8–9, Henry
2007).
[54] See West 1992: 122–6 on *krotala* used for cult worship; he treats these separately from the
krotala in *Hypsipyle* and Sappho fr. 44 Voigt, which he takes to be more pedestrian contexts,
even though the same term is used. For the music of Cybele's cult see Holzman 2016: 541.
[55] Σ Ar. *Ran.* 1305b (p. 147 Chantry).
[56] Thus the third-century BC historian Myrsilus of Methymna (*BNJ* 477 F 7a). While Myrsilus'
version certainly postdates the archaic period, it seems to reflect elements of Lesbian citharodic
tradition (Power 2010: 385–93).
[57] Verbs in –ιάζειν commonly refer to bodily deportment and behaviour, but in Ar. fr. 930 *PCG*,
two such verbs, σιφνιάζειν and χιάζειν, are used specifically for musical styles. Cf. Dover 1993 on
Ran. 1308.
[58] For a reconstruction of the recovery of the seven-toned (heptatonic) cithara through Lydia see
Franklin 2002, 2008: 194–6.
[59] Power 2010: 26, 378–85.

Lesbos specifically through an orientalising romanticism.[60] If then we take *lesbiazein* in a musical sense, a Lesbianising style of Hypsipyle's perform-ance would reflect a cultic tradition that Athens and Lemnos shared, rooting Euripides' New Musical experiment in an already ancient lore surrounding the kind Orphic *kitharôidia* that he aims to aetiologise in *Hypsipyle*. Aristophanes' 'Lesbianising' joke (1308) turns on a parallel between poetic style and desire, a fact that reflects Hypsipyle's Sapphic persona as a singer 'desirous' for music. *Frogs* itself pointedly pitches its comic play between poetic and sexual appetites in the opening scene between Dionysus and Heracles (52–67). In a further stylistic critique, the joke about oral sex in particular (where a ravenous desire centres on the mouth) is consistent with Aristophanes' feminised, sophistic characterisation of Euripides as a 'mouth-worker' (στοματουργός, 826) and 'chatter-collector' (στωμυλιοσυλλεκτάδη, 841).[61]

From Thiersch's nineteenth-century *foedissima meretrix* ('a most foul whore'), to Rogers's 'flaunting harlot', critics have tended to view Euripides' Muse – and the New Musical style associated with her – through the deliberately exaggerated lens that Aristophanes and his Aeschylus provide, reading their own era's moral outrage against 'the filthiest tricks of harlotry' – in Rogers's terms – as an apt assessment of Euripidean musical innovation.[62] Taking the fragments of *Hypsipyle* into account, Borthwick's more recent evaluation casts Euripides' Muse as 'the ancient equivalent of a "go-go girl"' and retains his predecessors' bias against the New Music: 'Aristophanes, while obviously recalling to the audience the *Hypsipyle* scene, thus demonstrates the sort of performance that such cheap café music really suits'.[63]

In view of Hypsipyle's monody, Aristophanes' caricature can be read in a more stylistic vein as a trenchant jab at the poetically self-conscious heroine's musical style. The slave woman playing castanets and singing about the music she desires is comically exaggerated as a sex worker entertaining symposiasts: her *krotala* become cheap ostraca; her poetic desire is transformed to one associated with a sympotic prostitute; her style turns on an alternate meaning for *lesbiazein* that locates her sexualised desire in the mouth, probably to pointed literary-critical effect. Aristophanes' caricature of the 'Muse of Euripides' thus amounts to an emphatic lowering

[60] [Plut.] *On Music* 1133c; Power 2010: 26–7.
[61] Worman 2015: 117 n. 43; also 2008: 96–105.
[62] Thiersch 1830: I 252, Rogers 1902: 199.
[63] Borthwick 1994: 27 = 2015: 201, 202.

of the tragic register in exaggeration of stylistic traits that are consistently targeted throughout the comic literary critique. As a critical aspect of Hypsipyle's performance, however, the 'Lesbianising' style resonates with the specific kind of 'Asian', Orphic *kitharôidia* that the play celebrates.

As the character Euripides claims in Aristophanes' *Frogs*, monody is the substance on which he nourished the tragic genre he had slimmed down. I have suggested that Hypsipyle's monody musically embodies the cultic form that the play as a whole works to regenerate through the virtuosic New Musical performance of its lead female character. If the path that Hypsipyle charts westward from Lemnos to Nemea ultimately reaffirms Athenian ties with these critical sites, as Martin Cropp has suggested, I submit that this trajectory is especially felt in the music of Hypsipyle's performance and its further resonances throughout the play.[64] As a woman from the eastern Aegean whose son establishes the Athenian cult of Dionysus Melpomenos, Hypsipyle herself is brought to these significant sites where she sings about the 'Asian' *kitharôidia* of her homeland. But Hypsipyle's performance does more than simply disseminate this musical form. Between its mimetic aural effects, its enacted Sapphic priamel and the synaesthetic window into Orphic performance that it opens up, this monody connects the audience with the music Hypsipyle desires. Euripides thus positions this Lemnian princess as Athens' Muse, inviting the city to participate in the kind of Orphic, Dionysian cultic *mousikê* that Athens shares with her allies. In style and content, this performance makes Hypsipyle a New Musical figure, connecting ancient cultic lore with contemporary musical practices through the vivid stylistic techniques illustrative of late fifth-century musical innovation. From the fragments of her monody and its refraction through the parodic lens Aristophanes provides, Hypsipyle thus emerges as the decidedly New Musical Muse of Euripidean style.

[64] Cropp 2003: 143.

11 | Fragmented Self and Fragmented Responsibility

Pasiphae in Euripides' Cretans

LUIGI BATTEZZATO

Sex with animals is an embarrassing topic, even in liberal modern societies. Yet Pasiphae, in a fragmentary play of Euripides, speaks exactly about that, as a woman in a society that greatly restricted the freedom of women (sexual, political and otherwise). This chapter will discuss her shocking speech not simply as an early instance of 'immoral' art,[1] but as an exploration the dynamics of self-control, regret and human responsibility in the face of external (divine) intervention.

Pasiphae's Speech

Pasiphae talks about her sexual congress with a bull in public, in front of her husband. Her way of talking is even more shocking than her tale. She explains what she did without uttering a single word of repentance. A modern critic thus finds that 'she is incapable of the normal human sentiments, of regret and repentance' and is 'a morally inferior person'.[2] Yet Pasiphae's story, perhaps because of the titillation of her scandalous sexual adventure, was hugely attractive to ancient writers, visual artists and audiences alike.[3] This is the text of the speech:[4]

> ἀρνουμένη μὲν οὐκέτ᾽ ἂν πίθοιμί σε,
> πάντως γὰρ ἤδη δῆλον ὡς ἔχει τάδε.   5
> ἐγ[ὼ] γὰρ εἰ μὲν ἀνδρὶ προὔβαλον δέμας
> τοὐμὸν λαθραίαν ἐμπολωμένη Κύπριν,
> ὀρθῶς ἂν ἤδη μάχ[λο]ς οὖσ᾽ ἐφαινόμην·
> νῦν δ᾽, ἐκ θεοῦ γὰρ προσβολῆς ἐμηνάμην,
> ἀλγῶ μέν, ἐστὶ δ᾽ οὐχ ἑκο[ύσ]ιον κακόν.   10

---

[1] For immorality and aesthetic value see Jacobson 1997, Kieran 2005.

[2] Reckford 1974: 321, 322.

[3] Papadopoulos 1994; also Cantarella 1964: 37–42, Webster 1967: 299, Collard 1995a, Cozzoli 2001: 15–18, Kannicht *TrGF* v/I 503, Armstrong 2006: 261–98, Collard and Cropp 2008: 1 532–3.

[4] Edition and translation from Collard and Cropp 2008: 1 546–9, occasionally slightly adapted; translations of Euripidean fragments throughout come from the same source.

ἔχει γὰρ οὐδὲν εἰκός· ἐς τί γὰρ βοὸς
βλέψασ' ἐδήχθην θυμὸν αἰσχίστηι νόσωι;
ὡς εὐπρεπὴς μὲν ἐν πέπλοισιν ἦν ἰδεῖν,
πυρσῆς δὲ χαίτης καὶ παρ' ὀμμάτων σέλας

15   οἰνωπὸν ἐξέλαμπε περ[καί]νων γένυν;
οὐ μὴν δέμας γ' εὔρ[υθμον — × ν]υμφίου·
τοιῶνδε λέκτρω[ν εἴνεκ' εἰς] πεδοστιβῆ
ῥινὸν καθισ.[× —◡—×—◡]ται;
ἀλλ' οὐδὲ παίδων.[—◡—×—] πόσιν

20   θέσθαι· τί δῆτα τῆι[δ' ἐμαι]νόμην νόσωι;
δαίμων ὁ τοῦδε κἄμ' ἐ[νέπλησεν κα]κῶν,
μάλιστα δ' οὗτος οισε[—×—◡]ῶν·
ταῦρον γὰρ οὐκ ἔσφαξ[εν ὅνπερ ηὔ]ξατο
ἐλθόντα θύσειν φάσμα [πο]ντίω[ι θε]ῶι.

25   ἐκ τῶνδέ τοί σ' ὑπῆλθ[ε κἀ]πετείσ[ατο
δίκην Ποσειδῶν, ἐς δ' ἔμ' ἔσκηψ[εν νόσον.
κᾆπειτ' αὐτεῖς καὶ σὺ μαρτύρηι θεοὺς
αὐτὸς τάδ' ἔρξας καὶ καταισχύνας ἐμέ;
κἀγὼ μὲν ἡ τεκοῦσα κοὐδὲν αἰτία

30   ἔκρυψα πληγὴν δαίμονος θεήλατον,
σὺ δ', εὐπρεπῆ γὰρ κἀπιδείξασθαι καλά,
τῆς σῆς γυναικός, ὦ κάκιστ' ἀνδρῶν φρονῶν,
ὡς οὐ μεθέξων πᾶσι κηρύσσεις τάδε.
σύ τοί μ' ἀπόλλυς, σὴ γὰρ ἡ 'ξ[αμ]αρτία,

35   ἐκ σοῦ νοσοῦμεν. πρὸς τάδ' εἴτε ποντίαν
κτείνειν δοκεῖ σοι, κτε[ῖ]ν'· ἐπίστασαι δέ τοι
μιαιφόν' ἔργα καὶ σφαγὰς ἀνδροκτόνους·
εἴτ' ὠμοσίτου τῆς ἐμῆς ἐρᾶις φαγεῖν
σαρκός, πάρεστι· μὴ 'λλίπηις θοινώμενος.

40   ἐλεύθεροι γὰρ κοὐδὲν ἠδικηκότες
τῆς σῆς ἕκατι ζημ[ία]ς ὀλούμεθα.

Denials from me will no longer convince you; for the facts are now quite
clear. If I had thrown myself at a man in love's furtive commerce, I should
rightly now be revealed as lascivious. As it is, because my madness was a
god's onslaught, I hurt, but my trouble is not voluntary. Why, it has no
probability! What did I see in a bull to have my heart eaten away by a
most shaming affliction? Was it that it was handsome to the eye in robes,
and threw out a bright beam from its ruddy hair and eyes, the beard on its
cheeks darkly red? Certainly it wasn't the (lissom *or* well-formed?) body
of a bridegroom! Was it for a union like that . . . of an animal's hide . . .?
Nor (to get) children . . . to make it my husband! Why then was I
(maddened) by this affliction? It was this man's destiny that (brought)

me too (my fill) of trouble, and he especially . . . since he did not slaughter (that) bull (which) he vowed to sacrifice to the sea-god when it was manifested. This is the reason, I tell you, why Poseidon undermined you and exacted punishment, but launched (the affliction) upon me. And then you cry out and call the gods to witness, when you did this yourself and brought shame upon me? While I, who gave birth and was at fault in nothing, concealed the god's stroke launched by heaven, you – fine and splendid things to put on show! – you proclaimed them to all, as if you want no part in your wife, you worst of men (*or* husbands) in your intention! It is you who have destroyed me! Yours was the wrongdoing! You are the cause of my affliction! So either, if you have decided to kill me by drowning, go on and kill me – indeed you understand acts of foul murder and the slaughtering of men! – or, if you desire to eat my flesh raw, here it is: don't go short on your banquet! Because of the punishment upon you, we are to die, who are free and quite innocent of wrongdoing.

Eur. Cretan Women fr. 472e.4–41

The very survival of her speech is a fluke that mirrors Pasiphae's fragmentary status. The speech is preserved by a single leaf of a parchment codex, probably from the third century AD, which contained a complete text of the play. The surviving section 'may have well have been deliberately preserved from a complete text, as a rhetorical *tour-de-force* and model'.[5] Had it been transcribed on different pages, we would probably not have it.

Pasiphae is, for us, a fragment: we do not know what she said before or after her big speech. However, her actions are a fragment for Pasiphae herself: she has no idea why she did what she did. Her shocking experience leaves her with apparently no memory of the reasons that caused her actions. She presents herself as a simple puppet of the gods.[6] Of course we, like Minos in the play, may decide not to believe her. But what she says poses complex philosophical and ethical problems: can the responsibility of human action be divorced from the agent? Do external influences free the agent from responsibility? How do we know that the person speaking now is the same 'self' as the person who did the act? How can she be the same, if she acted under external influences, and has no access to the reasons that prompted her to that action? And finally: when is a person a self?[7]

[5] Collard 1995a: 72. For a palaeographical and codicological discussion see Carrara 2009: 452–4.
[6] Cf. Pl. *Leg.* 644de with Schofield 2016.
[7] Sorabji 2006. For specifically female agency in tragedy see also CHONG-GOSSARD.

Euripides' *Cretans*: The Plot and the Myth of Pasiphae

Cretans is an early play of Euripides. The evidence provided by Euripides' metrical practice in handling iambic trimeters places it in the period 455–428.[8] It is close in subject matter to Euripides' *Cretan Women* of 438, a play that staged the story of Aerope, an adulteress who has sex with a servant.[9]

Pre-Euripidean sources for the myth of Pasiphae are not very helpful, and Euripides' account is probably quite different from them.

The versions in the *Catalogue of Women* attributed to Hesiod and in Pindar are very fragmentary and divergent. 'Hesiod' mentions the bull coming from the sea, the bull's desiring gaze for Pasiphae and the birth of the Minotaur, but not the intercourse between Pasiphae and the bull; Hirschberger suggests that the birth of the Minotaur is due to the 'sight' of the bull at the moment of conception (a common folkloric motif), not to sexual intercourse between Pasiphae and the bull.[10] As for Pindar, according to a version attributed to him by Porphyry, it was Zeus, in form of a bull, not a 'real bull', who had intercourse with Pasiphae.[11]

Bacchylides mentions the involvement of Aphrodite in causing Pasiphae's desire for the bull and Daedalus' help for Pasiphae, but (unlike Euripides) he does not mention Minos' fault.[12]

Scholars normally reconstruct the plot of *Cretans* from the narratives of Apollodorus and, in part, Hyginus: they do this because some of the narrative details, especially in Apollodorus, match the story as reported in Euripides' fragments,[13] and because on other occasions Apollodorus and

---

[8] Cropp and Fick 1985: 70, 82. This date range is generally accepted, by e.g. Collard 1995a: 58, Cozzoli 2001: 9–11 (she favours the period 442–432, and in particular 433, accepting a suggestion by Cantarella 1964: 103–7), Kannicht *TrGF* v/I 504 (who suggests 431, in the same trilogy as *Medea*), Collard and Cropp 2008: I 532.

[9] For the similarities between the two plays see Pohlenz 1954: I 250, Cantarella 1964: 104, Collard 1995a: 58. For *Cretan Women* see Kannicht *TrGF* v/1 494–501, Collard and Cropp 2008: I 516–27. For the Aerope myth and its treatment in archaic and classical literature see Finglass 2011 on Soph. *Aj.* 1295–7.

[10] [Hes.] fr. 145 M–W (with their note in the 1967 edition on line 10, which refers to the bull sent from the 'roaring' sea); for the motif in folklore where the shape of the foetus is influenced by what the woman sees, especially at the moment of intercourse, cf. Heliodorus 10.14.7, *Genesis* 30.37–43, Hirschberger 2004: 316.

[11] Pind. fr. 91 S–M.

[12] See Bacchylides 26 S–M with Maehler 1997: 44–5, 278–80 for a commentary on Bacchylides' poem and for other references to the sources. For a survey of the sources see Cantarella 1964: 157–71, Papadopoulos 1994: 193–4.

[13] Cantarella 1964: 15, 17, 48, 50, Webster 1967: 89, Maehler 1997: 268, Cozzoli 2001: 11–13, 53, Kannicht *TrGF* v/I 502–3, Collard and Cropp 2008: I 530.

Hyginus depend on prose summaries of Euripides' plays. Apollodorus and Hyginus do not passively or invariably depend on these plot summaries,[14] but a degree of dependence is likely when their accounts match the remains of the text of a play.

Apollodorus' and Hyginus' versions differ in one crucial detail: the responsibility for Pasiphae's erotic desire. In Apollodorus (*Bibl.* 3.1.3–4), the culprit is Minos: he refuses to sacrifice a bull to Poseidon, and the god punishes Minos by making his wife desire the bull. This corresponds exactly with what Pasiphae claims in Euripides' play (fr. 472e.23–4). Apollodorus does not mention Aphrodite. One can speculate that Poseidon asked her to cause Pasiphae's love, as many other Greek gods do under similar circumstances,[15] but we have no positive evidence, and some scholars rule out any explicit involvement of Aphrodite in Euripides.[16]

In Hyginus, the responsibility is Pasiphae's.[17] She neglected to make sacrifices to Aphrodite, and the goddess caused her love for the bull in retaliation. In this version Pasiphae behaves like Hippolytus in Euripides' play; similarities with *Hippolytus* have been pointed out by many scholars.[18] Should we suppose that Aphrodite played a role in Euripides' play? Hartung and Webster supposed that Pasiphae was punished by Aphrodite for neglecting to make sacrifices, but this is no more than speculation.[19]

Several scholars suggest that Pasiphae's speech was part of an *agôn*.[20] An *agôn* may seem likely since Helen uses similar arguments in the first speech of an *agôn* in *Trojan Women* (924–50), followed by a refutation speech delivered by Hecuba. However, in *Cretans*, Pasiphae's speech is followed by a comment of the chorus leader (fr. 472e.42–3), by a very short and brutal[21]

---

[14] Meccariello 2014: 88–90, following Huys 1997b in playing down the influence of *hypotheseis* of Euripides' plays on Apollodorus. For Hyginus see below, n. 17.

[15] See especially Hera in *Il.* 14.187–223 (deceiving Aphrodite).

[16] Cozzoli 2001: 30–1.

[17] Hyg. *Fab.* 40. Huys 1996, 1997a and Meccariello 2014: 86–8 are somewhat sceptical on the extent of the influence of the *hypotheseis* to Euripides' plays on Hyginus. Finglass 2014: 70–1 shows that the link is strong in the case of the two *Fabulae* that are explicitly stated (in their titles) to give the plot of a Euripidean play, even if Hyginus may introduce changes; the relationship is similar to that of Apollodorus' text with the *hypotheseis* (above, n. 14).

[18] Cantarella 1964: 105–6, Reckford 1974, Collard 1995a: 55, 57, Cozzoli 2001: 39–41.

[19] Hartung 1843: 105–6, Webster 1967: 89; they also suppose that Aphrodite spoke the prologue of Euripides' *Cretans*, as in *Hippolytus*. See also Cantarella 1964: 113 (prologue by Poseidon and Aphrodite).

[20] Duchemin 1968: 90, Cozzoli 2001: 102, Paduano 2005: 135.

[21] This is a typical trait of Minos' character in Attic tragedies, according to the pseudo-Platonic dialogue *Minos* (see especially 318d9–11 ... φασιν ... τὸν ... Μίνων ἄγριόν τινα καὶ χαλεπὸν καὶ

reply by Minos (44–9), by a second comment from the chorus leader (50–1), and by a firm statement by Minos about the future punishment of Pasiphae (52). The fragment stops at this point. In his replies, the king does not reject Pasiphae's narrative, nor does he claim that she made false statements. Since Euripides' *agônes* all follow a rather fixed structure, it is unlikely that Minos gave a whole speech after this exchange.[22] The second *agôn* speech normally follows immediately after the choral comment at the end of the first speech.[23] Minos' remarks may correspond to the short angry replies that follow the last speech of an *agôn*[24] or to the remarks of the 'judge' of the *agôn*.[25] However, the *agônes* of Euripides do not present a choral reply at that point, as found here (50–1), but rather a reply by the other speaker, normally part of an exchange between the two speakers, with no choral interventions.[26] This is another element that suggests that this section is not part of an *agôn*. Moreover, as Collard points out,[27] Pasiphae's speech is preceded by a *lyric* comment by the chorus (2–3): this is again unparalleled in Euripides' *agôn* scenes, where the choral 'tag' is in trimeters.[28] Finally, Pasiphae's speech does not refer to her opponent's previous speech, as it is normal in Euripidean *agônes*.[29]

Pasiphae's speech is thus unlikely to be part of an *agôn* and/or to be followed by a full reply by Minos. The end of Pasiphae's speech was the moment to challenge her claims. If Minos did not do it at this point, it does not seem likely that he contested Pasiphae's claims at all. Of course, this does not rule out the idea that, at some point earlier in the play, Minos accused Pasiphae in a dialogue or in a speech; Minos may even have replied, after Pasiphae's speech, when Pasiphae was not on stage any more.

ἄδικον. ΣΩ. Ἀττικόν ... λέγεις μῦθον καὶ τραγικόν, 'they say ... that Minos was a brutal, harsh and unjust kind of person.' (Socrates) 'The story you tell is an Attic tragedy'). Cf. Cozzoli 2001: 14, 110, Kannicht *TrGF* v/I 503, Collard and Cropp 2008: I 532.

[22] For the structure of *agônes* see Strohm 1957: 3–49, Duchemin 1968, Lloyd 1992, Dubischar 2001, Mastronarde 2010: 222–45, Battezzato 2017 (especially p. 164 n. 2 for further bibliography).

[23] There is one exception, which is however clearly motivated. As Denniston 1939 on Eur. *El.* 1055 ff. notes, 'Electra runs a great risk by indulging in the crushing invective' that she is about to deliver and needs to ask Clytemnestra for confirmation of permission to speak freely (1055–9); this explains the unusual form of the *agôn*.

[24] *Alc.* 708–9, *Med.* 579–87, *Hipp.* 1038–40, *Andr.* 234–5.

[25] *Hcld.* 236–52, *Hec.* 1240–51, *Tro.* 1036–41. In some cases, the 'judge' who delivers angry threats is also one of the speakers: see e.g. *Her.* 238–51.

[26] For the typical structure, with a dialogue between the two speakers of the *agôn*, without interventions of the chorus leader, cf. *Alc.* 710–40, *Med.* 588–626, *Hipp.* 1041–1101, *Andr.* 236–72; also the analyses in the works cited above, n. 22.

[27] Collard 1995a: 72–3, commentary on fr. 472e.2–3.

[28] E.g. *Alc.* 673–4. For full references and complete analyses see the works cited above, n. 22.

[29] E.g. *Alc.* 675–8.

We simply do not know. In this situation, the best course of action for us as interpreters is to make sense of Pasiphae's speech as it is, in the context of the literary practices and ethical principles presented in the tragic genre. If we do that, we can identify some character models that Pasiphae is following.

We do not know much else about the plot of Euripides' play.[30] The parodos (fr. 472) was sung by initiates of Zagreus, a chthonic god variously identified with Hades (Aesch. fr. 5), the son of Hades (fr. 228) or Dionysus (Call. fr. 43b.34 Harder).[31] A dialogue followed, possibly between the Nurse and Minos, on the birth and nature of the Minotaur (Eur. fr. 472b). We then have Pasiphae's well-preserved extensive speech, which will be discussed below. We also know that Icarus was a 'rather bold' character in the play and sang a monody (fr. 472g). Collard and Cropp suggest that he could have sung a monody before his fatal flight.[32] Alternatively, Van Looy supposes that his monody lamented the imprisonment of his father Daedalus.[33]

Pasiphae is by far the best-preserved figure from this play.

Pasiphae's Speech and the Excuse of Irresistible Love: Eur. fr. 472e

Pasiphae's argument is divided into two sections. In lines 6–20 (first section), she claims that her actions go against her plausible self-interest and must have been caused by a divine agent; this implies that she did not act willingly and is not responsible for her actions. In lines 21–35 (second section), she claims the fault is Minos': he offended a divine agent, who took revenge on him through his wife.

The first section can be seen as yet another instance of the well-known ancient tradition of the argument about human incapability to resist divine intervention, an argument that starts with Agamemnon's apology in the *Iliad*, and is found in Helen's defence in Euripides and Gorgias.[34] Many

[30] Collard 1995a, Diggle, *TrGFS* pp. 115–19, Cozzoli 2001, Di Benedetto 2001 = 2007: III 1343–65, Kannicht *TrGF* v/I 502–16, Collard and Cropp 2008: I 529–55.
[31] Collard 1995a: 69 and Cozzoli 2001: 85 argue for an identification with Dionysus in Eur. fr. 472.
[32] Collard and Cropp 2008: I 531; for a similar reconstruction see Collard 1995a: 54–5.
[33] Van Looy *ap.* Jouan and Van Looy 2000: 316–17.
[34] Hom. *Il.* 19.86–94, Eur. *Tro.* 948–50, Gorgias' *Helen*. Cf. Dodds 1951: 1–27, de Romilly 1976, B. Williams 1993: 50–5. For discussions of 'double motivation' (human and divine) see Lesky 1961 ≈ De Jong 1999: II 384–403 ≈ Cairns 2001: 170–202, Lesky 1966, Battezzato 2019.

modern interpreters suggest that here Euripides is simply echoing a 'traditional symbolism' that does not correspond to his beliefs nor to those of his audience,[35] or that he is mocking or showing the inadequacies of an 'archaic' modality of thought,[36] or that Pasiphae is fundamentally insincere.[37] De Romilly perceptively suggests that the motif of invincible love, here used in modified form by Pasiphae (an example not discussed by de Romilly), became a 'simple alibi' that proved the 'moral degradation' of characters.[38]

These perspectives, however, fail to account for Pasiphae's words, and do not have a basis in the text as transmitted: Pasiphae's argument is not self-contradictory, nor is it refuted by other characters. Pasiphae's speech is indeed similar to Helen's in *Trojan Women*,[39] but the context is different. In *Trojan Women*, Hecuba attacks Helen's argument, defending the reputation of the goddesses (969–70), denying any divine intervention (971–87) and claiming that Helen acted freely, of her own will (988–97): 'on seeing him [*sc.* Paris], your mind became Aphrodite' (ὁ σὸς δ' ἰδὼν νιν νοῦς ἐποιήθη Κύπρις, 988). Interpretations of this scene vary, but, even if not all interpreters agree that Hecuba's case is overwhelmingly persuasive, they all accept that she at least casts strong doubts on Helen's version of the facts.[40] Pasiphae's speech, as we saw (above, pp. 183–5), is not followed by a refutation denying divine intervention, and we have no reason to import this approach into this play; nor is divine intervention in human minds an 'archaic' approach rejected by Euripides, since divine intervention is central to the plot of *Hippolytus* and *Bacchae*, and no one can deny its effectiveness.[41]

Pasiphae's formulation is distinctive for several reasons: she is attentive to the ethical implications of divine intervention, is apparently unable to have access to her own inner psychological processes, and detects divine intervention from 'probable causes' rather than from access to the divine

---

[35] Dodds 1951. 186, followed by e.g. Dolfi 1984: 137.

[36] For a survey of similar interpretations, see Cozzoli 2001: 26–35; for the idea that Euripides criticises 'archaic' thought in that way see Goossens 1962: 152–4.

[37] Reckford 1974.

[38] de Romilly 1976: 319–20 'on voit en effet le respect des lois divines céder peu à peu la place au rejet égoïste des responsabilités humaines. L'invincible amour était une grande force du monde: il devient un simple alibi'; she talks of 'dégradation morale, dont la tragédie offre le reflet'. See also Paduano 2005: 128–33.

[39] For a balanced overview of the similarities see Lloyd 1984: 308.

[40] Stinton 1976: 70–2 = 1990: 248–50, de Romilly 1976: 317, Lloyd 1984, Meridor 2000. Lloyd and Meridor point out weaknesses or deliberate distortions in Hecuba's rhetoric.

[41] For the gods in Euripides see Mastronarde 2010: 153–206, Lefkowitz 2016.

realm. The second section, a 'counter-accusation', corresponds to a strategy used in other legal and tragic texts, as, for instance, in Antiphon's second tetralogy, *On an Accidental Murder (Oration* 3).[42] This argument is generally considered a simple (and unconvincing) rhetorical ploy.[43] However, in this case, the 'counter-accusation' is in fact necessary for the ethical and philosophical logic of Pasiphae's argument, and cannot be dismissed as a simple rhetorical artifice: her argument would collapse without it.

Divine Intervention and Human Guilt

Archaic and classical Greek literature has a long tradition of discussions on guilt, voluntary action, divine intervention and responsibility.[44] Some scholars, such as Snell and Dodds, created a narrative of progress: ethical thinking evolved from the archaic age to 'modern' conceptions that emerged in the classical age.[45] This evolutionary view has been contested by many recent scholars,[46] but retains its fascination. In fact, Pasiphae is both more modern and more 'archaic' than other tragic characters such as Phaedra. She is apparently 'archaic' in suggesting divine intervention, but 'modern' in using 'invincible love' as an excuse.

She seems to allude to the ethical principle of alternative possibilities: 'I am responsible for an action only if I can act otherwise'.[47] Simonides already voiced this principle:

πάντας δ' ἐπαίνημι καὶ φιλέω,
ἑκὼν ὅστις ἔρδηι
μηδὲν αἰσχρόν· ἀνάγκαι δ'
οὐδὲ θεοὶ μάχονται.

So long as he does nothing shameful willfully, I give my praise and love to any man. Not even the gods can fight necessity.

Simon. fr. 542.27–30 *PMG* = 260.27–30 Poltera[48]

---

[42] Gagarin 1997: 144–60. Dolfi 1984 analyses rhetorical similarities between Pasiphae's defence and Antiphon's speeches.
[43] Duchemin 1968: 207–8.
[44] See above, n. 34.
[45] Snell 1948, 1953, 1975, Dodds 1951, Irwin 1983, and below, n. 74.
[46] B. Williams 1993; also A. Schmitt 1990, Lawrence 2013.
[47] Frankfurt 1969: 829 (offering powerful arguments against this principle). For further discussion see Widerker and McKenna 2003, Michon 2011: 41. For this principle in relation to Greek tragedy, with special consideration for Aeschylus, see Battezzato 2019.
[48] Transl. Beresford 2008: 244. For interpretations of this controversial text see Most 1994, Hutchinson 2001: 291–306, Beresford 2008, Manuwald 2010.

Gorgias states the same principle in his *Encomium of Helen*. He considers Helen to be free from blame and of responsibility if anything (love, discourse, force, divine intervention) interfered with her will (20):[49]

> πῶς οὖν χρὴ δίκαιον ἡγήσασθαι τὸν τῆς Ἑλένης μῶμον, ἥτις εἴτ᾽ ἐρασθεῖσα εἴτε λόγωι πεισθεῖσα εἴτε βίαι ἁρπασθεῖσα εἴτε ὑπὸ θείας ἀνάγκης ἀναγκασθεῖσα ἔπραξεν ἃ ἔπραξε, πάντως διαφεύγει τὴν αἰτίαν;

> How then ought one consider the blame for Helen as being just, given that, whether she did what she did because she had fallen in love or had been persuaded by speech (*logos*) or had been seized with force or had been constrained by divine constraint, on every count she is acquitted of the accusation?

Gorgias thus combines the 'principle of alternative possibilities' with a strict definition of 'free action': an action is free if and only if nothing at all interferes with the will of the human agent (e.g. influence by other people through speech). This view is in fact close to Snell's view of human freedom, a view itself close to existentialist freedom: an action is free if its causation resides only within the mind of the individual, and is not influenced by external considerations or interventions (such as divine obligation or materialistic concerns). An action, in this existentialist view, is free only if it lacks a cause, even causes that are present within the agent's mind. This view of human freedom is strongly contested by Williams.[50]

Pasiphae, on the other hand, realises that she might be rightly held responsible for her actions even if they were caused by the gods. In her caution, she understands that she needs to use stricter standards if she is to have any hope of convincing her hearers of her innocence. Pasiphae begins by demonstrating that she did not act 'willingly' (472e.10 ἐστὶ δ᾽ οὐχ ἑκο[ύσ]ιον κακόν). If she did not act willingly, someone else must have interacted with her mind: a god. She makes this crucial point in a parenthesis, as if it were an obvious point.[51] This is rhetorically effective: the audience is more likely to accept this as an established fact, and it does not invite refutation.

Pasiphae understands that she cannot escape blame for her conduct unless she can prove that she acted because of divine intervention. She could have gone on arguing that divine intervention makes her innocent,

---

[49] Text and translation from Laks and Most 2016: 184–5.
[50] A. Schmitt 1990, B. Williams 1993.
[51] 9 ἐκ θεοῦ γὰρ προσβολῆς ἐμηνάμην. The English translation quoted above transforms this into a causal sentence 'because my madness was a god's onslaught', for clarity.

according to the principle of alternative possibilities: divine intervention makes her not simply an 'unwilling' agent, but also 'not responsible'. This is Helen's approach in *Trojan Women*.[52] However, Pasiphae knows that this is not enough. Greek gods often make human beings act against rationality, morality and law precisely to provide a reason to punish them, as claimed in a famous saying of Aeschylus:

> θεὸς μὲν αἰτίαν φύει βροτοῖς,
> ὅταν κακῶσαι δῶμα παμπήδην θέληι

> When god wishes to ruin a family completely, he plants a cause among its members

> Aesch. *Niobe* fr. 154a.15–16,
> transl. Sommerstein 2008: III 165

In quoting the line, Plato condemns this view as immoral,[53] but Pasiphae's version of divine intervention is perfectly ethical. Gods 'plant causes' not simply because they are cruel and ruthless, but because of other previous reprehensible (or unholy, immoral, etc.) acts of human beings. The very language she uses is typical of a tradition of thought that considered human beings responsible for their actions, even if the actions were caused by the gods. She talks of 'a god's attack' (ἐκ θεοῦ . . . προσβολῆς, 9). This is the word used by Apollo's oracle to describe the punishment Orestes faces unless he punishes the killers of his father. The 'attacks of the Furies' (Aesch. *Cho.* 283 προσβολὰς Ἐρινύων) are presented as divine punishment for failure to act in accordance to divine orders.[54] Antiphon explicitly states the principle that divine 'attacks' are meant as a means to bring about justice:

> εἰ δὲ δὴ θεία κηλὶς τῶι δράσαντι προσπίπτει ἀσεβοῦντι, οὐ δίκαιον τὰς θείας προσβολὰς διακωλύειν γίγνεσθαι.

> But if in fact pollution sent from the gods falls on the person who is guilty of an impious act, it is not right to prevent the attacks of the gods from happening.   Antiphon 3.3.8

The word 'attack' (προσβολή) is used in this meaning, in a similar context, also in in Aristophanes.[55] Pasiphae later paraphrases this 'attack' as a 'blow

---

[52] *Tro.* 948–50. Helen also makes the impious claim that Menelaus should 'punish the goddess' (948 τὴν θεὸν κόλαζε).

[53] Pl. *Resp.* 380a.

[54] For Orestes' ethical dilemma see Battezzato 2019.

[55] Ar. *Pax* 39–40 'and I do not know which of the gods attacked me' (χὥτου ποτ' ἐστὶ δαιμόνων ἡ προσβολὴ | οὐκ οἶδ').

from the *daimôn*' (πληγὴν δαίμονος, fr. 472e.30). This too echoes the traditional language of divine intervention. The chorus of Aeschylus' *Agamemnon* claims that the Trojans are punished because of their injustice and wickedness in assisting Paris' crime: 'They can speak of the blow struck by Zeus' (Διὸς πλαγὰν ἔχουσιν εἰπεῖν, 367). This tradition is taken up by Sophocles. The chorus of *Ajax* speaks of 'Zeus's blow' (πληγὴ Διός, 137) and of 'a blow from God' ('κ θεοῦ | πληγή, 278–9):[56] they assume that the madness of Ajax was caused by the hero's failure to accomplish ritual duties towards one of the gods, such as Artemis or Enyalios (172–181/2).

In this view, human culpability is not reduced by divine intervention: neither 'overdetermination' nor 'double motivation' save human wrong-doers.[57] Divine intervention *per se* would not free Pasiphae from guilt: compare the version of Hyginus where Pasiphae is punished for her disregard of Aphrodite (above, p. 183). Divine intervention is presented by Pasiphae as a means of punishing other, previous wrongdoings: in particular, previous wrongdoings by her husband Minos (fr. 472e.21, 27–8). She does not simply assess Minos' behaviour as a ritual fault, but as 'guilt' (σὴ γὰρ ἡ 'ξ[αμ]αρτία, 34) that is punished by the gods (τῆς σῆς . . . ζημ[ία]ς, 41). The *antenklêma* (counter-accusation) is thus essential for the ethical argument and juridical argumentation.[58] Divine intervention as a punishment for Minos' fault does free her from responsibility. Only at this point can she claim that she is completely free from guilt/responsibility (κοὐδὲν αἰτία, 29) and that she has 'done nothing wrong' (κοὐδὲν ἠδικηκότες, 40).

Regret

But should we believe Pasiphae when she declares herself free from guilt? And, even if she is not responsible for the causal chain that lead to her acts, does she feel regret or sorrow for her unwilling actions?

---

[56] See Finglass 2011 on Soph. *Aj.* 137–40, 278–80; also fr. 961 'a mortal cannot dodge a blow from a god' (θεοῦ δὲ πληγὴν οὐχ ὑπερπηδᾶι βροτός).

[57] For these concepts see Battezzato 2019.

[58] Hermogenes, *Περὶ Στάσεων* (*On Issues*) 2.7 (p. 14 Patillon, with his n. 3) γίνεται . . . ἀντέγκλημα, ὅταν ὁμολογῶν ὁ φεύγων πεποιηκέναι τι ὡς ἀδίκημα ἀντεγκαλῆι τῶι πεπονθότι ὡς ἀξίωι παθεῖν, ἃ πέπονθεν ('a counter-accusation occurs when the person on trial admits that he committed an action that can be considered unjust, but in response accuses the victim of deserving to suffer what he suffered').

Some interpreters consider Pasiphae's fault an instance of *akrasia* ('lack of self-control', that is the incapability of mastering one's own will and action) and compare her to Phaedra. Reckford 1974: 322 claims that

> her *adikos logos* betrays a demoralized, indeed god-afflicted personality. It embodies what Rivier has called, in a notable phrase, 'le pouvoir de transgression:' the way in which certain human beings depart from right and ordinary human limits, against their better inclination, bringing disaster upon themselves and upon those close to them.

He further remarks (p. 321)

> she is incapable of the normal human sentiments, of regret and repentance

This reading implies that her entire speech is completely false and unreliable.[59] Pasiphae claims the exact opposite of what Reckford says. We have no way of knowing whether the rest of the play demonstrated Pasiphae's insincerity, as in the case of Helen's speech in *Trojan Women* (924–50); however, it is extremely unlikely that the facts she remembers were at complete variance from the version accepted from other characters.[60]

So why does Pasiphae does not express regret? Lack of regret is considered damning: 'one should not do bad things, and if one does, feeling remorse for them may help to remedy the situation, even if only a little'.[61] It is true that Pasiphae does not explicitly mention 'shame' as her emotion, but gives strong indications that she condemns her past actions. She uses evaluative words, such as 'most shameful malady' (αἰσχίστηι νόσωι, 12), in reference to her previous states of mind and actions (below, p. 193). As we saw, this is in keeping with the tradition; Bacchylides already called Pasiphae's actions and states of mind a 'malady' (νόσον, 26.8; above, p. 182). In Euripides, she claims that she tried to 'conceal' her actions (ἔκρυψα, 30) and accuses Minos of 'having brought shame' on her (καταισχύνας ἐμέ, 28) when he revealed her actions (εὐπρεπῆ γὰρ κἀπιδείξασθαι καλά, 31).[62] So 'shame', 'dishonour' (αἰσχύνη) is her condition. Pasiphae does not explicitly state that she *feels* 'shame' (*aidôs* or *aischunê*), but attributes shame to the action and the

---

[59] Duchemin 1968: 207–8, Dolfi 1984: 137.

[60] See above, p. 186.

[61] Fulkerson 2013: 6. See Konstan 2010: 11 on the lack of interest in 'inward change of character as a condition for reconciliation' in ancient Greek culture and thought. For the relation between shame and guilt see Cairns 1993: 14–47.

[62] For the relation between 'shame' and the need to 'conceal' shameful actions cf. Eur. *Hipp.* 243–4 πάλιν μου κρύψον κεφαλήν, | αἰδούμεθα γὰρ τὰ λελεγμένα μοι ('cover my head again, because I feel shame at what I said').

person, Minos, who caused her suffering. She describes her emotion as 'hurt' (ἀλγῶ, 10). Like Orestes, Pasiphae admits that her action cannot be denied:

ἔκτεινα· τούτου δ' οὔτις ἄρνησις πέλει.

I killed her: there can be no denying that.
Aesch. *Eum.* 588[63]

ἀρνουμένη μὲν οὐκέτ' ἂν πίθοιμί σε·

Denials from me will not convince you.
Eur. *Cretan Women* fr. 472e.4

Neither Orestes nor Pasiphae admit to feeling shame, but they do feel hurt:[64]

ἀλγῶ μὲν ἔργα καὶ πάθος γένος τε πᾶν,
ἄζηλα νίκης τῆσδ' ἔχων μιάσματα.

I do grieve for her deeds, and for her suffering, and for my whole famly, having acquired an unenviable pollution from this victory
Aesch. *Cho.* 1016–17

ἀλγῶ μέν, ἐστὶ δ' οὐχ ἐκο[ύσ]ιον κακόν

I hurt, but my trouble is not voluntary
Eur. *Cretan Women* fr. 472e.10

Orestes does not feel shame, nor does he think his actions caused him dishonour. Pasiphae clearly implies that her actions brought dishonour to her, but only because they were made known to others, because of Minos. She puts the blame on Minos, and dissociates herself from her previous actions, not simply because she was not responsible for them, but because they would not have brought her dishonour had they been concealed. She thus does not seem to feel 'agent regret' at what she did: she does not feel the emotion that many human beings feel for the (negative) consequences of an entirely blameless action committed by them, especially when the action involuntarily causes great suffering or injustice.[65] Her dissociation from her past actions is thus complete.

---

[63] Transl. Sommerstein 2008; so also subsequent translations of Aeschylus.

[64] For 'hurt' as emotion of tragic characters cf. Eur. *El.* 1118 ἀλγῶ γάρ· ἀλλὰ παύσομαι θυμουμένη ('Yes, for I am in pain. But I shall stop being angry', transl. Kovacs 1994–2002), *Ba.* 1327–9 τὸ μὲν σὸν ἀλγῶ, Κάδμε· σὸς δ' ἔχει δίκην | παῖς παιδὸς ἀξίαν μέν, ἀλγεινὴν δὲ σοί ('I feel grief at your misfortune, Cadmus. As for your grandson, he has received justice, however painful it is for you', transl. Kovacs), Soph. *Aj.* 377 τί δῆτ' ἂν ἀλγοίης ἐπ' ἐξειργασμένοις; ('Why, then, should you grieve over what is accomplished?', transl. Finglass 2011).

[65] For the concept of 'agent regret' see B. Williams 1976: 123–7 ≈ 1981: 27–31.

Pasiphae and Phaedra: Desire, Diseases and Demons

Pasiphae presents her condition as a kind of 'disease' (νόσωι, 20; νοσοῦμεν, 35), and more specifically as a disease of the mind, a kind of 'madness' (ἐμηνάμην, 9; ἐμαι]νόμην, 20). Both Pasiphae and Phaedra try to conceal their *erôs* (fr. 472e.30 ἔκρυψα πληγὴν δαίμονος θεήλατον, 'I concealed the god's stroke launched by heaven'; *Hipp.* 394 κρύπτειν νόσον, 'to conceal the disease'). Pasiphae's psychological situation is the converse of her daughter's Phaedra in *Hippolytus*. Their erotic passions are both described as 'illness' (νόσος),[66] and explicitly presented as similar by Phaedra herself.[67] Phaedra, unlike Pasiphae, is unable to understand the divine origin of her 'illness'; however, Phaedra has access to the psychological path of her affliction and of her reactions to love.[68] She is able to explain the different steps she took in her attempt to resist love (391–9).

Pasiphae, on the contrary, speaks as if she had no access to her own motivations or experiences, and no way to oppose her absurd desire for the bull. This is so precisely because she is able to understand the divine origin of her desire, unlike Phaedra, who rejects the divine aspect of *erôs*.[69] Recognising the divine origin of this particular erotic passion rules out the possibility of resistance or even access to the reasons that make her act this way. Pasiphae rules out the possibility of having experienced pleasure from her erotic encounter with the bull; this claim is not presented as something she can tell out of her own experience but is based on logical inference and 'probability' (ἔχει γὰρ οὐδὲν εἰκός, 11). A logical proof from 'probability' (εἰκός) is more convincing, in the eyes of a hostile jury, than her own testimony. However, she does not even use her own testimony as a side argument. She does not seem to be aware of her own internal process of reflection, nor does she seem to have access to her mental images. Pasiphae does not seem to have a will of her own. She does not even have a *daimôn* of her own: it is Minos' *daimôn* that determines her fate. She thus dissociates herself from her actions: 'It was this man's destiny that

---

[66] Eur. *Hipp.* 394, 405, 477, 766, 1306, Barrett 1964 on *Hipp.* 476–7, Goff 1990: 1, 40, 50. Some characters in Euripides claim that love impulses are 'not self-chosen … nor a voluntary affliction' (fr. 339.3–4 οὐκ αὐθαίρετοι | … οὐδ' ἑκουσία νόσος) but rather 'necessary afflictions sent by the gods' (fr. 339.6 θεῶν ἀνάγκας).

[67] Barrett 1964 on Eur. *Hipp.* 337–8.

[68] For the text and interpretation of Phaedra's controversial speech at Eur. *Hipp.* 373–430 see Barrett 1964 *ad loc.*, Willink 1968: 11–26 = 2010: 3–25, Kovacs 1980, Cairns 1993: 321–40, Craik 1993, B. Williams 1993: 225–30, Furley 1996.

[69] See especially Eur. *Hipp.* 403–506.

(brought) me too (my fill) of trouble'.[70] She discusses her own behaviour as if it were a series of actions enacted by someone else, and reads her own actions as 'symptoms' of a disturbance in the order of things: 'a symptom is a disruption – without obvious cause and often, though not always, painful – either to the experience of self or to the outward presentation of self'.[71] Pasiphae recognises the interference of an external, divine agent from 'signs'. On the other hand, she is able to present a projection of her own erotic identity and of female desire. She claims that is illogical for her to feel desire for the bull: the bull was not 'attractive thanks to beautiful clothes' (εὐπρεπὴς ... ἐν πέπλοισιν, 13), did not have 'ruddy hair' (πυρσῆς ... χαίτης, 14), a 'sparkle in its eyes' (παρ' ὀμμάτων σέλας, 14),[72] a 'darkly red beard' (οἰνωπὸν ... γένυν, 15), a 'lissom body' (δέμας γ' εὔρ[υθμον, 16) nor was the bull chosen in view of procreation of 'children' (παίδων, 19). No other woman in Greek tragedy expresses reasons for desire so explicitly, not even hypothetically; exceptions do occur in the comic genre and, to some extent, in Sappho's poetry, but are usually avoided in serious genres, since merely expressing them in detail would go beyond what a polite and morally respectable woman could entertain in her thoughts.[73] The old Hecuba, in reacting to Helen's speech in *Trojan Women*, lists similar, but more generic, characteristics of her son Paris that kindled Helen's desire: extraordinary physical beauty (κάλλος ἐκπρεπέστατος, 987), exotic clothes (βαρβάροις ἐσθήμασι, 991), gold (χρυσῶι 992). Hecuba's mention of the elements that spark off female desire is however meant as a damning condemnation of Helen, who fell prey to desire. Pasiphae's speech anticipates both Helen's and Hecuba's speeches in *Trojan Women*: Helen's in stressing divine intervention, Hecuba's in articulating female desire (above, p. 186).

Pasiphae's articulation of female desire does not characterise her as an 'immoral' woman. Rather, it is a crucial step in her philosophical approach. Her argument rests on a hedonistic premise: all human beings act rationally and acting rationally means acting in order to maximise pleasure.

---

[70] 21 δαίμων ὁ τοῦδε κἄμ' ἐ[νέπλησεν κα]κῶν (for the text see above, n. 3). 'His *daimôn*' here is apparently used to mean 'the divine power that controls Minos' (Pl. *Phaedo* 107d6 ὁ ἑκάστου δαίμων, 'the *daimôn* of each person', Lys. 2.78), not simply his 'divinely-apportioned fate', for which sense see Finglass 2007 on Soph. *El.* 917 (cf. 999–1000, 1156–7, 1305–6).

[71] Holmes 2010: 2.

[72] Hippodamia in Sophocles' *Oenomaus* mentions Pelops' erotic gaze (fr. 474); see SOMMERSTEIN, pp. 65–7. For the 'attractiveness' of the bull see Paduano 2005: 142–4.

[73] For desire in Greek literature and thought see Nussbaum 1994, Gaca 2003; for the strong constraints against the expression of female desire in tragedy see Mastronarde 2010: 260.

This hedonistic premise is shared by most ancient ethical thinkers, includ-ing Socrates as portrayed by Plato.[74] From this hedonistic premise, Pasiphae logically infers that sex, like all human actions, is motivated by pleasure, in particular erotic pleasure and the pleasure at the prospect of procreation. Pasiphae the speaking character argues that 'Pasiphae' (the woman who mated with the bull, to whose internal reasoning and feelings Pasiphae does not have access) could not have acted because of erotic pleasure or in view of procreation. Therefore, 'Pasiphae' did not act to maximise pleasure. Therefore, she was motivated by an external agent (a god). Pasiphae 'the speaker' infers the nature of her action from external criteria, as if she were judging another person, 'Pasiphae' the woman who had sex with a bull. The only escape of Pasiphae 'the speaker' consists in self-effacement.

Bruno Snell offered a 'Socratic' narrative of philosophical development from Euripides' Medea to his Phaedra, as steps in a discussion over the moral problem of *akrasia*: both Medea and Phaedra claim, with different arguments taken from their own psychological experience, that it is not only possible to act against one's better judgment, but that the soul is divided and different parts of the soul may take prominence in guiding human decisions, even at the cost of choosing a path of action that reduces the happiness of the subject.[75] Pasiphae in many ways undermines Snell's Socratic narrative of progress, in a play earlier than *Medea* and *Hippolytus*. She has already committed acts that she judges shameful, and must explain them. She rejects the possibility of 'irrational' action, not aimed at pleasure: consequently, she seems to reject completely the possibility of *akrasia*, like Socrates. Her presupposition is that if a human agent acts in a way that does not further his or her hedonistic goals, he or she must act unwillingly, under the influence of an external agent. Her rejection of the possibility of *akrasia* is remarkable because she is a woman: many Greek texts, including some by Euripides (especially *Medea*), presuppose that women are especially prone to *akrasia*, much more so than men.[76] Aristotle even claimed that the 'deliberative capacity' of women is *akuron*, that is that it 'lacks power'.[77] According to Fortenbaugh's influential and, in this respect, convincing interpretation, Aristotle's claim implies that a woman's 'deliberative capacity . . . is often overruled by her emotions or alogical side.

---

[74] Irwin 1977, especially 102–14, 1983, 1995, especially 83–91.

[75] Snell 1948.

[76] Dillon 1997. For akrasia in Greek philosophy see Bobonich and Destrée 2007.

[77] Arist. *Pol.* 1260a12–13 ὁ μὲν γὰρ δοῦλος ὅλως οὐκ ἔχει τὸ βουλευτικόν, τὸ δὲ θῆλυ ἔχει μέν, ἀλλ' ἄκυρον ('For the slave has not got the deliberative part at all; the female has it, but it is without mastery', transl. Parker 2012: 94).

Her decisions and actions are too often guided by pleasures and pains'.[78]
Pasiphae, however, by adopting ethical hedonism, skilfully manipulates
these misogynistic stereotypes: it would have been reasonable for her to
yield to erotic attraction in the case of a 'lissom' bridegroom with 'ruddy
hair' (fr. 472e.13–16) but she could not have felt any erotic attraction for a
bull. She presents herself as possibly attracted by pleasure, but stresses that
rational choice of pleasure and rejection of pain is the basis for her actions.
In the absence of pleasure, she cannot be guilty of *akrasia*, and must have
been compelled to irrational action by external overwhelming forces.

Passivisation is thus crucial to Pasiphae's argument, and she extends this
to her fate after the speech, where she freely offers herself as a completely
passive object of Minos' punishment:

35
πρὸς τάδ᾽ εἴτε ποντίαν
κτείνειν δοκεῖ σοι, κτε[ῖ]ν᾽· ἐπίστασαι δέ τοι
μιαιφόν᾽ ἔργα καὶ σφαγὰς ἀνδροκτόνους·
εἴτ᾽ ὠμοσίτου τῆς ἐμῆς ἐρᾶις φαγεῖν
σαρκός, πάρεστι· μὴ ᾽λλίπηις θοινώμενος.
40
ἐλεύθεροι γὰρ κοὐδὲν ἠδικηκότες
τῆς σῆς ἕκατι ζημ[ία]ς ὀλούμεθα.[79]

So either, if you have decided to kill me by drowning, go on and kill me –
indeed you understand acts of foul murder and the slaughtering of men! –
or, if you desire to eat my flesh raw, here it is: don't go short on your
banquet! Because of the punishment upon you, we are to die, who are free
and quite innocent of wrongdoing.

Pasiphae's 'freedom' (40 ἐλεύθεροι 'free') consists in willingly accepting
Minos' punishment. Her 'fantasy of willing self-sacrifice'[80] will be re-
enacted by Polyxena in Euripides' *Hecuba*. Polyxena's words closely recall
Pasiphae's: they both list a series of imperatives directed against their
killers (or would-be killers), issuing orders to people who have mastery
over them, and paradoxically reversing the power structure of reality; they
both claim that their body is available (πάρεστι, fr. 472e.39; *Hec.* 565) to
their executioners.

---

[78] Fortenbaugh 1977: 138 = 2006: 245. As Karbowski 2014b: 98–101 notes, some passages in
Aristotle's works on biology (especially *HA* 608a33–b15) offer a degree of support for
Fortenbaugh's argument. For more detailed, and less sympathetic, assessments of Aristotle's
views on the deliberative capacity of women see Parker 2012, Karbowski 2014a and 2014b
(critical of Fortenbaugh), with further references to other interpretations.

[79] ὀλούμεθα 'we are to die' was conjectured (and rejected) by Wilamowitz, who preferred another
conjecture with the same meaning, θανούμεθα; the papyrus has ονουμεθα.

[80] Coo, p. 54.

ὦ τὴν ἐμὴν πέρσαντες Ἀργεῖοι πόλιν,
ἑκοῦσα θνήισκω· μή τις ἅψηται χροὸς
τοὐμοῦ· παρέξω γὰρ δέρην εὐκαρδίως.
ἐλευθέραν δέ μ᾽, ὡς ἐλευθέρα θάνω,   550
πρὸς θεῶν, μεθέντες κτείνατ᾽·

. . .

ἰδού, τόδ᾽ εἰ μὲν στέρνον, ὦ νεανία,
παίειν προθυμῆι, παῖσον, εἰ δ᾽ ὑπ᾽ αὐχένα
χρήιζεις, πάρεστι λαιμὸς εὐτρεπὴς ὅδε.   565

You Argives who have sacked my city, I die willingly; let no one touch my
person; I shall offer my neck with good courage. Let me go freely, I beg
you by the gods, when you kill me, so that I may die free: as a princess
I shame to be called slave among the dead . . . See, here, young man, if you
are eager to strike my breast, strike here; but if into my neck is your desire,
here is my throat, here and ready.

Eur. *Hec.* 547–51, 563–5
(transl. Collard 1991)

Pasiphae appears to us as series of fragments of different characters: a mix
of Orestes (Aeschylus' *Choephori* and *Eumenides*), Phaedra (*Hippolytus*),
Helen (*Trojan Women* and Gorgias' *Encomium of Helen*) and Polyxena
(*Hecuba*). This is our modern perspective: we already know the road that
Euripides' text will take in presenting female guilt and shame. However,
fragmentation of conscience is also the main theme of Pasiphae's own
speech and self-perception. How do we know that we are exactly the
same self as the body that acted in the past, in ways that we cannot
explain ourselves? Does regret presuppose the unity of the self? Or can
it occur only if the present suffering self and the previous acting self
are felt as unity?[81] This sense of alienation from one's previous actions
is famously explored in many modern works of art and philosophical
discussions; Heraclitus (or Cratylus, or Hippocrates, or Plato) noted that
one cannot bathe twice in the same river, not simply because the river
changes, but because the person bathing changes and is not the same.[82]
Pasiphae seems to presuppose the same view: external (divine) intervention fragments the self, and makes it different from the self that
performed the action. Euripides in this play again uses a female character
to explore the fragmentation of the self as an ethical, philosophical and
dramatic theme.

---

[81] Sorabji 2006.
[82] Colvin 2007, Benati 2017.

12 | Female Agency in Euripides' *Hypsipyle*

JAMES H. KIM ON CHONG-GOSSARD

Euripides is well known for exploring female subjectivity and female agency in his tragedies. His fragmentary *Hypsipyle* is a fascinating example of this, in that its complicated plot – a princess in slavery is responsible for the accidental death of her infant charge, but as a result is reunited with her long-lost twin sons – hinges on the interconnectedness of decisions made by women, even decisions made independently of one another. Euripides utilises the title role's subjective point of view to illustrate the nature of fortune itself: that one person's suffering can lead unwittingly to another's good fortune; and that people's sudden prosperity can be the unintended outcome of decisions made long ago by themselves, or by others whom they have never even met. Importantly in this play, all the people in question are women.

This interconnectedness of women's decisions can be visualised by considering an Apulian volute-krater dated to the 330s and attributed to the Darius Painter that clearly illustrates Euripides' *Hypsipyle*.[1] Dominating the top of the vase-painting is a three-bay portico with a figure in each bay; the figures are labelled, so the identification is certain. At the far left stands Hypsipyle, her knees slightly bent, facing and gesturing towards the two characters to the viewer's right. In the centre stands the queen Eurydice in a thoughtful pose, her left arm draped over her bosom, her right elbow bent and resting on her hip, and her right hand resting below her chin, as if she were toying with a necklace; she gazes towards Hypsipyle. To the right stands Amphiaraus dressed in a short belted tunic, sporting a crested helmet and boots; in his left hand he holds a vertical spear, and he lifts his right hand while looking at the two women. In Taplin's words, 'This is not "simply the story" [of Hypsipyle], but Euripides' dramatization of the story.'[2] Other elements of the play's plot – such as the funeral of Archemorus – are depicted elsewhere on the vase, but Hypsipyle's 'trial' scene and her defence by Amphiaraus take pride of place, confirming that

---

[1] Naples, Museo Archeologico Nazionale 81934 (H3255). See Taplin 2007: 211–14 for a fuller discussion of this vase, including an illustration.

[2] Taplin 2007: 213.

this was the moment that – in the mind of the artist or his customer, at least – defined the play. Furthermore, the length of the play has been estimated at around 1,742 lines.[3] Therefore Amphiaraus' arrival at line 853 in order to rescue the accused Hypsipyle would have occurred at nearly the midpoint.[4] Hypsipyle is accused of murdering Opheltes, her nursling and Eurydice's son; Amphiaraus has arrived to prevent Eurydice from killing Hypsipyle, since he was a witness to Opheltes' accidental death. The artist of the Apulian vase placed Eurydice – not Hypsipyle – in the centre of the triptych because it is her reaction to Amphiaraus' speech that plays the decisive role in the outcome of the drama. It is Eurydice who has the important choice to make, and the power to make it. Yet Eurydice's decision-making is not the first in this play, nor in this myth. Hypsipyle also makes choices, and has made choices in the past, all of which had unforeseen consequences, just as Eurydice's choice will have. And another woman – Amphiaraus' wife, Eriphyle – is remembered for another disastrous choice. Moreover, had Eriphyle not chosen to accept a golden necklace in exchange for convincing Amphiaraus to join the expedition against Thebes, not only would Amphiaraus not be here in Nemea at this moment to plead Hypsipyle's case, but neither (perhaps) would the child Opheltes be dead in the first place. By the play's end, the peculiar nature of fortune is revealed: events unfold because of significant actions taken by individuals at specific junctures – and those individuals are women.

What Is Female Agency in Greek Tragedy?

In Greek myth, men's stories involve adventures outside the home, such as the Achillean model of killing various noble enemies hand-to-hand in wartime and thereby achieving fame, or the Odyssean model of battling

---

[3] W. Cockle 1987: 23: 'It has been possible to determine that the roll contained 30 columns of play text, amounting to *c.* 1742 lines. Known column heights vary between 55 lines (frr. 64 ii+) and 62 (frr. 60 i+)'. The roll in question is P.Oxy. 852, discovered in 1906 and first published by Grenfell and Hunt 1908. P.Oxy. 852 contains the text of Euripides' *Hypsipyle* on one side, written in a hand dating to the late second or early third century AD. On the other side (P.Oxy. 985) is a wine merchant's account of receipts and expenditures during the reign of Domitian (late first century AD).

[4] Because P.Oxy. 852 preserves marginal stichometric letters indicating every hundredth line, fr. 757.800–949 and fr. 759a.1579–1632 are confidently cited with the line numbers of the play (which Kannicht in *TrGF* provides) rather than the line numbers of the fragments themselves. Collard and Cropp's Loeb edition (2008), which provides 'approximate' line numbers in other portions of the play, will also be cited with a tilde (~).

monsters and outwitting obstacles during a homeward journey. Women's stories, in contrast, are about endurance, both physical and emotional, in many forms: unhappy marriage, rape and abduction, being sold into slavery, the agony of childbirth, the painful survival after the death of loved ones, even being ritually sacrificed as a virgin. When Euripides' Medea chides men for saying that women lead a danger-free life in the house while men themselves fight with the spear, and retorts that she would rather stand with a shield three times than give birth even once (*Med.* 248–51), her words have multiple meanings. Of course, Medea really does seem the sort of woman who would rather fight with the spear than have children; but she also argues convincingly that women's achievements, women's sufferings, women's stories, women's 'dangers', are just as valid and worthy of remembrance – and dramatisation – as men's.

From the 1990s onwards, the study of female agency has been an important aspect of feminist approaches to Greek tragedy. Taking as their starting point the fact that tragedy does not represent 'real' women, feminist scholars have analysed how tragedy instead used the myths of legendary women to explore social issues pertinent to the Athenians themselves. As Victoria Wohl explains it, scholars began 'focusing on female agency and analyzing the ways in which the dramatization of a woman's subjective experience can complicate her structural position within the institutions and relations of tragedy's masculine world'.[5] Among the must-read authors from this period of work on tragic female agency are Nancy Sorkin Rabinowitz, Victoria Wohl, Kirk Ormand and Helene P. Foley. Rabinowitz's *Anxiety Veiled. Euripides and the Traffic in Women* (1993) analysed Euripidean heroines according to two Freudian polarities: the fetish and the uncanny. Self-sacrificing virgins like Polyxena, Macaria and Iphigenia represent the fetish, whereby their willingness to die in support of patriarchal values was a fetishising comfort to the male viewer, obscuring their sex difference from men. Murderous mothers such as Medea and Hecuba represent the monstrous uncanny and the capacity for women to castrate and destroy men. In this way, Rabinowitz argued that tragedy was a project of patriarchy that reinforced the subjectivity of its male audiences. Euripides 'ultimately ... recuperates the female figures for patriarchy ... their experience is shaped to the end of supporting male power'.[6] In contrast, by examining gendered subjectivities in *Intimate Commerce. Exchange, Gender, and Subjectivity in Greek Tragedy* (1998),

---

[5] Wohl 2005: 153. For female agency in tragedy see also BATTEZZATO.
[6] Rabinowitz 1993: 14.

Wohl came to see 'tragedy's frequent dramatization of the female psyche as part of its attempt to develop a language and theory of the self'.[7] To this end, she evaluated the exchange of women in three plays (*Women of Trachis, Agamemnon* and *Alcestis*), and included a study of silent female characters occupying 'a site of potential resistance'.[8] In *Exchange and the Maiden: Marriage in Sophoclean Drama* (1999), Kirk Ormand studied tragic women's experience of alienation within the institution of marriage in five Sophoclean plays. Since marriage both creates female subjectivity and economic exchange between men, there is an inevitable conflict for women who consider themselves more central to marriage than their husbands. Helene P. Foley's *Female Acts in Greek Tragedy* (2001) observed that the ethical choices made by tragic women are often predicated on women's social roles in the community, as virgin, wife or mother, and not solely on universal principles.[9] As a result, female agency in tragedy begs an audience to question whether public and private moral conflicts can be resolved on the same terms, since with female subjectivity the tragedians are 'experimenting with what one might call alternative moralities'.[10] As Wohl herself explains in her excellent chapter 'Tragedy and feminism' (2005), scholarship that engages with female agency in Greek tragedy must also contend with other trends that continue to debate the connection between tragedy and Athenian society, specifically whether tragedy as part of an annual festival served to reinforce civic ideology (and gender ideology within that), or whether it posed challenges by 'exposing the rifts and fissures within Athens' dominant ideology'.[11] Anatole Mori describes the *communis opinio* (at least in 2012) about fifth-century drama as follows:

> it seems fair to say that dramatic festivals in Athens presupposed an audience that was dominated by masculinist perspectives and for whom dramatizations of female agency, whether tragic or comic, were hypothetical 'what if?' scenarios and perversions of 'how things really and rightly are'. The scripted behavior of female protagonists bore little resemblance to social reality, and the drama, in short, was a locus for experimentation.[12]

---

[7] Wohl 2005: 154.
[8] Wohl 1998: xxi.
[9] Foley 2001: 109–44.
[10] Foley 2001: 119.
[11] Wohl 2005: 155.
[12] Mori 2012: 6.

Even so, not all tragic women are the same, and it would be unfair to see all instances of female agency as 'perversions.' Euripides' *Hypsipyle* is an exciting test case for this idea because its plot (at least, what can be reconstructed) is quite unlike other plays where tragic conflict ends in death that can be blamed on female acts arising from the failure of men and women to inhabit gender norms fully (as in *Medea* or Euripides' *Electra*). Nor is there an elaborate escape plot (as in *Helen* or *Iphigenia among the Taurians*) that might require the stereotypical deviousness of a woman, or the complicity of a female chorus.[13] Although Hypsipyle is a slave, she is neither a prisoner of war nor a concubine, so the plot does not involve her negotiation of any sexual or pseudo-marital role (as in *Andromache* or *Trojan Women*). What characterises *Hypsipyle* instead are tragic conflicts that result in women choosing clemency or kindness – although more negative outcomes are certainly alluded to in the background story of Eriphyle. As in so many other tragedies, and in keeping with Helene Foley's observations, the agency of women in Euripides' *Hypsipyle* seems inseparable from women's familial roles as daughters, mothers and wives, and from the social expectations of those roles. Or to put it another way, the agency of women in Euripides' *Hypsipyle* is consistent with Sheila Murnaghan's observations about women in Greek tragedy more generally:

> these plays do spring from and respond to a highly polarized world with sharply distinguished male and female spheres of action, and the values that animate female characters reflect their identification with the household and its private concerns.[14]

Male and female spheres of action are polarised in *Hypsipyle*, too. From the male perspective, the events that unfold in Nemea – the accidental death of Opheltes, the establishment of games in his honour and the recognition of Hypsipyle's long-lost sons – form a prelude to the great military expedition called the Seven Against Thebes. From the female perspective, the Argive army and their march through the Nemean meadow are considered a spectacle worth watching by the chorus (fr. 752f.29–39, ~216–26), something for women to appreciate aesthetically, but not partake in themselves. And it is the women's perspective that dominates since, apparently, only women are at home today, and there is not a single Nemean man who

[13] Hypsipyle does consider escaping Nemea, but in the surviving fragment (fr. 754b, ~668–83) the chorus women are finding reasons that would prevent an escape, and in any case Eurydice arrives too soon for Hypsipyle to attempt one.
[14] Murnaghan 2005: 239.

speaks on stage.[15] Hypsipyle, Eurydice (without her husband) and the chorus women represent the Nemean palace, and the drama that unfolds this day is of a private nature. It is in this context that we can begin to appreciate the importance of female agency and the actions of individual women to the plot.

Hypsipyle

Hypsipyle herself begins the play at the tail end of her own personal story. Once the daughter of the king of Lemnos, abducted by pirates, sold into slavery, taken to Nemea and transformed into a nursemaid, she is now reduced to singing lullabies to the infant Opheltes, child of Zeus's priest, Lycurgus and his wife, Eurydice. Hypsipyle's past history, however, begins with two important decisions: first, to entertain Jason and his Argonauts on Lemnos,[16] to become Jason's lover and to allow him to take their twin sons with him on his journey to Colchis after they were weaned (an event alluded to at the play's end, fr. 759a.1614–15); and second, to spare the life of her father, King Thoas (a son of Dionysus), on the fateful night when the women of Lemnos killed all the men on the island. It is not known whether this second part of Hypsipyle's history was mentioned elsewhere in the play, but the details (fr. 759a.1593–1609) are preserved only during the recognition scene near the end. Although somewhat vague, they can be interpreted as follows. At 1593 Hypsipyle cries αἰαῖ for the φυγὰς ἐμέθεν ἃς ἔφυγον ('my flights which I fled', a cognate accusative structure that makes more sense in English as 'my exile which I had to endure'), which refers as a whole to Hypsipyle's experiences since her abduction from 'sea-girt Lemnos' (Λήμνου ποντίας, 1594). At 1595, πολιὸν ὅτι πατέρος οὐκ ἔτεμον κάρα ('because I did not cut the grey head of my father'), she confirms that her exile was caused (such is the force of ὅτι) by her decision to spare Thoas' life. Her son Euneus asks the leading question whether the other women of Lemnos really ordered her to kill her father (1596). Hypsipyle's reliving of the fear of that night (1597) when the women, like Gorgons,

---

[15] The male household slaves who have bound Hypsipyle (she addresses them at fr. 757.851) are mute roles. There was also surely a Messenger to describe events at the first Nemean games, but we do not know whether he was part of the palace's household or attached to the Argive army.

[16] The chorus women (fr. 752f.19–21, ~206–8) imply that Hypsipyle is well known for singing nostalgically about the Argo. Hypsipyle describes her memories of the Argonauts at fr. 752g.2–15 (~251–63), and invokes the Argo's prow at fr. 757.844–5.

killed their husbands in their beds (1598–9) confirms Euneus' question. When Euneus asks how Hypsipyle stole away so that she did not die, her reply about making her way to the lonely seashore (1601–3) explains how she escaped the murderous hands of the other Lemnian women, her own subjects. She leaves out the details of what happened to her father. In the best-known version of the myth, as told in Apollonius of Rhodes' *Argonautica* (1.620–6), Hypsipyle placed Thoas in a hollow chest at the seashore and set him afloat in the water, so that he could be carried away to safety. But she is silent on the matter here, and the surviving fragments do not indicate the full story of what happened to Thoas on that memorable night. In any case, while Hypsipyle was on the shore, pirates arrived and abducted her. She refers to them as ναῦται κώπαις ('sailors [who came] with oars', 1605), which is similar in imagery to her memories of the Argonauts. Although she is not explicit about it here, one can imagine Hypsipyle's joy, on the very night of the massacre, at seeing what she thought was the Argo approaching Lemnos on its return voyage, ready to rescue her from a night of murder – and her sudden fear and sorrow to realise that pirates had arrived instead. They abducted her and sold her into slavery at Nauplion harbour in the Peloponnese (1606–9). If this sequence of events from Hypsipyle's song has been construed correctly, then her abduction was both accidental and an unintended consequence of her decision to save her father's life by taking him to the seashore. Her story is not one of simply being in the wrong place at the wrong time; her ethical decision to be the 'good' daughter put her in the opportune place for terrible consequences to herself.

When the play begins, Hypsipyle is a slave in the palace of Nemea, and much older. One might ask, as a slave, what agency does she really have? Yet Euripides gives her quite a bit. She might not have power over her own person *qua* slave, but she has agency over her duties. These duties appear twofold: first, she maintains the front of the palace. The chorus women begin their entrance song by asking Hypsipyle (fr. 752f.16–18, ~203–5) whether she is sweeping the entrance of the house, or casting water on the ground, οἷά τε δοῦλα ('as a slave-woman does'), which suggests that these are tasks they have seen her perform before. Second, babysitting is Hypsipyle's chief responsibility; in fact, she is singing a lullaby to Opheltes (fr. 752f.2–14, ~188–201) just before the chorus women make their entrance. With regard to her first duty, that of maintaining the front of the house, Hypsipyle performs two important acts within the first 450 lines of the play. First, she shows hospitality to Thoas and Euneus when they knock on the palace door and ask for shelter (fr. 752d.2–10, ~132–40), while not recognising them (of course) as her long-lost sons.[17] Second, she agrees to show the stream of Achelous to the Argives (fr. 753, quoted in Macrobius, *Saturnalia* 5.18.2).[18] This enables the army to have running water to pour pure libations to the gods, as Amphiaraus had explained at fr. 752h.29–31, ~338–40). There is significance to the fact that Hypsipyle, a slave, performs these acts herself: there is apparently no one at home today. Hypsipyle explains to Thoas and Euneus that 'the house happens to be masterless of males' (ἀδέσ]ποτος μ[ὲν ο]ἶκ[ο]ς ἀρσένων κυ[ρεῖ, fr. 752d.11, ~141). In Amphiaraus' case, not enough of the play survives to indicate why Hypsipyle (and no one else) takes the Argives to the sacred spring. On the one hand, it is very likely that there was no one else to ask. On the other, acquiring water was an essentially female act in Greek culture, so if Amphiaraus was to learn from anyone where fresh water could be found, it would logically be from a woman.[19]

Hypsipyle's second duty as Opheltes' nurse is referred to multiple times. In fr. 752d, as she enters the stage (line 1, ~131) to answer the front door, she is telling the baby that something (perhaps ἀ]θύρμα[τ]α 'toys', 2, ~132) will calm his mind from crying (3, ~133), implying that she is carrying him. At fr. 752f she tells the baby ἰδοὺ κτύπος ὅδε κορτάλων (8, ~194), a stage direction that she picks up some *krotala* (hand-held percussion instruments often translated 'clappers' or 'castanets') and plays them for the child. She refers to her own song as something that serves for the sleep (εἰς ὕπνον, 11, ~198) or the charming or the tending (ἢ χάριν ἢ θεραπεύματα, 12, ~199) of a little boy, a good indication that the child is asleep. When the child's mother Eurydice later arrives in search of him, she asks the chorus whether he is sleeping pleasantly by the doorway (maybe in a crib?), or whether Hypsipyle is stopping his tears by holding him in her arms (fr. 754c.11–12, ~702–3), confirming that this is the kind of care that Hypsipyle is known to give the baby, and most likely what she is doing at the play's beginning.

---

[17] *Pace* Taplin 1977: 341 n. 1, who is doubtful that Hypsipyle herself answers the door, and questions whether the door is even knocked on. He notes that the hypothesis in P.Oxy. 2455 fr. 14 lines 193–4 (test. iiia) suggests that Eurydice answers the door, and that the reconstruction πύλα]ς at fr. 752d.4 (~134) is not certain enough to prove that the palace door was knocked on.

[18] Cropp 2004: 198 argues that fr. 753 'probably belong[s] within the next thirty lines' after the Δ marking for the play's four hundredth line, which itself is part of Hypsipyle and Amphiaraus' *stichomythia*.

[19] For the task of fetching water as potentially degrading for a man see Finglass 2013: 10–13 as it applies to the character of Epeius in Steisichorus' *Sack of Troy* (fr. 100 F.).

Yet Hypsipyle's decision to act in accordance with her first duty (to the house) is put in conflict with her second duty (to pay full attention to the baby Opheltes). She chooses, or at least allows herself to be persuaded, to accompany the Argives to the sacred spring – in Amphiaraus' words, κρηναῖον [γά]νος | δεῖξαι ('to point out the brightness of the spring', fr. 757.891–2). In so doing, she puts the child down on the ground in Zeus's sacred grove, and he is strangled by a snake. One of the essential qualities of 'agency' in tragedy is the capacity to be held accountable for the consequences of one's actions. As Ruby Blondell phrases it: 'Agency entails responsibility, and responsibility entails susceptibility to blame and, most important, punishment.'[20] Blondell is referring to *Iliad* 3, where Paris and Menelaus will fight over Helen without asking her about it. Helen is objectified as Paris' victim, rather than acknowledged as an agent in her departure from Sparta, so she is herself blameless. But Blondell's comment could also be applied to Hypsipyle. Agency implies responsibility and blame and punishment, so does blame confirm agency? In Hypsipyle's case, she fears punishment for her negligence and the child's death (fr. 754b.7, ~672) and contemplates fleeing Nemea (fr. 754b.5, ~676).[21] And she is right to fear it, since Eurydice clearly accuses Hypsipyle of deliberate murder. The remains of fr. 757.835 can be constructed]μοι παιδί θ' ὃν διώ[λεσας ('for me and my son whom you have destroyed'), and Hypsipyle explains to Amphiaraus explicitly φησὶ δ' ἥδ' ἑκουσίως | κτανεῖν μ[ε π]αῖδα κἀπιβουλεῦσαι δόμοις ('But she says that I willingly killed the child and plotted against the house', 866–7).[22]

It is this belief on Eurydice's part that Hypsipyle could be capable of murder – that she did not love the child – that causes Hypsipyle great distress. She says as much:

ὡς τοῦ θανεῖν μὲν οὕνεκ' οὐ μέγα στ[έν]ω,
εἰ δὲ κτανεῖν τὸ τέκνον οὐκ ὀρθῶς δοκῶ,
τοὐμὸν τιθήνημ', ὃν ἐπ' ἐμαῖσιν ἀγκάλαις
πλὴν οὐ τεκοῦσα τἄλλα γ' ὡς ἐμὸν τέκνον
στέργουσ' ἔφερβον, ὠφέλημ' ἐμοὶ μέγα.

[20] Blondell 2013: 60.
[21] The approximate line numbering of this passage follows the transposition of lines 5–8 according to Wecklein 1909: 25–6.
[22] I follow W. Cockle 1987 and Collard and Cropp 2008 in printing φησί where Kannicht, *TrGF* prints φῆσι.

> I do not groan so greatly about dying, but if I am wrongly believed to have
> killed the child, my nursling, whom I fed in my own arms, loving him as
> my own child in every way except that I did not bear him, a great benefit
> to me.
>
> Eur. *Hypsipyle* fr. 757.839–43

Here gender truly makes a difference. Since these thoughts trigger Hypsipyle's invocation of the Argo and her twin sons (844–5), it becomes clear
that her love for Opheltes was a kind of substitute motherhood, replacing
the intimacy with children that she might have had in younger, freer days.
Hypsipyle appeals to Eurydice as if they were both Opheltes' mother.
Hypsipyle's argument is that it is inconceivable that she would have killed
the child since she loved him and cared for him as if he were her own; her
appeal to Eurydice as mother, as woman, is meant to breach the social
distance between the two. It is not the kind of argument that a man could
make, since a man would never be in the role of a nurse. All the social
baggage that is attached to motherhood and women's role as nurturers is
called forth by Hypsipyle's appeal to a solidarity that mothers have with
each other, regardless of free or slave status. Unfortunately this tactic of
solidarity does not work. In fact, Eurydice has already shut down communication, and indeed Hypsipyle had remarked on her mistress's silence
(838). It takes the intervention of a witness – who happens to be both a
man, and a well-known prophet – to get a response out of Eurydice.

Eurydice

Eurydice's agency takes the form of arresting something she had started;
namely, she has Hypsipyle bound and is determined to kill her (836), yet
she is persuaded by Amphiaraus to relent. Eurydice's change of heart,
as stated above, was perhaps the most memorable scene of the play.
Amphiaraus arrives at line 853, immediately after Hypsipyle had given
up hope of his arrival and ordered the attendants to lead her away (851).
Amphiaraus' first words – 'Stop, oh you who are sending this woman to
her slaughter!' – are addressed to Eurydice (the gender of the participle
πέμπουσα, 'sending', makes this clear). He then addresses her as mistress of
the house, claiming (854–5) that because of her seemly appearance he can
'attribute free birth to you in your nature (φύσις)'. Hypsipyle interrupts and
supplicates him to save her by telling Eurydice what happened to her son
(856–67). His defence of Hypsipyle is a combination of a narration of the

child's death and the role of the Argives in it, and a consolation that death is a normal aspect of life, but that Opheltes can nonetheless win fame with athletic games established in his honour. Elsewhere I have argued that Eurydice's choice to forgive, to be persuaded not to kill Hypsipyle out of revenge, is a testament to Amphiaraus' skills as a consoler.[23] Here I argue that Eurydice's refusal to take revenge can also be understood as agency. The capacity to decide not to act when one can is a paradoxical sign of power. Crucially Eurydice, and Eurydice alone, can decide not to kill her slave Hypsipyle. Amphiaraus, the male who comes to the rescue, can attempt to persuade her, but cannot force her to relent.

Eurydice's initial response to Amphiaraus' greeting establishes that she will be receptive to what he will say. Amphiaraus' reputation precedes him. Eurydice knows that he lives near Argos (881), and she has heard from everyone that he is σώφρων ('discreet', 'moderate', 882), which confirms Amphiaraus' boast that all Hellas acknowledges his discreet eye (σῶφρον … ὄμμα, 875). She also permits him to look into her own ὄμμα (883), which indicates that she has uncovered her head (which Amphiaraus invited her to do at 874). It is this trust in Amphiaraus as a σώφρων individual that inspires her willingness to listen to him (884); but she also foreshadows a desire to explain things to him in turn (ἐκδιδάσκειν, 885).

For fifty-eight lines, Eurydice is silent, perhaps adopting the pensive pose depicted on the Apulian volute-krater, while Amphiaraus tries to persuade her not to kill Hypsipyle. His arguments are that he is looking to the interests of justice (τὸ τῆς δ[ί]κης ὁ[ρ]ῷν, 888), the child's death was accidental, death is necessary in any case and part of human nature (921–7), the child will be memorialised (μνησθήσετα[ι, 938), and ultimately Hypsipyle is blameless (ἀναιτία γάρ, 941). Then, where one might expect a chorus-leader to interject a rejoinder, Eurydice herself speaks.[24] Her first address is to her deceased son (ὦ παῖ, 944), rather than to Amphiaraus, but then quickly her speech becomes a self-reflection. Eurydice says that one must examine (σκοπεῖν) three things in people (946–7): their natures (φύσεις), their actions (πράγματα) and their manner of life (διαίτας). These three aspects of what one might call a person's 'character' align seamlessly with one another. One's nature (φύσις) is visible through one's actions

---

[23] Chong-Gossard 2009: 18–20.

[24] P.Oxy. 852 indicates a change of speaker with a *paragraphos* (a short horizontal line), but not the name of the speaker. Most scholars have attributed lines 944–7 to Eurydice. However, Scatena 1950: 11 and Wiles 2005: 204 (an English translation for the stage) attribute them to the chorus, and admittedly the words do sound like the generic statements made in choral rejoinders.

(πράγματα) – one's agency – and determined by the way one lives one's life (δίαιτα). At the same time, the semantics of φύσις hover between one's social status, in the way that Amphiaraus attributes free birth to Eurydice's φύσις at 855; the nature of human life, as in Amphiaraus' rhetorical question about why we should lament the things which we must endure κατὰ φύσιν ('through our very nature', 927); and the nature of one's mind, which seems to be the point of looking at the φύσεις of both wicked and good people.

But what people does Eurydice have in mind to examine? Hypsipyle? Amphiaraus? Given that she was about to send Hypsipyle to her death before Amphiaraus interrupted her, one might initially expect Eurydice to be asking herself how she judges Hypsipyle. Eurydice's criterion of πράγματα ('actions') also recalls Hypsipyle's earlier dismay that Eurydice has determined to kill her 'before properly understanding this πρᾶγμα' (πρὶν ὀρθῶς πρᾶγμ[α] διαμαθε[ῖν τόδε, 837), in which πρᾶγμα can have the sense of 'my action', as well as the generic sense of an 'occurrence', and (according to Bond) the legal meaning of a 'case'.[25] Is Eurydice now describing how she will examine Hypsipyle's case? How do Hypsipyle's nature, actions and manner of life testify to whether she is innocent of wilful murder or not, to whether she should live or not? But then Eurydice's next lines change the focus: one should have trust in (or even 'let oneself be persuaded by', πειθὼ ἔχειν) those who are σώφρων (948) and not consort with τοῖς μὴ δικαίοις ('those who are unjust', 949). These lines sound like the outcome of the examination of others; once one has sorted people into two types – the σώφρονες and the μὴ δίκαιοι – based on their natures, actions and lifestyles, one should trust the former and avoid the latter. A conclusion like this, which repeats the key word σώφρων, implies that Eurydice has been examining Amphiaraus' character and has decided to take his advice, to be persuaded by him. After all, did not Amphiaraus himself admit ταύτην ἐγὼ 'ξέπεισα κρηναῖον [γά]νος | δεῖξαι, 'I myself persuaded this woman to point out the brightness of the spring' (891–2)? If Hypsipyle yielded to the persuasion of the σώφρων seer, should Eurydice not do so too?

Yet the sheer beauty of Euripides' gnomic statements is their applicability to almost anyone in a drama, including the speaker. Thus Eurydice could just as easily be examining herself. She may have decided at this very point that it is desirable for her to be σώφρων (echoing the chorus women's

---

[25] Bond 1963: 104 on his fr. 60.6.

earlier desire to be counted ἐν σώφροσιν, 830). Eurydice chooses not to be reckoned among τοῖς μὴ δικαίοις ('the unjust'), the sort of people who would not respect the interests of justice (δίκη) that Amphiaraus claimed he was looking to (888). She may recognise in her own φύσις the cruelty with which Amphiaraus accused her of behaving (ἀγρίως φέρουσαν, 887). Eurydice is no Clytemnestra who kills her husband to avenge the ritual sacrifice of their child, no Hecuba who maims her son's murderer; nor is Hypsipyle an Agamemnon or a Polymestor, since the death of Eurydice's son was an accident. Nor is Eurydice a Merope who tries to kill her dead son's assassin (or so Merope believes).[26] Instead, Eurydice decides that her φύσις ('nature') – to which Amphiaraus attributed free birth (855) – is capable of an act of forgiveness, which is in keeping with her manner of life. She chooses to be the gentle and lenient (ἤπιος, 887) woman that Amphiaraus wanted to make her. Sadly we have lost the rest of Eurydice's speech and may never know whether she 'explained things in turn' (ἐκδιδάσκειν, 885) as she had promised to.[27] But by choosing to spare Hypsipyle, Eurydice is making a momentous statement about revenge. Fiona McHardy has proposed that 'the vengeful women of tragedy become embodiments of uncivilized values which cannot be condoned in civilized democratic Athens'.[28] Eurydice proposes the alternative, and her choice of forgiveness is a tremendous leap that expands the definition of female agency in Greek tragedy.

Eriphyle

The role of Eriphyle in the myth of Amphiaraus and the Seven Against Thebes is reducible to a single act: bribery. In the well-known version, Eriphyle's brother Adrastus, king of Argos and her husband Amphiaraus agreed to let her be the judge in any dispute between them.[29] When they disagreed on whether they should lead an Argive army to restore Adrastus' son-in-law Polynices to power in Thebes, and Amphiaraus refused because he foretold that he would die if he joined in the campaign, Eriphyle judged in Adrastus' favour, which compelled Amphiaraus to march. But she

---

[26] See Collard and Cropp 2008: I 493–5 for a plot summary of Euripides' *Cresphontes*.

[27] See Cropp 2004: 173–5 on the scholarly agreement that, at this point where the text is lost, Eurydice accepts Amphiaraus' advice and releases Hypsipyle.

[28] McHardy 2004: 111.

[29] This version is recorded in Σ Pind. *N.* 9.30b (III 153.19–154.5 Drachmann), as well as by Diodorus Siculus (4.65.5–6) in the first century.

judged in this way because she had been bribed by Polynices to do so, with a golden necklace that had been passed down from Harmonia, daughter of the goddess Aphrodite. Amphiaraus agreed to march, but before he left Argos, he asked his son Alcmaeon to kill Eriphyle after his death.[30] In his conversation with Hypsipyle in fr. 752k (~375–90), Amphiaraus apparently introduces the story of his wife, Eriphyle. Tantalising in its patchy state, the conversation is nonetheless relatively easy to reconstruct. Polydorus (9, ~380) was the son of Cadmus (the founder of Thebes) and Harmonia, the daughter of a goddess (10, ~381), Aphrodite. Polydorus' descendants (11, ~382) include Polynices. Amphiaraus explains that it was necessary that he himself join the Argive expedition (χρὴ γὰρ στρατεύειν μ', 15, ~386) because Eriphyle willingly accepted a bribe. This, at least, is the implication of the subsequent fragments ἐ]δέξατ' οὖν ἑκοῦσα ('Did she then willingly accept … ?', 16, ~387), probably a question asked by Hypsipyle, and the following line, ἐδέ]ξαθ', ἥκω δ' [οὔ]ποτ' ἐκ[('She accepted it, and I shall never come (back) from …', 17, ~388), which editors interpret as Amphiaraus' response.[31]

If Amphiaraus is indeed informing Hypsipyle (who, by the way, is a complete stranger to him, and a household slave) that he is marching against Thebes because of the bribery of his wife, then a few thematic points become clear. First, Amphiaraus' knowledge of his own mortality and imminent death make his later consolation of Eurydice more poignant. It is clear that Amphiaraus knows he will not return from Thebes, since Hypsipyle confirms as much when she asks him, τί δῆτα θύειν δεῖ σε κατθανούμενον; ('Why, then, must you sacrifice if you are going to your death?' 20, ~391, preserved in Plutarch, *On How Young Men Should Listen to Poetry* 20d). Therefore when Amphiaraus asks Eurydice to spare Hypsipyle because it is necessary that everyone must die (fr. 757.921–3), he speaks from personal experience and foreknowledge of his own fate.[32] Amphiaraus does not, apparently, mention Eriphyle in his consolation speech; but such a narrative might have detracted from the general points Amphiaraus is trying to make. It is enough for an audience to recognise that, when it comes to the topic of the inevitability of death, Amphiaraus knows what he is talking about.

---

[30] See Sommerstein 2012: 26–34, Davies and Finglass 2014: 344–8, on the ancient sources for the Eriphyle myth, which include Diodorus Siculus, Apollodorus, Hyginus and Cicero.

[31] *Paragraphoi* indicating a change of speaker in every line appear consistently in col. 7 of P.Oxy. 852, but the speakers are not named. Context alone determines who is speaking which line in this *stichomythia*.

[32] Chong-Gossard 2009: 19.

Second, apparently absent from his conversation with Hypsipyle is the next part of the story: that before Amphiaraus left Argos, he commanded his son Alcmaeon to kill Eriphyle after Amphiaraus' own death in Thebes. This part of Amphiaraus' myth would surely have been familiar to Euripides' audience, not least because of his own treatment of the Alcmaeon myth in 438 with *Alcmaeon in Psophis*.[33] But in the surviving fragments of Euripides' *Hypsipyle* there is no overt mention of Amphiaraus' injunction to his son to have Eriphyle killed. By leaving his own plans for revenge unsaid, Amphiaraus complicates his appeals to Eurydice for forgiveness. An implicit comparison is drawn between two passionate queens, Eurydice and Eriphyle. Eriphyle is persuaded by bribery; will Eurydice allow herself to be persuaded by reason? Amphiaraus was unable to persuade his wife to relent from sending him to Thebes; will he succeed in persuading Eurydice? At the same time, Eurydice's statement that 'One must look to the natures and the actions and the manners of life of the wicked and the good' has an additional significance by suggesting how Amphiaraus has judged his own situation. Do Eriphyle's actions and manner of life attest that she is among the μὴ δίκαιοι whom one should not consort with? Although Amphiaraus does not mention Eriphyle in his consolation speech, perhaps she is all the more conspicuous for her omission. Because Amphiaraus knows Eriphyle's wicked motive and judges that she must die, he can discern that Opheltes' death was an accident and therefore does not rightfully require revenge.

Finally, from the perspective of agency, Eriphyle lurks in the background of the narrative as a woman whose decision to act is revealed to have unforseen consequences. Although it is not explicitly stated in the fragments, one suspects that Eriphyle must have known that Amphiaraus was doomed to die if he were to march against Thebes, but that she chose to send him there anyway; otherwise, why would the bribe be necessary, and why would Amphiaraus feel compelled to punish her, and at the hands of her own son? If this is the case, then her own death would be the obvious unforeseen consequence of Eriphyle's act; but it would be a consequence taking place after the events of the play, and one not overtly referenced.

---

[33] See Collard and Cropp 2008: I 77–81, 87–9 on *Alcmaeon in Psophis* (performed 438) and *Alcmaeon in Corinth* (performed 405, posthumously). Amphiaraus is also mentioned in Soph. *Electra* 836/7–848. See Sommerstein 2012: 26–34, Davies and Finglass 2014: 344–8, on further sources, including Sophocles' *Alcmaeon* and *Eriphyle*, whose performance dates are unknown; and the *Alcmaeonis*, part of the now-lost epic Theban Cycle, which original audiences of Euripides might very well have known.

Instead, the play's ending reveals a further unintended consequence of Eriphyle's agency – namely, Hypsipyle's happy reunion with her sons.

The Play's Ending

The final long section of *Hypsipyle* preserved on P.Oxy. 852 (fr. 759a) is a recognition duet between Hypsipyle and her sons, Euneus and Thoas (although Thoas is mute at this point), the very men to whom she had shown hospitality at the play's beginning. The duet is preceded by Amphiaraus' parting words as he heads off to Thebes. All the instances of female agency in this play achieve closure in this final scene. The papyrus fragment becomes legible at 1579, part of the last five lines of a lyric passage that editors assign to Hypsipyle. The sentiment of her song is clear: all has turned out well at the end of a single day. Something brought Hypsipyle and her sons along a single path (1579–80); and although it swerved them into different directions, one fearful, and another glad (1581–2), in the end it turned out to be, literally, a 'good day' (εὐάμερος, 1583). On the one hand, her comments are a summary of the play's events from her perspective. On the other, they are also a précis of the message of the drama itself: that one woman's suffering can give rise to another woman's good fortune, and one woman's happiness can be the unintended result of decisions made by herself long ago, or by others whom she has never met.

As noted earlier, it is during the recognition duet that Hypsipyle relives her memories of the night when the Lemnian women killed all their men, and she spared her father's life (1593–1603), and how on the shore of Lemnos she was abducted by pirates and sold into slavery (1604–9). The duet is also the opportunity for her (and perhaps the audience) to learn her sons' hidden history. She learns that Jason died long ago, perhaps in Colchis (1611–16), and that Orpheus took her sons back to Thrace and raised them there (1619–23). Then the most exciting news is revealed: her father King Thoas conveyed his grandsons to Lemnos (1626), presumably to search for her. When Hypsipyle asks whether Thoas was indeed saved (the sentence can be reconstructed ἦ γὰ[ρ] σέσ[ω]τ[α]ι̣;, 1627), Euneus confirms it was by the contrivances of Dionysus (Βα[κ]χ[ίου] γε μηχαναῖς, 1626), Thoas' own father. Whether or not the Hypsipyle of Euripides' play ever put her father in a hollow chest on the seashore to rescue him, it is evident that until now Hypsipyle never learned whether her father survived the Lemnian massacre.

All the connections between events and their causation are finally revealed. Hypsipyle's reunion with her adult sons would not have been possible had she not spared her father's life on Lemnos (since it is Thoas who conveys the sons on their search for their mother); nor would it have been possible without the institution of the Nemean games (at which the sons were recognised), which would not have happened without the death of Opheltes (in whose honour the games were established), which would not have happened if Hypsipyle had not chosen to direct Amphiaraus to the sacred spring, which would not have happened without Eriphyle's acceptance of Polynices' bribe that necessitated Amphiaraus' participation in the expedition against Thebes; nor would Hypsipyle's reunion with her sons have happened if Eurydice had not decided to relent in punishing her and allowed the games to be set up, which itself would not have happened if Amphiaraus had not arrived and repaid Hypsipyle for her act of kindness to him; nor would Hypsipyle's reunion with her sons have happened if she had not shown shelter to the wandering Thoas and Euneus at the play's very beginning. Hypsipyle's agency in the past, Eurydice's agency today, and even Eriphyle's agency in far-away Argos have all led to the momentous resolution of Hypsipyle's story of endurance. Having lost the nursling that she loved as her own, she is restored to motherhood once again to her biological sons. And she owes this convoluted sequence of events to Eurydice, Eriphyle and herself.

Conclusion

In the mythology of Euripides' *Hypsipyle*, decisions by women have long-reaching consequences that are not fully realised except in the fullness of time. Instead of focussing on battles or war prizes or debates about heroism – the topics of an epic, male world – this play focuses on the female perspective and the significance of women's choices. A series of women's decisions, some generous and some self-serving – to show hospitality, to refrain from killing, to do a favour for a soldier, to accept a bribe – are what propel the story to its climax.

Clearly Euripides' interest in female subjectivity is at work – but to what end? Those who interpret tragedy as a project of patriarchy might argue that this play's female agency nonetheless serves patriarchal interests. Eurydice's decision to spare Hypsipyle allows the Nemean Games to be established, which are athletic contests for men, not women. Hypsipyle's reunion with her sons could be what a male audience expects from women – that motherhood is woman's proper place, even a mother reunited with adult children who no longer need her nurturing. Eriphyle could be interpreted as a negative female stereotype, the wife who loves finery more than her husband's life. Those who interpret tragedy itself as reinforcing civic ideology might note that all the women are in their proper place by the play's end. Hypsipyle is a mother again. The orphaned Eurydice took a man's rational advice with grace and is not making a fuss; she might even try to have more children, which Amphiaraus at 922 says is part of human nature. And Eriphyle, the audience knows, will be killed by her own son in due course, which society might say is just what she deserves. All of these interpretations are possible. But the observation being made here is one of fascination with this under-studied fragmentary play. In *Hypsipyle*, Euripides reinforces a difference between the lived experiences of women and men. For the men, the events in Nemea have been the first omen – the first sign of death (hence Opheltes' cult name 'Archemorus') – in a long saga called the Seven Against Thebes. Men will fight, men will suffer, men will even compete in games. But Euripides imagines a women's world happening alongside that, a world that might seem to the male characters like an interlude, but which is characterised by lifetimes of endurance that are just as momentous, just as worthy of memory, and just as tragic as the battles and adventures of men.

13 | Making Medea Medea

MATTHEW WRIGHT

'The play dodges the part that makes Medea Medea'. Thus Lloyd Evans in his review of Rachel Cusk's stage adaptation at the Almeida Theatre, London, of Euripides' *Medea*.[1] What he means is that Cusk downplayed Medea's agonised decision to kill her own children, in contrast to Euripides' version, which puts the infanticide at the heart of the plot, along with a powerful focus on Medea's disturbed psychological state.[2] But what 'made Medea Medea' for ancient Greek theatregoers? The question cannot be answered simply with reference to Euripides' play. Its main character has come to be regarded as the definitive Medea – indeed, as *the* quintessential tragic heroine.[3] But the ancient mythical and literary tradition incorporated other retellings of her story, and Euripides' tragedy of 431 was just one of many.

This chapter attempts to answer the question by examining the other theatrical versions of Medea from fifth- and fourth-century Greece. The evidence is exiguous, but nonetheless we can see that these various incarnations of Medea differed significantly from Euripides' 431 version and from one another. Several dramatised incidents from Medea's early life in Colchis or her adventures in Iolcus, including her killing of Pelias and her own brother Apsyrtus, and her career as a magician or witch (for instance, Aeschylus' *Nurses*, Sophocles' *Women of Colchis*, *Root-Cutters* and *Scythians*, and Diogenes of Sinope's *Medea*). Some tragedians, such as Melanthius and Neophron, were particularly interested in the relationship between Medea and Jason, though they presented both characters in unexpected ways. Certain plays (including the *Medea*s by Carcinus, Dicaeogenes and Neophron) were obviously similar to Euripides' *Medea*: this leads us to consider the exact relationship between different versions, and the extent to which Euripides' play was already a significant model or point of departure for other classical writers. Euripides himself created

---

[1] *The Spectator*, 10 October 2015.

[2] Cf. how Cusk maintains that Euripides' play 'is about divorce, not motherhood' (*The Guardian*, 3 October 2015).

[3] Aélion 1986: 244, Boedeker 1997.

more than one Medea, treating an aspect of her early history in his first tragedy, *Daughters of Pelias* (455), echoes of which can be detected in his *Medea*, and yet another aspect of her character and myth in his *Aegeus*. Papyrus evidence has even been taken as indicating that the *Medea* of 431 was a revised version of an earlier Euripidean *Medea*. Much remains obscure about these lost plays, but careful study of the fragments can help us to give a richer and more nuanced account of this fascinating character.

What Made Medea Medea?

Here I survey all known classical Greek tragedies that featured Medea,[4] drawing attention to the presentation of the myth and the characterisation of Medea, and emphasising the range and multiplicity of variants current during the fifth and fourth centuries.[5]

Aeschylus, *Nurses* (frr. 246a–d *TrGF*)

According to an ancient hypothesis to Euripides' *Medea*, Aeschylus' *Nurses* depicted Medea as a sorceress, boiling human bodies to rejuvenate them. Unlike other versions, in which Pelias, Jason or Aeson were boiled, in Aeschylus the bodies in question belonged to Dionysus' nurses (Thracian nymphs) and their husbands.[6] This odd detail (the connection between Medea and Dionysus is not seen elsewhere) may indicate that *Nurses* was a satyr-play rather than a tragedy;[7] the presence of nurses points to the motif of motherhood and child-bearing so important for Medea's story elsewhere.

   This play may mark Medea's first appearance in Athenian drama.[8] It displayed the grotesque and magical aspects of Medea's character, perhaps in a fashion absurd (if satyr-drama) or terrifying (if tragedy). Surprisingly,

---

[4] Cf. Melero 1996, Mastronarde 2002: 44–57, Mossman 2011: 14–28.

[5] This section revises and expands certain portions of Wright 2016, 2019. I am grateful to Bloomsbury Publishing for freely granting me permission to do this.

[6] Hyp. I Eur. *Med.* (= Aesch. fr. 246a), comparing Pherecydes (fr. 113 *EGM*) and Simonides (fr. 548 *PMG* = 270 Poltera). Aesch. fr. 361, which mentions the rejuvenation of an old man, was ascribed to *Nurses* by Hartung.

[7] Sommerstein 2008: III 248–9; see further Radt *ad loc.*, R. Germar and R. Krumeich *ap.* Krumeich et al. 1999: 197–202.

[8] Melero 1996: 59.

Aeschylus does not seem to have put Medea on stage elsewhere, despite her rich dramatic appeal.[9]

Anonymous, (?) *Medea* (Tr. Adesp. fr. 701 *TrGF*)

A second century AD papyrus (P.Berol. 17203) preserves part of a song from a tragedy about Medea and Jason. Probably from a choral ode or a lyric *kommos* between Medea and the chorus, these verses evoke a scenario in which Medea and Jason are at odds. Reference is made to 'an exile, apart from good people' (δίχ' ἀγαθῶν φυγάς, 2), a marriage bed (3), something or someone Thessalian (3), weeping children (3–4), a Scythian woman (5) and an ungrateful Jason (7); someone, no doubt Medea, is described as 'raving' (μαν<ε>ῖσα, 6) and 'bereft' (8), and the singer apparently laments her wretched state (φεῦ μογερά, 12). This scenario resembles Euripides' *Medea,* at least in broad detail, but nothing can be said about its date or authorship.

Anonymous, (?) *Medea* (*CGFPR* fr. dub. 350 = Tr. Adesp. fr. 667a *TrGF*)

Another papyrus, dating from the second or third century AD, is from a drama set in Corinth featuring Medea, Jason, Aegeus and Creon. Identified variously as tragic, comic or satyric, recent scholars tend to agree that it comes from a tragedy of the fourth century or later.[10] The date is suggested by the performance direction χοροῦ (after line 112), which indicates a detachable choral interlude functioning as an act-division (in contrast to the fully integrated choral odes of fifth-century drama). The papyrus contains a conversation concerning the fate of Medea and her children; their death might be described.[11] As with Tr. Adesp. fr. 701 *TrGF* above, the fragment may or may not belong to one of the other plays discussed below.

---

[9] Aélion 1986: 148.

[10] Snell considered it comic and excluded it from *TrGF* ii, but see his later remarks, reported by Austin in *CGFPR ad loc.*, and see R. Hunter 1981 for full discussion. The fragment was included by Kannicht in the addenda to *TrGF* ii at the end of *TrGF* v/2 (pp. 1137–42). The possibility that it preserves part of Neophron's *Medea* is rejected by Martina 2000.

[11] See line 105 κοίμησον ἠρεθισμ[ένη, supplemented by Snell *ap.* Austin and interpreted as referring to Medea's killing the children in anger (he compares Soph. *Aj.* 832 for euphemistic use of κοιμίζω).

Antiphon, *Jason* (*TrGF* 1 55 F 1a)

Antiphon was active in the first half of the fourth century; his plays include a *Jason*, the only attested tragedy with this title. Unfortunately, the single surviving word (διετίθουν, 'they disposed') reveals nothing about its contents. Perhaps the play dramatised Jason's adventures in Colchis or Corinth and his relationship with Medea, but it might have dealt with any portion of Argonautic myth;[12] perhaps Medea did not feature at all.

Aphareus, *Daughters of Pelias* (*TrGF* 1 73 F 1)

Aphareus won third prize at the City Dionysia of 341 with a trilogy consisting of *Daughters of Pelias*, *Orestes* and *Auge*.[13] All that we have to go on is the play's title, which may indicate a plot similar to Euripides' tragedy of the same name (see below). Perhaps Aphareus consciously designed his play as some sort of response, or 'sequel', to the Euripidean version (the other plays in the trilogy also share titles with Euripidean tragedies), but there is no actual evidence to support such a view. At any rate, it seems that Aphareus' Medea appeared, as elsewhere, in the guise of sorceress or witch, boiling up bodies and persuading Pelias' daughters to kill their father.

Biotus, *Medea* (*TrGF* 1 205 F 1)

The anthologist Stobaeus quotes a couple of gnomic verses about love-charms and the birth and rearing of children, attributing them to 'the *Medea* of Biotus'. Nothing else is known about this play or its author.

Carcinus, *Medea* (*TrGF* 1 70 F 1e)

The heroine of Carcinus' *Medea* (a version of the story from the mid-fourth century) did not kill her children, as Aristotle reveals:[14]

οἷον ἐν τῆι Καρκίνου Μηδείαι οἱ μὲν κατηγοροῦσιν ὅτι τοὺς παῖδας ἀπέκτεινεν, οὐ φαίνεσθαι γοῦν αὐτούς (ἥμαρτε γὰρ ἡ Μήδεια περὶ τὴν

---

[12] Cf. Aesch. *Argo* (or *Oarsmen*), Soph. *Phineus*, and Eur. *Hypsipyle*, and some plays mentioned below. See Aélion 1986: 119–35, Deforge 1987.

[13] *IG* II–III² 2325A col. i.46, 2320 col. ii.13; Millis and Olson 2012: 149, 67.

[14] Wright 2016: 112–14.

ἀποστολὴν τῶν παίδων), ἡ δ' ἀπολογεῖται ὅτι οὐ τοὺς παῖδας ἀλλὰ τὸν Ἰάσονα ἂν ἀπέκτεινεν· τοῦτο γὰρ ἥμαρτεν ἂν μὴ ποιήσασα, εἴπερ καὶ θάτερον ἐποίησεν.

In Carcinus' *Medea*, for instance, some characters accuse Medea of having killed her children – or, at any rate, they had disappeared – for Medea made the mistake of sending them out of the way. Medea says in her defence that she would not have killed her children but would have killed Jason instead; for indeed it would have been a mistake not to have done this, if she had actually done the other killings of which she was accused.

Arist. *Rhet.* 1400b10–15

Carcinus' Medea sent her children away from Corinth to protect them, fearing that Jason's new wife Glauce or others among the Corinthians would do them harm; when the children disappeared, the other characters concluded that Medea had killed them. The play must have included some sort of *agôn* or trial scene, in which Medea offered a rhetorically polished self-defence speech to her accusers. Furthermore, Aristotle shows us that the characterisation and psychology of Medea were handled differently from in Euripides' version.

No confirmed fragments of Carcinus' *Medea* survive, but a second-century papyrus plausibly belongs to it.[15] The fragment preserves tragic dialogue between Jason, Medea and another character (probably Creon); the situation dramatised corresponds with Aristotle's description. West's reconstruction permits appreciation of the meaning. Jason begins by saying to Medea: 'If, . . . as you say, you did not kill the children, [save] yourself: produce these ones you have not killed, let us see them.' Medea replies: 'I swear to you that . . . I have not destroyed the boys that I myself bore, but sent them away to safety in the care of an aged(?) nurse.' Creon, or some other hostile character, repeats the accusation against Medea, saying that she is clearly guilty: 'The Colchian woman has killed Glauce with fire – she admits as much – so there is no doubt that she has done [this too], killed the children. [So] what are you waiting for, Jason? You are free to take this barbarian woman to be executed.' Thus Medea's own life was apparently in danger. But the fragment gives no further clues as to how the action resolved itself.

A non-infanticidal Medea will surprise a modern audience because Euripides' *Medea* has so shaped our expectations. The effect upon

---

[15] P.Louvre (Antiquités égyptiennes inv. E 10534), first published in Bélis 2004. For a revised edition, translated above, see West 2007 = 2011–13: II 334–50. West also discusses the musical notation, on which see further Taplin 2014: 151–3.

Carcinus' original audience is harder to gauge. The characters within the play did not expect to encounter an innocent Medea, since the scenario evoked by Aristotle and the papyrus depends on their assumption that Medea murdered the boys: perhaps a self-conscious intertextual response to Euripides' *Medea*? But we cannot take for granted that a child-murdering Medea represented the norm for Carcinus' audience; his play may have reflected other pre-existing variants of the myth, such as versions in which the children were killed by the Corinthians for political reasons, or taken by Medea to the sanctuary at Eleusis.[16]

Dicaeogenes, *Medea* (*TrGF* I 52 F 1a)

Known only from a reference in a Euripidean scholion, this fourth-century tragedy dealt with Medea's murder of her brother, thus situating the action in Colchis (unless the fratricide was merely mentioned in a passing allusion or flashback).[17] Medea's brother, elsewhere Apsyrtus, was named Metapontius; such mythical innovation might hint that Medea's killing of Metapontius was handled unexpectedly in other respects.[18]

Diogenes of Sinope, *Medea* (*TrGF* I 88 F 1e)

This play by the fourth-century Cynic philosopher Diogenes radically reimagined Medea's character and actions. Like Sophocles' *Root-Cutters*, Euripides' *Daughters of Pelias* and Aeschylus' *Nurses*, the play centred on Medea's exploits as a witch in Iolcus. Unlike these other plays, however, Diogenes' tragedy rationalised the myth, offering a new explanation of Medea's supposed supernatural powers, as a plot-summary preserved by Stobaeus makes clear:[19]

---

[16] Attested only in later sources, including vase-painting, these variants may have been current in the fourth century or earlier (see West 2007: 5–6 = 2011–13: II 342, citing Creophylus of Ephesus fr. 3 *EGM* and Σ Eur. *Med.* 9 = II 142.10–20 Schwartz, and Taplin 2014: 150–3, citing an Apulian red-figure volute-krater ascribed to the Darius painter, Princeton University Art Museum inv. 1983.13 = Taplin 2007: 238–40), perhaps even before 431 (see McHardy 2005: 136–7, citing in addition Eumelus fr. 20, 23 *GEF* = Paus. 2.3.10–11, Σ Pind. *O.* 13.74 = I 373–4 Drachmann, Σ Eur. *Med.* 264 = II 159.16–160.9 Schwartz = Parmeniscus fr. 13 Breithaupt).

[17] *TrGF* I 52 F 1a. For Dicaeogenes see Wright 2016: 146–8.

[18] For other accounts see Soph. *Colchian Women*, Pherecydes fr. 32 *EGM*, Ap. Rh. 4.305–481, Apollod. *Bibl.* 1.9.24, Ov. *Her.* 6.129–30, Gantz 1993: 363–4.

[19] Similar accounts, almost certainly related to Diogenes' play, are given by Palaephatus, *Peri Apistôn* (*On Incredible Things*) 4 and Dio of Prusa 16.10: Wright 2016: 153–63.

ὁ Διογένης ἔλεγε τὴν Μήδειαν σοφήν, ἀλλ' οὐ φαρμακίδα γενέσθαι. λαμβά-
νουσαν γὰρ μαλακοὺς ἀνθρώπους καὶ τὰ σώματα διεφθαρμένους ὑπὸ
τρυφῆς ἐν τοῖς γυμνασίοις καὶ τοῖς πυριατηρίοις διαπονεῖν καὶ ἰσχυροὺς
ποιεῖν σφριγῶντας· ὅθεν περὶ αὐτῆς ῥυῆναι τὴν δόξαν, ὅτι τὰ κρέα ἕψουσα
νέους ἐποίει.

Diogenes said that while Medea may have been clever, she was not a
sorceress. That is, she took on weak and feeble people, whose bodies had
been ruined through overindulgence, and she made them strong and
vigorous again by means of gymnastic exercises and steam baths. It is
for this reason that the story arose that she boiled people's flesh and
rejuvenated them.

Diogenes *TrGF* I 88 F 1e

Such a play might seem provocative or wilfully outrageous.[20] But Diogenes'
intellectual outlook seems to have had a serious aim – that of shocking
people into re-examining settled opinions. His *Medea* may have been
intended to undermine the accepted truth about Medea and uncover problems inherent in the mythical tradition. After all, Diogenes did not downplay
or ignore the more grotesque or bizarre aspects of Medea's character (as
Euripides had done). Rather, he drew attention to them, offering a rational,
down-to-earth explanation. Diogenes' Medea is no witch but a sensible,
practical, woman. Even her 'cleverness', an ambivalent quality in Euripides,
is reconfigured as practical intelligence instead of something more dangerous.[21] Diogenes' literary agenda parallels that of Euripides: *viz.* the transformation of a potentially monstrous or marginal figure into a human,
sympathetic person to whom his audience could relate.

Euripides, *Aegeus* (frr. 1–13 *TrGF*)

This play dramatised a late stage in Medea's story: her sojourn in
Athens under the Aegeus' protection following her flight from Corinth.
Of uncertain date,[22] the play can be tentatively reconstructed from later
mythographic narratives as well as from contemporary vase-paintings.[23] Its
main action centred on the arrival in Athens of Theseus, a stranger to his

---

[20] For Diogenes as *provocateur* (and other aspects of his life and thought) see Dudley 1937,
Desmond 2008. For the notion that his tragedies were transgressive, anti-tragic, parodic or
quasi-comic, see López Cruces 2003, Sluiter 2005, Noussia 2006.

[21] For *sophia* in Euripides' *Medea* see López Férez 1996, Gibert 2016.

[22] The metrical evidence is inconclusive: Cropp and Fick 1985: 70–1, Melero 1996: 64–5, Kannicht
(*TrGF* v/1 152).

[23] Apollod. *Bibl.* 3.16.1, *Ep.* 1.5–6, Plut. *Thes.* 12.2–3. See further Kannicht *ad loc.*

father Aegeus. Recognising Theseus, Medea convinced Aegeus that he had come with hostile purpose, and persuaded him to give the newcomer a cup of poisoned wine; at the last moment Aegeus recognised Theseus' identity by means of his distinctive sword, and banished Medea from Athens.

Evidently Euripides could put on stage utterly different versions of the same character. The Medea of *Aegeus* seems to have been a clever, cunning woman, influencing men by persuasion or guile, an expert in drugs and poisons (as in her traditional Colchian guise) and a dangerous outsider; perhaps her barbarian status was given particular emphasis, if vase-paintings indicate the play's costumes or themes.[24] There has been some doubt whether Apollodorus used Euripides' play as a source,[25] but some fragments correspond to his account. In particular, fr. 3 contrasts weak men with powerful women, fr. 4 comments on dangerous step-mothers and both fr. 3 and fr. 5 deal with potentially dangerous speech: all plausibly relate to Medea's character and situation. Fr. 12a also confirms that this play dealt with Medea's murder of her brother Apsyrtus. But how prominent Medea was in comparison with Aegeus or Theseus is unclear.

Euripides, *Daughters of Pelias* (frr. 601–16 *TrGF*)

This tragedy is of particular interest because it was not only Euripides' first attempt to put Medea on stage; it was also his first play, produced in 455. The prologue's opening line was Μήδεια πρὸς μὲν δώμασιν τυραννικοῖς ('Medea near the royal palace', fr. 601), which means that 'Medea' was the first word from the pen of Euripides that the public ever heard. Its early date means that *Peliades* may have influenced several of the other Medea-tragedies, including the versions by Sophocles, but there is no way of knowing whether this is true. Indeed, one of the most frustrating aspects of our evidence is that it provides no way of determining the relative chronology of most of these plays, even though the question of influence or intertextuality is bound to recur.

As elsewhere, the basic outline has to be reconstructed from other texts, on the basis that later writers will almost certainly have known Euripides' play and that Apollodorus and others used tragedy as a source

---

[24] Several vases from *c.* 460 into the mid-fourth century depict Aegeus, Theseus and the Bull of Marathon with a woman (probably Medea) in oriental costume: Simon 1954, Shefton 1956, Kron 1981: 360–1, 364–5, Guirard 1996.

[25] Hahnemann 1999, 2003 believes that Apollodorus reflects Sophocles' *Aegeus*, but, as Mills 2003 points out, the Sophoclean fragments do not correspond as well to his narrative, and there is no definite evidence that Medea appeared in Sophocles' play.

of mythological material.[26] This play was based on Medea's exploits in Iolcus, and it depicted her as a witch, first of all rejuvenating a ram by boiling it and later inducing Pelias' daughters to kill their father by boiling him;[27] it also seems to have dramatised Medea's relationship with Jason and the couple's escape to Corinth.[28] Beyond the bare bones of the plot, it is hard to say anything else for definite about the play or its characterisation of Medea. Her role in the action demands that she must possess supernatural or magical powers, but it is impossible to say how Euripides handled other aspects of her character, or to what degree Medea was made to appear barbaric, grotesque, alien, dangerously feminine or otherwise unsympathetic.

The play was often quoted within antiquity, but most of the surviving quotations take the form of gnomic generalisations about the inferiority of women to men (fr. 603), power (604), tyranny (605), divine justice (606), self-interest (607) and friendship (608–9). Perhaps these verses reflect some of the broad thematic preoccupations of the play, but not much more can be said. Fr. 610 is more interesting in that it shows that a characteristic Euripidean motif, the contrast between words and actions, was already present in his work right from the beginning.[29]

Fr. 602 is identical to line 693 of *Medea*: τί χρῆμα δράσας; φράζε μοι σαφέστερον ('by doing what? Tell me more clearly'). This self-quotation is unusual and slightly puzzling, since the verse in question does not seem significant or striking.[30] Did any of the audience or readers of *Medea* notice the verse and identify its source? If so, it suggests that Euripides wanted to remind them of *Daughters of Pelias* and make them aware of a relationship (of some sort) between his earlier and later plays on the same subject. In that case, the self-quotation in fr. 602 was probably not unique: if *Daughters of Pelias* survived we would probably be able to trace other intertextual echoes between the two plays. It may even be that *Medea* was even deliberately designed as a 'sequel' to *Daughters of Pelias*.[31] In that case,

---

[26] Apollod. *Bibl.* 1.9.27, Paus. 8.11.2–3, Hyg. *Fab.* 24; other sources collected by Kannicht, *TrGF* v/2 608–9.

[27] This is confirmed by P.Oxy. 2455 fr. 18 col. II (test. iiia), part of a narrative hypothesis.

[28] Suggested by Moses of Chorene, *Progymnasmata* 3.4 (test. iiib).

[29] φθείρου· τὸ γὰρ δρᾶν οὐκ ἔχων λόγους ἔχεις ('Away with you! Even though you have plenty of words, you don't have the capacity for action').

[30] For repeated lines in tragedy see Rutherford 2012: 400 n. 2.

[31] Melero 1996: 62 notes other possible thematic/verbal echoes. For the Euripidean 'sequel' as a phenomenon seen elsewhere see Wright 2006.

the presentation of Medea in the later play will have depended in part on the audience's knowledge of the earlier plays, and the character will have been constructed specifically on the basis of similarity to or difference from these alternative versions.[32]

? Euripides, Medea I (earlier version)

Two separate papyrus fragments have been taken as evidence that the *Medea* of 431 was a revised version of an earlier *Medea* by Euripides. One of them, from a collection of dramatic hypotheses dating from the second century AD, contains the following lines:[33]

>]ετο τὴν Ἰωλκὸν.[
>]ποιήσας αὐτὸς δὲ τη[
> Β̄ Μήδεια, ἧς ἀρχ[ή·
> ε]ἴθ' ὤφελ' Ἀργοῦς μὴ δι[απτάσθαι σκάφος. Ἰάσων δι–
>]ὰ τὸν Πελίου φόνον.[

> ... Iolcus ...
> ... but (him)self having made (written? done?) the ...
> 2 *Medea*, of which the first line is:
> 'If only the Argo had never winged its way ...'
> Jason on account of the murder of Pelias ...

Obviously the hypothesis writer is quoting the opening of the surviving *Medea*, but the heading Β̄ Μήδεια is unexpected. It was interpreted by Wolfgang Luppe as 'the second *Medea*' (who compared other Euripidean dramas, such as *Hippolytus* and *Phrixus*, that existed in earlier and later versions); if that is correct, the two lines above that heading may represent the end of a hypothesis of 'the first *Medea*' (i.e., Ā Μήδεια). Certainly a play about Medea or Jason is suggested by the word Ἰωλκόν in the first line, indicating that the play was set in (or alluded to) Iolcus.[34] Nevertheless, as Daniela Colomo has pointed out, no parallel can be found for the use of Β̄ Μήδεια (as opposed to Μήδεια Β̄ to refer to a revised play:) the numeral ought to come after the title, not before. It is more likely that the heading

---

[32] Cf. Goldhill 1990 on intertextuality and characterisation.

[33] P.IFAO inv. PSP 248: Van Rossum-Steenbeek 1998: 16–17, 198–9 (§9), Meccariello 2014: 239–43.

[34] Luppe 2010.

indicates that the hypothesis to *Medea* was the second hypothesis in the author's collection.[35]

The other relevant piece of evidence is a recently published papyrus that explicitly describes the circumstances in which Euripides' first *Medea* came to be revised and quotes some verses attributed to the earlier version.[36] It is said (col. iv. 1–11) that the original *Medea* represented the infanticide on stage, thus horrifying and scandalising the audience:

ἐδυσχέρα]ναν οὖν τὴν ὄψιν καλῶς γε ποιοῦντες. ὅθεν ἐπανορθωσάμενος τοῦτο το μέρος Εὐριπίδης καὶ τοὺς στίχους ἐκεινους ὧν μέμνηνταί τινες διαγράψας·

ποῖ δῆτα μητρὸς χεῖρα δεξ[ι]ὰν στυγῶν

φεύγεις, ἀνάνδρου βήματος τιθεὶς ἴχνος;

καθόλου τε τὴν οἰκονομίαν ἀλλάξας ἔνδον ἀμφοτέρους κατέσφαξεν ὡς μετριωτέρας ἐσομένης τῆς τεκνοκτονίας εἰ μὴ ἐν φανερῶι πραχθείη, καὶ τότε οὐδὲν ἧττον ἐνικήθη.

So they felt disgust at the spectacle, rightly. Hence Euripides, correcting this part, and crossing out those lines that some people recall – 'Where then do you flee, hating your mother's right hand, placing the footprint of a coward step?' – and changing the plot on the whole, slaughtered both sons indoors, as if the child-murder would be less striking of it were not carried out in public – and then he was defeated none the less.

(edition and translation from Colomo 2010b: 107–8)

Thus it seems that Euripides was persuaded to revise the play to make it less shocking (just as he is said to have revised his *Hippolytus* and *Melanippe* plays for a similar reason).

If we accept this evidence, it substantially alters our view of the surviving *Medea* and gives an insight into the play's genesis. However, in her *editio princeps* of the papyrus, Colomo denies that it contains any truth. She assigns the text to the category of 'rhetorical epideixis', and links it to some sort of educational context of the Second Sophistic; it is assumed that it represents the type of simplistic, quasi-biographical anecdote and invention found in other declamatory or scholarly texts.[37]

Colomo is probably right to question the authenticity of this evidence, but a few doubts linger. As Colomo herself admits, it is entirely unclear

---

[35] Colomo 2011a: 47–8 (citing numerous examples); cf. Meccariello 2014: 240–1. This was originally the interpretation of Luppe 1986.

[36] P.Oxy. 5093; Colomo 2011b.

[37] Colomo 2011b: 90–1; cf. Colomo 2011a: 48–50, Finglass 2016b: 78–9.

what genre of text is preserved here.[38] Furthermore, as she points out, other writers in antiquity seem to have known a text of *Medea* that differs from our own,[39] and there is nothing about the quoted verses that would rule out Euripidean authorship. Thus the possibility that there really was an earlier version of *Medea* cannot entirely be rejected.

When we consider this question it is all too easy to be swayed by the assumption – shared by most scholars – that the surviving *Medea* is a classic and unique work; the existence of a flawed first draft might seem to diminish its status as a perfectly realised work of art. But in any case we are not obliged to view P.Oxy. 5093 as a rhetorical exercise. Even if the biographical anecdote is invented, it may be that the writer is quoting verses that were genuinely thought to be the work of Euripides. Another possible explanation is that there has been a mix-up between the work of two tragic playwrights of the same name. Was the supposed '*Ur-Medea*' of Euripides actually the *Medea* of Euripides II (see below)? One can imagine a scenario in which scholars in later antiquity, confronted with a 'Euripidean' *Medea* different from (or inferior to) the famous *Medea* of 431, might have assumed it to be an earlier, discarded version rather than the work of a long-forgotten homonymous author.

Euripides II, *Medea* (*TrGF* I 17 T 1)

Somewhat confusingly, there were three tragedians named Euripides, though the work and reputation of two of them (an uncle and a nephew, apparently not related to their more famous namesake) quickly fell into obscurity.[40] The nephew, conventionally referred to as 'Euripides II', wrote a *Medea*, but nothing is known about this work except its title, included in the poet's entry in the *Suda*.[41] The same source implies that Euripides II was roughly contemporary with the famous Euripides (since it is said that 'Euripides I', the uncle, was older), and thus it is possible that his *Medea* was produced before 431.

---

[38] Colomo 2011b: 89.

[39] E.g. Σ Ar. *Ach.* 119 (p. 25 Wilson) cites ὦ θερμόβουλον σπλάγχνον (Eur. fr. 858) as from Euripides' *Medea*, but this phrase is absent from the transmitted manuscripts (Wilson emends the name of the play to *Têmenidae*, presumably for that reason). Cic. *Fam.* 7.6.2 quotes from Ennius' *Medea* (221 Jocelyn) a phrase not in the extant *Medea* of Euripides (*qui ipse sibi sapiens prodesse non quit nequiquam sapit*): Colomo 2011b: 112–13.

[40] *TrGF* I 16 ('Euripides I'), 17 ('Euripides II'); Sutton 1987: 16–17, Wright 2016: 96.

[41] *Suda* ε 3694 (*TrGF* I 17 T 1); cf. 3693 (II 468.6–10 Adler).

Melanthius, *Medea* (*TrGF* I 23 T 4a, F 1)

This tragedy is parodied by Aristophanes in *Peace*, which means that it can be dated to 423 or earlier, though it is impossible to say whether it pre- or post-dated Euripides' *Medea*. The character Trygaeus satirises Melanthius and imagines a scenario in which he acts out part of his own *Medea*:[42]

> κᾆτα Μελάνθιον
> ἥκειν ὕστερον εἰς τὴν ἀγοράν,
> τὰς δὲ πεπρᾶσθαι, τὸν δ' ὀτοτύζειν,
> εἶτα μονῳδεῖν ἐκ Μηδείας·
> "ὀλόμαν, ὀλόμαν ἀποχηρωθεὶς
> τᾶς ἐν τεύτλοισι λοχευομένας."

> and then let Melanthius arrive late at the market and find that everything has been sold, and let him wail in his despair, and then sing a monody from his *Medea*: 'I am ruined! I am ruined and bereft of her that gave birth among the beetroots!'

This joke reveals several important facts. First, Melanthius' *Medea* was based on the same basic story as Euripides' *Medea*, viz. Jason and Medea's arrival in Corinth, Jason's abandonment of Medea in favour of Glauce and Glauce's death at Medea's hands. Secondly, the passage above includes an altered quotation from Melanthius' play (ὀλόμαν, ὀλόμαν ἀποχηρωθεὶς τᾶς ... λοχευομένας); the reference to beetroots is a humorous replacement for some more tragic phrase.[43] It has been suggested, plausibly, by Douglas Olson that the lines originally appeared in the mouth of Jason, mourning his new wife's death: 'the implication would be that she died in childbirth ..., doubtless murdered by Medea (with drugs ostensibly intended to ease her labour?)'.[44] Thirdly, and most interestingly, the verses quoted come from a *monody*. This fact is significant in terms of the play's characterisation of Jason, because the great majority of solo songs in tragedy were performed by female or barbarian characters. Thus Melanthius was attempting something striking here: for a central male character to express heightened emotion in a passionate lyric outburst, especially one with strong overtones of a ritual lament, would have come

---

[42] Ar. *Pax* 1009–14 (*TrGF* I 23 T 4a).

[43] Such as ἐν πέπλοισι, 'in her robes', supplied *exempli gratia* by Pellegrino 2008: 209–10. Doubt has been expressed about the attribution of the fragment. Snell prints it as *TrGF* I 29 F 1, attributed to Morsimus; Nauck had previously included it as Tr. Adesp. fr 6 in Nauck, *TrGF²*. But the Aristophanic context makes it clear that Melanthius is the author.

[44] Olson 1998: 263.

across as an unexpected gesture.[45] This use of performance conventions would have coloured the audience's understanding of the relationship and power dynamic between Jason and Medea, and it shows us that Melanthius' version of this relationship was different from that of Euripides in at least one crucial respect.

Neophron, *Medea* (*TrGF* 1 15 FF 1–3)

Neophron's play (traditionally dated to the early or mid-fifth century[46]) seems to have been similar to Euripides' *Medea*, in that its main focus was on the deterioration of Medea and Jason's marriage and Medea's killing of their children. Here too Jason's masculinity was undermined; but whereas Melanthius' Jason performed solo lyrics, Neophron's Jason was feminised by the circumstances of his death, as predicted by Medea in the following words:[47]

> τέλος φ<θ>ερεῖς γὰρ αὐτὸν αἰσχίστωι μόρωι
> δέρηι βροχωτὸν ἀγχόνην ἐπισπάσας.
> τοία σε μοῖρα σῶν κακῶν ἔργων μένει,
> δίδαξις ἄλλοις μυρίας ἐφ' ἡμέρας
> θεῶν ὕπερθε μήποτ' αἴρεσθαι βροτούς.

> In the end you will kill yourself and meet a most shameful fate, tying a knotted noose around your neck – this is the sort of destiny that awaits you in return for your evil deeds, and acts as a lesson to others for countless days to come: that mortals should never try to raise themselves above gods.

This unique version of the myth alters our view of Jason's character and situation. Rather than being left to suffer for a prolonged period without relief, as in Euripides or Seneca, Jason is made to destroy himself, in grief or in remorse, while Medea lives on. The manner of Jason's death is clearly meant to diminish him, since hanging was regarded as a female method of suicide.[48] Medea emphasises the grotesque and sordid nature of his death by lingering pleonastically on the gruesome details. By her stress on 'fate' or

---

[45] This is not to say that Jason's masculinity is necessarily diminished: Suter 2008a, Finglass 2014: 75.
[46] Based on the evidence of the *Suda* (ν 218) and Dicaearchus and Aristotle, as cited in the Hypothesis to Euripides' *Medea* (*TrGF* 1 15 TT 1–2), but not all scholars accept these testimonia: pp. 237–8 below.
[47] *TrGF* 1 15 F3 (quoted by Σ Eur. *Med.* 1386, which indicates the speaker and context). For a more detailed discussion see Wright 2016: 36–45.
[48] Michelini 1989: 125, Loraux 1985 ≈ 1987, especially 31–43 ≈ 7–17.

'destiny' she makes it seem as if superhuman powers are responsible for Jason's end, and implies that there is a grim inevitability about this outcome. Medea – though a murderess – presents herself as in the right, on the side of the gods and fate, while Jason is seen as being firmly in the wrong. These lines obviously come from the very end of the play, and it may be that Medea delivered them *ex machina,* as in Euripides' version. At any rate, there is a quasi-divine tone to Medea's words – in their apparent omniscience, their ability to foretell the future, their lofty pronouncements about 'mortals' in relation to the gods and their identification of a moral lesson or message underlying the action.

As in other versions, Medea was depicted by Neophron as a clever, resourceful woman. It is unclear whether, as elsewhere, she was an expert in magic, but her skills here included an ability to decipher oracles. This detail (alongside the fragment above) makes her seem quite different from the Euripidean Medea, who shows little hint of prophetic skills or omniscience until the very end of the play. During the play (F 1) Aegeus visited Medea in order to find out the meaning of an oracle, whereas in Euripides, by contrast, Medea meets Aegeus by chance on the road to Troezen (a coincidence regarded by Aristotle and others as a violation of probability or dramatic necessity).

Medea's agonised decision to murder her sons was articulated in a powerful monologue, fifteen lines of which survive (F 2):

εἶέν· τί δράσεις, θυμέ; βούλευσαι καλῶς
πρὶν ἐξαμαρτεῖν καὶ τὰ προσφιλέστατα
ἔχθιστα θέσθαι. ποῖ ποτ' ἐξῆιξας τάλας;
κάτισχε λῆμα καὶ σθένος θεοστυγές.
5   καὶ πρὸς τί ταῦτα δύρομαι, ψυχὴν ἐμὴν
ὁρῶσ' ἔρημον καὶ παρημελημένην
πρὸς ὧν ἐχρῆν ἥκιστα; μαλθακοὶ δὲ δή
τοιαῦτα γιγνόμεσθα πάσχοντες κακά;
οὐ μὴ προδώσεις, θυμέ, σαυτὸν ἐν κακοῖς;
10   οἴμοι, δέδοκται· παῖδες, ἐκτὸς ὀμμάτων
ἀπέλθετ'· ἤδη γάρ με φοινία μέγαν
δέδυκε λύσσα θυμόν. ὦ χέρες χέρες,
πρὸς οἷον ἔργον ἐξοπλιζόμεσθα· φεῦ,
τάλαινα τόλμης, ἣ πολὺν πόνον βραχεῖ
15   διαφθεροῦσα τὸν ἐμὸν ἔρχομαι χρόνωι.

Well, then – what will you do, my heart? Think hard before you slip up and turn your dearest friends into bitterest enemies. Wretched heart, whither have you rushed forth? Restrain your impulse and your terrible strength that is hateful to the gods.

> And why is it that I am crying about all this, when I can see my soul desolate and forsaken by those who least of all ought to have abandoned me? Am I, then, to become weak, indeed, as I undergo such awful sufferings? My heart! Do not betray yourself, even among such evils!
>
> [*She sighs.*] Alas! My mind is made up.
>
> [*Speaking to her children*] Out of my sight, boys! Get away from here! For by now a murderous madness has already sunk deep within my heart.
>
> Oh, hands! My hands! What sort of deed is this to which we are steeling ourselves! Ah! I am wretched even in my daring, I who now set out to destroy my long travail in a short moment.

Here Neophron is attempting to convey a complex psychological state in (for its time) unusually vivid and explicit language. Perhaps one might detect a certain clumsiness in Medea's diction or turn of phrase, but no doubt this reflects the distress and desperation in which she finds herself; or perhaps all these inchoate sentences, internal contradictions and abrupt changes of direction are signs of a disordered mentality.

Two features of Medea's language are of particular interest. First, Medea explicitly informs us that madness (λύσσα) has entered her heart. This establishes an implicit tension between passionate emotion and rational thought, and it makes us wonder just how far Medea is in control of her own words or actions. Secondly, it is not clear whom Medea is addressing here. At times she seems to be talking to an imaginary third party; at times she seems to be talking to her sons (who may or may not be present on stage to hear these terrifying words); but at other times she is apostrophising herself (either in a general sense, or in terms of specific individual parts such as her heart or hands). Medea blurs together these different imaginary addressees in an ambiguous manner. Sometimes the grammar adds to the sense of confusion, as Medea jumbles together nominative and vocative forms, or first-person singular and plural verbs, when referring to herself. But it seems that Neophron's aim is to represent a sense of a divided self, as if Medea conceives of her own personality or identity as a fragmented entity.

It is obvious that this monologue has many features in common with Euripides' *Medea* – to such an extent that most of the scholarship, from antiquity onward, has centred on the question of which author influenced the other.[49] I return to this question below (pp. 237–8). But for the time being let us note that the central elements of Medea and Jason's characters were presented here in a way that had similarities to *and* differences from

---

[49] Thompson 1944, Snell 1971: 199–205, Manuwald 1983, Michelini 1989, Mastronarde 2002: 57–64, Diggle 2008.

the Euripidean version. The differences are equally significant, but they have been ignored or downplayed by scholars whose main concern is to establish the debt of one author to the other. It should also be stressed that, apart from the fragments discussed above, there is no evidence for the plot of Neophron's *Medea*. We do not know how the play began or ended, or what happened to Medea eventually, or whether Medea succeeded in her attempt to kill the children.

Sophocles, *Aegeus* (frr. 19–25a)

Almost nothing is known about this tragedy except that it dramatised a mythical episode similar to that in Euripides' *Aegeus* (see above). Apollodorus' and Plutarch's narratives about Aegeus and Theseus, conventionally linked to Euripides' play, may also have been inspired by Sophocles' treatment, but there is no way of knowing for certain.[50] The scanty fragments allude to Theseus' fight with the Bull of Marathon, but there is nothing here about Medea, which means that we cannot confirm whether she appeared in the play.

Sophocles, *Women of Colchis* (frr. 337–49 TrGF)

This play dramatised an episode from the Argonauts' exploits in Colchis, including Jason's meeting with Medea and his acquisition of the Golden Fleece. Medea helped Jason and told him how to succeed in the dangerous task imposed by Aeetes.[51] The play included Medea's murder of her own brother Apsyrtus, though this detail was handled differently from the narrative in Apollonius' *Argonautica,* in which Apsyrtus was killed at sea while pursuing the Argonauts: here Apsyrtus was a mere child, and he was killed in Aeetes' palace.[52] Since we do not know which version was prevalent in the fifth century, we cannot know whether or not Sophocles' version represents a desire for mythical innovation, but the effect of this detail would have been to reinforce the image of Medea as a child-killer.[53]

It is not clear to what extent sorcery or witchcraft were crucial elements in Medea's portrayal here,[54] but the overall situation and her developing

---

[50] Radt *ad loc.* (*TrGF* IV 123); cf. Hahnemann 1999, 2003, Mills 2003.

[51] Σ Ap. Rh. 3.1040c (*TrGF* IV 316).

[52] Fr. 343; SOMMERSTEIN, pp. 67–9.

[53] Cf. Bremmer 1997 on Medea as 'the kin-killer par excellence' (p. 100).

[54] Fr. 340 ὑμεῖς μὲν οὔκ ἄρ' ἦιστε τὸν Προμηθέα ('so you did not know that Prometheus') has been taken to refer to the drug 'Prometheion', which Medea gives to Jason in Ap. Rh. 3.828–87. If so,

relationship with Jason requires that Medea must have been presented with some degree of sympathy and humanity. Unfortunately, the surviving fragments tell us nothing about the play's central characters. The only fragment that arguably relates to Medea is fr. 339 ἦ φὴς ὑπομνὺς ἀνθυπουργῆσαι χάριν; ('Do you promise on your oath to do one good turn in exchange for another?'); it has been suggested that this line was spoken by Medea to Jason, and that the 'good turn' in question was marriage.[55]

Sophocles, *Root-Cutters* (frr. 534–6 *TrGF*)

The fragments of this play provide a vivid glimpse of Medea as a barbarian witch, boiling up strange potions and crying out loud as she performs rituals to Hecate:

> ἡ δ' ἐξοπίσω χερὸς ὄμμα τρέπουσ'
> ὀπὸν ἀργινεφῆ στάζοντα τομῆς
> χαλκέοισι κάδοις δέχεται …
> … αἱ δὲ καλυπταὶ
> κίσται ῥιζῶν κρύπτουσι τομάς,
> ἃς ἥδε βοῶσ' ἀλαλαζομένη
> γυμνὴ χαλκέοις ἦμα δρεπάνοις

And she [Medea], with a backward glance, received the juice, with its white cloud of foam, in bronze pots … And hidden boxes concealed the cut portions of roots, which this woman, naked and crying out loud, severed with bronze sickles … (fr. 534)

XO. Ἥλιε δέσποτα καὶ πῦρ ἱερόν,
      τῆς εἰνοδίας Ἑκάτης ἔγχος,
      τὸ δι' Οὐλύμπου προπολοῦσα φέρει
      καὶ γῆς ἀνιοῦσ' ἱερὰς τριόδους,
      στεφανωσαμένη δρυΐ καὶ πλεκταῖς
      ὠμῶν σπείραισι δρακόντων

O Helios, master and sacred fire, the spear of Hecate *Einodia*, which she bears as she attends her mistress in the sky and as she inhabits the sacred crossroads of the earth, crowned with oak and the woven coils of savage dragons (fr. 535)

---

the play may have depicted Medea as a witch or pharmacist, but this interpretation is uncertain (Radt, *TrGF* iv 318).

[55] Cf. Euripides' *Medea* (especially 20–3, 160–3, 169–70, 209, 439–40, 488–98), Mossman 2011: 40–4 for the motif of oaths and (thwarted) reciprocity.

Apart from its characterisation of Medea, all other details about this play are obscure, including its plot and setting. It would be reasonable to suppose that Sophocles was writing about the boiling of the ram and killing of Pelias, but the play might equally have dramatised an earlier episode from Medea's life in Colchis.[56] The only other fragment is a reference to someone being 'annihilated in fire' (κόρον ἀϊστώσας πυρί, fr. 536): this enhances the flavour of sorcery and ritual but makes it no easier to imagine the plot or characters.[57]

Sophocles, *Scythians* (frr. 546–52)

This tragedy treated a part of the Argonautic legend similar to *Women of Colchis*, which prompts speculation about the relationship between these two plays. Did Sophocles conceive of them as thematically connected? Was one written as a 'sequel' to the other? The remains are so scanty that such speculation cannot take us very far. Two or three fragments refer to geographical locations and coastal features, which have been taken as signs that 'this play dealt with the voyage of the Argonauts, in all probability with the return voyage'.[58] The only plot detail that is certain is that *Scythians*, like *Women of Colchis*, showed Medea as the murderer of her brother Apsyrtus. In fr. 546 someone points out that Medea and Apsyrtus were only half-siblings (they had the same father, Aeetes, but different mothers), though it is hard to assess how this would have affected the play's presentation of events. The same fragment describes Apsyrtus as 'the Nereid's child' (ὁ μὲν Νηρηΐδος | †τέκνον), which may imply that here (as in *Women of Colchis*) Apsyrtus was only a small child when he was killed, but the unmetrical text cannot be trusted.

Theodorides, *Medea* (*TrGF* i 78A, DID A 2b, 94)

A little-known tragedian called Theodorides won second prize at the Lenaea in 363 with a suite of plays including *Medea*. This fact is known solely from epigraphic evidence, and nothing can be said about the play itself.[59] Nevertheless, this play, along with those of Antiphon, Aphareus,

[56] Lloyd-Jones 2003: 268–9.
[57] Who or what is being burnt? (Jason? A wax doll?) See Radt, *TrGF* iv 411 for various attempts to explain or emend fr. 536.
[58] Lloyd-Jones 2003: 274; see especially frr. 547–9.
[59] *SEG* xxvi 203 col. ii.10–11, with Millis and Olson 2012: 118–21; cf. Wright 2016: 192.

Carcinus, Dicaeogenes and Diogenes, provides further evidence of the continuing popularity of Medea as a tragic character throughout the fourth century.

***

What we see here is an extraordinary multiplicity of Medeas. All of these plays can be said to reflect Medea's character, but the sort of reflection they give is like the proliferation of images in a hall of mirrors. It is impossible to say which of these versions, if any, was regarded within antiquity as offering the definitive portrayal. Indeed, it may well be that the search for a 'definitive' Medea is a misguided enterprise from the start. It seems rather that in the ancient world no one ever created, or set out to create, a truly definitive version of the character or her story.

As modern scholars have pointed out, by the standards of Greek myth Medea is an unusually complex and elusive figure, and her mythical tradition (not just in tragedy) encompasses many separate strands.[60] It is not simply that there are many parts to Medea's story – her birth and early life in Colchis, her association with Jason and the Argonauts, her voyages to Iolcus, Corinth and Athens, and her subsequent adventures. There are also many different aspects to her character – as Scythian, sorceress, wise woman, prophetess, lover, wife, mother and murderer. At times Medea elicits both sympathy and revulsion; at times she seems to exemplify or to transcend the characteristics of her gender; at times she appears either Greek or barbarian, human or superhuman. It has proved frustratingly difficult to interpret Medea as a character or to understand what she represents. Perhaps 'what makes Medea Medea' is, above all, her many-sidedness. She cannot be pinned down to a single appearance in a single play.

Who Made Medea Medea?

It will now be apparent that approximately twenty Greek tragedies featured Medea as a central character. This is a hugely significant figure, because it means that, as far as we can tell, Medea's story was the most popular subject in the whole tragic genre.[61] Given that this was so, it is worth asking

---

[60] For the Medea myth in literature and art see Schmidt 1992; cf. Moreau 1994, Clauss and Johnston 1997.

[61] Other recurrently popular subjects were Oedipus (dramatised by Aeschylus, Sophocles, Euripides, Achaeus, Xenocles, Carcinus the Younger, Timocles, Theodectes, Diogenes of Sinope

why Euripides' *Medea* of 431 should be seen as such an important work –
or, at any rate, it is worth questioning whether the extant play, so greatly
admired in later times, was already regarded as definitive in the classical
period itself.

There is no reason to see Euripides' *Medea* as unique or uniquely
influential within antiquity. Its originality, singularity and influence have
been overstated, no doubt because it is the only play on the subject to have
survived and because it is undeniably great. It is often claimed that it
attained 'classic' status almost immediately, but there is no actual proof
that this was so.[62] Indeed, comedy and vase-painting tell a different story.
Even within Euripides' own oeuvre, as we have seen, the 431 *Medea* is just
one among several different attempts to imagine the character and her
myth. In other words, as far as fifth- and fourth-century Greeks were
concerned, it was not Euripides' *Medea* of 431, in particular, that 'made
Medea Medea'.

Existing interpretations of *Medea* in relation to the other, fragmentary
plays tend to be coloured by questionable hierarchical assumptions
regarding literary history and canonicity – that is, the prior notions that
Medea is a 'classic' work of art and that Euripides is a 'major' tragedian, in
contrast to other 'minor' playwrights. This is not necessarily an assumption
that would have been made by fifth- and fourth-century audiences.
Because all these other tragedies are lost, any sort of qualitative criticism
is now impossible. But these so-called 'minor' playwrights were not all
non-entities: some were no doubt better than others (judged by some
criterion or other), but in their own time many of them were prominent,
celebrated figures whose work was widely performed and won prizes.[63]
Euripides himself was not *yet* a classic: the quasi-canonical triad of
Aeschylus–Sophocles–Euripides was only established towards the end
of the fourth century.[64] For its contemporary audience and for
many decades later, Euripides' *Medea* was just one play among many

and Meletus: see Finglass 2018: 26–7), Alcmeon (Achaeus, Sophocles, Euripides, Agathon,
Astydamas the Younger, Theodectes, Timotheus and Chaeremon), and Achilles (Aeschylus,
Aristarchus, Iophon, Astydamas the Younger, Carcinus the Younger, Chaeremon, Cleophon,
Euaretus, Diogenes of Sinope); see Wright 2016: 203–5 for further lists.
[62] There is no definite evidence that the play was reperformed, in Athens or elsewhere, during the
fifth or fourth centuries: see Vahtikari 2014: 172–5 for an open-minded summary of the
evidence (most of which could relate to any of the Medea-tragedies mentioned above).
[63] Wright 2016, especially ix–xix.
[64] Hanink 2014.

others on the same subject. It did not even win first prize: Euripides came in last place in 431.[65]

A good example of the way in which one's reading of the evidence can be affected by preconceptions about 'classic' versus 'non-classic' status is provided by Neophron's *Medea*, a work that has been studied exclusively in relation to Euripides' *Medea*. All existing discussions have taken a compare-and-contrast approach, rather than discussing Neophron's play as a work in its own right, and almost all these discussions involve explicitly pejorative critical assessment of Neophron's work. Since only twenty-four lines of Neophron's play survive, a true critical judgement or comparison is ruled out; so it seems that such assessments depend on the assumption that Neophron's lost play must inevitably have been 'worse' than Euripides' play (though what might count as 'bad' or 'good' tragedy is not usually spelt out in so many words).

We have observed the *prima facie* similarity between the two tragedies. Several ancient scholars, considering these similarities, came to the conclusion that Euripides was influenced by Neophron – or that he had 'plagiarised' his work.[66] It seems likely that what these scholars were highlighting was not plagiarism as such, but some more complex form of intertextual relationship between the two poets' dramas. Maybe Euripides' version was designed as a critique of Neophron, or as an implicit judgement on some aspect of his dramatic technique or handling of myth, or as an act of homage to a famous predecessor.[67] Euripides' *Medea* looks rather different if we approach it as a play openly and self-consciously written in dialogue with the work of another tragedian.

However, the majority of modern critics have tried to defend Euripides from this charge, most commonly by reversing the order of these two plays and suggesting that Neophron, not Euripides, was the 'plagiarist'. This is a radical interpretation – or rather a complete rejection – of the evidence. Denys Page re-dated Neophron to the fourth century,[68] while Donald Mastronarde has suggested that the fragments we possess are not from Neophron's *Medea* but some other, post-Euripidean *Medea* later misattributed to Neophron.[69] There is no way of disproving this sort of

[65] According to Aristophanes of Byzantium (Hyp. II Eur. *Med.*); but as Wright 2009 argues, prizes are not a reliable guide to a work's quality or reputation.
[66] Hyp. I Eur. *Med.*, *Suda* ν 218, Diog. Laert. 2.134 (*TrGF* I 15 TT 1–3).
[67] This sort of technique is well attested in Euripides' other plays, notably *Electra*, *Orestes*, *Helen*, *Phoenician Women*, *Children of Heracles*: Torrance 2013.
[68] Page 1938: xxx–xxxvi.
[69] Mastronarde 2002: 57–64.

scenario, but once again it seems to be based on questionable preconceptions about literary quality: in this case not just the relative merits of Euripides and Neophron, but also the assumption that the label 'fourth-century' is synonymous with 'inferior'.[70] Furthermore, it seems clear that the enterprise of re-dating Neophron to the fourth century is based on a desire to attribute the greatest possible originality to Euripides – as if 'classic' status depended on originality. But even if one removes Neophron from the equation, it is impossible to identify any aspects of Euripides' *Medea* that are definitely original. Euripides may have invented some of the motifs that seem to mark out his play as distinctive, but any of them could have been inherited or reworked from earlier poetry or drama now lost.[71]

Much of the scholarship centres on the question of the poetic quality or aesthetic value of each poet's work, as if that were a decisive factor in the argument. Could it really be that the 'classic' Euripides was influenced by a 'minor' or 'inferior' playwright? Most critics think not. James Diggle, for instance, emphasises six times in a seven-page-long article that Neophron was a 'bad' or 'very bad' poet. Listing several striking verbal similarities between the *Medeas* of Neophron and Euripides (not just in Medea's monologue but elsewhere), he concludes that 'it is not believable that Euripides would remember such bad poetry so well that he would allow the memory of it to creep into other parts of his play too'.[72] But is it unbelievable? Even if we concede that Neophron's poetry was really so bad (and I do not think this is self-evident), it is perfectly plausible that it was striking enough for Euripides to remember it and to be influenced in some way by its form or content – to imitate or improve it as it might be.

The case of Neophron illustrates some of the problems inherent in the ancient and modern critical reception of tragedy, but it is not unique. Questions of intertextuality and influence also arise in relation to the tragedies that are definitely known to have been produced after 431. It is normally assumed that the status of Euripides' *Medea* was already so well established that all these later plays must have been based on it. Even when the details do *not* correspond with Euripides' *Medea,* it is usually thought that the 'classic' play must nevertheless have been the main model or point of departure. But this is not really an objective or logical way of

---

[70] For criticism of this problematic assumption see Wright 2016: 117–22; cf. Easterling 1993, Csapo *et al.* 2014.

[71] A point well made by Mastronarde 2002: 52.

[72] Diggle 2008: 411, citing Eur. *Med.* 16, 572–3 (cf. Neophron *TrGF* I 15 F 2.2–3), 1236 (F 2.10), 1242 (F 2.13).

approaching the evidence. The most obvious objection is that we know almost nothing about any of these plays, so we are almost never in a position to make confident pronouncements of this sort. But even if some of the details are demonstrably similar to or different from Euripides' version, this does not necessarily imply that these later poets are consciously responding to his *Medea*. It may just mean that they have selected different strands within the mythical tradition, in an attempt to entertain their audiences by reimagining the myth afresh each time.

Some major details in fourth-century *Medea*-tragedies were quite different from Euripides' version. For example, in Carcinus' play, Medea did not murder her children. If one approaches this material with Euripides' *Medea* firmly in mind, it is bound to seem surprising. Sure enough, Euripides' *Medea* is normally assumed to be the main source or model for Carcinus. Taplin argues that 'there could hardly be a bolder departure from the authority of the Euripidean version', and he goes so far as to call Carcinus' tragedy 'anti-canonical'.[73] But these statements are too confident. There is nothing in the remains of Carcinus' *Medea* to mark any definite connection with Euripides, and there is no reason to assume that Euripides' play was *already* canonical, or that it already represented the 'authorised version' of the myth, in Carcinus' time. We have to keep firmly in mind the fact that a very large number of other tragedies also treated this well-known story. There is no justification for regarding Carcinus' *Medea* as an 'anti-canonical' tragedy. Indeed, it need not be seen as a response to any *specific* earlier play, by Euripides or by anyone else.

It is easy to suppose, on the basis of his later reception history, that Euripides represented the 'classic' tragedian *par excellence* for Carcinus and his contemporaries. But Euripides was only one among many tragedians. Even if it could be demonstrated that in the mid-fourth century he was already the best-known author of tragedy, it is not plausible that all these epigonal writers would invariably choose the best-known play for intertextual reworking. Some of these poets, especially the more bookish ones, will surely have made use of lesser-known works, in order to show off their knowledge and appeal to a similarly learned contingent within their audience.

Similar questions and problems present themselves in relation to the Greek comedies on the Medea theme, including works by Strattis, Eubulus, Cantharus and Antiphanes. It is universally assumed that all these works

---

[73] Taplin 2014: 151.

are parodies of Euripides' *Medea*, but once again there is no evidence to confirm this assumption.[74] There is always a degree of doubt whether these comedies should be called paratragic or 'mythological burlesque': perhaps they do not even have a specific literary model or target.[75] But even if we accept that they are parodies of a specific earlier work, why should we automatically assume that that work was Euripides' *Medea*? There could be at least nineteen other possible candidates. (If we extend our scope to include comedies about Medea from Sicily and the Greek West, it seems likely that there would have been an even wider range of influences available.[76]) Indeed, there is clear evidence that other versions of the Medea myth apart from Euripides' *Medea* did influence the comedians: Diphilus' comedy *Daughters of Pelias* was based on another source, as was a fragmentary comedy probably by Antiphanes apparently featuring Medea giving a bath to Pelias.[77]

Quotations or allusions to Euripides' *Medea* are found in a number of Athenian comedies from the fifth century onwards.[78] All these examples are limited to single verses or short phrases (quoted to lend a broadly paratragic tone rather than to make a point about the play itself), and there is no evidence of sustained parody. Such passages confirm that Euripides' play was well known to Athenian audiences in the fifth century and later; but they do not suggest that the play was especially popular, and they do not rule out the possibility that other Medea-dramas were equally well known. As we have seen, Aristophanes also quotes from Melanthius' *Medea*, and it may well be that his and other comedians' work contained many more (now undetectable) quotations and allusions to other lost tragedies.

---

[74] The most recent scholar to survey the material dissociates himself from 'an excessively "Euripidean" vision' ('una visione eccessivamente "euripidea"', Pellegrino 2008: 203), but even his treatment of the evidence is coloured by the view that Euripides' *Medea* is an undisputed classic. R. Hunter 1983: 149 states that 'all of these dramas were *probably deeply* indebted to Euripides' *Medea*' (my italics), a self-undermining statement that draws attention to the lack of evidence for such a claim.

[75] Nesselrath 1990: 204–41.

[76] Nothing substantial is known about comedies called *Medea* attributed to Epicharmus (test. 35 PCG), Dinolochus (test. 3, frr. 4–5) and Rhinthon (fr. 7).

[77] Diphilus fr. 64 PCG, Antiphanes fr. 239.

[78] Ar. *Knights* 813 (*Med.* 168), *Clouds* 662 (*Med.* 404), 1397 (*Med.* 1317), *Thesm.* 1130 (*Med.* 298), *Frogs* 1382 (*Med.* 1), *Wealth* 114 (*Med.* 625), 601 (*Med.* 168); Eupolis, *Cities* fr. 106 PCG (*Med.* 395, 398); Philemon, *Soldier* fr. 82.1–2 (*Med.* 57–8); Theognetus, *Ghost* fr. 1.9 (*Med.* 57). Plato, *Festivals* fr. 29, a joke about Euripides' sigmatism, may evoke lines such as *Med.* 476 ἔσωσά σ' ὡς ἴσασιν Ἑλλήνων ὅσοι, as the scholia to that line note (ιι 169.33–170.5 Schwartz); cf. Eubulus, *Dionysius* fr. 26.

The fragments of those comedies that took Medea as their main focus are few. But no trace is to be found of any quotation from Euripides' play, nor any other clear sign of Euripidean influence. The only significant fragment of Cantharus' *Medea* mentions 'an Arabian lyre-player in this chorus' (fr. 1 *PCG*), perhaps hinting at an orientalising tone, but this is an aspect of Medea downplayed, by contrast, in Euripides' version. The sole surviving fragment of Antiphanes' *Medea* (fr. 151) is a reference to linen underclothes, but it would take a leap of the imagination to identify this detail with anything in Euripides' play. Eubulus' *Medea* is also represented by a single fragment, which describes someone eating eels wrapped in beetroot (fr. 64): this is unrelated to anything in Euripides, but it may be connected, in some obscure and irrecoverable sense, with the *Medea* of Melanthius, a connection suggested by the fact that Aristophanes' parody of Melanthius' play describes the dead Glauce as having given birth among beetroots.[79]

The contents of Strattis' *Medea* are hard to reconstruct on the basis of the surviving remains, but one fragment (fr. 34) has been seen as particularly significant in relation to Euripides:[80]

> καὶ λέγ' ὅτι φέρεις αὐτῆι μύρον
> τοιοῦτον, οἷον οὐ Μέγαλλος πώποτε
> ἥψησεν, οὐδὲ Δεινίας Αἰγύπτιος
> οὔτ' εἶδεν οὔτ' ἐκτήσατο.

> and tell her that you're bringing her a scented ointment, such as Megallus himself never boiled up, and such as Deinias the Egyptian never saw or got hold of.

According to Mastronarde, 'fr. 34 mentions gifts to a bride and so it is likely that this comedy exploited Eur[ipides'] tragedy'.[81] But on both counts this claim is questionable. It is likely only if we already assume that Euripides' *Medea* was bound to be foremost in the mind of Strattis and his audience. Even if the fragment does allude to the wedding of Jason and Glauce, there are at least four other known models that Strattis might have been evoking (i.e. the *Medea*s of Melanthius and Neophron and the plays represented by the two anonymous papyrus fragments). But in any case

---

[79] *TrGF* 1 23 T4a (Ar. *Pax* 1014): see above. R. Hunter 1983: 150 draws attention to this 'strange coincidence'; cf. Pellegrino 2008: 208–9.
[80] The fragment is quoted by Athenaeus (*Deipn.* 15.690f), who gives no clue to its context or meaning.
[81] Mastronarde 2002: 65.

fr. 34 does not mention gifts to a bride; what it does mention is a perfume or ointment (μύρον), not, as in Euripides, a robe and gold crown smeared with poison.[82] Even if we assume that Strattis altered his source for comic effect, it has to be admitted that the details simply do not match up. Given the fragment's reference to 'boiling' (ἥψησεν), and its emphasis on the extraordinary properties of the μύρον, it is possible that Strattis had in mind any of the other tragedies in which Medea's potions and magical powers are prominent. The only other surviving fragment of Strattis' play features Creon (fr. 35), but it tells us nothing about the treatment of this character: it could reflect Euripides' *Medea*, but it could equally reflect any of the other Corinthian Medea-tragedies.

In general, then, what the comedians show us is that Medea continued to be a popular subject for drama throughout the fifth and fourth centuries; they do not prove that Euripides' *Medea* was an especially or uniquely influential model. The same is true of the evidence from vase-painting of the same period. A number of Greek and Italian vases depict scenes from Medea's story in a manner that suggests the influence of drama, and they have usually been interpreted in relation to Euripides rather than Melanthius, Carcinus, Neophron or any other playwrights.[83] These images have been widely discussed, most recently by Taplin, who points out that they actually contain a wide variety of motifs and details, many of which do not match up with Euripides' play.[84] Nonetheless, Taplin's view is that the vase-paintings are to be seen as 'reflecting Euripides' version in various ways, yet also distinctly departing from it', and that 'Euripides' play generally seems to have had a crucial impact on the presentation of Medeia in the visual arts.'[85] This approach to the evidence is based on the assumption that Euripides' unique influence can be taken for granted. But it is not the only possible reading of the evidence. If the iconographic details do not correspond with Euripides' play, it is impossible to prove that the play influenced the vase-painters at all, let alone that its impact was 'crucial'. All that we can say for certain is that Euripides' play – along with any of the other lost Medea-tragedies – *may* have had some sort of impact

---

[82] Eur. *Med.* 784–9.

[83] Sourvinou-Inwood 1997.

[84] Taplin 2007: 114–25; also Melero 1996: 66, and cf. Vahtikari 2014: 9, 174.

[85] Taplin 2007: 114; cf. p. 120, where it is said that all other dramatic versions of the Medea story were 'inevitably influenced by Euripides'. Taplin elsewhere concedes (167, 238–40) that plays other than *Medea* (such as Euripides' *Aegeus* or Carcinus' *Medea*) may have influenced the iconography.

on the iconography. Many have even doubted whether there is any direct connection at all between drama and visual art.[86]

✷✷✷

The evidence of fragments suggests that the impact of Euripides' *Medea* on fifth- and fourth-century audiences has been overstated. Tragedy's subsequent survival, transmission and reception make it difficult to interpret the evidence with an open mind, since modern views of Greek tragedy are dominated by the later status of Euripides' classic work. But Euripides should be viewed alongside these other fragmentary tragedians rather than as an extraordinary or unique figure. These playwrights seem to have had similar preoccupations, in that they were imaginatively responding to a character who was part of their complex mythical heritage – a mythical icon who did not belong to any one author, but provided endless fascination precisely because she offered so many different aspects and inconsistencies.

Perhaps the most revealing piece of evidence of all comes from Diodorus Siculus, who ends his summary of the different strands in the Medea story by saying (4.56.1):

> καθόλου δὲ διὰ τὴν τῶν τραγωιδῶν τερατείαν ποικίλη τις διάθεσις καὶ διάφορος ἱστορία περὶ Μηδείας ἐξενήνεκται.

> In general, it is because of the tragedians' penchant for marvellous stories that so varied and changeable an account of Medea has been handed down.

For Diodorus, the crucial aspects are the plurality of the myth and the many-sidedness of Medea's character, both of which are ideally explored on the tragic stage. *The tragedians* (plural) have provided their audiences with variety and entertainment by returning to Medea; Euripides' name is not even mentioned. In other words, Diodorus regards Medea as essentially a product of the whole tragic genre. It was Greek tragedy – including the lost plays – that made Medea Medea.

---

[86] Guirard 1996; cf. the comparison of 'iconocentric' versus 'philodramatic' approaches in Taplin 2007: 2–37, on which see further Coo 2013b.

Bibliography

Abbattista, A. 2018. 'The vengeful lioness in Greek tragedy: a posthumanist perspective', in Dawson and McHardy 2018 (eds.), 203–20.

Aélion, R. 1986. *Quelques grands mythes héroïques dans l'oeuvre d'Euripide*. Paris.

Ahrens, E. A. J. 1846. *Aeschyli et Sophoclis tragoediae et fragmenta*. Paris.

Alaux, J. 1995. *Le liège et le filet. Filiation et lien familial dans la tragédie athénienne du vᵉ siècle av. J.-C.* No place.

Alexiou, M. 2002. *The Ritual Lament in the Greek Tradition*, revised by D. Yatromanolakis and P. Roilos. Lanham, Boulder, New York, Oxford. [1st edn London, 1974].

Allan, W., and Kelly, A. 2013. 'Listening to many voices: Athenian tragedy as popular art', in Marmodoro and Hills 2013 (eds.), 77–122.

Armstrong, R. 2006. *Cretan Women. Pasiphae, Ariadne, and Phaedra in Latin Poetry*. Oxford.

Auger, D., and Peigney, J. 2008 (eds.). *Phileuripidès. Mélanges offerts à François Jouan*. Paris.

Bachvarova, M. R. 2015. 'Migrations in the Anatolian narrative traditions', in Stampolidis 2015 (eds.), 145–83.

2016. *From Hittite to Homer. The Anatolian Background of Ancient Greek Epic*. Cambridge.

Bailey, C. et al. 1936. *Greek Poetry and Life. Essays Presented to Gilbert Murray on his Seventieth Birthday, January 2, 1936*. Oxford.

Baltussen, H., and Olson, S. D. 2017. 'Epilogue: a conversation on fragments', in Derda *et al.* 2017 (eds.), 393–406.

Bañuls, J. V., and Crespo, P. 2008. 'La *Fedra* de Sófocles', in Pociña and López 2008 (eds.), 15–83.

Barnes, J., Schofield, M., and Sorabji, R. 1977 (eds.). *Articles on Aristotle. 2: Ethics and Politics*. London.

Barrett, W. S. 1964. *Euripides. Hippolytos*. Oxford.

2007. *Greek Lyric, Tragedy, and Textual Criticism. Collected Papers*, assembled and edited by M. L. West. Oxford.

Barringer, J. M. 1995. *Divine Escorts. Nereids in Archaic and Classical Greek Art*. Ann Arbor.

Bastianini, G., and Casanova, A. 2005 (eds.). *Euripide e i papiri. Atti del Convegno Internazionale di Studi, Firenze, 10–11 giugno 2004*. Studi e Testi di Papirologia NS 7. Florence.

2013 (eds.). *I papiri di Eschilo e di Sofocle. Atti del convegno internazionale di studi, Firenze, 14–15 giugno 2012.* Edizioni dell'Istituto Papirologico "G. Vitelli" 2. Florence.

Battezzato, L. 2005. 'La parodo dell'*Ipsipile*', in Bastianini and Casanova 2005 (eds.), 169–203.

2017. 'Change of mind, persuasion, and the emotions: debates in Euripides from *Medea* to *Iphigenia at Aulis*', *Lexis* 35: 164–77.

2018. *Euripides. Hecuba.* Cambridge.

2019. 'Oreste nelle *Coefore*: la doppia motivazione da Omero a Eschilo', in Cavallo and Medaglia 2019 (eds.), 163–88.

Beissinger, M., Tylus, J., and Wofford, S. 1999 (eds.). *Epic Traditions in the Contemporary World. The Poetics of Community.* Berkeley, Los Angeles, London.

Belfiore, E. S. 2000. *Murder among Friends. Violation of* Philia *in Greek Tragedy.* New York and Oxford.

Bélis, A. 2004. 'Un papyrus musical inédit au Louvre', *Comptes rendus des séances de l'Académie des Inscriptions et Belles-Lettres* 148: 1305–29.

Benati, E. 2017. 'La teoria del flusso nel *Cratilo* e nel *Timeo* di Platone: il problema di un mondo in divenire e il rapporto con Eraclito', *Studi Classici e Orientali* 63: 73–89.

Beresford, A. 2008. 'Nobody's perfect: a new text and interpretation of Simonides *PMG* 542', *Classical Philology* 103: 237–56.

Bernabé, A., Herrero de Jáuregui, M., Jiménez San Cristóbal, A. I., and Martín Hernández, R. 2013 (eds.). *Redefining Dionysos.* MythosEikonPoiesis 5. Berlin and Boston.

Bers, V. 1997. *Speech in Speech. Studies in Incorporated* Oratio Recta *in Attic Drama and Oratory.* Lanham, Boulder, New York, London.

Bierl, A., and Möllendorff, P. von 1994 (eds.). *Orchestra. Drama, Mythos, Bühne. Festschrift für Hellmut Flashar anläßlich seines 65. Geburtstages.* Stuttgart and Leipzig.

Blass, F. 1880. 'Neue Fragmente des Euripides und andrer griechischer Dichter', *Rheinisches Museum* NF 35: 74–93, 278–97.

Blondell, R. 2013. *Helen of Troy. Beauty, Myth, Devastation.* Oxford and New York.

Blondell, R., and Ormand, K. 2015 (eds.). *Ancient Sex. New Essays.* Columbus, OH.

Boardman, J. 1975. *Athenian Red Figure Vases. The Archaic Period. A Handbook.* London.

Bobonich, C., and Destrée, P. 2007 (eds.). Akrasia *in Greek Philosophy. From Socrates to Plotinus.* Philosophia Antiqua 106. Leiden and Boston.

Bodiou, L., Brulé, P., and Pierini, L. 2005. 'En Grèce antique, la douloureuse obligation de la maternité', *Clio* 21: 17–42.

Boedeker, D. 1997. 'Becoming Medea: assimilation in Euripides', in Clauss and Johnston 1997 (eds.), 127–48.

Bond, G. W. 1963. *Euripides. Hypsipyle.* Oxford.

Borthwick, E. K. 1994. 'New interpretations of Aristophanes *Frogs* 1249–1328', *Phoenix* 48: 21–41. [= 2015: 196–214]

2015. *Greek Music, Drama, Sport, and Fauna. The Collected Classical Papers of E. K. Borthwick*, ed. C. Maciver. Collected Classical Papers 4. Prenton.

Bothmer, D. von 1987. *Greek Vase Painting*. New York.

Bouvrie, S. des 1990. *Women in Greek Tragedy. An Anthropological Approach.* Symbolae Osloenses supplement 27. Oslo and Oxford.

2004 (ed.). *Myth and Symbol II. Symbolic Phenomena in Ancient Greek Culture. Papers from the Second and Third International Symposia on Symbolism at the Norwegian Institute at Athens, September 21–24, 2000 and September 19–22, 2002*. Papers from the Norwegian Institute at Athens 7. Bergen.

Bremer, J. M., Radt, S. L., and Ruijgh, C. J. 1976 (eds.). *Miscellanea Tragica in Honorem J. C. Kamerbeek*. Amsterdam.

Bremmer, J. N. 1976. 'Avunculate and fosterage', *Journal of Indo-European Studies* 4: 65–78.

1983. 'The importance of the maternal uncle and grandfather in archaic and classical Greece and early Byzantium', *Zeitschrift für Papyrologie und Epigraphik* 50: 173–86.

1997. 'Why did Medea kill her brother Apsyrtus?', in Clauss and Johnston 1997 (eds.), 83–100.

Brown, A. S. 1997. 'Aphrodite and the Pandora Complex', *Classical Quarterly* NS 47: 26–47.

Budelmann, F. 2009 (ed.). *The Cambridge Companion to Greek Lyric*. Cambridge.

Budelmann, F., and Michelakis, P. 2001 (eds.). *Homer, Tragedy and Beyond. Essays in Honour of P. E. Easterling*. London.

Burgess, J. S. 2009. *The Death and Afterlife of Achilles*. Baltimore.

Burkert, W. 1966. 'Greek tragedy and sacrificial ritual', *Greek, Roman, and Byzantine Studies* 7: 87–121. [transl. S. R. West; = 2001: 1–36 = 2001–11: VII 1–36]

Burkert, W. 1979. *Structure and History in Greek Mythology and Ritual*. Sather Classical Lectures 47. Berkeley, Los Angeles, London.

1994. 'Orpheus, Dionysos und die Euneiden in Athen: das Zeugnis von Euripides' *Hypsipyle*', in Bierl and von Möllendorff 1994 (eds.), 44–9. [= 2001–11: III 112–19]

2001. *Savage Energies. Lessons of Myth and Ritual in Ancient Greece*, transl. P. Bing and S. R. West. Chicago and London.

2001–11. *Kleine Schriften*, 8 vols. Hypomnemata supplement 2. Göttingen.

Burnett, A. P. 1968. Review of Webster 1967, *Classical Philology* 63: 310–13.

1998. *Revenge in Attic and Later Tragedy*. Sather Classical Lectures 62. Berkeley, Los Angeles, London.

Bushnell, R. 2005 (ed.). *A Companion to Tragedy*. Malden, MA, Oxford, Carlton, VIC.

Butler, J. 2000. *Antigone's Claim. Kinship between Life and Death*. New York.

Butler, S., and Purves, A. 2013a. 'Introduction: synaesthesia and the ancient senses', in *id*. 2013 (eds.), 1–7.

2013b (eds.). *Synaesthesia and the Ancient Senses*. Durham.

Buxton, R. G. A. 1982. *Persuasion in Greek Tragedy. A Study of* Peitho. Cambridge.

1995. *Sophocles*². Greece and Rome New Surveys in the Classics 16. Oxford. [1st edn 1984]

2009. *Forms of Astonishment. Greek Myths of Metamorphosis*. Oxford.

Cairns, D. L. 1993. Aidōs. *The Psychology and Ethics of Honour and Shame in Ancient Greek Literature*. Oxford.

2001 (ed.). *Oxford Readings in Homer's* Iliad. Oxford.

2016. 'Metaphors for hope in archaic and classical Greek poetry', in Caston and Kaster 2016 (eds.), 13–44.

Cairns, D. L., and Liapis, V. 2006 (eds.). *Dionysalexandros. Essays on Aeschylus and his Fellow Tragedians in Honour of Alexander F. Garvie*. Swansea.

Calame, C. 1986. 'Facing otherness: the tragic mask in ancient Greece', *History of Religions* 26: 125–42.

2011. 'Myth and performance on the Athenian stage: Praxithea, Erechtheus, their daughters, and the etiology of autochthony', *Classical Philology* 106: 1–19.

Cameron, A., and Kuhrt, A. 1983 (eds.). *Images of Women in Antiquity*. London and Canberra.

Canciani, F. 1994. 'Protesilaos', *Lexicon Iconographicum Mythologiae Classicae* vii/1: 554–60.

Cantarella, R. 1964. *Euripide. I Cretesi*. Classici Greci e Latini Sezione Testi e Commenti 1. Milan.

Capasso, M., and Pernigotti, S. 2001 (eds.). *Studium atque urbanitas. Miscellanea in onore di Sergio Daris*. Papyrologica Lupiensia 9/2000. Lecce.

Carden, R. 1974. *The Papyrus Fragments of Sophocles*. Texte und Kommentare 7. Berlin and New York.

Carlisle, M., and Levaniouk, O. 1999 (eds.). *Nine Essays on Homer*. Lanham, MD, Boulder, New York, Oxford.

Carpenter, T. H., and Faraone, C. A. 1993 (eds.). *Masks of Dionysus*. Ithaca, NY and London.

Carrara, P. 1977. *Euripide. Eretteo*. Papyrologica Florentina 3. Florence.

2009. *Il testo di Euripide nell'antichità. Ricerche sulla tradizione testuale euripidea antica (sec.* iv *a.C. – sec.* viii *d.C.)*. Studi e Testi 27. Florence.

Casanova, A. 2007. 'I frammenti della *Fedra* di Sofocle', in Degl'Innocenti Pierini *et al*. 2007 (eds.), 5–22.

Caston, R. R., and Kaster, R. A. 2016 (eds.). *Hope, Joy, and Affection in the Classical World*. Oxford and New York.

Catenaccio, C. 2017. *Monody and Dramatic Form in Late Euripides*. Diss. Columbia.

Cavallo, G., and Medaglia, S. 2019 (eds.). *Reinterpretare Eschilo. Verso una nuova edizione dei drammi*. Rome.

Chanter, T., and Kirkland, S. D. 2014 (eds.). *The Returns of Antigone. Interdisciplinary Essays*. Albany.

Chesi, G. M. 2014. *The Play of Words. Blood Ties and Power Relations in Aeschylus' Oresteia*. Trends in Classics supplement 26. Berlin and Boston.

Chong-Gossard, J. H. K. O. 2008. *Gender and Communication in Euripides' Plays. Between Song and Silence*. Mnemosyne supplement 296. Leiden and Boston.

  2009. 'Consolation in Euripides' *Hypsipyle*', in Cousland and Hume 2009 (eds.), 11–22.

Christ, M. R. 2004. 'Draft evasion onstage and offstage in classical Athens', *Classical Quarterly* NS 54: 33–57.

Clark, A. C. 2003. '*Tyro Keiromene*', in Sommerstein 2003 (ed.), 79–116.

Clark, P. 1998. 'Women, slaves, and the hierarchies of domestic violence: the family of St Augustine', in Joshel and Murnaghan 1998 (eds.), 109–29.

Clauss, J. J., and Johnston, S. I. 1997 (eds.). *Medea. Essays on Medea in Myth, Literature, Philosophy, and Art*. Princeton.

Cockle, W. E. H. 1987. *Euripides. Hypsipyle. Text and Annotation based on a Re-examination of the Papyri*. Testi e Commenti 7. Rome.

Cohen, D. 1991. *Law, Sexuality, and Society. The Enforcement of Morals in Classical Athens*. Cambridge.

Collard, C. 1991. *Euripides. Hecuba*. Warminster.

  1995a. 'Cretans', in *id. et al.* 1995: 53–78.

  1995b. '*Stheneboea*', *ibid.* 79–97.

  2004a. '*Oedipus*', in *id. et al.* 2004: 105–32.

  2004b. '*Antiope*', in *id. et al.* 2004: 259–329.

  2017. 'Fragments and fragmentary plays', in McClure 2017 (ed.), 347–64.

Collard, C., and Cropp, M. J. 2008. *Euripides. Fragments*, 2 vols. Loeb Classical Library 504, 506. Cambridge, MA and London.

Collard, C., Cropp, M. J., and Gibert, J. 2004. *Euripides. Selected Fragmentary Plays. Volume* II. Alexandros *(together with* Palamedes *and* Sisyphus), Oedipus, Andromeda, Antiope, Hypsipyle, Archelaus. Warminster.

Collard, C., Cropp, M. J., and Lee, K. H. 1995. *Euripides. Selected Fragmentary Plays. Volume* I. Telephus, Cretans, Stheneboea, Bellerophon, Cresphontes, Erectheus, Phaethon, Wise Melanippe, Captive Melanippe. Warminster.

Collins, B. J., Bachvarova, M. R., and Rutherford, I. C. 2008 (eds.). *Anatolian Interfaces. Hittites, Greeks and Their Neighbours. Proceedings of an International Conference on Cross-Cultural Interaction, September 17–19, 2004, Emory University, Atlanta, GA*. Oxford.

Colomo, D. 2011a. 'Euripides' *Ur-Medea* between *hypotheseis* and declamation', *Zeitschrift für Papyrologie und Epigraphik* 176: 45–51.

  2011b. '5093. Rhetorical epideixeis', *The Oxyrhynchus Papyri* 76: 84–171.

Colvin, M. 2007. 'Heraclitean flux and unity of opposites in Plato's *Theaetetus* and *Cratylus*', *Classical Quarterly* NS 57: 759–69.

Compton-Engle, G. 2015. *Costume in the Comedies of Aristophanes*. Cambridge.

Coo, L. 2011a. *Sophocles' Trojan Fragments. A Commentary on Selected Plays*. Diss. Cambridge.

  2011b. 'Wrestling with Aphrodite: a re-evaluation of Sophocles fr. 941', in Millett *et al.* 2011 (eds.), 11–26.

  2013a. 'A tale of two sisters: studies in Sophocles' *Tereus*', *Transactions of the American Philological Association* 143: 349–84.

  2013b. 'A Sophoclean slip: mistaken identity and tragic allusion on the Exeter pelike', *Bulletin of the Institute of Classical Studies* 56: 67–88.

Coray, M. 2016. *Homers Ilias. Gesamtkommentar. Band* XI. *Achtzehnter Gesang* (Σ). *Faszikel 2: Kommentar*. Berlin and Boston.

  2018. *Homer's Iliad. The Basel Commentary – Book XVIII*. transl. B. Millis and S. Strack. Berlin.

Cosgrove, C. H. 2005. 'A woman's unbound hair in the Greco-Roman world, with special reference to the story of the "sinful woman" in Luke 7:36–50', *Journal of Biblical Literature* 124: 675–92.

Cousland, J. R. C., and Hume, J. R. 2009 (eds.). *The Play of Texts and Fragments. Essays in Honour of Martin Cropp*. Mnemosyne supplement 314. Leiden and Boston.

Cox, C. A. 1996. 'Hipponicus' trapeza: humour in Andocides 1.130–1', *Classical Quarterly* NS 46: 572–5.

  1998. *Household Interests. Property, Marriage Strategies, and Family Dynamics in Ancient Athens*. Princeton.

Cozzoli, A.-T. 2001. *Euripide. Cretesi*. Test e Commenti 15. Pisa and Rome.

Craik, E. M. 1993. 'ΑΙΔΩΣ in Euripides' *Hippolytos* 373–430: review and reinterpretation', *Journal of Hellenic Studies* 113: 45–59.

Cropp, M. J. 1995. 'Erectheus', in Collard *et al.* 1995: 148–94.

  2003. 'Hypsipyle and Athens', in Csapo and Miller 2003 (eds.), 129–45.

  2004. '*Hypsipyle*', in Collard *et al.* 2004: 169–258.

  2019. *Minor Greek Tragedians. Volume 1: The Fifth Century. Fragments from the Tragedies with Selected Testimonia*. Liverpool.

Cropp, M., and Fick, G. 1985. *Resolutions and Chronology In Euripides. The Fragmentary Tragedies*. Bulletin of the Institute of Classical Studies supplement 43. London.

Cropp, M., Fantham, E., and Scully, S. E. 1986 (eds.). *Greek Tragedy and Its Legacy. Essays presented to D. J. Conacher*. Calgary.

Csapo, E. 1999–2000. 'Later Euripidean music', *Illinois Classical Studies* 24–5: 399–426.

  2003. 'The dolphins of Dionysus', in *id.* and Miller 2003 (eds.), 69–98.

  2004. 'The politics of the new music', in Murray and Wilson 2004 (eds.), 207–48.

  2008. 'Star choruses: Eleusis, Orphism, and New Musical imagery and dance', in Revermann and Wilson 2008 (eds.), 262–90.

Csapo, E., and Miller, M. C. 2003 (eds.). *Poetry, Theory, Praxis. The Social Life of Myth, Word and Image in Ancient Greece. Essays in Honour of William J. Slater*. Oxford.

Csapo, E., and Wilson, P. 2009. 'Timotheus the new musician', in Budelmann 2009 (ed.), 277–93.

Csapo, E., Goette, H. R., Green, J. R., Wilson, P. 2014 (eds.). *Greek Theatre in the Fourth Century B.C.* Berlin and Boston.

Curley, D. 2003. 'Ovid's *Tereus*: theater and metatheater', in Sommerstein 2003 (ed.), 163-97.

2013. *Tragedy in Ovid. Theater, Metatheater, and the Transformation of a Genre.* Cambridge.

Damet, A. 2011. 'Le sein et le couteau. L'ambiguïté de l'amour maternel dans l'Athènes classique', *Clio* 34: 17–40.

D'Angour, A. 2006. 'The new music: so what's new?', in Goldhill and Osborne 2006 (eds.), 264–83.

Dasen, V. 1997. 'Multiple births in Graeco-Roman antiquity', *Oxford Journal of Archaeology* 16: 49–63.

2005. 'Blessing or portent? Multiple births in ancient Rome', in Mustakallio *et al.* 2005 (eds.), 62–73.

Davidson, J. 2005. 'Theatrical production', in Gregory 2005 (ed.), 194–211.

Davies, M. 1986. 'Who speaks at Sophocles *Antigone* 572?', *Prometheus* 12: 19–24.

Davies, M., and Finglass, P. J. 2014. *Stesichorus. The Poems.* Cambridge Classical Texts and Commentaries 54. Cambridge.

Dawson, L., and McHardy, F. 2018 (eds.). *Revenge and Gender in Classical, Medieval and Renaissance Literature.* Edinburgh.

Deacy, S., and McHardy, F. 2013. 'Uxoricide in pregnancy: ancient Greek domestic violence in evolutionary perspective', *Evolutionary Psychology* 11: 994–1010.

Deforge, B. 1987. 'Eschyle et la légende des Argonautes', *Revue des Études Grecques* 100: 30–44.

Degl'Innocenti Pierini, R., Lambardi, N., Magnelli, E., Mattiacci, S., Orlando, S., and Pace Pieri, M. 2007 (eds.). *Fedra. Versioni e riscritture di un mito classico. Atti del Convegno AICC Firenze, 2–3 aprile 2003.* Il Diaspro: Piccola Biblioteca de la Fortezza 3. Florence.

Demand, N. 1994. *Birth, Death, and Motherhood in Classical Greece.* Baltimore and London.

De Martino, F., and Morenilla, C. 2010 (eds.). *Teatro y sociedad en la antigüedad clásica. La redefinición del rôle de la mujer por el escenario de la guerra.* El teatro clásico en el marco de la cultura griega y su pervivencia en la cultura occidental 13. le Rane Collana di Studi e Testi 55. Bari.

Dendrinos, C., Harris, J., Harvalia-Crook, E., and Herrin, J. 2003 (eds.). *Porphyrogenita. Essays on the History and Literature of Byzantium and the Latin East in Honour of Julian Chrysostomides.* Aldershot and Burlington, VT.

Denniston, J. D. 1939. *Euripides. Electra.* Oxford.

Derda, T., Hilder, J., and Kwapisz, J. 2017 (eds.). *Fragments, Holes, and Wholes. Reconstructing the Ancient World in Theory and Practice.* The Journal of Juristic Papyrology Supplement 30. Warsaw.

Deschamps, H. 2010. 'Achille d'Homère à Eschyle. Transposition d'un héros épique sur la scène tragique', *Gaia: revue interdisciplinaire sur la Grèce archaïque* 13: 177–204.

De Simone, M. 2008. 'The "Lesbian" muse in tragedy: Euripides Μελοποιός in Aristoph. *Ra.* 1301–28', *Classical Quarterly* NS 58: 479–90.

Desmond, W. 2008. *Cynics*. Berkeley and Los Angeles.

Di Benedetto, V. 2001. Review of Cozzoli 2001, *Rivista di Filologia e di Istruzione Classica* 129: 210–30. [= 2007: III 1343–65]

2007. *Il richiamo del testo. Contributi di filologia e letteratura*, 4 vols. Anthropoi: Biblioteca di Scienza dell'Antichità 1–4. Pisa.

Diggle, J. 1970. *Euripides*. Phaethon. Cambridge Classical Texts and Commentaries 12. Cambridge.

2008. 'Did Euripides plagiarize the *Medea* of Neophron?', in Auger and Peigney 2008 (eds.), 405–13.

Dijkstra, P., and Buunk, B. P. 1998. 'Jealousy as a function of rival characteristics: an evolutionary perspective', *Personality and Social Psychology Bulletin* 24: 1158–66.

Dillon, J. M. 1997. 'Medea among the philosophers', in Clauss and Johnston 1997 (eds.), 211–18.

Dodds, E. R. 1951. *The Greeks and the Irrational*. Sather Classical Lectures 25. Berkeley, Los Angeles, London.

Dolfi, E. 1984. 'Su *I Cretesi* di Euripide: passione e responsabilità', *Prometheus* 10: 121–38.

Dougherty, C., and Kurke, L. 2003 (eds.). *The Cultures within Ancient Greek Culture. Contact, Conflict, Collaboration*. Cambridge.

Dover, K. J. 1993. *Aristophanes*. Frogs. Oxford.

Dowden, K., and Livingstone, N. 2011 (eds.). *A Companion to Greek Mythology*. Malden, MA, Oxford, Chichester.

Downing, C. 1988. *Psyche's Sisters. ReImagining the Meaning of Sisterhood*. San Francisco etc.

Dubischar, M. 2001. *Die Agonszenen bei Euripides. Untersuchungen zu ausgewälhten Dramen*. Drama: Beiträge zum antiken Drama und seiner Rezeption 13. Stuttgart and Weimar.

Duchemin, J. 1968. *L'ἀγών dans la tragédie grecque*[2]. Paris. [1st edn 1945]

Dudley, D. R. 1937. *A History of Cynicism from Diogenes to the 6th Century A.D.* London.

Dué, C. 2002. *Homeric Variations on a Lament by Briseis*. Lanham, MD, Boulder, New York, Oxford.

2006. *The Captive Woman's Lament in Greek Tragedy*. Austin.

2012. 'Lament as speech act in Sophocles', in Ormand 2012 (ed.), 236–50.

Dugdale, E. 2015. 'Who named me? Identity and status in Sophocles' *Oedipus Tyrannus*', *American Journal of Philology* 136: 421–45.

Dyson, M. 1988. 'Alcestis' children and the character of Admetus', *Journal of Hellenic Studies* 108: 13–23.

Easterling, P. E. 1982. *Sophocles*. Trachiniae. Cambridge.

  1987. 'Women in tragic space', *Bulletin of the Institute of Classical Studies* 34: 15–26.

  1991. 'Men's κλέος and women's γόος: female voices in the *Iliad*', *Journal of Modern Greek Studies* 9: 145–51.

  1993. 'The end of an era? Tragedy in the early fourth century', in Sommerstein *et al.* 1993 (eds.), 559–69.

  1997 (ed.). *The Cambridge Companion to Greek Tragedy*. Cambridge.

  2003. 'Sophocles and the Byzantine student', in Dendrinos *et al.* 2003 (eds.), 319–34.

  2005. '*Agamemnon* for the ancients', in Macintosh *et al.* 2005 (eds.), 23–36.

  2013. 'Perspectives on antiquity and tragedy', *Classical Receptions Journal* 5: 184–9.

Easterling, P., and Hall, E. 2002 (eds.). *Greek and Roman Actors. Aspects of an Ancient Profession*. Cambridge.

Easterling, P. E., and Knox, B. M. W. 1985 (eds.). *The Cambridge History of Classical Literature* I. *Greek Literature*. Cambridge.

Ebbott, M. 1999. 'The wrath of Helen: self-blame and nemesis in the *Iliad*', in Carlisle and Levaniouk 1999 (eds.), 3–20.

Edwards, M. W. 1991. *The* Iliad: *a Commentary. Volume* V: *Books 17–20*. Cambridge.

Engelmann, R. 1890. 'Tyro', *Jahrbuch des Kaiserlich Deutschen Archäologischen Instituts* 5: 171–9. [≈ 1900: 40–51]

  1900. *Archäologische Studien zu den Tragikern*. Berlin.

Engelstein, S. 2011. 'Sibling logic; or, Antigone again', *PMLA* 126: 38–54.

  2017. *Sibling Action. The Genealogical Structure of Modernity*. New York.

Fantuzzi, M. 2012. *Achilles in Love. Intertextual Studies*. Oxford.

Farmer, M. C. 2017. *Tragedy on the Comic Stage*. Oxford and New York.

Fearn, D. 2007. *Bacchylides. Politics, Performance, Poetic Tradition*. Oxford.

Finglass, P. J. 2007. *Sophocles*. Electra. Cambridge Classical Texts and Commentaries 44. Cambridge.

  2011. *Sophocles*. Ajax. Cambridge Classical Texts and Commentaries 48. Cambridge.

  2013. 'How Stesichorus began his *Sack of Troy*', *Zeitschrift für Papyrologie und Epigraphik* 185: 1–17.

  2014. 'A new fragment of Euripides' *Ino*', *Zeitschrift für Papyrologie und Epigraphik* 189: 65–82.

  2015a. 'Ancient reperformances of Sophocles', *Trends in Classics* 7/2. [= Lamari 2015 (ed.), 207–23].

  2015b. Reperformances and the transmission of texts', *Trends in Classics* 7/2. [= Lamari 2015 (ed.), 259–76].

  2016a. 'Mistaken identity in Euripides' *Ino*', in Kyriakou and Rengakos 2016 (eds.), 299–315.

2016b. 'A new fragment of Sophocles' *Tereus*', *Zeitschrift für Papyrologie und Epigraphik* 200: 61–85.

2017a. 'Euripides' *Oedipus*: a response to Liapis', *Transactions of the American Philological Association* 147: 1–26.

2017b. 'Sophocles' *Ajax* and the polis', *Polis. The Journal for Ancient Greek Political Thought* 34: 306–17.

2017c. 'Further notes on the Euripides *Ino* papyrus (*P. Oxy.* 5131)', *Eikasmos* 28: 61–5.

2017d [2015 on journal]. 'Agamemnon's death: a reply to Nova', *Aevum Antiquum* 15: 89–94.

2018. *Sophocles*. Oedipus the King. Cambridge Classical Texts and Commentaries 57. Cambridge.

2019a. *Sophocles*. Greece and Rome New Surveys in the Classics 44. Cambridge.

2019b. Euripides' *Medea* in context', in Pociña *et al.* 2019 (eds), 11–20.

Finglass, P. J., Collard, C., and Richardson, N. J. 2007 (eds.). *Hesperos. Studies in Ancient Greek Poetry Presented to M. L. West on His Seventieth Birthday*. Oxford.

Fitzpatrick, D., and Sommerstein, A. H. 2006. '*Tereus*', in Sommerstein *et al.* 2006: 141–95.

Foley, H. P. 1981a (ed.). *Reflections of Women in Antiquity*. New York, London, Paris.

1981b. 'The conception of women in Athenian drama', in *ead.* 1981a (ed.), 127–68.

1982. 'The "female intruder" reconsidered: women in Aristophanes' *Lysistrata* and *Ecclesiazusae*', *Classical Philology* 77: 1–21.

1985. *Ritual Irony. Poetry and Sacrifice in Euripides*. Ithaca, NY and London.

1993. 'The politics of tragic lamentation', in Sommerstein *et al.* 1993 (eds.), 101–143. [≈ 2001: 19–55]

2001. *Female Acts in Greek Tragedy*. Princeton and Oxford.

2015. *Euripides*. Hecuba. London and New York.

Fortenbaugh, W. W. 1977. 'Aristotle on slaves and women', in Barnes *et al.* 1977 (eds.), 135–9. [= 2006: 241–7]

2006. *Aristotle's Practical Side. On His Psychology, Ethics, Politics and Rhetoric*. Philosophia Antiqua 101. Leiden and Boston.

Fournier-Finocchiaro, L. 2006 (ed.). *Les Mères de la patrie. Représentations et constructions d'une figure nationale*. Cahiers de la MRSH 45. Caen.

Foxhall, L. 1989. 'Household, gender and property in classical Athens', *Classical Quarterly* NS 39: 22–44.

Foxhall, L., and Salmon, J. 1998 (eds.). *When Men Were Men. Masculinity, Power and Identity in Classical Antiquity*. Leicester–Nottingham Studies in Ancient Society 8. London and New York.

Frank, J. 2006. 'The *Antigone*'s law', *Law, Culture and the Humanities* 2: 336–40.

Frankfurt, H. G. 1969. 'Alternate possibilities and moral responsibility', *The Journal of Philosophy* 66: 829–39.

Franklin, J. C. 2002. 'Diatonic music in Greece: a reassessment of its antiquity', *Mnemosyne* 4th ser. 55: 669–702.

2008. '"A feast of music": the Greco-Lydian musical movement on the Assyrian periphery', in Collins *et al.* 2008: 191–201.

2013. '"Songbenders of circular choruses": dithyramb and the "demise of music"', in Kowalzig and Wilson 2013 (eds.), 213–36.

Frede, D., and Inwood, B. 2005 (eds.). *Language and Learning. Philosophy of Language in the Hellenistic Age. Proceedings of the Ninth Symposium Hellenisticum.* Cambridge.

Fulkerson, L. 2013. *No Regrets. Remorse in Classical Antiquity.* Oxford.

Furley, W. D. 1996. 'Phaidra's pleasurable *aidos* (Eur. *Hipp.* 380–7)', *Classical Quarterly* NS 46: 84–90.

Gaca, K. L. 2003. *The Making of Fornication. Eros, Ethics, and Political Reform in Greek Philosophy and Early Christianity.* Hellenistic Culture and Society 40. Berkeley, Los Angeles, London.

Gagarin, M. 1997. *Antiphon. The Speeches.* Cambridge.

Gantz, T. 1993. *Early Greek Myth. A Guide to Literary and Artistic Sources.* Baltimore and London.

Garvie, A. F. 1994. *Homer.* Odyssey. Books VI–VIII. Cambridge.

Garzya, A. 1995. 'Sui frammenti dei *Frigî* di Eschilo', *Cuadernos de Filología Clásica. Estudios griegos e indoeuropeos* 5: 41–52.

Gastaldi, E. C. 2010. 'L'isola di Lemnos attraverso la documentazione epigrafica', *Annuario della Scuola Archeologica di Atene e delle Missioni Italiane in Oriente* 89: 347–64.

Gentili, B., and Perusino, F. 1995 (eds.). *Mousike. Metrica, ritmica e musica Greca in memoria di Giovanni Comotti.* Studi di Metrica Classica 11. Pisa and Rome.

Ghidini, M. T. 2013. 'Dionysos versus Orpheus?', in Bernabé *et al.* 2013 (eds.), 144–58.

Gibert, J. 1999–2000. 'Falling in love with Euripides (*Andromeda*)', *Illinois Classical Studies* 24–5: 75–91.

2003. 'Apollo's sacrifice: the limits of a metaphor in Greek tragedy', *Harvard Studies in Classical Philology* 101: 159–206.

2004. '*Andromeda*', in Collard *et al.* 2004: 133–68.

2016. 'The wisdom of Jason', in Kyriakou and Rengakos 2016 (eds.), 105–20.

Gilhuly, K. 2015. 'Lesbians are not from Lesbos', in Blondell and Ormand 2015b (eds.), 143–76. [≈ 2018: 92–116]

2018. *Erotic Geographies in Ancient Greek Literature and Culture.* Abingdon and New York.

Giudice, F. 1981. 'Aiolos', *Lexicon Iconographicum Mythologiae Classicae* 1/1: 398–9.

Goerschen, F. C. 1975. 'Sophokles' Eurypylos: Inhalt, Aufbau und Aufführungszeit', *Rendiconti della Accademia di Archeologia Lettere e Belle Arti* NS 50: 55–115.

Goff, B. E. 1990. *The Noose of Words. Readings of Desire, Violence and Language in Euripides'* Hippolytos. Cambridge.

1995 (ed.). *History, Tragedy, Theory. Dialogues on Athenian Drama*. Austin.

2004. *Citzen Bacchae: Women's Ritual Practice in Ancient Greece*. Berkeley.

Golden, M. 1990. *Children and Childhood in Classical Athens*. Baltimore and London.

2015. *Children and Childhood in Classical Athens. Second Edition*. Baltimore.

Goldhill, S. 1987. 'The Great Dionysia and civic ideology', *Journal of Hellenic Studies* 107: 58–76. [≈ Winkler and Zeitlin 1990 (eds.), 97–129]

1990. 'Character and action, representation and reading: Greek tragedy and its critics', in Pelling 1990 (ed.), 100–27.

1991. 'Violence in Greek tragedy', in Redmond 1991 (ed.), 15–33.

2006. 'Antigone and the politics of sisterhood', in Zajko and Leonard 2006 (eds.), 141–61.

2012. *Sophocles and the Language of Tragedy*. Oxford.

2014. 'Antigone: an interruption between feminism and Christianity', *International Journal of the Classical Tradition* 21: 309–16.

Goldhill, S., and Osborne, R. 1999 (eds.). *Performance Culture and Athenian Democracy*. Cambridge.

2006 (eds.). *Rethinking Revolutions through Ancient Greece*. Cambridge.

Goossens, R. 1962. *Euripide et Athènes*. Académie royale de Belgique classe des lettres mémoires 55/4. Brussels.

Gould, T. 1991. 'The uses of violence in drama', in Redmond 1991 (ed.), 1–13.

Gould, T. F., and Herington, C. J. (eds.). *Greek Tragedy*. Yale Classical Studies 25. Cambridge.

Gredley, B. 1987. 'The place and time of victory: Euripides' *Medea*', *Bulletin of the Institute of Classical Studies* 34: 27–39.

Gregory, J. 1999. *Euripides*. Hecuba. American Philological Association Textbook Series 14. Atlanta.

2005 (ed.). *A Companion to Greek Tragedy*. Malden, MA, Oxford, Carlton, VIC.

2007. 'Donkeys and the equine hierarchy in archaic Greek literature', *Classical Journal* 102: 193–212.

Grenfell, B. P., and Hunt, A. S. 1908. '852. Euripides, *Hypsipyle*', *The Oxyrhynchus Papyri* 6: 19–106.

Griffin, J. 1999 (ed.). *Sophocles Revisited. Essays Presented to Sir Hugh Lloyd-Jones*. Oxford.

Griffith, M. 1983. *Aeschylus*. Prometheus Bound. Cambridge.

1999. *Sophocles*. Antigone. Cambridge.

2001. 'Antigone and her sister(s): embodying women in Greek tragedy', in Lardinois and McClure 2001 (eds.), 117–36.

2006a. 'Sophocles' satyr-plays and the language of romance', in De Jong and Rijksbaron 2006 (eds.), 51–72.

2006b. 'Horsepower and donkeywork: equids and the ancient Greek imagination. Part two', *Classical Philology* 101: 307–58.

Gruber, M. A. 2009. *Der Chor in den Tragödien des Aischylos. Affekt und Reaktion*. Drama: Studien zum antiken Drama und zu seiner Rezeption NS 7. Tübingen.

Guirard, H. 1996. 'La figure de Médée sur les vases grecs', *Pallas* 45: 207–18.

Hadjicosti, I. 2007. *Aischylos and the Trojan Cycle. The Lost Tragedies*. Diss. UCL.

Hahnemann, C. 1999. 'Zur Rekonstruktion und Interpretation von Sophokles' *Aigeus*', *Hermes* 127: 385–96.

2003. 'Sophokles' *Aigeus*: plaidoyer for a methodology of caution', in Sommerstein 2003 (ed.), 201–18.

2012. 'Sophoclean fragments', in Ormand 2012 (ed.), 169–84.

Hall, E. 1989. *Inventing the Barbarian. Greek Self-Definition through Tragedy*. Oxford.

1993. 'Asia unmanned: images of victory in classical Athens', in Rich and Shipley 1993 (eds.), 108–33.

1999. 'Actors' song in tragedy', in Goldhill and Osborne 1999 (eds.), 96–122. [≈ 2006: 288–320]

2002. 'The singing actors of antiquity', in Easterling and Hall 2002 (eds.), 3–38.

2006. *The Theatrical Cast of Athens. Interactions between Ancient Greek Drama and Society*. Oxford.

Halleran, M. R. 1995. *Euripides. Hippolytus*. Warminster.

Hanink, J. 2014. *Lycurgan Athens and the Making of Classical Tragedy*. Cambridge.

Harder, A. 2006. 'Praxithea: a perfect mother?', in Lardinois *et al.* 2006 (eds.), 146–59.

Harder, M. A., Regtuit, R. F., and Wakker, G. C. 2006 (eds.). *Beyond the Canon*. Hellenistica Groningana 11. Leuven, Paris, Dudley, MA.

Hardie, A. 2012. '*Hypsipyle*, Dionysus Melpomenos and the Muse in tragedy', *Papers of the Langford Latin Seminar* 15: 143–89.

Harrison, G. W. M., and Liapis, V. 2013a (eds.). *Performance in Greek and Roman Theatre*. Mnemosyne supplement 353. Leiden and Boston.

2013b. 'Making sense of ancient performance' in *id.* 2013a (eds.), 1–42.

Hartman, G. 1969. 'The voice of the shuttle: language from the point of view of literature', *The Review of Metaphysics* 23: 240–68. [= 1970: 337–55]

1970. *Beyond Formalism. Literary Essays 1958–1970*. New Haven and London.

Hartung, J. A. 1843. *Euripides restitutus sive scriptorum Euripidis ingeniique censura. Volumen prius*. Hamburg.

Hawley, R. 1998. 'The dynamics of beauty in classical Greece', in Montserrat 1998 (ed.), 37–54.

Henderson, J. 1987. 'Older women in Attic old comedy', *Transactions of the American Philological Association* 117: 105–29.

1991. *The Maculate Muse. Obscene Language in Attic Comedy*. Oxford and New York. [1st edn New Haven and London, 1975]

1998–2008. *Aristophanes*, 5 vols. Loeb Classical Library 178–80, 488, 502. London and Cambridge, MA.

Henrichs, A. 2000. 'Drama and *dromena*: bloodshed, violence, and sacrificial metaphor in Euripides', *Harvard Studies in Classical Philology* 100: 173–88.

Henry, W. B. 2007. 'Pindaric accompaniments', in Finglass *et al.* 2007 (eds.), 126–31.

Heubner, S. forthcoming (ed.). *Missing Mothers: Maternal Absence in Antiquity*. Louvain.

Hexter, R., and Selden, D. 1992 (eds.). *Innovations of Antiquity*. New York and London.

Higgins, L. A., and Silver, B. R. 1991 (eds.). *Rape and Representation*. New York.

Hirschberger, M. 2004. *Gynaikōn Katalogos und Megalai Ēhoiai. Ein Kommentar zu den Fragmenten zweier hesiodeischer Epen*. Beiträge zur Altertumskunde 198. Munich and Leipzig.

Hofmann, H. 1991 (ed.). *Fragmenta Dramatica. Beiträge zur Interpretation der griechischen Tragikerfragmente und ihrer Wirkungsgeschichte*. Festschrift Radt. Göttingen.

Holland, L. 2003. 'Πᾶς δόμος ἔρροι: myth and plot in Euripides' *Medea*', *Transactions of the American Philological Association* 133: 255–79.

Holmes, B. 2010. *The Symptom and the Subject. The Emergence of the Physical Body in Ancient Greece*. Princeton and Oxford.

Holzman, S. 2016. 'Tortoise-shell lyres from Phrygian Gordion', *American Journal of Archaeology* 120: 537–64.

Honig, B. 2011. 'Ismene's forced choice: sacrifice and sorority in Sophocles' *Antigone*', *Arethusa* 44: 29–68.

2013. *Antigone, Interrupted*. Cambridge.

Hourmouziades, N. C. 1975. "Ἀνόμοιοι δίδυμοι στο θέατρο τοῦ Εὐριπίδη", in *Φίλτρα. Τιμητικός τόμος Σ. Γ. Καψωμένου* (Thessaloniki), 201–20. [= 2003: 105–34]

2003. *Θεατρικές Διαδρομές*. Athens.

Hunter, R. L. 1981. 'P. Lit. Lond. 77 and tragic burlesque in Attic comedy', *Zeitschrift für Papyrologie und Epigraphik* 41: 19–24.

1983. *Eubulus. The Fragments*. Cambridge Classical Texts and Commentaries 24. Cambridge.

Hunter, V. J. 1994. *Policing Athens. Social Control in the Attic Lawsuits, 420–320 B.C.* Princeton.

Hurst, A. C., Alquist, J. L., and Puts, D. A. 2016. 'Women's fertility status alters other women's jealousy and mate guarding', *Personality and Social Psychology Bulletin* 43: 191–203.

Hutchinson, G. O. 2001. *Greek Lyric Poetry. A Commentary on Selected Larger Pieces*. Oxford.

Huys, M. 1996. 'Euripides and the "Tales from Euripides": sources of the *Fabulae* of Ps-Hyginus? (Part 1)', *Archiv für Papyrusforschung* 42: 168–78.

1997a. 'Euripides and the "Tales from Euripides": sources of the Fabulae of Ps-Hyginus? (Part 2)', *ibid.* 43: 11–30.

1997b. 'Euripides and the "Tales from Euripides": sources of Apollodoros' *Bibliotheca*?', *Rheinsiches Museum* NF 140: 308–27.

Iovine, G. 2016. 'A survey of wormholes in Soph. frr. 206–213 R.^{2} (*P.Oxy.* IX 1175 + XVII 2081[b], frr. 1–8 Hunt)', *Archiv für Papyrusforschung* 62: 317–36.

2017. 'Defying the fragments. Some notes about Sophocles' **Εὐρύπυλος (frr. 210, 211 R.^{2})', *Rivista di Cultura Classica e Medioevale* 59: 299–310.

Irigaray, L. 1974. *Speculum de l'autre femme*. Paris.

1985. *Speculum of the Other Woman*, transl. G. C. Gill. Ithaca, NY.

Irwin, T. H. 1977. *Plato's Moral Theory. The Early and Middle Dialogues*. Oxford.

1983. 'Euripides and Socrates', *Classical Philology* 78: 183–97.

1995. *Plato's Ethics*. New York and Oxford.

Jacobson, D. 1997. 'In praise of immoral art', *Philosophical Topics* 25/1: 155–99.

Janko, R. 1979. 'The etymology of σχερός and ἐπισχερώ: a Homeric misunderstanding', *Glotta* 57: 20–3.

Jebb, R. C. 1892. *Sophocles. The Plays and Fragments. Part V:* The Trachiniae. Cambridge.

Jones, H. L. 1969. *The Geography of Strabo. Volume V*. Loeb Classical Library 211. Cambridge, MA and London.

Jones Roccos, L. 1994. 'Perseus', *Lexicon Iconographicum Mythologiae Classicae* VII/1: 332–48.

Jong, I. J. F. de 1999 (ed.). *Homer. Critical Assessments*. London and New York.

Jong, I. J. F. de, and Rijksbaron, A. 2006 (eds.). *Sophocles and the Greek Language. Aspects of Diction, Syntax and Pragmatics*. Mnemosyne supplement 269. Leiden and Boston.

Jong, I. J. F. de, and Sullivan, J. P. 1994 (eds.). *Modern Critical Theory and Classical Literature*. Mnemosyne supplement 130. Leiden, New York, Cologne.

Joshel, S. R., and Murnaghan, S. 1998 (eds.). *Women and Slaves in Greco-Roman Culture. Differential Equations*. London and New York.

Jouan, F. 1992. 'Dionysos chez Eschyle', *Kernos* 5: 71–86.

Jouan, F., and Looy, H. van 1998 (eds.). *Euripide. Tome* VIII. *1re partie. Fragments. Aigeus–Autolykos*. Paris.

2000. *Euripide. Tome* VIII. *2e partie. Fragments. Bellérophon–Protésilas*. Paris.

Jouanna, J. 2007. *Sophocle*. Paris.

2018. *Sophocles. A Study of His Theater in Its Political and Social Context*, transl. S. Rendall. Princeton and Oxford.

Juffras, D. M. 1991. 'Sophocles' *Electra* 973–85 and tyrannicide', *Transactions of the American Philological Association* 121: 99–108.

Kambitsis, J. 1972. *L'Antiope d'Euripide*. Athens.

Kamerbeek, J. C. 1991. 'En relisant les fragments de l'Erechthée d'Euripide', in H. Hofmann 1991 (ed.), 111–16.

Kapsomenos, S. G. 1963. *Sophokles' Trachinierinnen und ihr Vorbild. Eine Literargeschichtliche und Textkritische Untersuchung*. Griechische Humanistiche Gesellschaft Zweite Reihe: Studien und Untersuchungen 2. Athens.

Karamanou, I. 2012. 'Euripides' "family reunion plays" and their socio-political resonances', in Markantonatos and Zimmermann 2012 (eds.), 241–52.

Karbowski, J. 2014a. 'Aristotle on the deliberative abilities of women', *Apeiron* 47: 435–60.

2014b. 'Deliberating without authority: Fortenbaugh on the psychology of women in Aristotle's *Politics*', *Philosophical News* 8: 88–104.

Kassel, R. 1991a. 'Fragmente und ihre Sammler', in Hofmann 1991 (ed.), 243–53. [= 1991b: 88–98 ≈ McHardy *et al.* 2005 (eds.), 7–20]

1991b. *Kleine Schriften*. Berlin and New York.

Kazantzidis, G., and Spatharas, D. 2018 (eds.). *Hope in Ancient Literature, History, and Art*. Trends in Classics supplement 63. Berlin and Boston.

Kearns, E. 1990. 'Saving the city', in Murray and Price 1990 (eds.), 323–44.

Keen, A. G. 2005. 'Lycians in the *Cares* of Aeschylus', in McHardy *et al.* 2005 (eds.), 63–82.

Kelly, A. 2015. 'Aias in Athens: the worlds of the play and the audience', *Quaderni Urbinati di Cultura Classica* ns 111: 61–92.

Kieran, M. 2005. 'Art and morality', in Levinson 2005 (ed.), 451–70.

Kilburn, K. 1959. *Lucian*, vol. vi. London and Cambridge, MA.

Kirkpatrick, J. 2011. 'The prudent dissident: unheroic resistance in Sophocles' *Antigone*', *The Review of Politics* 73: 401–24.

Kiso, A. 1977. 'Notes on Sophocles' *Epigoni*', *Greek, Roman, and Byzantine Studies* 18: 207–26.

Kitzinger, M. R. 2012. 'The divided worlds of Sophocles' *Women of Trachis*', in Ormand 2012 (ed.), 111–25.

Klindienst Joplin, P. 1984. 'The voice of the shuttle is ours', *Stanford Literature Review* 1: 25–53. [= Higgins and Silver 1991 (eds.), 35–64 = McClure 2002 (ed.), 259–86.]

Knox, B. M. W. 1977. 'The *Medea* of Euripides', in Gould and Herington 1977 (eds.), 193–225. [= 1979: 295–322]

1979. *Word and Action. Essays on the Ancient Theatre*. Baltimore and London.

Konstan, D. 2010. *Before Forgiveness. The Origins of a Moral Idea*. Cambridge.

2013. 'Propping up Greek tragedy: the right use of *opsis*', in Harrison and Liapis 2013a (eds.), 63–75.

Kovacs, D. 1980. 'Shame, pleasure, and honor in Phaedra's great speech. Euripides, *Hippolytus* 375–87)', *American Journal of Philology* 101: 287–303.

1994–2002. *Euripides*, 6 vols. Loeb Classical Library 9–12, 484, 495. London and Cambridge, MA.

2016. 'Notes on a new fragment of Euripides' *Ino* (P. Oxy. 5131)', *Zeitschrift für Papyrologie und Epigraphik* 199: 3–6.

Kowalzig, B. 2013. 'Dancing dolphins on the wine-dark sea. Dithyramb and social change in the archaic Mediterranean', in *ead.* and Wilson 2013 (eds.), 31–58.

Kowalzig, B., and Wilson, P. 2013 (eds.). *Dithyramb in Context*. Oxford.

Krappe, A. H. 1924. 'Euripides' *Alcmaeon* and the *Apollonius Romance*', *Classical Quarterly* 18: 57–8.

Kron, U. 1981. 'Aigeus', *Lexicon Iconographicum Mythologiae Classicae* I/1: 359–67.

Krumeich, R., Pechstein, N., and Seidensticker, B. 1999 (eds.). *Das griechische Satyrspiel*. Texte zur Forschung 72. Darmstadt.

Kurtz, D., and Sparkes, B. 1982 (eds.). *The Eye of Greece. Studies in the Art of Athens*. Cambridge.

Kyriakou, P., and Rengakos, A. 2016 (eds.). *Wisdom and Folly in Euripides*. Trends in Classics supplement 31. Berlin and Boston.

Lacan, J. 1986. *Le Seminaire. Livre VII: L'ethique de la psychanalyse, 1959–1960*, ed. J.-A. Miller. Paris.

  1992. *The Ethics of Psychoanalysis, 1959–1960. The Seminar of Jacques Lacan: Book VII*, transl. D. Porter. London and New York.

Laks, A., and Most, G. W. 2016. *Early Greek Philosophy. Volume* VIII: *Sophists. Part 1*. Loeb Classical Library 531. Cambridge, MA and London.

Lamari, A. A. 2012. 'The return of the father: Euripides' *Antiope, Hypsipyle*, and *Phoenissae*', in Markantonatos and Zimmermann 2012 (eds.), 219–39.

  2015 (ed.), *Reperformances of Drama in the Fifth and Fourth Centuries* BC. *Authors and Contexts*. Trends in Classics 7/2. Berlin and Boston.

  2017. *Reperforming Greek Tragedy. Theater, Politics, and Cultural Mobility in the Fifth and Fourth Centuries* BC. Trends in Classics supplement 52. Berlin and Boston.

Lambert, S. D. 2011 (ed.). *Sociable Man. Essays on Ancient Greek Social Behaviour, in Honour of Nick Fisher*. Swansea.

Lardinois, A., and McClure, L. 2001 (eds.). *Making Silence Speak. Women's Voices in Greek Literature and Society*. Princeton and Oxford.

Lardinois, A. P. M. H., Poel, M. G. M. van der, and Hunink, V. J. C. 2006 (eds.). *Land of Dreams. Greek and Latin Studies in Honour of A. H. M. Kessels*. Leiden and Boston.

Larson, J. 1995. *Greek Heroine Cults*. Madison and London.

Lawrence, S. 2013. *Moral Awareness in Greek Tragedy*. Oxford.

Leduc, C. 2011. 'Mère et fils dans la cité démocratique des Athéniens', *Pallas* 85: 97–118.

Lefkowitz, M. 2016. *Euripides and the Gods*. Oxford.

Leitao, D. D. 2012. *The Pregnant Male as Myth and Metaphor in Classical Greek Literature*. Cambridge and New York.

Lesky, A. 1961. *Göttliche und menschliche Motivation im homerischen Epos*. Sitzungs-berichte der Heidelberger Akademie der Wissenschaften, Philosophisch-historische Klasse 1961/4. Heidelberg. [≈ De Jong 1999: II 384–403 ≈ Cairns 2001: 170–202].

1966. 'Decision and responsibility in the tragedy of Aeschylus', *Journal of Hellenic Studies* 86: 78–85.

LeVen, P. A. 2014. *The Many-Headed Muse. Tradition and Innovation in Late Classical Greek Lyric Poetry*. Cambridge.

Levinson, J. 2005 (ed.). *The Oxford Handbook of Aesthetics*. Oxford and New York.

Lewis, S. 2011. 'Women and myth', in Dowden and Livingston 2011 (eds.), 443–58.

Liapis, V. 2014. 'The fragments of Euripides' *Oedipus*: a reconsideration', *Transactions of the American Philological Association* 144: 307–70.

Libatique, D. 2018. 'The speaker and the addressee of Sophocles' *Tereus* fr. 588 Radt and the context of fr. 583', *Classical Quarterly* NS 68: 707–12.

Llewellyn-Jones, L. 2002 (ed.). *Women's Dress in the Ancient Greek World*. London and Oakville, CT.

2011. 'Domestic abuse and violence against women in ancient Greece', in Lambert 2011 (ed.), 231–66.

Lloyd, M. 1984. 'The Helen scene in Euripides' *Troades*', *Classical Quarterly* NS 34: 303–13.

1992. *The* Agon *in Euripides*. Oxford.

Lloyd-Jones, H. 1957. 'Addendum: new text of fr. 50', in Smyth 1957: 599–603.

1992. 'Helikaon (Sophocles, fr. 10e, 8; fr. 210, 47–53)', *Zeitschrift für Papyrologie und Epigraphik* 92: 55–8. [= 2005: 106–9]

1997. *Sophocles*. Ajax. Electra. Oedipus Tyrannus. Loeb Classical Library 20. Cambridge MA and London. [Corrected version of 1994 impression]

1998. *Sophocles*. Antigone. Women of Trachis. Philoctetes. Oedipus at Colonus. Loeb Classical Library 21. Cambridge MA and London. [Corrected version of 1994 impression]

2003. *Sophocles. Fragments*. Loeb Classical Library 483. Cambridge, MA and London. [Corrected version of 1996 impression]

2005. *The Further Academic Papers of Sir Hugh Lloyd-Jones*. Oxford.

López Cruces, J. L. 2003. 'Diógenes y sus tragedias a la luz de la comedia', *Ítaca. Quaderns Catalans de Cultura Clàssica* 19: 47–69.

2010. 'Religión y saber femenino en la *Antíope* de Eurípides', in De Martino and Morenilla 2010 (eds.), 123–48.

2011. 'Dionysiac elements in *Antiope* and P. Oxy. 3317', *Maia* 63: 460–81.

López Férez, J. A. 1996. 'Sophía-sophós dans la *Médée* d'Euripide', *Pallas* 45: 139–51.

Loraux, N. 1985. *Façons tragiques de tuer une femme*. <Paris>.

1987. *Tragic Ways of Killing a Woman*, transl. A. Forster. Cambridge, MA and London.

1998. *Mothers in Mourning. With the Essay 'Of Amnesty and Its Opposite'*, transl. C. Pache. Ithaca, NY and London.

Luppe, W. 1981. 'Das neue Euripides-Fragment P. Oxy. 3317', *Zeitschrift für Papyrologie und Epigraphik* 42: 27–30.

1984. 'Euripides-Hypotheseis in den Hygin-Fabeln "Antiope" und "Ino"?', *Philologus* 128: 41–59.

1986. 'Die Μήδεια-Hypothesis', *Anagennesis* 4: 37–58.

1989. 'Nochmals zur Zuordnung des Tragiker-Fragments P. Oxy 3317', *Zeitschrift für Papyrologie und Epigraphik* 77: 13–17.

2010. 'Ein weiteres Zeugnis für zwei Μήδεια-Dramen des Euripides', *Zeitschrift für Papyrologie und Epigraphik* 173: 15–16.

Luppe, W., and Henry, W. B. 2012. '5131. Tragedy (Euripides, *Ino*)?', *The Oxyrhynchus Papyri* 78: 19–25.

Luschnig, C. A. E. 2007. *Granddaughter of the Sun. A Study of Euripides' Medea*. Mnemosyne supplement 286. Leiden and Boston.

Lyons, D. 2003. 'Dangerous gifts: ideologies of marriage and exchange in ancient Greece', *Classical Antiquity* 22: 93–134.

2012. *Dangerous Gifts. Gender and Exchange in Ancient Greece*. Austin.

Machon, J. 2009 *(Syn)aesthetics. Redefining Visceral Performance*. Basingstoke and New York.

Macintosh, F., Michelakis, P., Hall., E., Taplin, O. 2005 (eds.). Agamemnon *in Performance 458* BC *to* AD *2004*. Oxford.

MacKinnon, J. K. 1971. 'Heracles' intention in his second request of Hyllus: *Trach.* 1216–51', *Classical Quarterly* NS 21: 33–41.

Mac Sweeney, N. 2013. *Foundation Myths and Politics in Ancient Ionia*. Cambridge.

Maehler, H. 1997. *Die Lieder des Bakchylides. Zweiter Teil. Die Dithyramben und Fragmente*. Mnemosyne supplements 167. Leiden, New York, Cologne.

Maitland, J. 1992. 'Dynasty and family in the Athenian city state: a view from Attic tragedy', *Classical Quarterly* NS 42: 26–40.

Manuwald, B. 1983. 'Der Mord an den Kindern: Bermerkungen zu den Medea-Tragödien des Euripides und des Neophron', *Wiener Studien* NF 17: 27–61.

2010. 'Ist Simonides' Gedicht an Skopas (*PMG* 542) vollständig überliefert?', *Rheinsiches Museum* NF 153: 1–24.

March, J. 2003. 'Sophocles' *Tereus* and Euripides' *Medea*', in Sommerstein 2003 (ed.), 139–61.

Marconi, C. 2007. *Temple Decoration and Cultural Identity in the Archaic Greek World. The Metopes of Selinus*. Cambridge.

Markantonatos, A. 2012 (ed.). *Brill's Companion to Sophocles*. Leiden and Boston.

Marmodoro, A., and Hills, J. 2013 (eds.). *The Author's Voice in Classical and Late Antiquity*. Oxford.

Marshall, C. W. 2006. *The Stagecraft and Performance of Roman Comedy*. Cambridge.

2014. *The Structure and Performance of Euripides'* Helen. Cambridge.

Martin, R. P. 1989. *The Language of Heroes. Speech and Performance in the* Iliad. Ithaca, NY and London.

2003. 'The pipes are brawling: conceptualizing musical performance in Athens', in Dougherty and Kurke 2003 (eds.), 153–80.

Martina, A. 2000. 'PLitLond 77, i frammenti della *Medea* di Neofrone e la *Medea* di Euripide', in Capasso and Pernigotti 2000 (eds.), 247–75.

Martino, G. 1996. 'La *Tyro* e l'*Elettra* di Sofocle: due tragedie a lieto fine?', *PdelP* 51: 198–212.

Masciadri, V. 2004. 'Hypsipyle et ses soeurs. Notes d'analyse structurale et historique', in des Bouvrie 2004 (ed.) 221–41.

Mastronarde, D. J. 1979. *Contact and Discontinuity. Some Conventions of Speech and Action on the Greek Tragic Stage.* University of California Publications in Classical Studies 21. Berkeley, Los Angeles, London.

1990. 'Actors on high: the skene roof, the crane, and the gods in Attic drama', *Classical Antiquity* 9: 247–94.

1999–2000. 'Euripidean tragedy and genre: the terminology and its problems', *Illinois Classical Studies* 24–5: 23–39.

2002. *Euripides. Medea.* Cambridge.

2010. *The Art of Euripides. Dramatic Technique and Social Context.* Cambridge.

Mattison, K. 2015. 'Sophocles' *Trachiniae*: lessons in love', *G&R* 2nd ser. 62: 12–24.

Mauthner, M. L. 2002. *Sistering. Power and Change in Female Relationships.* Basingstoke and New York.

2005. 'Distant lives, still voices: sistering in family sociology', *Sociology* 39: 623–42.

McClure, L. K. 1999. *Spoken Like a Woman. Speech and Gender in Athenian Drama.* Princeton.

2002. *Sexuality and Gender in the Classical World. Readings and Sources.* Malden, MA, Oxford, Carlton, VIC.

2017 (ed.). *A Companion to Euripides.* Malden, MA, Oxford, Chichester.

McCoskey, D. E. 1998. '"I, whom she detested so bitterly": slavery and the violent division of women in Aeschylus' *Oresteia*', in Joshel and Murnaghan 1998 (eds.), 35–55.

McCoskey, D. E., and Zakin, E. 2009 (eds.). *Bound by the City. Greek Tragedy, Sexual Difference, and the Formation of the* Polis. Albany.

McHardy, F. 2004. 'Women's influence on revenge in ancient Greece', in McHardy and Marshall 2004 (eds.), 92–114.

2005. 'From treacherous wives to murderous mothers: filicide in tragic fragments', in *ead. et al.* 2005 (eds.), 129–50.

2008a. *Revenge in Athenian Culture.* London.

2008b. 'The "trial by water" in Greek myth and literature', *Leeds International Classical Studies* 7.1.

2018. '"The power of our mouths": gossip as a female mode of revenge', in Dawson and McHardy 2018 (eds.), 160–80.

forthcoming. 'The risk of violence towards motherless children in ancient Greece', in Heubner forthcoming (ed.).

McHardy, F., and Marshall, E. 2004 (eds.). *Women's Influence on Classical Civilization*. London and New York.

McHardy, F., Robson, J., and Harvey, D. 2005 (eds.). *Lost Dramas of Classical Athens. Greek Tragic Fragments*. Exeter.

McLaughlin, E. 2005. *The Greek Plays*. New York.

Meccariello, C. 2014. *Le hypotheseis narrative dei drammi euripidei. Testo, contesto, fortuna*. Pleiadi 16. Rome.

Meineck, P. 2011. 'The neuroscience of the tragic mask', *Arion* 19.1: 113–58.

Melero, A. 1996. 'Les autres Médées du théâtre grec', *Pallas* 45: 57–68.

Mendelsohn, D. 2002. *Gender and the City in Euripides' Political Plays*. Oxford and New York.

Meridor, R. 2000. 'Creative rhetoric in Euripides' *Troades*: some notes on Hecuba's speech', *Classical Quarterly* NS 50: 16–29.

Mette, H. J. 1963. *Der verlorene Aischylos*. Deutsche Akademie der Wissenschaften zu Berlin Schriften der Sektion für Altertumswissenschaft 35. Berlin.

Michelakis, P. 2002. *Achilles in Greek Tragedy*. Cambridge.

Michelini, A. N. 1987. *Euripides and the Tragic Tradition*. Madison.

   1989. 'Neophron and Euripides' *Medeia* 1056–80', *Transactions of the American Philological Association* 119: 115–35.

Michie, H. 1992. *Sororophobia. Differences Among Women in Literature and Culture*. New York and Oxford.

Michon, C. 2011. *Qu'est-ce que le libre arbitre?* Paris.

Mierow, H. E. 1946. 'Euripides' first play', *Classical Journal* 42: 106–8.

Millett, P., Oakley, S. P., and Thompson, R. J. E. 2011 (eds.). *Ratio et res ipsa. Classical Essays Presented by Former Pupils to James Diggle on His Retirement*. Cambridge Classical Journal supplement 36. Cambridge.

Millis, B. W., and Olson, S. D. 2012. *Inscriptional Records for the Dramatic Festivals in Athens. IG* II^2 *2318–2325 and Related Texts*. Leiden and Boston.

Mills, S. 1997. *Theseus, Tragedy, and the Athenian Empire*. Oxford.

   2003. 'Sophocles' *Aegeus* and *Phaedra*', in Sommerstein 2003 (ed.), 219–32.

Milo, D. 2008. *Il* Tereo *di Sofocle*. Bibliotheca Antiqua 2. Naples.

Mitchell-Boyask, R. 2006. 'The marriage of Cassandra and the *Oresteia*: text, image, performance', *Transactions of the American Philological Association* 136: 269–97.

Monsacré, H. 1984. *Les larmes d'Achille. Le héros, la femme et la souffrance dans la poésie d'Homère*. Paris.

Montiglio, S. 2000. *Silence in the Land of Logos*. Princeton.

Montserrat, D. 1998 (ed.). *Changing Bodies, Changing Meanings. Studies on the Human Body in Antiquity*. London and New York.

Moodie, G. 2003. 'Sophocles' *Tyro* and late Euripidean tragedy', in Sommerstein 2003 (ed.), 117–38.

Moreau, A. 1994. *Le mythe de Jason et Médée. Le va-nu-pied et la sorcière*. Paris.

1996. 'Eschyle et les tranches des repas d'Homère: la trilogie d'Achille', *Cahiers du GITA* 9: 3–29.

Morgan, R. 1970 (ed.). *Sisterhood Is Powerful. An Anthology of Writings from the Women's Liberation Movement.* New York.

1984 (ed.). *Sisterhood Is Global. The International Women's Movement Anthology.* Garden City, NY.

2003 (ed.). *Sisterhood Is Forever. The Women's Anthology for a New Millennium.* New York.

Mori, A. 2012. 'Mediation vs. force: thoughts on female agency in Apollonius Rhodius' *Argonautica'*, *Aitia. Regards sur la culture hellénistique au XXIe siècle* 2. https://journals.openedition.org/aitia/337 (accessed 15.3.20)

Mossman, J. 2001. 'Women's speech in Greek tragedy: the case of Electra and Clytemnestra in Euripides' *Electra'*, *Classical Quarterly* NS 51: 374–84.

2005. 'Women's voices', in Gregory 2005 (ed.), 352–65.

2011. *Euripides.* Medea. Oxford.

2012. 'Women's voices in Sophocles', in Markantonatos 2012 (ed.), 491–506.

Most, G. W. 1994. 'Simonides' ode to Scopas in contexts', in De Jong and Sullivan 1994 (eds.), 127–52.

2009. 'On fragments', in Tronzo 2009 (ed.), 9–20.

Mueller, M. 2016. *Objects as Actors. Props and the Poetics of Performance in Greek Tragedy.* Chicago and London.

2017. 'Gender', in McClure 2017 (ed.), 500–14.

Mülke, C. 2007. '4807. Sophocles, Ἐπίγονοι', *The Oxyrhynchus Papyri* 71: 15–26.

Murnaghan, S. 1999. 'The poetics of loss in Greek epic', in Beissinger *et al.* 1999 (eds.), 203–20.

2005. 'Women in Greek tragedy', in Bushnell 2005 (ed.), 234–50.

Murray, O., and Price, S. 1990 (eds.). *The Greek City from Homer to Alexander.* Oxford.

Murray, P., and Wilson, P. 2004 (eds.). *Music and the Muses. The Culture of 'Mousikē' in the Classical Athenian City.* Oxford.

Mustakallio, K., Hanska, J. Sainio, H.-L., and Vuolanto, V. 2005 (eds.). *Hoping for Continuity. Childhood, Education and Death in Antiquity and the Middle Ages.* Acta Instituti Romani Finlandiae 33. Rome.

Neil, R. A. 1901. *The Knights of Aristophanes.* Cambridge: Cambridge University Press.

Nesselrath, H.-G. 1990. *Die attische mittlere Komödie. Ihre Stellung in der antiken Literaturkritik und Literaturgeschichte.* Untersuchungen zur antiken Literatur und Geschichte 36. Berlin and New York.

Newby, Z. 2016. *Greek Myths in Roman Art and Culture. Imagery, Values and Identity in Italy, 50 BC–AD 250.* Cambridge.

Newton, R. M. 1989. 'Medea's passionate poison', *SyllClass* 1: 13–20.

Nicolosi, C. 1976. 'L'*Euripilo* di Sofocle e il fr. 91 in *Pap. Oxyrh.* IX', *Sileno* 2: 99–106.

Noussia, M. 2006. 'Fragments of Cynic "tragedy"', in Harder *et al.* 2006 (eds.), 229–47.

Nussbaum, M. C. 1994. *The Therapy of Desire. Theory and Practice in Hellenistic Ethics.* Martin Classical Lectures NS 2. Princeton.

Obbink, D. 2001. 'Vanishing conjecture: lost books and their recovery from Aristotle to Eco', in Obbink and Rutherford 2011 (eds.), 20–49.

Obbink, D., and Rutherford, R. B. 2011 (eds.). *Culture in Pieces. Essays on Ancient Texts in Honour of Peter Parsons.* Oxford.

O'Connor-Visser, E. A. M. E. 1987. *Aspects of Human Sacrifice in the Tragedies of Euripides.* Amsterdam.

Olson, S. D. 1998. *Aristophanes. Peace.* Oxford.

  2014 (ed.). *Ancient Comedy and Reception. Essays in Honor of Jeffrey Henderson.* Berlin and Boston.

  2017. 'Some unattributed fragments of Eupolis: problems and possibilities', in Derda *et al.* 2017 (eds.), 127–38.

Ormand, K. 1999. *Exchange and the Maiden. Marriage in Sophoclean Tragedy.* Austin.

  2009. 'Electra in exile', in McCoskey and Zakin 2009 (eds.), 247–73.

  2012 (ed.). *A Companion to Sophocles.* Malden, MA, Oxford, Chichester.

  2015. 'Buying babies in Euripides' *Hippolytus*', *Illinois Classical Studies* 40: 237–61.

Orth, C. 2015. *Nikochares – Xenophon. Einleitung, Übersetzung, Kommentar.* Fragmenta Comica 9.3. Heidelberg.

O'Sullivan, N. 1992. *Alcidamas, Aristophanes and the Beginnings of Greek Stylistic Theory.* Hermes Einzelschriften 60. Stuttgart.

Ozbek, L. 2006. 'L'*Euripilo* di Sofocle: i modelli intertestuali del fr. 210 R (P. Oxy. 1175, fr. 5) e un'ipotesi di datazione dell'opera', *Zeitschrift für Papyrologie und Epigraphik* 158: 29–42.

Pabst, A. 2011. 'Zwei Frauen unter einem Dach. Beobachtungen zu Euripides' Andromache', *Archiv für Papyrusforschung* 57: 318–30.

Paco Serrano, D. M. de 2011. 'Cassandra e le donne tragiche', *Myrtia* 26: 123–39.

Padel, R. 1983. 'Women: model for possession by Greek daemons', in Cameron and Kuhrt 1983 (eds.), 3–19.

  1992. *In and Out of the Mind. Greek Images of the Tragic Self.* Princeton.

Paduano, G. 2005. 'L'apologia di Pasifae nei *Cretesi*', in Bastianini and Casanova 2005 (ed.), 127–44.

Page, D. L. 1938. *Euripides. Medea.* Oxford.

Papadopoulos, J. K. 1994. 'Pasiphae', *Lexicon Iconographicum Mythologiae Classicae* VII/1: 193–200.

Parker, H. N. 2012. 'Aristotle's unanswered questions: women and slaves in *Politics* 1252a–1260b', *Eugesta* 2: 71–122.

Parsons, P. J. 1974. '3013. Argument of a *Tereus*?', *The Oxyrhynchus Papyri* 42: 46–50.

Pellegrino, M. 2008. 'Il mito di Medea nella rappresentazione parodica dei com-mediografi greci', *Estudios griegos e indoeuropeos* 18: 201–16.

Pelling, C. 1990 (ed.). *Characterization and Individuality in Greek Literature.* Oxford.

Perkell, C. 2008. 'Reading the laments of *Iliad* 24', in Suter 2008a (ed.), 93–117.

Petersen, L. H., and Salzman-Mitchell, P. 2012 (eds.). *Mothering and Motherhood in Ancient Greece and Rome.* Austin.

Phelan, P. 1997. *Mourning Sex. Performing Public Memories.* London and New York.

Phillips, T., and D'Angour, A. 2018 (eds.). *Music, Text, and Culture in Ancient Greece.* Oxford.

Pociña, A., and López, A. 2008 (eds.). *Fedras de ayer y de hoy. Teatro, poesía, narrativa y cine ante un mito clásico.* Biblioteca de humanidades Estudios clásicos 25. Granada.

Pociña, A., López, A. Morais, C., Silva, M. de F., and Finglass, P. J. 2019 (eds). *Portraits of Medea in Portugal during the 20th and 21st Centuries.* Meta-forms 14. Leiden and Boston.

Pohlenz, M. 1954. *Die griechische Tragödie*[2], 2 vols. Göttingen. [1st edn Leipzig 1930]

Poli-Palladini, L. 2001. 'Some reflections on Aeschylus' *Aetnae(ae)*', *Rheinsiches Museum* n.F. 144: 287–325.

Post, C. R. 1922. 'The dramatic art of Sophocles as revealed by the fragments of the lost plays', *Harvard Studies in Classical Philology* 33: 1–63.

Powell, A. 1990 (ed.). *Euripides, Women, and Sexuality.* London and New York.

Power, T. 2010. *The Culture of* Kitharôidia. Hellenic Studies 15. Cambridge, MA and London.

Rabinowitz, N. S. 1993. *Anxiety Veiled. Euripides and the Traffic in Women.* Ithaca, NY and London.

Rawlinson, M. C. 2014. 'Beyond Antigone: Ismene, gender, and the right to life', in Chanter and Kirkland 2014 (eds.), 101–21.

2016. *Just Life. Bioethics and the Future of Sexual Difference.* New York and Chichester.

Reckford, K. J. 1974. 'Phaedra and Pasiphae: the pull backward', *Transactions of the American Philological Association* 104: 307–28.

Redmond, J. 1991 (ed.). *Violence in Drama.* Themes in Drama 13. Cambridge.

Rehm, R. 1988. 'The staging of suppliant plays', *Greek, Roman, and Byzantine Studies* 29: 263–307.

1994. *Marriage to Death. The Conflation of Wedding and Funeral Rituals in Greek Tragedy.* Princeton.

Restani, D. 1995. 'I suoni del telaio. Appunti sull'universo sonoro degli antichi Greci', in Gentili and Perusino 1995 (eds.), 93–109.

Revermann, M. 2006. *Comic Business. Theatricality, Dramatic Technique, and Performance Contexts of Aristophanic Comedy.* Oxford.

Revermann, M., and Wilson, P. 2008 (eds.). *Performance, Iconography, Reception. Studies in Honour of Oliver Taplin*. Oxford.

Rich, J., and Shipley, G. 1993 (eds.). *War and Society in the Greek World*. London and New York.

Ridgway, B. S. 1977. *The Archaic Style in Greek Sculpture*. Princeton.

Robert, C. 1916. 'Tyro', *Hermes* 51: 273–302.

Robertson, M. 1957. 'Europa', *Journal of the Warburg and Courtauld Institutes* 20: 1–3.

    1988. 'Europe I', *Lexicon Iconographicum Mythologiae Classicae* iv/1: 76–92.

Robson, J. 2013. 'Beauty and sex appeal in Aristophanes', *Eugesta* 3: 43–66.

Rocconi, E. 2003. *Le parole delle Muse. La formazione del lessico tecnico musicale nella Grecia antica*. Quaderni dei Seminari Romani di Cultura Greca 5. Rome.

Rogers, B. B. 1902. *The Comedies of Aristophanes in Six Volumes. Volume V. IX. The Frogs. X. The Ecclesiazusae*. London.

Roisman, H. M. 2006. 'Helen in the *Iliad*; *causa belli* and victim of war: from silent weaver to public speaker', *American Journal of Philology* 127: 1–36.

    2018. 'The two sisters', in Stuttard 2018 (ed.), 63–77.

Roisman, J. 1999. 'How can an Agamemnon be an Achilles? Drama in the Athenian courts', *The Ancient History Bulletin* 13: 157–61.

Romilly, J. de 1976. 'L'excuse de l'invincible amour dans la tragédie grecque', in Bremer *et al.* 1976 (eds.), 309–21.

    1983 (ed.). *Sophocle*. Entretiens sur l'antiquité classique 29. Vandoeuvres and Geneva.

Romm, J. 1998. *Herodotus*. New Haven and London.

Rood, N. J. 2010. 'Four silences in Sophocles' *Trachiniae*', *Arethusa* 43: 345–64.

Rossum-Steenbeek, M. van 1998. *Greek Readers' Digests? Studies on a Selection of Subliterary Papyri*. Mnemosyne supplement 175. Leiden, New York, Cologne.

Rutherford, R. B. 2012. *Greek Tragic Style. Form, Language and Interpretation*. Cambridge.

    2019. *Homer*. Iliad *Book XVIII*. Cambridge.

Sammons, B. 2017. *Device and Composition in the Greek Epic Cycle*. Oxford and New York.

Sancisi-Weerdenburg, H. 1983. 'Exit Atossa: images of women in Greek historiography on Persia', in Cameron and Kuhrt 1983 (eds.), 20–33.

Sanders, E. 2013. 'Sexual jealousy and *erôs* in Euripides' *Medea*', in *id. et al.* 2013 (eds.), 41–57.

    2014. *Envy and Jealousy in Classical Athens. A Socio-Psychological Approach*. Oxford and New York.

Sanders, E., Thumiger, C., Carey, C., and Lowe, N. J. 2013 (eds.). Erôs *in Ancient Greece*. Oxford.

Scafuro, A. 1990. 'Discourses of sexual violation in mythic accounts and dramatic versions of "The Girl's Tragedy"', *differences. A Journal of Feminist Cultural Studies* 2.1: 126–59.

Scatena, U. 1950. 'Contributo ad una ricostruzione dell' *Ipsipile* euripidea', *Dioniso. Bolletino dell'Istituto Nazionale del Dramma Antico* NS 13: 3–17.

Scattolin, P. 2013. 'Le notizie sul Tereo di Sofocle nei papiri', in Bastianini and Casanova 2013 (eds.), 119–41.

Schaps, D. M. 2006. 'Zeus the wife-beater', *Scripta Classica Israelica* 25: 1–24.

Schauenburg, K. 1981. 'Andromeda I', *Lexicon Iconographicum Mythologiae Classicae* I/1: 774–90.

Schmid, W. 1946. *Geschichte der griechischen Literatur. Erster Teil: Die klassische Periode der griechischen Literatur. Vierter Band: Die griechische Literatur zur Zeit der attischen Hegemonie nach dem Eingreifen der Sophistik. Zweite Hälfte, Erster Abschnitt.* Handbuch der Altertumswissenschaft VII/1/4. Munich.

Schmidt, M. 1992. 'Medeia', *Lexicon Iconographicum Mythologiae Classicae* VI/1: 386–98.

Schmitt, A. 1990. *Selbständigkeit und Abhängigkeit menschlichen Handelns bei Homer. Hermeneutische Untersuchungen zur Psychologie Homers.* Akademie der Wissenschaften und der Literatur, Mainz, Abhandlungen der geistes- und sozialwissenschaftlichen Klasse 1990/5. Stuttgart.

Schmitt, J. 1921. *Freiwilliger Opfertod bei Euripides. Ein Beitrag zu seiner dramatischen Technik.* Giessen.

Schofield, M. 2016. 'Plato's marionette', *Rhizomata* 4: 128–53.

Schulze, W. 1918. 'Beiträge zur Wort- und Sittengeschichte. I–III', *Sitzungsberichte der Königlich Preussischen Akademie der Wissenschaften* 320–32, 481–511, 769–91. [= 1966: 148–210]

   1966. *Kleine Schriften*². Göttingen. [1st edn 1934]

Scodel, R. 1982. 'P. Oxy. 3317. Euripides' *Antigone*', *Zeitschrift für Papyrologie und Epigraphik* 46: 37–42.

   1997. 'Teichoscopia, catalogue, and the female spectator in Euripides', *Colby Quarterly* 33: 76–93.

Seaford, R. 1987. 'The tragic wedding', *Journal of Hellenic Studies* 107: 106–30. [= 2018: 257–99, with Postscript]

   1989. 'Homeric and tragic sacrifice', *Transactions of the American Philological Association* 119: 87–95. [= 2018: 3–14, with Postscript]

   1990. 'The imprisonment of women in Greek tragedy', *Journal of Hellenic Studies* 110: 76–90.

   1994. *Reciprocity and Ritual. Homer and Tragedy in the Developing City-State.* Oxford.

   2018. *Tragedy, Ritual and Money in Ancient Greece. Selected Essays*, ed. R. Bostock. Cambridge.

Sebillotte Cuchet, V. 2006. 'La place de la maternité dans la rhétorique patriotique de l'Athènes classique (V^e–IVe siècles avant notre ère): autour de Praxithéa', in Fournier-Finocchiaro 2006 (ed.), 237–50.

Segal, C. 1985. 'Choral lyric in the fifth century', in Easterling and Knox 1985 (eds.), 222–44.

  1993. *Euripides and the Poetics of Sorrow. Art, Gender, and Commemoration in* Alcestis, Hippolytus, *and* Hecuba. Durham, NC and London.

  1995. *Sophocles' Tragic World. Divinity, Nature, Society.* Cambridge, MA and London.

Seidensticker, B. 1995. 'Women on the tragic stage', in Goff 1995 (ed.), 151–73.

Shaw, M. 1975. 'The female intruder: women in fifth-century drama', *Classical Philology* 70: 255–66.

Shefton, B. B. 1956. 'Medea at Marathon', *American Journal of Archaeology* 60: 159–63.

Sifakis, G. M. 2013. 'The misunderstanding of *opsis* in Aristotle's *Poetics*', in Harrison and Liapis 2013a (eds.), 45–61.

Simon, E. 1954. 'Die Typen der Medeadarstellung in der antiken Kunst', *Gymnasium* 61: 203–27.

  1963. 'Ein Anthesterien-Skyphos des Polygnotos', *Antike Kunst* 6: 6–22.

  1982. 'Satyr-plays on vases in the time of Aeschylus', in Kurtz and Sparkes 1982 (eds.), 123–48.

Slater, N. W. 2018. 'Up from tragicomedy: the growth of hope in Greek comedy', in Kazantzidis and Spatharas 2018 (eds.), 85–110.

Slattery, S. 2016. '5292. Sophocles' *Tereus*', *The Oxyrhynchus Papyri* 82: 8–14.

Sluiter, I. 2005. 'Communicating cynicism: Diogenes' gangsta rap', in Frede and Inwood 2005 (eds.), 139–63.

Smarczyk, B. 1986. *Bündnerautonomie und athenische Seebundspolitik im Dekeleischen Krieg.* Beiträge zur klassischen Philologie 177. Frankfurt.

  1990. *Untersuchungen zur Religionspolitik und politischen Propaganda Athens im Delisch-Attischen Seebund.* Quellen und Forschungen zur antiken Welt 5. Munich.

Smyth, H. W. 1922–6. *Aeschylus*, 2 vols. London and New York.

  1957. *Aeschylus*, vol. ii. London and Cambridge, MA.

Snell, B. 1948. 'Das frühste Zeugnis über Sokrates', *Philologus* 97: 125–34.

  1953. *The Discovery of the Mind. The Greek Origins of Eurpean Thought*, transl. T. G. Rosenmeyer. Oxford.

  1971. *Szenen aus griechischen Dramen.* Berlin.

  1975. *Die Entdeckung des Geistes. Studien zur Entstehung des europäischen Denkens bei den Griechen*^{4}. Göttingen. [1st edn Hamburg 1946]

Sommerstein, A. H. 1981. *The Comedies of Aristophanes: vol. 2. Knights.* Warminster.

  1990–3. 'Soph. *Ant.* 572 ("Dearest Haimon")', *Museum Criticum* 25–8: 71–6. [= 2010b: 202–8]

1996. *The Comedies of Aristophanes: vol. 9.* Frogs. Warminster.

2002a. 'The titles of Greek dramas', *SemRom* 5: 1–16. [= 2010b: 11–29, with addenda]

2003 (ed.). *Shards from Kolonos. Studies in Sophoclean Fragments.* le Rane Collana di Studi e Testi 34. Bari.

2004. 'Violence in Greek drama', *Ordia Prima. Revista de Estudios Clásicos* 3: 41–56. [= 2010b: 30–46]

2006a. 'Rape and consent in Athenian tragedy', in Cairns and Liapis 2006 (eds.), 233–51.

2006b. '*Polyxene*', in *id. et al.* 2006: 41–83.

2008. *Aeschylus,* 3 vols. Loeb Classical Library 145, 146, 505. Cambridge, MA and London.

2010a. *Aeschylean Tragedy².* London. [1st edn Bari 1996]

2010b. *The Tangled Ways of Zeus and other Studies in and around Greek Tragedy.* Oxford.

2012. 'The Epigoni or *Eriphyle*', in Sommerstein and Talboy 2012: 25–74.

2014. 'Menander's *Samia* and the Phaedra theme', in Olson 2014 (ed.), 167–79.

2019. *Aeschylus.* Suppliants. Cambridge.

Sommerstein, A. H., and Talboy, T. H. 2012. *Sophocles. Selected Fragmentary Plays. Volume* ɪɪ. The Epigoni, Oenomaus, Palamedes, The Arrival of Nauplius, Nauplius and the Beacon, The Shepherds, Triptolemus. Oxford.

Sommerstein, A. H., Fitzpatrick, D., and Talboy, T. 2006. *Sophocles. Selected Fragmentary Plays. Volume* ɪ. Hermione, Polyxene, The Diners, Tereus, Troilus, Phaedra. Oxford.

Sommerstein, A. H., Halliwell, S., Henderson, J., and Zimmermann, B. 1993 (eds.). *Tragedy, Comedy and the Polis. Papers from the Greek Drama Conference Nottingham, 18–20 July 1990.* le Rane Collana di Studi e Testi 11. Bari.

Sonnino, M. 2010. *Euripidis Erechthei quae exstant.* Biblioteca Nazionale serie dei Classici Greci e Latini 19. Florence.

Sorabji, R. 2006. *Self. Ancient and Modern Insights about Individuality, Life, and Death.* Chicago.

Sourvinou-Inwood, C. 1997. 'Medea at a shifting distance: images and Euripidean tragedy', in Clauss and Johnston 1997 (eds.), 253–96.

2003. *Tragedy and Athenian Religion.* Lanham, MD, Boulder, New York, Oxford.

2005. *Hylas, the Nymphs, Dionysos and Others. Myth, Ritual, Ethnicity.* Acta Instituti Atheniensis Regni Sueciae 8° 19. Stockholm.

2011. *Athenian Myths and Festivals. Aglauros, Erechtheus, Plynteria, Panathenaia, Dionysia,* ed. R. Parker. Oxford.

Staltmayr, M. 1991. 'Aischylos und die Phryger', *Hermes* 119: 367–74.

Stampolidis, N. C., Maner, Ç., and Kopanias, K. 2015 (eds.). *Nostoi. Indigenous Culture, Migration and Integration in the Aegean Islands and Western Anatolia during the Late Bronze and Early Iron Age.* Istanbul.

Stieber, M. 2011. *Euripides and the Language of Craft*. Mnemosyne supplement 327. Leiden and Boston.

Stinton, T. C. W. 1976. '"Si credere dignum est": some expressions of disbelief in Euripides and others', *Proceedings of the Cambridge Philological Society* NS 22: 60–89. [= 1990: 236–64]

    1990. *Collected Papers on Greek Tragedy*. Oxford.

Strohm, H. 1957. *Euripides. Interpretationen zur dramatischen Form*. Zetemata 15. Munich.

Strubbe, J. H. M. 1993. 'Meter ametor. Persoonlijke relaties in Sophocles Electra', *Lampas* 26: 296–313.

Stuttard, D. 2018 (ed.). *Looking At* Antigone. London etc.

Suter, A. 2004. 'The myth of Prokne and Philomela', *New England Classical Journal* 31: 377–86.

    2008a. 'Male lament in Greek tragedy', in *ead.* 2008b (ed.), 156–80.

    2008b (ed.). *Lament. Studies in the Ancient Mediterranean and Beyond*. Oxford and New York.

Sutton, D. F. 1984. *The Lost Sophocles*. Lanham, MD and London.

    1987. 'The theatrical families of Athens', *American Journal of Philology* 108: 9–26.

Swift, L. A. 2009. 'Sexual and familial distortion in Euripides' *Phoenissae*', *Transactions of the American Philological Association* 139: 53–87.

Synodinou, K. 1987. 'The threats of physical abuse of Hera by Zeus in the *Iliad*', *Wiener Studien* 100: 13–22.

Talboy, T. H., and Sommerstein, A. H. 2006. '*Phaedra*', in Sommerstein *et al.* 2006: 248–317.

    2012. '*Oenomaus*', in Sommerstein and Talboy 2012: 75–109.

Taplin, O. 1972. 'Aeschylean silences and silences in Aeschylus', *Harvard Studies in Classical Philology* 76: 57–97.

    1977. *The Stagecraft of Aeschylus. The Dramatic Use of Exits and Entrances in Greek Tragedy*. Oxford.

    1978. *Greek Tragedy in Action*. London.

    1997. 'The pictorial record', in Easterling 1997 (ed.), 69–90.

    2007. *Pots and Plays. Interactions between Tragedy and Greek Vase Painting of the Fourth Century* BC. Los Angeles.

    2014. 'How pots and papyri might prompt a re-evaluation of fourth-century tragedy', in Csapo *et al.* 2014 (eds.), 141–55.

Thiersch, B. 1830. *Aristophanis comoediae. Tomus VI continens P. I. Ranas et P. II. Ecclesiazusas*, two parts. Leipzig and London.

Thomas, B. M. 2002. 'Constraints and contradictions: whiteness and femininity in ancient Greece', in Llewellyn-Jones 2002 (ed.), 1–16.

Thompson, E. A. 1944. 'Neophron and Euripides' *Medea*', *Classical Quarterly* 38: 10–14.

Thumiger, C. 2013. 'Mad *erôs* and eroticized madness in tragedy', in Sanders *et al.* 2013 (eds.), 27–40.

Todd, S. C. 2007. *A Commentary on Lysias, Speeches 1–11*. Oxford.

Toepffer, J. 1889. *Attische Genealogie*. Berlin.

Torrance, I. 2013. *Metapoetry in Euripides*. Oxford.

Trendall, A. D., and Webster, T. B. L. 1971. *Illustrations of Greek Drama*. London and New York.

Tronzo, W. 2009. *The Fragment. An Incomplete History*. Los Angeles.

Tsagalis, C. 2004. *Epic Grief. Personal Laments in Homer's Iliad*. Untersuchungen zur antiken Literatur und Geschichte 70. Berlin and New York.

2014. 'γυναίων εἵνεκα δώρων: interformularity and intertraditionality in Theban and Homeric epic', *Trends in Classics* 6: 357–98.

Tzanetou, A. 2012. 'Citizen-mothers on the tragic stage', in Petersen and Salzman-Mitchell 2012 (eds.), 97–120.

Unwin, N. C. 2017. *Caria and Crete in Antiquity. Cultural Interaction between Anatolia and the Aegean*. Cambridge.

Vahtikari, V. 2014. *Tragedy Performances outside Athens in the Late Fifth and the Fourth Centuries* BC. Papers and Monographs of the Finnish Institute at Athens 20. Helsinki.

Vernant, J.-P., and Vidal-Naquet, P. 1972. *Mythe et tragédie en Grèce ancienne*. Paris. 1988. *Myth and Tragedy in Ancient Greece*, transl. J. Lloyd. New York.

Vester, C. 2009. 'Bigamy and bastardy, wives and concubines: civic identity in *Andromache*', in Cousland and Hume 2009 (eds.), 293–305.

Vidal-Naquet, P. 1972. 'Chasse et sacrifice dans l'*Orestie* d'Eschyle', in Vernant and *id.* 1972: 133–58.

1988. 'Hunting and sacrifice in Aeschylus' *Oresteia*', in Vernant and *id.* 1988: 141–59.

Visser, M. 1986. 'Medea: daughter, sister, wife and mother. Natal family *versus* conjugal family in Greek and Roman myths about women', in Cropp *et al.* 1986 (eds.), 149–65.

Volscus, A. 1481. *Epistulae Heroides*. Venice.

Wagner, F. W. 1852. *Poetarum tragicorum graecorum fragmenta. Volumen I. Aeschyli et Sophoclis perditarum fabularum fragmenta*. Breslau.

Watson, P. A. 1995. *Ancient Stepmothers. Myth, Misogyny and Reality*. Mnemosyne supplement 143. Leiden, New York, Cologne.

Webster, T. B. L. 1936a. 'Sophocles' *Trachiniae*', in Bailey *et al.* 1936: 164–80. 1936b. *An Introduction to Sophocles*. Oxford. 1967. *The Tragedies of Euripides*. London.

Wecklein, N. 1909. *Über die Hypsipyle des Euripides*. Sitzungsberichte der Königlich Bayerischen Akademie der Wissenschaften, Philosophisch-philologische und historische Klasse 1909/8. Munich.

Wees, H. van 1998. 'A brief history of tears: gender differentiation in archaic Greece', in Foxhall and Salmon 1998 (eds.), 10–53.

Weil, H. 1879. *Un papyrus inédit de la Bibliothèque de M. Ambroise Firmin-Didot. Nouveaux fragments d'Euripide et d'autres poètes grecs.* Paris.

Weiss, N. A. 2017. 'Noise, music, speech: the representation of lament in Greek tragedy', *American Journal of Philology* 138: 243–66.

2018. *The Music of Tragedy. Performance and Imagination in Euripidean Theater.* Oakland, CA.

Welcker, F. G. 1824. *Die Aeschylische Trilogie Prometheus und die Kabirenweihe zu Lemnos nebst Winken über die Trilogie des Aeschylus überhaupt.* Darmstadt.

Wescoat, B. D. 2012. *The Temple of Athena at Assos.* Oxford.

West, M. L. 1990. *Studies in Aeschylus.* Beiträge zur Altertumskunde 1. Stuttgart.

1992. *Ancient Greek Music.* Oxford.

2000. '*Iliad* and *Aethiopis* on the stage: Aeschylus and son', *Classical Quarterly* NS 50: 338–52. [= 2011–13: II 227–49]

2007. 'A new musical papyrus: Carcinus, *Medea*', *Zeitschrift für Papyrologie und Epigraphik* 161: 1–10. [= 2011–13: II 334–50]

2011–13. *Hellenica. Selected Papers on Greek Literature and Thought,* 3 vols. Oxford.

West, S. 1999. 'Sophocles' *Antigone* and Herodotus book three', in Griffin 1999 (ed.), 109–36.

Whitehead, D. 2003. 'Εὐφορίων', www.stoa.org/sol-entries/epsilon/3800 (accessed 15.3.20).

Widerker, D., and McKenna, M. 2003 (eds.). *Moral Responsibility and Alternative Possibilities. Essays on the Importance of Alternative Possibilities.* Aldershot and Burlington, VT.

Wilamowitz-Moellendorff, U. 1921. 'Melanippe', *Sitzungsberichte der Preussischen Akademie der Wissenschaften* 63–80. [= 1935–72: I 440–60]

1935–72. *Kleine Schriften,* 6 vols. Berlin and Amsterdam.

Wiles, D. 2005. 'ΗΥ]Ψ[ΙΡΥΛΕ: a version for the stage', in McHardy *et al.* 2005 (eds.), 189–207.

2007. *Mask and Performance in Greek Tragedy. From Ancient Festival to Modern Experimentation.* Cambridge.

Wilkins, J. 1990. 'The state and the individual: Euripides' plays of voluntary self-sacrifice', in Powell 1990 (ed.), 177–94.

Williams, B. A. O. 1976. 'Moral luck', *The Aristotelian Society. Supplementary Volume* 50: 115–35. [≈ 1981: 20–39]

1981. *Moral Luck. Philosophical Papers 1973–1980.* Cambridge.

1993. *Shame and Necessity.* Sather Classical Lectures 57. Berkeley, Los Angeles, London.

Williams, J. 1997. *Interpreting Nightingales. Gender, Class and Histories.* Sheffield.

Willink, C. W. 1968. 'Some problems of text and interpretation in the *Hippolytus*', *Classical Quarterly* NS 18: 11–43. [= 2010: 3–49]

2010. *Collected Papers on Greek Tragedy*, ed. W. B. Henry. Leiden and Boston.

Wilson, P. 1999. 'The *aulos* in Athens', in Goldhill and Osborne 1999 (eds.), 58–95.

Winkler, J. J., and Zeitlin, F. I. 1990 (eds.). *Nothing to Do with Dionysos? Athenian Drama in its Social Context*. Princeton.

Winnington-Ingram, R. P. 1980. *Sophocles. An Interpretation*. Cambridge.

1983. 'Sophocles and women', in de Romilly 1983 (ed.), 233–49.

Wohl, V. 1998. *Intimate Commerce. Exchange, Gender, and Subjectivity in Greek Tragedy*. Austin.

2005. 'Tragedy and feminism', in Bushnell 2005 (ed.), 145–60.

2015. *Euripides and the Politics of Form*. Princeton and Oxford.

Woodhouse, W. J. 1930. *The Composition of Homer's Odyssey*. Oxford.

Worman, N. 2008. *Abusive Mouths in Classical Athens*. Cambridge.

2015. *Landscape and the Spaces of Metaphor in Ancient Literary Theory and Criticism*. Cambridge.

Wright, M. 2005. 'The joy of Sophocles' *Electra*', *G&R* 2nd ser. 52: 172–94.

2006. '*Orestes*, a Euripidean sequel', *Classical Quarterly* NS 56: 33–48.

2009. 'Literary prizes and literary criticism in antiquity', *Classical Antiquity* 28: 138–77.

2012. *The Comedian as Critic. Greek Old Comedy and Poetics*. London and New York.

2016. *The Lost Plays of Greek Tragedy. Volume 1: Neglected Authors*. London and New York.

2019. *The Lost Plays of Greek Tragedy. Volume 2: Aeschylus, Sophocles and Euripides*. London and New York.

Wyles, R. 2011. *Costume in Greek Tragedy*. London.

Xanthakis-Karamanos, G. 1986. '*P.Oxy.* 3317: Euripides' *Antigone* (?)', *Bulletin of the Institute of Classical Studies* 33: 107–11.

Yoon, F. 2016. 'Against a *Prometheia*: rethinking the connected trilogy', *Transactions of the American Philological Association* 146: 257–80.

Zacharia, K. 2001. '"The rock of the nightingale": kinship diplomacy and Sophocles' *Tereus*', in Budelmann and Michelakis 2001 (eds.), 91–112.

Zagdoun, M.-A., and Gondicas, D. 1988. 'Eurypylos I', *Lexicon Iconographicum Mythologiae Classicae* IV/1: 109–10.

Zajko, V., and Leonard, M. 2006 (eds.). *Laughing with Medusa. Classical Myth and Feminist Thought*. Oxford.

Zeitlin, F. I. 1965. 'The motif of the corrupted sacrifice in Aeschylus' *Oresteia*', *Transactions of the American Philological Association* 96: 463–508.

1978. 'The dynamics of misogyny: myth and mythmaking in the *Oresteia*', *Arethusa* 11: 149–84. [≈ 1996: 87–119]

1985. 'Playing the other: theater, theatricality, and the feminine in Greek drama', *Representations* 11: 63–94. [≈ 1996: 341–74 ≈ Winkler and Zeitlin 1990 (eds.), 63–96]

1992. 'The politics of Eros in the Danaid trilogy of Aeschylus', in Hexter and Selden 1992 (eds.), 203–52. [≈ 1996: 123–71]

1993. 'Staging Dionysus between Thebes and Athens', in Carpenter and Faraone 1993 (eds.), 147–82.

1996. *Playing the Other. Gender and Society in Classical Greek Literature.* Chicago and London.

2008. 'Intimate relations: children, childbearing, and parentage on the Euripidean stage', in Revermann and Wilson 2008 (eds.), 318–32.

General Index

Acusilaus, 145–6
[Aeschylus]
    Prometheus Bound, 122
Aeschylus
    Achilleis trilogy, 13–14, 105–24
    Agamemnon, 25–6, 87–91, 100–1, 190
    Carians or *Europa*, 11, 125–38
    Eumenides, 58, 122–3
    Hypsipyle, 70
    Myrmidons, 13–14, 105–11
    Nereids, 13–14, 105–8, 113–21
    Niobe, 189
    Nurses, 217–18
    Persians, 127
    Phrygians or *The Ransoming of Hector*,
        13–14, 105–8, 111–13
    Suppliant Women, 47–8, 122–3
    Women of Aetna, 123
agôn, tragic, 183–4
akrasia, 195–6
Andocides
    On the Mysteries, 25
anonymous versions of *Medea*, 218
Antiphon (orator), 189
Antiphon (tragedian)
    Jason, 219
Aphareus
    Daughters of Pelias, 219
Aristophanes, 9–10, 85
    Frogs, 62, 174–6
    Peace, 228
    Thesmophoriazusae, 73
Athens
    commemoration of war dead, 58–9
    contrast with Thrace, 99
    and Lemnos, 162, 176–7
    royal family, 52

Biotus
    Medea, 219

Carcinus
    Medea, 219–21, 239

comedies
    about Medea, 240–2

Dicaeogenes
    Medea, 221
Diogenes of Sinope
    Medea, 221–2

Easterling, Pat, 2, 13, 121
envy, *see* women, sexual rivalry
Euphorion, 11, 131–2
Euripides
    Aegeus, 222–3
    Aeolus, 79–81
    Alcestis, 26–8
    Alcmaeon at Corinth, 28–30
    Andromache, 20, 23–5
    Andromeda, 73–4, 83–4
    Antigone, 82–3
    Antiope, 34–7
    Cretans, 14, 179–97
    Daughters of Pelias, 223–5
    Erechtheus, 51–9, 142–3
    Hecuba, 196–7
    Hippolytus plays, 62–3
    Hypsipyle, 11, 14–15, 76–7, 162–78, 198–215
    Ino, 29, 141
    Medea, 15, 21–3, 135, 141, 216–17, 235–43
    Medea I, 225–7
    Meleager, 81–2
    Oedipus, 77–9
    Phoenix, 71
    Protesilaus, 74–6, 86
    Scyrians, 143
    Stheneboea, 62
    Suppliant Women, 143
    Theseus, 79
Euripides II
    Medea, 227

family, *see* husbands; uncles; women as mothers;
        women as sisters (to brothers); women
        as sisters (to sisters); women as

277

Index of main female characters discussed